Praise for *Bad Religion*

Winner of the 2013 *Christianity Today* Book Award

Chosen as one of *The Christian Century*'s Five Notable
Religion Books of 2012

"A brilliantly reasoned argument for orthodox Christianity and the need
for vibrant faith in society. In this perceptive and timely work, Ross
Douthat extolls the 'vital center' of belief while calling out the fashionable
heretics among us. This is one 'Bad Religion' we can all believe in."

—Raymond Arroyo, *New York Times* bestselling author,
host of EWTN's *The World Over Live*

"Not only is Ross Douthat's account of orthodox Christianity's decline
provocative, but his critique of today's ascendant heresies is compelling.
This volume is a sustained proof of Chesterton's thesis that when people
turn from God, 'they don't believe in nothing—they believe in anything.'
Everyone who is interested in why the church is faring as it is in U.S. culture today needs to get this book."

—Timothy Keller, Redeemer Presbyterian Church,
New York City

"*Bad Religion* is superb: sharply critical of the amazing variety of American
religious pathologies, but fair; blunt in diagnosis, but just; telling a dark
tale, but telling it hopefully. For those trying to understand the last half-
century or more of American religion, and to strive for a better future, it is
an indispensable book."

—Alan Jacobs, author of *The Narnian: The Life and Imagination
of C. S. Lewis*

"Ross Douthat's thoughtful, articulate, wide-ranging, sometimes contrarian and always provocative new book asks a tough question: Why has Christianity been so misunderstood, and so misused, in the past few decades? From those who (foolishly) watered down the most basic Christian beliefs, to those who (falsely) promised worldly success to the followers of Jesus, the values of orthodoxy (literally, "right belief") have often been blithely set aside. With an impressive command of both history and contemporary social trends, Douthat shows not only how we ended up with a Christianity of our own making, but also how we can reclaim an adherence to the teachings of the real Jesus—not just the convenient one."

—James Martin, SJ, author of *The Jesuit Guide to (Almost) Everything*

"*Bad Religion* is nothing short of prophetic. In a time of religious, political, and cultural upheaval, Ross Douthat tells the American faithful—liberals, conservatives, and everybody in between—not what we want to hear, but what we desperately need to hear. With this provocative and challenging work that no thoughtful Christian can afford to ignore, Douthat assures his place in the first rank of his generation's public intellectuals."

—Rod Dreher, author of *The Little Way of Ruthie Leming*

ALSO BY ROSS DOUTHAT

Privilege: Harvard and the Education of the Ruling Class

Grand New Party: How Republicans Can Win the Working Class
and Save the American Dream (with Reihan Salam)

BAD RELIGION

HOW WE BECAME
A NATION OF HERETICS

ROSS DOUTHAT

FREE PRESS

NEW YORK   LONDON   TORONTO   SYDNEY   NEW DELHI

For Abby

Free Press
A Division of Simon & Schuster, Inc.
1230 Avenue of the Americas
New York, NY 10020

First Free Press trade paperback edition April 2013

FREE PRESS and colophon are trademarks of Simon & Schuster, Inc.

For information about special discounts for bulk purchases, please contact Simon & Schuster Special Sales at 1-866-506-1949 or business@simonandschuster.com.

The Simon & Schuster Speakers Bureau can bring authors to your live event. For more information or to book an event contact the Simon & Schuster Speakers Bureau at 1-866-248-3049 or visit our website at www.simonspeakers.com.

Designed by Akasha Archer

Manufactured in the United States of America

10   9   8   7

Library of Congress Cataloging-in-Publication Data

Douthat, Ross Gregory.
    Bad religion : how we became a nation of heretics / by Ross Douthat.—1st Free Press hardcover ed.
        p.   cm.
        1. Christianity—United States. 2. Catholic Church—United States. 3. Theology, Doctrinal—United States. 4. United States—Religious life and customs. I. Title.
    BR526.D68 2012
    277.3'083—dc23
    2011043081

ISBN 978-1-4391-7830-0
ISBN 978-1-4391-7833-1 (pbk)
ISBN 978-1-4391-7834-8 (ebook)

There is almost no human action, however particular one supposes it, that does not arise from a very general idea that men have conceived of God, of his relations with human race, of the nature of their souls, and of their duties toward those like them. One cannot keep these ideas from being the common source from which all the rest flow.

—Alexis de Tocqueville, *Democracy in America*

Man is *homo religiosus*, by "nature" religious: As much as he needs food to eat and air to breathe, he needs a faith for living. . . . But—and this is the challenging word of Jewish-Christian faith—so long as he pursues this quest in self-sufficiency, relying on his own virtue, wisdom, or piety, it will not be God that he finds, but an idol—the self, or some aspect of the self, writ large, projected, objectified, and worshiped.

—Will Herberg, *Protestant–Catholic–Jew*

The confusion avenges itself and becomes its own punishment. The forgetting of the true God is already itself the breaking loose of his wrath against those who forget Him.

—Karl Barth, *The Epistle to the Romans*

CONTENTS

X CONTENTS

BAD RELIGION

PROLOGUE

A NATION OF HERETICS

After the great crash of 2008, Americans awoke and saw their country the way anti-Americans have always seen it: spendthrift, decadent, and corrupt. The city on a hill had become a mismanaged empire; the land of self-reliance was buried in debt. Our political class had run up enormous deficits at home and entangled us in never-ending military operations overseas. Our financial elites had been exposed as reckless, self-deluded speculators who had gambled away the country's economic future and then gone begging for a bailout. And the whole mess had been made possible by middle America's relentless appetite—for bigger houses, bigger portfolios, bigger government programs, bigger everything, and damn the long-term cost.

During the 2008 election season, the extraordinary unpopularity of George W. Bush made him an obvious scapegoat for these debacles, and the charisma of Barack Obama made him a convenient savior figure. By the fall of 2010, it was Obama's turn to take the blame, while the Tea Party offered a right-wing version of hope and change. But even as Americans turned the parties into and out of office, most of them understood that the rot ran deeper than the White House and Capitol Hill, and that there were trends at work that couldn't be reversed by simply dispatching a more talented set of leaders to Washington, D.C.

Thus the ongoing search for more comprehensive theories of American decline. Some of these theories are ideological: Conservatives denounce liberals as free-spending socialists, while liberals denounce conservatives for championing a cult of deregulated dog-eat-dog. Some theories are structural: On the left, in particular, there is a widespread sense that America's creaky eighteenth-century institutions are no longer capable of responding to the challenges of a polarized country and a globalized world. And some theories are frankly conspiratorial, involving perfidious foreigners and conniving corporations, villainous ex-Weathermen and dissembling Straussians, controlled demolitions on 9/11 and forged birth certificates in 1960s Hawaii.

The most potent theories, though, involve religion. This is as it should be because, at the deepest level, every human culture is religious—defined by what its inhabitants believe about some ultimate reality, and what they think that reality demands of them. The reality doesn't have to be a personal God: It can be the iron laws of Marxism, the religion of blood and soil, the Gaia hypothesis, the church of the free market, the cult of the imperial self. But Bob Dylan had it right: *You gotta serve somebody,* and every culture does.

This insight forms the basis for two of the most popular explanations for America's current predicament—one offered by the Christian right, the other by the secular left. The first holds that Americans have lost their way because they've fallen away from the faith of their fathers, or else been bullied into apostasy by secular elites. The more simplistic version of this argument insists that the United States was founded as an explicitly "Christian nation" and, like Israel of old, has lost God's favor by straying from this covenant. The more sophisticated version follows Alexis de Tocqueville in suggesting that American democracy, while formally secular, has always depended on religion to provide a moral framework for its citizens—and so the eclipse of Christian belief has led, inevitably, to the eclipse of public morality and private virtue alike.

But both the populists and the intellectuals in this camp share the same basic understanding of our national predicament. Their America is a nation in which religious faith has been steadily marginalized, with increasingly disastrous results. Their scapegoats include progressive educators, activist judges, Hollywood elites, and the deophobic media. Their prescription, from the 1970s to the present day, has been a religious counterrevolution, aimed at restoring faith to its rightful place at the center of American culture, politics, and law.

For a time this narrative dominated the conversation about religion and American decline. In the last decade, however, an alternative story came into its own—first as a stinging critique of George W. Bush's administration, and then as a broader account of the American situation. Against the idea that the United States has lost touch with its religious roots, a growing chorus began insisting that the United States is in decline because it's *excessively* religious. On issue after issue, these critics made Christian belief the problem in and of itself, casting the political controversies of the 2000s as an apocalyptic struggle between science and ignorance, reason and superstition, the light of progress and the medieval dark.

Sometimes this argument has been couched as an attack on the so-called theocracy that Christian conservatives are supposedly bent on setting up. (Thus the spate of Bush-era books attacking "Christian fascists," "Christian nationalists," and "Christianists," culminating in Kevin Phillips's bestselling jeremiad *American Theocracy*.) At other times it has taken the form of a straightforward assault on belief in a God, advanced by atheists who shared Christopher Hitchens's sweeping assessment that religion "poisons everything." Either way, the portrait of contemporary America is roughly the same: a once-great nation brought low by piety and zeal.

These two visions seem mutually contradictory—but both contain an element of truth. America has indeed become less traditionally Christian across the last half century, just as religious conservatives insist, with unhappy consequences for our national life. But certain kinds of religious faith are as influential as ever, just as secular critics and the new atheists contend—and they're right, as well, that to the extent that there's an ongoing crisis in American culture, the excesses of the faithful probably matter more than the sins of unbelievers.

That's because America's problem isn't too much religion, or too little of it. It's *bad* religion: the slow-motion collapse of traditional Christianity and the rise of a variety of destructive pseudo-Christianities in its place. Since the 1960s, the institutions that sustained orthodox Christian belief—Catholic and Protestant alike—have entered a state of near-terminal decline. The churches with the strongest connection to the Christian past have lost members, money, and authority; the elite that was once at least sympathetic to Christian ideas has become hostile or indifferent; and the culture as a whole has turned its back on many of the faith's precepts and demands.

The United States remains a deeply religious country, and most Americans are still drawing some water from the Christian well. But a growing number are inventing their own versions of what Christianity means, abandoning the nuances of traditional theology in favor of religions that stroke their egos and indulge or even celebrate their worst impulses. These faiths speak from many pulpits—conservative and liberal, political and pop-cultural, traditionally religious and fashionably "spiritual"—and many of their preachers call themselves Christian or claim a Christian warrant. But they are increasingly offering distortions of traditional Christianity, not the real thing.

Locked in conflict, neither religious conservatives nor their secular antagonists have come to grips with this transformation. The secular mistake has been to assume that every theology tends inevitably toward the same follies and fanaticisms, and to imagine that a truly postreligious culture is even possible, let alone desirable. The religious mistake has been to fret over the threat posed by explicitly anti-Christian forces, while ignoring or minimizing the influence that the apostles of pseudo-Christianity exercise over the American soul. Along the way, both sides have embraced a wildly simplified vision of our culture, in which the children of light contend with the children of darkness, and every inch of ground is claimed by absolute truth or deplorable error.

The real story is what's happening in the vast America in between, where papal encyclicals rarely penetrate and the works of Richard Dawkins pass unread. That's where you'll find the reality of contemporary religion, and the roots of our present crisis. It's an America that remains the most religious country in the developed world, as God-besotted today as ever; a place where Jesus Christ is an obsession, God's favor a birthright, and spiritual knowledge an all-consuming goal. But it's also a place where traditional Christian teachings have been warped into justifications for solipsism and anti-intellectualism, jingoism and utopianism, selfishness and greed.

In this America, the ancient Christian teaching that the Scriptures are simultaneously divinely inspired and open to multiple interpretations has become an either/or choice instead. You're either a rigid fundamentalist who believes that dinosaurs just missed hitching a ride on Noah's Ark, or a self-consciously progressive believer for whom the Bible is a kind of refrigerator magnet poetry, awaiting rearrangement by more enlightened minds. As a result, the Jesus of the New Testament, whose paradoxical mix of qualities and commandments presents a challenge to every ideology and faction, has been replaced in the hearts and minds of many Americans with a more congenial figure—a "choose your own Jesus" who better fits their own preconceptions about what a savior should and shouldn't be.

Likewise, in this America the traditional Christian attempt to balance the belief that God desires human happiness with the reality of human suffering has been transformed into the simpler teaching that God wants everyone to get rich—that your house or car or high-paying job was intended for you from before the foundation of the world, and that the test of true faith is the rewards that it reaps for believers here on earth. The result is a country where religion actively encourages the sort of recklessness that produced our current economic meltdown, rather than serving as a brake on materialism and a rebuke to avarice.

In this America, too, the Christian teaching that every human soul is unique and precious has been stressed, by the prophets of self-fulfillment and gurus of self-love, at the expense of the equally important teaching that every human soul is fatally corrupted by original sin. Absent the latter emphasis, religion becomes a license for egotism and selfishness, easily employed to justify what used to be considered deadly sins. The result is a society where pride becomes "healthy self-esteem," vanity becomes "self-improvement," adultery becomes "following your heart," greed and gluttony become "living the American dream."

Finally, in this America the Christian view that God desires justice but that it's wrong to expect utopia in this lifetime has given way to a more optimistic vision, in which the spread of democracy is part of the divine plan, the doctrine of American exceptionalism is a kind of Eleventh Commandment, and political leaders are expected to achieve an approximation of heaven here on earth. The results: an overreaching foreign policy under both Republicans and Democrats, a domestic government that tries to be all things to all people no matter which party is in power, and a polarized mood in which the two political coalitions oscillate between messianic delusions and apocalyptic fears depending on whether or not they control the levers of government.

This is the real story of religion in America. For all its piety and fervor, today's United States needs to be recognized for what it really is: not a Christian country, but a nation of heretics.

But haven't we always been a nation of heretics? Wasn't our country founded as a religious sanctuary and a haven for experimenters of all stripes—Pilgrims and Quakers, Methodists and Baptists, Jehovah's Witnesses and Seventh-day Adventists, and a parade of more exotic sects? In the stories we tell about ourselves, aren't the heroes usually iconoclasts and freethinkers, not sticklers for dogma and theological correctness?

Indeed they are. Since the first settlers arrived in Jamestown and Plymouth, our common life has been shaped by a succession of fascinating, only-in-America faiths: the chilly Deism of the eighteenth century and the warm metaphysical bath of Ralph Waldo Emerson's Transcendentalism; the Mormon theocracy of the nineteenth century and the New Age movements of the 1960s; Mary Baker Eddy's Christian Science and L. Ron Hubbard's Scientology; and many, many more.

But there's another story to tell about religion in the United States, one that gives the dogmatists their due. You can't have fringes without a center, iconoclasts without icons, revolutionaries without institutions to rebel against. We have always been a nation of heretics, but heresy has never had the field to itself. Instead, the potency, creativity, and resilience of American faith have been a testament to both the boldness of our spiritual freelancers *and* the staying power of our religious establishments—the various denominations of mainstream Protestantism and then, as its presence in the United States grew apace, the Roman Catholic Church. A chart of the American religious past would look like a vast delta, with tributaries, streams, and channels winding in and out, diverging and reconverging—but all of them fed, ultimately, by a central stream, an original current, a place where all the waters start.

This river is Christian orthodoxy. Not the orthodoxy of any specific Christian church, whether Lutheran or Presbyterian or Roman Catholic, but the shared theological commitments that have defined the parameters of Christianity since the early Church. The constant struggles between this consensus and its critics—between existing churches and start-up faiths, between ancient doctrine and modern experimentation, between the belief that religious truth is handed down from the apostles and the belief that it's something that each believer needs to discover on his own—have played an immensely fruitful role in our religious history, and helped to make the American experiment such a remarkable success.

Time and again, America's heretics have tugged their Christian countrymen forward toward new ideas, new horizons, new visions of justice, and new experiences of the numinous. Think of the Founders themselves; many of them were Deists and Unitarians rather than orthodox Christians, and their distance from institutional Christianity helped guarantee the new nation's absolute commitment to freedom of religion. Think of self-appointed prophets like John Brown, violent and half-mad but also visionary in his absolutist condemnation of chattel slavery. Think of the late-nineteenth-century Social Gospel, which aimed—in tension with traditional Christian emphases and understandings—to build the kingdom of God on earth, and succeeded in curbing some of the worst excesses of industrialization. Think of twentieth-century Pentecostalism, doctrinally suspect from the perspective of many Christian churches, but also responsible for reviving the strangest and most ancient form of Christian worship—the wild ecstasy of glossolalia.

But now consider orthodox Christianity's contribution to America as well. From the beginning, the existence of a Christian center—first exclusively Protestant, and then eventually accommodating Catholicism as well—has helped bind together a teeming, diverse, and fissiparous nation. This binding has often been tangible and concrete: The hierarchy, discipline, and institutional continuity of Mainline Protestantism and Catholicism helped build hospitals and schools, orphanages and universities, and assimilated generation upon generation of immigrants. But our religious center has bound us together in a more mysterious fashion as well. In a country without a national church, the kind of "mere Christianity" has frequently provided an invisible mortar for our culture and a common vocabulary for our great debates. As Jody Bottum put it in a 2008 essay, the major Christian churches have operated "as simultaneously the happy enabler and the unhappy conscience of the American republic—a single source for both national comfort and national unease."[1]

That "unease" has been particularly important. In a country where religious enthusiasms tend to run ahead of common sense, the insistence on continuity with the Christian past has saved many churches from captivity to whatever fad or fashion happened to be passing through at the moment—and often helped save America as well. In this sense, orthodoxy hasn't just provided a moral and theological center for Americans. It has also often provided a means of necessary dissent—dissent from the intellectual overconfidence of the Age of Reason and the anti-intellectualism of nineteenth-century revivalism, dissent from the cold scientism of the Gospel According to Darwin and the crass materialism of the Gospel According to the Robber Barons, dissent from the desiccated rationalism of modernist theology and the dreary literalism of fundamentalism.

But, for the last five decades, with the decline of institutional Christianity, the river of orthodoxy has gradually been drying up. Americans, steeped in the ideal of religious freedom, take it for granted that orthodoxy without room for heresy is dangerous. Think of the Inquisition, they say, or the trial of Galileo, or (a little closer to home) the Puritan witch hunts. Yet heresy without room for orthodoxy turns out to be dangerous as well. Many of the overlapping crises in American life, from our foreign policy disasters to the housing bubble to the rate of out-of-wedlock births, can be traced to the impulse to emphasize one particular element of traditional Christianity—one insight, one doctrine, one teaching or tradition—at the expense of all the others. The goal is always progress: a belief system that's simpler or more reasonable, more authentic or more up-to-date. Yet the results often vindicate the older Christian synthesis. Heresy sets out to be simpler and more appealing and more rational, but it often ends up being more extreme.

Such extremism isn't a new thing in American life. Today's heretics are all eminently American, the heirs of Jefferson and Joseph Smith, Emerson and Eddy, the Victorian prosperity preachers and the religious intellectuals of the Progressive Era. Pushing Christianity to one extreme or another is what Americans have always done. We've been making idols of our country, our pocketbooks, and our sacred selves for hundreds of years.

What's changed today, though, is the weakness of the orthodox response.

*   *   *

A sign of this weakness is the extent to which the very terms *orthodoxy* and *heresy* have become controversial in today's religious conversation—either dismissed as anachronisms, or shunned for their historical associations with bigotry and persecution. In the modern age, there's an assumption that theological debates are really just struggles for power, that the lines between heresy and orthodoxy are inherently arbitrary, and that religious belief is too fluid and complicated to fit any sort of binary interpretation.

These assumptions aren't entirely wrong. Any theory of Christianity, my own included, has to allow that the line between orthodox and heretical beliefs often will be apparent more in theory than in practice, and clearer in hindsight than in the heat of controversy and debate. The definition of heresy proposed by Alister McGrath is a useful one: A Christian heresy is "best seen as a form of Christian belief that, more by accident than design, ultimately ends up subverting, destabilizing or even destroying the core of Christian faith." But McGrath's cautionary follow-up is also useful: "Both this process of destabilization and the identification of its threat may be spread out over an extended period of time."[2] This means that the last word on a particular controversy can take generations to be written. Reformers may be damned in one generation and rehabilitated in the next. Apparent heresiarchs are sometimes remembered as faithful Christians who attacked abuses, rather than as wreckers who threatened the essence of the faith. Mystics who were burned for heresy, as was Joan of Arc, may reemerge as saints.

But we should be able to recognize these complexities, and the crucial role that heresy has played in the history of the faith, without going to the extreme of denying that Christianity has a theological core at all. However blurry matters get on the periphery, a Christian center still exists—one that dates to the earliest centuries of the faith and that's still shared by most of the divided churches of Christendom today. Even as decisive a break as the Reformation, with all its hurled anathemas and "whore of Babylon" polemics, didn't shatter this common Protestant-Catholic connection to what Thomas Oden calls "the consensus of the early church."[3] The major Reformation-era debates were over how to interpret an existing consensus, both ancient and medieval, not about whether the consensus should be binding in the first place.

This consensus includes the basic dogmas of the faith: Christ's incarnation and atonement, the Trinity and the Virgin Birth, the forgiveness of sins and the possibility of everlasting life. It includes a belief in the divine inspiration and authority of a particular set of sacred scriptures, the Old and New Testaments, with no additional revelations added on and nothing papered over or rejected. It includes an adherence to the moral vision encoded in the Ten Commandments and expanded and deepened in the New Testament: a rejection of violence and cruelty, a deep suspicion of worldly wealth and power, and a heavy stress on chastity. It includes a commitment to the creeds of the ancient world—Nicene, Apostolic, Athanasian—and to the idea that a church, however organized and governed, should guarantee and promulgate them. And it includes the *idea* of orthodoxy—the belief that there exists "a faith once delivered to the saints," and that the core of Christianity is an inheritance from the first apostles, rather than being something that every believer can and should develop for himself.

What defines this consensus, above all—what distinguishes orthodoxy from heresy, the central river from the delta—is a commitment to mystery and paradox. Mysteries abide at the heart of every religious faith, but the Christian tradition is uniquely comfortable preaching dogmas that can seem like riddles, offering answers that swiftly lead to further questions, and confronting believers with the possibility that the truth about God passes all our understanding.

Thus orthodox Christians insist that Jesus Christ was divine and human all at once, that the Absolute is somehow Three as well as One, that God is omnipotent and omniscient and yet nonetheless leaves us free to choose between good and evil. They propose that the world is corrupted by original sin and yet somehow also essentially good, with the stamp of its Creator visible on every star and sinew. They assert that the God of the Old Testament, jealous and punitive, is somehow identical to the New Testament's God of love and mercy. They claim that this same God sets impossible moral standards and yet forgives every sin. They insist that faith alone will save us, yet faith without works is dead. And they propose a vision of holiness that finds room in God's Kingdom for all the extremes of human life—fecund families and single-minded celibates, politicians and monastics, queens as well as beggars, soldiers and pacifists alike.

Time and again, in the early centuries Anno Domini, the councils of the Church had the opportunity to resolve the dilemmas and shore up the fragile syntheses—to streamline Christianity, rationalize it, minimize the paradoxes and the difficulties, make it more consistent and less mysterious. They could have joined the movement that we call Gnosticism in attempting to minimize the problem of theodicy—of how a good God can allow evil to endure—by simply declaring this pain-filled world the work of a foolish or wicked demigod, and portraying Jesus as an emissary from a more perfect deity than the one who made our wounded earth. They could have fallen in line behind the second-century theologian Marcion's perfectly reasonable attempt to resolve the tensions between the Gospels and the Hebrew scriptures by abandoning Christianity's Jewish roots entirely. They could have listened to the earnest British moralist Pelagius instead of to Saint Augustine, and replaced the mysteries of grace and original sin with the more commonsensical vision of a God whose commandments can be obeyed through straightforward exertion.

In each instance, and in many more as well, they chose the way of mystery instead—or else they were bullied and arm-twisted into it, by mobs and emperors and polemicizing intellectuals. The process seemed haphazard at the time, but in hindsight it looks providential. In the choices they made and the arguments they rejected, the Fathers of the Church forged a faith whose doctrines speak to the intuition, nearly universal among human beings, that the true nature of the world will always remain just beyond our grasp. But they accomplished this without surrendering to an unintelligible mysticism or a crude anti-intellectualism. Indeed, this is perhaps the greatest Christian paradox of all—that the world's most paradoxical religion has cultivated rationalism and scientific rigor more diligently than any of its rivals, making the Christian world safe for philosophy as well as fervor, for the study of nature as well as the contemplation of divinity.

But if this spirit of paradox and mystery, of *both/and* rather than *either/ or,* has made Christianity extraordinarily adaptable, it has exposed the faith to a constant stream of criticism as well. One man's mystery is another man's incoherence, and the paradoxes of Christian doctrine have always been a source of scandal as well as strength—not only among atheists, but also among the many honest believers to whom orthodox Christian doctrine looks like a hopeless muddle or else transparent sophistry.

Jews and Muslims have argued as much for going on two thousand years. More significantly for our purposes, so have most heretics. The great

Christian heresies vary wildly in their theological substance, but almost all have in common a desire to resolve Christianity's contradictions, untie its knotty paradoxes, and produce a cleaner and more coherent faith. Heretics are often stereotyped as wild mystics, but they're just as likely to be problem solvers and logic choppers, well-intentioned seekers after a more reasonable version of Christian faith than orthodoxy supplies. They tend to see themselves, not irrationally, as rescuers rather than enemies of Christianity—saving the faith from self-contradiction and cultural irrelevance.

The nature of these rescue attempts varies according to which aspect of the Christian synthesis seems most incredible to a given culture at a given time and place. Amid the oracles and mystery cults of the early Roman Empire, for instance, the Gnostics sought to make Christianity more appealing by making it more overtly supernatural. Their Christ was a pure spirit disguised in mortal flesh, their vision of salvation an escape from physical suffering into an entirely disembodied plane. Eighteen centuries later, at the height of the Age of Reason, Deists and Unitarians went in the opposite direction, trying to rescue Christianity from the scorn of the scientific age by stripping away its supernatural aspects while leaving its ethical core intact. Their Christ was just a particularly insightful version of the species *Homo sapiens,* their God a distant watchmaker who had established physical and moral laws and then let His world unfold without any further intervention.

For many orthodox believers, these and all the other heresies are traps from which the faith has narrowly escaped. In G. K. Chesterton's vivid vision of Christian history, the fullness of truth is sustained in a perpetual balancing act, conducted at a wild gallop:

People have fallen into a foolish habit of speaking of orthodoxy as something heavy, humdrum, and safe. There never was anything so perilous or so exciting as orthodoxy. . . . It was the equilibrium of a man behind madly rushing horses, seeming to stoop this way and to sway that, yet in every attitude having the grace of statuary and the accuracy of arithmetic. The Church in its early days went fierce and fast with any warhorse; yet it is utterly unhistoric to say that she merely went mad along one idea, like a vulgar fanaticism. She swerved to left and right, so exactly as to avoid enormous obstacles. . . . To have fallen into any of those open traps of error and exaggeration which fashion after fashion and sect after sect set along the historic path of Christendom—that would indeed have been simple. It is always simple to fall; there are an infinity of angles at which one falls, only one at which one stands. To have fallen into any one of the fads from Gnosticism to Christian Science would indeed have been obvious and tame. But to have avoided them all has been one whirling adventure; and in my vision the heavenly chariot flies thundering through the ages, the dull heresies sprawling and prostrate, the wild truth reeling but erect.[4]

Yet perhaps this vision does not give heresy enough credit. "With no small amount of irony," Jonathan Wright points out "[heretics] did many favors to the cause of orthodoxy. Heresy was always orthodoxy's grumpy but indispensable twin."[5] Christianity's two thousand years of dynamism, its persistent and often unexpected vitality, owes something to the tight grip that the faith's leaders have kept on the reins of doctrine. But it owes a great deal to bold experimentation as well—to scholars who flirt with heterodoxy in the pursuit of a deeper understanding of the faith, to saints who rebel against the limits imposed by ecclesiastical authorities, to artists and poets who boldly go where popes and theologians fear to tread.

All of which is to say that Christian faith needs heresy, or at least the possibility of heresy, lest it become something rote and brittle, a compendium of doctrinal technicalities with no purchase on the human soul. Indeed, like flying buttresses around a great cathedral, the pull-and-push of competing heresies may be precisely the thing that keeps the edifice of Christian faith upright.

For most of our country's history, the American experience has vindicated this point. In many ways, the landscape of Christianity in America—where the faith is uncorrupted by state power and a thousand heresies are allowed to bloom—resembles the climate of the early Church, with all the furious theological ferment but (mercifully) none of the Roman persecution. What Christianity has offered to the United States has been matched by what the United States has offered to Christianity: a chance, in a nation with no establishment of religion, to recover the subversive power of its early centuries—a power that a religion founded on the crucifixion of a God-man alongside common criminals ought by rights to always possess.

In the nations of Europe, where orthodox belief was backed up by the force of law as well as by custom, the idea of what Robert Inchausti calls "subversive orthodoxy" often seemed like a contradiction in terms.[6] But in America, where heresies had free rein and established churches competed on a level playing field with start-up sects, the paradoxes of Christianity could regain their countercultural power. In America, religious gestures that would have been viewed as establishmentarian in the state-supported Christianity of Europe—becoming a priest or pastor or a monk, defending creeds and rituals and doctrinal exactness, seeking God through Holy Communion as well as in nature or philosophy—became radical once more. In America, because orthodoxy couldn't be taken for granted, orthodoxy came alive. In America, Chesterton's whirling adventure could become a real adventure once again.

For a time, at least. But if the American religious landscape has long resembled the world of early Christianity, then twenty-first-century America looks increasingly as if it's replaying that story with a very different ending—one in which orthodoxy slowly withers and only heresies endure.

How this came to pass is the subject of this book. The first chapter offers a portrait of American Christianity in the years following World War II—an era of intellectual confidence, artistic vitality, pews full to bursting, and a widespread sense that traditional Christian faith and contemporary liberal democracy were natural partners. Tracing the convergences between Mainline Protestantism, Evangelical Christianity, Roman Catholicism, and the African-American church, I discuss the emergence of what seemed at the time to be a rebuilt Christian center, at once steeped in the faith's oldest traditions and confidently engaged with modern thought and politics. In that lost world, only half a century gone, the Christian religion seemed to have passed through the fires of modernity and emerged scorched but stronger on the other side.

The next three chapters describe how this world came apart, and how an era of theological convergence gave way to a Christian civil war. They cover the divisions produced by controversies ranging from the Vietnam War to the debate over abortion; the efforts to accommodate Christian theology to the cultural revolutions of the 1960s and 1970s; the attempts at resistance by Protestants and Catholics alike; and the steady institutional decline—apparent in dwindling memberships, declining religious vocations, and diminished cultural clout—of the country's established churches in the wake of those revolutions. And they place special weight on the deeper reasons behind America's loss of confidence in orthodoxy, tracing developments in the late-modern West that have made basic Christian tenets seem less plausible than they did even in the very recent past.

In the second half of the book I consider American Christianity as it is today, in the wake of this slow-motion collapse, focusing on heresy's increasing dominance over our hyperreligious nation's way of faith. Some of these heresies can be associated with the careers of specific individuals—Joel Osteen and Dan Brown, Oprah Winfrey and Elizabeth Gilbert, Eckhart Tolle and Glenn Beck. Other heresies permeate our culture so completely that we take their premises for granted and don't think of them as distinctive theologies at all. Some offer direct critiques of orthodoxy, and define themselves explicitly as alternatives to historic Christianity; others undercut traditional Christian beliefs only implicitly, while noisily insisting on their own fidelity to Jesus Christ. But all of them exert a profound, and often profoundly negative, influence on our American society—on our intellectuals and our popular culture, our bedrooms and our boardrooms, the Democratic left and the Republican right alike. And, judging by spiritual trends within the rising generation, the future of American religion seems likely to be defined by Christian heresy even more completely than the present already is.

Given my own Catholic commitments, it will not be surprising that I would prefer to see a different American future—one where heresy's hold weakened and a more traditional Christianity was gradually renewed. But this book is not intended primarily as an apologia for my own religious beliefs. Obviously, I hope that my readers will be inspired to take a closer look at orthodox Christianity, and to reflect anew on its potential relevance for contemporary life. But I think that my analysis of how and why American Christianity has changed over the last fifty years, and what these changes mean for our national life today, will be compelling even to readers who are unconvinced that Jesus of Nazareth was resurrected from the dead.

As long as the United States remains a God-haunted country, secular as well as pious Americans will have a strong stake in the forms that American

religion takes. Both doubters and believers have benefited from the role
that institutional Christianity has traditionally played in our national life—
its communal role, as a driver of assimilation and a guarantor of social
peace, and its prophetic role, as a curb against our national excesses and a
constant reminder of our national ideals. Both doubters and believers stand
to lose if religion in the age of heresy turns out to be complicit in our fragmented communities, our collapsing families, our political polarization,
and our weakened social ties. Both doubters and believers will inevitably
suffer from a religious culture that supplies more moral license than moral
correction, more self-satisfaction than self-examination, more comfort than
chastisement.

This is the argument that I will advance in these pages. I am confident
that it can be received profitably by anyone—Christian or not, religious or
not—who cares about the state of this country, the challenges of the present moment, and the shape of things to come.

I

Christianity in Crisis

ONE

THE LOST WORLD

Somewhere in the dark years between Adolf Hitler's invasion of Poland and the turn of the Second World War's tide, Wystan Hugh Auden returned to his childhood faith. The poet was living in New York, having emigrated from England shortly before the outbreak of the war, and he began attending services at St. Mark's in the Bouwerie, an Episcopal parish and New York's second oldest church. He officially entered Anglican Communion in October 1940, but he would later describe that precise date as less important than the general drift in his thinking about matters of religion, which had been pressing him back toward Christianity for some time.

Some of the reasons for Auden's conversion were personal—in particular, the experience of being betrayed by his lover Chester Kallman, which Auden later wrote forced him to "know in person what it is like to feel oneself the prey of demonic powers, in both the Greek and Christian sense."[1] But he had other motives, intellectual and cultural, that were very particular to that specific historical time and place. These motives included the influence of his literary contemporaries. Along with Søren Kierkegaard, Auden would cite two of his fellow English writers, Charles Williams and C. S. Lewis—both members of a famous literary circle that also included J. R. R. Tolkien—as crucial to his return to religious belief, and once in America, he became fast friends with the Protestant theologian Reinhold Niebuhr and his wife, Ursula, as well.

Still more crucial, though, was the political context in which the poet found himself, and his reaction to the totalizing ideologies, Marxist and fascist, that were vying for mastery of Europe. In a 1957 essay on his re-conversion, Auden described a sojourn in Barcelona during the Spanish Civil War, at a time when the Republican struggle against Francisco Franco's fascists was a cause célèbre for the West's liberal intelligentsia. Following the example set by left-wing regimes from Mexico to Moscow, the Republicans had launched a campaign of persecution against the Spanish Catholic Church, and Auden arrived to find that all of the city's many churches had been closed and its priests exiled or killed. "To my astonishment," he wrote, "this discovery left me profoundly shocked and disturbed. . . . I could not help acknowledging that, however I had consciously ignored and rejected the Church for sixteen years, the existence of churches and what went on in them had all the time been very important to me."[2]

What he felt during his Spanish encounter with left-wing anti-Christianity was similar to his reactions to the anti-Christianity of the right. The "novelty and shock of the Nazis," Auden wrote, and the blitheness with which Hitler's acolytes dismissed Christianity "on the grounds that to love one's neighbor as oneself was a command fit only for effeminate weaklings," pushed him inexorably toward unavoidable questions. "If, as I am convinced, the Nazis are wrong and we are right, what is it that validates our values and invalidates theirs?" The answer to this question, he wrote later, was part of what "brought me back to the church."[3] When confronting the phenomenon of modern totalitarianism, he argued, "it was impossible any longer to believe that the values of liberal humanism were self-evident."[4] Humanism needed to be grounded in something higher than a purely material account of the universe, and in something more compelling than the hope of a secular utopia. Only religious premises could support basic liberal concepts like equality and human rights. Only God could ask human beings, as the poet put it, to "love their crooked neighbor with all their crooked heart."[5]

Auden being Auden, all of this was later summarized in verse, in two stanzas from his 1973 poem "Thanksgiving."

Finally, hair-raising things
that Hitler and Stalin were doing
forced me to think about God.

Why was I sure they were wrong?
Wild Kierkegaard, Williams and Lewis
guided me back to belief.[6]

The details of his pilgrimage were distinctive, but in its broad outlines, Auden's story was emblematic of his era. The disillusionment with the utopias of left and right, the sense of religion as a moral bulwark against totalitarianism, the influence of a generation of brilliant apologists and theologians, even the physical migration from the Old World to the New—these elements in Auden's return to Christian faith were also crucial elements in the larger postwar revival of American Christianity, which ushered in a kind of Indian summer for orthodox belief.

That age is lost to us now, almost beyond recall. It was the last moment in American life when the churches of the Protestant Mainline still composed something like a religious establishment capable of setting the tone for the culture as a whole. It was a period that saw the reemergence of Evangelical Protestantism as a significant force in American life, trading decades of self-imposed, often-paranoid isolation for cultural engagement and ecumenical revival. It was the peak, in certain ways, of the American Catholic Church, which had passed from a mistrusted immigrant faith to an institution almost unmatched in confidence and prestige, admired even by its fiercest Protestant rivals for the loyalty of its adherents and the vigor of its leaders. Most remarkably, perhaps, it was an era in which the black church, heretofore the most marginal of American Christian traditions, suddenly found itself at the center of the national story and claimed a moral authority unmatched before or since.

The strength of Christianity in this era rested on a foundation of swift demographic growth, as the steady, linear increase to which most American churches were accustomed gave way to a surge in membership and attendance that left denominations and parishes struggling to match supply to the newfound demand. In 1940, churchgoing rates hovered around 40 percent; by the late 1950s, they were close to 50 percent.[7] Religious identification increased more rapidly than usual as well, with church membership growing almost twice as fast as population growth. In 1930, 47 percent of Americans were formally affiliated with a church or denomination; the number had risen to 69 percent in 1960.[8] The prestige of religious leaders rose; for example, a poll from 1957 found that 46 percent of Americans described the clergy as the group "doing the most good" in the nation's common life, easily outstripping politicians, businessmen, and labor leaders.[9] Enrollments in seminaries and Sunday schools increased steadily, and there was a great surge in church construction: Americans spent $26 million on sacred architecture in 1945, $409 million in 1950, and a *billion* dollars in 1960.[10] "Not since the close of the Middle Ages," enthused one of the many advice books pitched to pastors and planning committees, "has there been promise of such able advance in the building arts of the church."[11] A British journalist, assessing America in the spirit of Alexis de Tocqueville, remarked that "we did not need the evidence of polls and church attendance to confirm what we could so easily observe—the walls of new churches rising in town and countryside wherever we went."[12]

The popular culture partook of the same revivalist spirit. "The theme of religion dominates the non-fiction best sellers," a *Publishers Weekly* analysis noted in 1953, "as it has in many of the preceding years."[13] Scripture sales soared: the distribution of Bibles rose 140 percent between 1949 and 1953.[14] The mutual antagonism between Christians and the entertainment industry lay in the future: From New Testament–themed sword-and-sandal epics like *The Robe* (1953), *Ben-Hur* (1959), and *Barabbas* (1961) to Old Testament dramas like *The Ten Commandments* (1956), spectacle and piety went hand in hand in postwar Hollywood. (Some of the more amusing casting choices from this era include Victor Mature as Samson, Gregory Peck as King David, and a young Joan Collins as Queen Esther.) Catholic influence in the movie industry was particularly potent, visible in the cooperation between motion picture executives and the Church on decency standards—the famous/infamous Hays Code was written by a Jesuit theologian—and the way that movie stars lined up to play heroic priests and nuns. (For a generation, Charles Morris writes, "the Hollywood priest archetype was the 'superpadre,' virile, athletic, compassionate, wise."[15]) One of the first celebrities in the new medium of television was a Catholic bishop, the great popularizer Fulton Sheen, who delivered a prime-time mix of apologetics and moral advice in a full cape, cassock, and pectoral cross. (Upon receiving an Emmy in 1952, he cracked, "I wish to thank my four writers—Matthew, Mark, Luke, and John."[16]) It was an era when "even the juke boxes and disc jockeys," Sydney Ahlstrom wrote, "provided evidence of a change in public attitudes."[17]

The Christian renaissance wasn't just a middlebrow affair. Taken on its own, the upsurge in church attendance could be chalked up to purely sociological factors (the return of veterans from war, the growth of the suburbs, the consequences of the baby boom), and the popular culture's religious turn to simple trend-chasing by publishers and movie executives. But there was a shift in the intellectual climate as well, which suggests that something deeper was happening—that the experience of the 1930s and 1940s had really prompted a broader reassessment of the modern story, and that the same feelings that had impelled Auden back to Christianity were at work in society as a whole. After the death camps and the gulag, it was harder to credit the naive progressive belief that the modern age represented a long march toward ever-greater enlightenment and peace, or that humanity was capable of relying for salvation on its own capacities alone. Instead, there was a sudden demand for writers who could revise the story that modernity told about itself—explaining what had gone wrong, and why, with reference to ideas and traditions that an earlier generation's intelligentsia had dismissed as irrelevant and out-of-date.

A host of thinkers answered this call. Not of all them were explicitly religious; their commitments ranged from the idiosyncratic European traditionalism of Eric Voegelin to the antitotalitarian liberalism of Hannah Arendt, from the continental socialism of Theodor Adorno to the very American conservatism of Richard Weaver and Russell Kirk. But they all contributed to a mood of historical and philosophical reassessment, in which the Christian past was mined for insights into the present situation, and the religious vision of a fallen world was suddenly more intellectually respectable than it had been for decades. Western liberalism originally sprang, in many ways, from Christian sources, and in the shadow of totalitarianism, the old Victorian-era debates over Darwinism, biblical criticism, and the like seemed less pressing than they once had, and the commonalities between the two traditions came rushing to the surface. From the halls of the United Nations (where the Catholic philosopher Jacques

Maritain played a small but crucial role in the writing of the Declaration on Human Rights) to the streets of the Jim Crow South (where ministers and priests were joining arms with left-wing activists in the name of human brotherhood), the intertwining causes of democracy, civil rights, and anti-Communism provided orthodox Christians and secular liberals with a set of common purposes and a temporary common ground.

The result was an era in which religious intellectuals such as C. S. Lewis, Paul Tillich, and John Courtney Murray regularly graced the cover of *Time* magazine; in which the prolific historians Christopher Dawson and Arnold Toynbee (another *Time* cover subject) attempted sweeping syntheses of Western history from a Christian point of view; in which the work of writers like William F. Buckley and Whittaker Chambers helped forge a conservative anti-Communism rooted in religious faith.

It was a golden age for Christian literature as well, a time when the Anglosphere's three greatest poets (Auden, Eliot, and the young Robert Lowell) were all Christian converts; when Evelyn Waugh and Graham Greene were at the height of their powers and Walker Percy and Flannery O'Connor were just coming into their own; when Lewis and Tolkien were publishing the twentieth century's two most enduring works of Christian fantasy. Catholicism had been a fossilized substrate in the works of Lost Generation novelists, but the midcentury literary scene was crowded with self-consciously Catholic writers, many of them unjustly neglected today: J. F. Powers, Jean Stafford, Edwin O'Connor, Caroline Gordon, Allen Tate, and Walter Miller. And not only novelists; the two greatest spiritual memoirs of the twentieth century were produced within five years of each other, when Thomas Merton's *The Seven Storey Mountain* (1948) was followed by Dorothy Day's *The Long Loneliness* in 1952.

Indeed, from the vantage point of the current religious moment, perhaps the most striking features of the midcentury revival are the ways in which mass-market faith and highbrow religiosity seemed to complement each other. The revival meetings in the Bible Belt coincided with what *Commentary*'s Will Herberg called the "religious stirring on campus"[18]; the surge in church attendance in the heartland was mirrored in a sudden tendency for intellectuals to identify themselves, if not necessarily as believers, then at least as what one journalist termed "fellow travelers of faith."[19] As a writer for the *Times Literary Supplement* put it in 1954, both "the social climate for religious living" and "the intellectual climate for religious thinking" became "much more congenial" in the years following World War II.[20]

Asked to assess "the revival of religion," a major American theologian took note of this parallelism: "Mass conversions under the ministrations of popular evangelists," he wrote in the Sunday *New York Times,* were suddenly proceeding at a pace unseen "since the days of Billy Sunday." At the same time, there was an unexpected "receptivity toward the message of the historic faiths" among intellectuals, "which is in marked contrast to the indifference or hostility of past decades." Among academic students of religion, especially, a "defensive attitude" about their subject has given way to a "conviction of the importance and relevance of the 'message' of the Bible, as distinguished from the message of, say, Plato, on the one hand, or Herbert Spencer, on the other."[21]

Or, as another observer put it: "The avante-garde is becoming old-fashioned; religion is the latest thing."[22]

A kind of Christian convergence was the defining feature of this era. In the postwar revival, the divided houses of American Christendom didn't just grow, they grew closer together, reengaged with one another after decades of fragmentation and self-segregation. Four figures in particular—a Protestant intellectual, an Evangelical preacher, a Catholic bishop, and an African-American prophet—embodied this convergence.

The intellectual was Reinhold Niebuhr, author of the *New York Times* essay quoted above and a thinker who embodied the trend that he was describing. Niebuhr was the ideal type of a species all but lost to us today: the public theologian, deeply engaged in a particular Christian tradition—in his case, a "neo-orthodox" Protestantism—but capable of setting the agenda for the secular world as well. There were many such figures in the postwar era, and many of them had some sort of continental pedigree, from Auden-esque émigrés like Jacques Maritain and Paul Tillich to Europeans whose ideas crossed the Atlantic, even if they themselves did not: Protestants Karl Barth, Dietrich Bonhoeffer, and Denis de Rougemont (Auden's favorable 1941 review of de Rougemont's *Love in the Western World* was one of the first public clues to his conversion); Catholics Etienne

Gilson, Yves Congar, and Henri de Lubac; the Eastern Orthodox philosopher Nikolai Berdyaev; the unclassifiable Simone Weil.

But the Missouri-born Niebuhr loomed over them all. He was the leading thinker of the Mainline Protestant establishment in its last years of cultural supremacy, the most sophisticated interpreter of the American soul at a moment when the United States had suddenly achieved global preeminence, the conscience of a deeply religious nation reckoning with the moral perils of the nuclear age. For a generation of intellectuals and academics, his preachings and writings offered a model of highbrow Christianity and a reason to look anew at religious faith. For a generation of American policy makers wrestling with the challenges of the Cold War, he supplied a compelling vocabulary for thinking about the relationship between morality and politics in a fallen world. In the popular religious culture, his Serenity Prayer was adopted by Alcoholics Anonymous (itself one of the most enduring institutional legacies of the midcentury revival), and soon claimed a place alongside the Our Father and the Hail Mary in the vernacular of American piety. In death, he has become a kind of universal intellectual, claimed as an inspiration by Protestants and Catholics, liberals and neoconservatives, believers and atheists alike.

He was an unlikely figure to become a pillar of the East Coast religious establishment. Born to a German Calvinist pastor in the Middle West of 1892, Niebuhr was educated in the middling academies of his denomination before making the leap to Yale's School of Religion during World War I. (On the Ivy League campus, he wrote to a friend, his lack of intellectual training or East Coast polish made him feel like a "mongrel among thoroughbreds."[23]) The first thirteen years of his public career were spent as the pastor of Bethel Evangelical Church on West Grand Boulevard in Detroit, where he gained a reputation for what one biographer, Larry L. Rasmussen, calls "volcanic activity": he was constantly preaching, writing, and traveling; throwing himself into the controversies of his city, his denomination, and his country. In the late 1920s, this activity brought him to the attention of Henry Sloane Coffin, dean of Union Theological Seminary in New York, the Mainline's flagship school, who decided to offer the thirty-something Niebuhr a teaching position despite his conspicuous lack of a Ph.D. The faculty was skeptical, and the young minister had his appointment approved by a mere one-vote margin. But as Richard Wightman Fox writes, his electric impact on the Union campus soon vindicated Coffin's judgment:

> Already a celebrity on the Protestant circuit, he instantly drew circles of students around him. They dogged his steps as he careered through the hallways, they sat wide-eyed in the Common Room after lunch and dinner while he issued rapid-fire commentary on world events, they struggled to record even a small portion of his lectures as his words raced ahead to keep up with his mind. They flocked to chapel to hear him roar and watch him gesticulate: his words rolled down like waters, his ideas like a never-ending stream. Thoughts piled up on other thoughts with such speed that sentences were often abandoned halfway through, overwhelmed by the more potent images that followed. He worked usually from a one-page outline, having long before found it difficult to read aloud from a text. . . . Certain vital items like Biblical passages or literary allusions he memorized. Otherwise it was the free flow of an inspired mind, summoning a favorite Old Testament verse in an affectionate whisper, playing excitedly with some key irony of human living or paradox of Christian belief, clamoring with fists clenched for an end to Christian complacency and the dawn of a militant church fighting eyeball to eyeball with the principalities and powers.[24]

When Niebuhr arrived at Union, the seminary and the denominations it served were dominated by modernist theology, which had been developed in the late Victorian era as a response to the twin challenges posed to Christianity by Darwinism and historical criticism of the Bible. The modernists' goal was to adapt Christianity to the new scientific and historical consensus, and to maintain the relevance of faith in an intellectual climate suddenly grown dismissive of the authority of Scripture. To this end, they stressed ethics rather than eschatology; social reform rather than confessional debate; symbolic and allegorical interpretations of the Bible rather than more literal readings. Their great project was the Social Gospel, which urged believers to embrace an "applied Christianity" that would put Jesus' commandments into practice here and now, through legislation as well as conversion, law as well as grace.

Some aspects of modernism were compatible with traditional Christianity, and many Protestants in the churches influenced by the modernist project retained a recognizably orthodox faith—albeit one that allowed room for Darwin-inspired doubts about the more literal interpretations of certain Bible passages, and that placed special stress on the obligation to convert societies as well as individuals to Christian ethics. But it was easy to go further. A famous cartoon from the era depicted theological liberals descending step by step from Christianity to atheism; the steps are labeled *Bible Not Infallible, No Virgin Birth,* and *No Resurrection*—and many modernists fit the caricature. They tried to strip away anything transcendent or mysterious in Christianity; they scoffed at the miraculous and dismissed creeds and confessions as irrelevant. They downgraded original sin and placed their faith in what Walter Rauschenbusch's *Christianity and the Social Crisis* (1907) rather overoptimistically called "the immense latent perfectability in human nature."[25] Instead of merely reconciling their faith to Darwinian science, they subordinated their faith to a vulgar Social Darwinism, which divinized capital-P Progress and treated the unfolding of secular history itself as the only dispositive revelation of God's purposes on earth.

In Europe, the modernist project died in the trenches of World War I, its utopianism gassed and machine-gunned and garroted on barbed wire. In the wake of that catastrophe, the young German theologian Karl Barth published his *Epistle to the Romans* (1922), a commentary on Saint Paul that doubled as a long attack on every kind of Christian accommodation—to history, to humanism, to the nation-state, to fashionable ideas of progress and development and reform. Barth preached a return to "the strange world of the Bible,"[26] a return to original sin and transcendent hope, a return to the idea of God as a mysterious Other whose purposes could not be comprehended by the fallen mortal mind. He emphasized the limits of human knowledge and the absolute demands of divine revelation, rejecting the confident rationalism of liberal theologians in favor of the existentialism of Luther, Kierkegaard, and Augustine. And he depicted World War I as the inevitable end point of a theology that made human aspirations rather than the biblical God the measure of all things. "They have wished to experience the known god of this world," Barth wrote of the modernists. "Well! They have experienced him!"[27]

Barth's "bombshell in the playground of the theologians," as his Catholic contemporary Karl Adam called it,[28] took some time to find an audience (or even a translator, for that matter) in the United States. But by the 1930s, with storm clouds gathering once again in Europe and our nation sunk in the Great Depression, the time was ripe for a reassessment of modernism's worldliness and for a return to aspects of Christianity that the liberal theologians had downgraded or ignored.

From his position at Union Seminary, Niebuhr became the central figure in this reconsideration. He had grown up with modernist theology, but the more he immersed himself in the political and social controversies of his era, the more overoptimistic and implausible the modernist project came to seem. "About midway in my ministry," he wrote in 1939, "which extends roughly from the peace of Versailles to the peace of Munich . . . I underwent a fairly complete conversion of thought which involved rejection of almost all the liberal theological ideals and ideas with which I ventured forth in 1915."[29]

In their place he championed what came to be known as *neo-orthodoxy* (Niebuhr preferred the term *prophetic Christianity*), which dismissed modernism's blithe cosmic optimism and insisted on the relevance of traditional Christian concepts like original sin and divine judgment. (In the much-quoted words of Niebuhr's brother, Richard, the modernists were guilty of believing that "a God without wrath brought men without sin into a kingdom without judgment through the ministrations of a Christ without a cross."[30]) The details differed from thinker to thinker, but the overall pattern of neo-orthodoxy held: a rejection of utopianism in all its forms; a return to Protestantism's Reformation roots; a renewed interest in creedal, confessional, and liturgical issues; a stress on the saving life and death (as opposed to just the ethical message) of Jesus Christ; and a demand for Christian humility in the face of the mysteries of God's purposes.

Niebuhr's particular emphasis was on humanity's irredeemable sinfulness—what his fellow Union professor John Bennett called "the stubbornness of evil in the human situation,"[31] which no philosophy can overcome and no political regime can legislate away. However, this pessimism did not lead him to abandon politics entirely, or even to break with the political left. (He famously rejected the pacifism of the interwar period, but he continued to call himself a socialist, and eventually embraced

Franklin Roosevelt's New Deal.) Instead, he preached a chastened form of Christian liberalism, which was alive to the possibility of social reform but constantly attuned to the realities of power and to the perpetual temptations of hubris, self-righteousness, and pride. "There is . . . no cultural or scientific task, and no social or political problem," he wrote in the 1940s, "in which men do not face new possibilities of the good and the obligation to realize them." But, at the same time, "every effort and pretention to complete life . . . or to eliminate the final corruptions of history must be disavowed."[32] For Niebuhr, the quest for reform was authentically Christian; the quest for utopia was a dangerous and destructive heresy.

This message found a wide audience in the world of the postwar revival. Sydney Ahlstrom writes, "If one looks to the remarkable way in which theology and theologians loomed up during the forties in the nation's moral, intellectual and cultural life . . . neo-orthodoxy becomes essential to an adequate explanation."[33] The movement's influence touched nearly every Mainline denomination, through figures such as Episcopalian theologian Walter Lowrie, Congregationalist Douglas Lawrie, Methodist Edwin Lewis, and many more. It reached upward to great ecumenical organizations like the Federal (later National) Council of Churches and the World Council of Churches, whose founding conference featured addresses from Niebuhr and Karl Barth, and downward to the parish level, where there was renewed emphasis in many Protestant churches on Scripture, creeds, and formal liturgy.

A Niebuhrian worldview also radiated outward into national politics, calling America's leaders to a sober realism, a reluctant shouldering of adult responsibilities in a world inevitably deformed by sin. George Kennan would later describe his famous "Long Telegram" from Moscow as a document written in the form of "a seventeenth-century Protestant sermon,"[34] and the entire American political class's understanding of their Cold War mission partook of the same spirit. In this climate, the classic image of an "American Adam," born innocent of the Old World's stamp of sin, gave way to an image of the United States as a post-Edenic Adam—Adam as "a tragic hero," Jason Stevens writes, "bearing History as his cross."[35]

Even among the secular intelligentsia, the idea of a Christian realism, neither innocent nor cynical, appealed to many people who had seen their utopian hopes dashed by the lived experience of fascism and (especially)

Communism. Many socialist intellectuals, Stevens points out, "had come from inherited religious backgrounds that they were either trying to lose or renovate." Once the realities of left-wing totalitarianism became apparent, their credulous former support for the Soviet Union inspired a potent sense of quasi-Christian guilt—which was often "peculiarly expressed," Stevens writes, in the "post-Edenic themes pronounced in American's Protestant past."[36] Sometimes this guilt carried them all the way back to Protestantism itself, as with Whittaker Chambers, Soviet spy turned Quaker memoirist. More often, though, it inspired a general sympathy for the neo-orthodox worldview that stopped somewhat short of actual Christian belief, a dynamic captured in Arthur Schlesinger Jr.'s famous crack that he intended to start a movement of "atheists for Niebuhr."

During this era the Protestant Mainline enjoyed a kind of twilight glow. The years of the Niebuhrs and neo-orthodoxy were the last years that Presbyterians and United Methodists and Episcopalians and Lutherans would see a sustained growth in membership, the last era during which Mainline churches conducted serious missionary efforts overseas, the last period when leadership seemed to care as much about evangelization as about political activism. This was the last era when the Mainline seemed to have a particular culture all its own—when magazines with names like *Presbyterian Life* and *The American Lutheran* reached millions of subscribers, when Mainline intellectuals had enough confidence in their faith to talk without embarrassment about "winning America" for Protestantism,[37] and when their denominations had enough money and manpower to build new churches almost as quickly as other branches of American Christianity.

Perhaps the emblematic project of this period was the National Council of Churches' new Manhattan headquarters, a nineteen-story skyscraper intended as a kind of "Protestant Vatican" that all Mainline churches could call home. The money for the Interchurch Center came from the Northern Baptist John D. Rockefeller Jr., who guaranteed the NCC a rent-free ninety-nine-year lease. The cornerstone had been excavated from the marketplace of ancient Corinth—the place, as the next day's *New York Times* noted, "where the New Testament reports the apostle Paul 'stayed a year and six months teaching the word of God.'"[38]

That stone was laid in the autumn of 1958 by Dwight D. Eisenhower himself, whose grand progress from Riverside Church to the construction site was joined by two hundred choristers, three hundred religious leaders, and thirty-seven banners representing the various denominational participants. The spirit of the ceremony was the spirit of the age: a celebration of Christian convergence and institutional vitality, in which thirty thousand people heard the president of the United States hail the nation's churches as "sturdy defenders of the Constitutional and God-given rights of each citizen," and describe religion itself as the "firm foundation" of the nation's moral life. Readers of the next day's *Times* were informed, by no less an authority than the president of the United Nations General Assembly, that the new center's main purpose was to "draw together the scattered sheep" of Jesus Christ.[39]

When it came time, some years later, for New York City to rename the street in front of the center, there was only one possibility. To this day, the section of West 120th Street between Broadway and Riverside Drive is known as Reinhold Niebuhr Place.

Less than a year before Eisenhower made his pilgrimage to Morningside Heights, New York City played host to a very different but equally emblematic gathering: Billy Graham's famous Manhattan crusade. Graham had been the nation's most celebrated revivalist for almost a decade, but even by his standards the New York event was an extraordinary undertaking; the nightly services featured a four-thousand-member choir, three thousand ushers, and thousands of counselors ready to assist anyone who came forward to answer Graham's call for conversion. For sixteen weeks, the famous evangelist preached at Madison Square Garden, drawing almost twenty thousand people a night in what was supposed to be the world's capital of scoffing, sophisticated skepticism. (The mass media was completely won over: ABC began broadcasting an hourlong segment from the revival, and the *New York Times* took to printing the texts of his sermons—"as though he were some international dignitary addressing the United Nations," David Aikman notes.[40]) In midsummer, Graham drew 100,000 people to Yankee Stadium, breaking the record set by the Joe Louis–Max Baer fight a decade earlier. On the final weekend, Labor Day of 1957, a similar number crowded Times Square to hear Graham exhort them to turn their hearts over to Jesus Christ, temporarily transforming

Forty-second and Broadway into a vast cathedral, pillared with skyscrapers and vaulted by the sky.

Graham's rise to eminence was even more unlikely than Niebuhr's. He was reared in Depression-era poverty in rural North Carolinia: His father was a dairy farmer with only three years of formal schooling, and Graham himself was an indifferent student who bounced from Bible college to Bible college in the 1930s before getting his diploma (and meeting his wife, Ruth, which was perhaps more crucial) at Illinois's Wheaton College in the early 1940s. By then he had discovered his gift for preaching, and he spent the rest of that decade making his way up the revival-circuit ladder, as a field representative for Youth for Christ and then as a celebrity preacher in his own right, who burst into the nation's consciousness (thanks in part to some boosterism from the Hearst newspaper chain) during a huge tent-meeting revival in Los Angeles in 1949. By the middle of the following decade, he had become the public face of American Christianity—an astonishing feat for a preacher from what was supposed to be a marginalized and fading religious tradition.

That tradition was Evangelical Christianity. In the nineteenth century, the term "evangelical" simply described the characteristic style of American Christianity in the aftermath of the Second Great Awakening: a Protestantism that emphasized biblical authority, personal conversion, and public evangelization. Prior to the rise of modernism, Evangelicals effectively *were* the Mainline. But the challenge of Darwinism and biblical criticism threw this style of faith into crisis. From the 1920s onward, American Evangelicals responded by retreating into the intellectual cul-de-sac of fundamentalism, losing a long battle with modernists for control of the major Protestant churches along the way. (Of the major Protestant bodies, only the Southern Baptist Convention remained a stronghold of Evangelical piety and belief.)

Just as many modernists saw themselves as loyal believers trying to make the Christian religion intelligible in an age of growing doubt, many of the Evangelicals who turned to fundamentalism during the 1910s and 1920s saw themselves as simply carrying on the unbroken traditions of their ancestors in faith. (The five "fundamentals" from which the fundamentalist movement took its name were mainly just a restatement of orthodox Christian beliefs—the divine inspiration of the Bible, the virgin birth and bodily resurrection of Christ, the historical reality of his miracles, and the atoning purpose of his crucifixion.) But, just as many modernists had slipped inexorably toward a quasi-Christian religion of progress, many fundamentalists gradually embraced interpretations of the Bible that would have been foreign to earlier Christian authorities, and looked untenable in the light of modern scholarship.

In their haste to defend scriptural authority against scoffing scientists and academic critics, fundamentalists adopted a radical literalism—including the deadly "six 24-hour days" reading of Genesis 1—that their Protestant forebears had traditionally rejected. ("He who would learn astronomy," John Calvin wrote of Genesis 1, "let him go elsewhere."[41]) Meanwhile, their political and cultural anxieties left them prey to millenarian scenarios, chief among them the "dispensationalist" reading of Scripture popularized in the 1910s by Cyrus Scofield's bestselling *Scofield Reference Bible*, which claimed to trace, with quasiscientific precision, a series of stages in salvation history that would soon culminate in the Second Coming of Christ. (This was the first time that the now-commonplace idea of a "Rapture" of believers entered Christian thought.)

Equipped with this mix of textual literalism and analytic pseudorigor, fundamentalism could claim to have a biblically based schematic for interpreting all of modern history—a kind of Christian version of Marxism, one might say, that offered all the answers to anyone willing to embrace its self-enclosed system of interpretation. This self-enclosure was cemented in the 1920s, when fundamentalists chose a courtroom in Dayton, Tennessee, as the central front in their battle against modernism, evolution in school textbooks as their enemy, and William Jennings Bryan as their general—and lost resoundingly.

In the aftermath of the Darwin wars, fundamentalists were either pushed to the margins of the major Protestant churches or else jumped ship to found their own denominations, and what remained of nineteenth-century Protestantism's institutional inheritance (seminaries and universities, especially) slipped permanently beyond their grasp. By the Depression era, the stigma of fundamentalism ensured that Evangelical Protestantism was increasingly defined as a religion of the marginalized and dispossessed, retrenching in the rural heartland while the progress of modern civilization continued without them. "Of course, most Americans were aware that in the back country there were hillbillies, rednecks, holy rollers, tent revivalists, Bible colleges, and evangelistic radio stations and publishing compa-nies," Martin Marty writes. "But these were segregated in the Bible Belts of the Midwest and especially the South. . . . Since they were out of step with modernity, they were expected increasingly to disappear."[42]

This was the world in which Graham came of age. His parents were Presbyterians who joined a dispensationalist church after the family lost its savings in a Depression-era bank failure, and Graham's theology in the early years of his ministry was for the most part an unvarnished fundamen-talism, literalist in its reading of Scripture and apocalyptic in its interpreta-tion of the signs of the times.

But his style was something else—ecumenical, openhanded, confident, American. The revivalists of fundamentalism's wilderness years were figures of fun for nonbelievers—Aimee Semple McPherson, the leading evangelist of the 1920s, was accused of faking her own kidnapping for publicity pur-poses—and by the early 1940s revivalism itself seemed to be on the verge of dying out. (In 1946, the dean of the Harvard Divinity School remarked that the hacks and hucksters of fundamentalism had "discredited the tradi-tion" of revivals entirely.[43]) But Graham almost singlehandedly revitalized the form, using it to carry an Evangelical message from the backwoods tent meetings to the nation's biggest cities and arenas—and then overseas as well, to Europe and the Third World and even behind the Iron Curtain.

As his audience grew and his horizons expanded, the trajectory of Graham's career led inexorably up from fundamentalism, and his example helped pull millions of his fellow Evangelicals upward with him. His big-city crusades required cooperation with Mainline Protestants and even Catholic leaders, and required him to abandon the radical separatism that many fundamentalist preachers demanded. (The people who answered the altar call at his massive urban rallies were referred to local churches after-ward—Mainline as well as Evangelical, Catholic as well as Protestant.) As the civil rights movement gathered steam, he invited blacks and whites to worship together at his rallies. Fifty years later, Bill Clinton remembered Graham's refusing a request from the city fathers of Little Rock to segregate his revival there in 1959: "I was just a little boy," Clinton said, "and I never forgot it, and I've loved him ever since."[44]

Visiting England in the mid-1950s, Graham was asked about his theo-logical convictions, and answered, "I am neither a fundamentalist nor a modernist."[45] Instead, he was on his way to becoming the prototypical *neo-evangelical*, a term coined by Harold Ockenga to describe Evangelicalism's midcentury reemergence from the fundamentalist ghetto. The neo-evangelical movement coalesced around a group of new religious institutions: the National Association of Evangelicals was founded in 1942; Fuller Theological Seminary opened its doors five years later (with its namesake, Charles E. Fuller, host of the "Old Fashioned Revival Hour" radio show, as its first president); Campus Crusade for Christ began ministering on UCLA's campus in 1951; *Christianity Today*, the movement's flagship periodical, was founded midway through Eisenhower's presidency and quickly claimed a readership in the hundreds of thousands. Like Graham's own ministry, these were all "parachurch" organizations, deliberately designed to transcend the fissiparous tendencies of Evangelicalism, and unify where too many fundamentalist churches had divided.

The key neo-evangelical text was Carl F. W. Henry's *The Uneasy Conscience of Modern Fundamentalism* (1947), which chastised fundamentalists for their separatism and anti-intellectualism, and called for Evangelicals to reengage with the nation's great political and social debates. Officially, Henry and his fellow neo-evangelicals were proposing a shift only in tactics, not in theology. "The 'uneasy conscience' of which I write," Henry insisted, "is not one troubled about the great Biblical verities . . . but rather one distressed by the frequent failure to apply them effectively to crucial problems confronting the modern mind."[46] But the neo-evangelical movement clearly had theological purposes as well. From its inception, its leaders were intent on detaching their cobelievers from the millenarian temptation— Evangelicalism must not preach an "imminent utopia," Henry warned, but rather, approach the future with "sober optimism"[47]—and returning them to their Reformation roots. And while the movement's first generation was at pains to emphasize its fidelity to the doctrine of biblical inerrancy, the process of intellectual engagement they set in motion led inexorably to a reevaluation of fundamentalism's insistence on a strict literalism in scriptural interpretation as well.

Graham himself was no intellectual, but he understood his moment and picked his allies wisely. He became a board member at Fuller Theological Seminary, a frequent attendee at NAE, a vocal supporter of the neo-evangelical movement's forays into political engagement. When

Christianity Today was launched, with Henry as its editor, it was under the umbrella of the Billy Graham Evangelistic Association. The new magazine, Graham promised, would "plant the evangelical flag in the middle of the road, taking the conservative theological position but a definite liberal approach to social problems."[48]

He understood his role in the wider culture as well. Just as Niebuhr's Christian realism fit the Cold War mood, so did Graham's call to national revival, his message of Christian hope in the shadow of the atom bomb, his emphasis on the salvation of nations as well as individuals. (The highbrow Niebuhr disdained the great revivalist, but they were working different ends of the same street.) Year after year, rally after rally, Graham took premises that fundamentalists had placed in the service of off-putting jeremiads and turned them, through the elixir of his charisma, in the service of a message of God's universal love. As Marty writes, "Paradoxically, this preacher of an exclusive Gospel—Jesus Saves! meant Only Jesus Saves!—came to be seen as an inclusivist who could figuratively wrap his long arms around Protestant-Catholic-Jew, around black and white, male and female America."[49]

Little more than a generation passed between the Scopes Monkey Trial and the great Manhattan crusade of 1957, but it might as well have been an eternity. With his command of mass media, his television broadcasts and stadium appearances and global tours, Billy Graham had done the near-impossible: he had carried Evangelical Christianity from the margins to the mainstream, making Evangelical faith seem respectable as well as fervent, not only relevant but *modern*.

The controversies that divided American Protestantism in the first decades of the twentieth century had also troubled the Roman Catholic Church, but among Catholics the papacy still had the last word, and it was delivered in Pope Pius X's sweeping 1907 condemnation of the entire modernist project. Calling modernism the "synthesis of all heresies," the pope listed sixty-five propositions that were incompatible with Catholic faith, and required that "all clergy, pastors, confessors, preachers, religious superiors, and professors in philosophical-theological seminaries" take an oath against modernism and its works. The sixty-fifth proposition, summarizing the thrust of the entire anathema, condemned the conceit that "modern

Catholicism can be reconciled with true science only if it is transformed into a non-dogmatic Christianity; that is to say, into a broad and liberal Protestantism."[50]

Notably, Pius's syllabus of modernist heresies did not directly reference evolutionary science or the proper interpretation of Genesis 1, sparing the Catholic Church from some of the dead ends explored by fundamentalists. Nonetheless, the atmosphere of purges, loyalty oaths, and forbidden books took an undoubted toll on Catholic intellectual life, driving the modernist tendency underground rather than engaging its errors and assimilating its insights. Pius's crackdown temporarily spared the Church from division and dissent, but his victory was inevitably impermanent, and he may have made later intra-Catholic civil wars that much more intense. In the years following the Second Vatican Council, the Catholic essayist James Hitchcock has noted, modernism would "haunt Catholicism like a repressed desire."[51]

With that being said, the conventional wisdom on this episode—"it was as though someone had pulled a switch and the lights had failed all across the American Catholic landscape," runs an analysis quoted in Jay Dolan's *The American Catholic Experience* (1992)[52]—seems perhaps overstated, given how little American Catholicism at midcentury seemed to have suffered from the suppression of the modernist impulse fifty years before. Quite the reverse; the postwar era was a kind of Catholic golden age, a time when the Church's demographic strength was unrivaled, its political influence unparalled, and its cultural footprint large and deep.

The architects of American Catholicism, nineteenth-century prelates like John Hughes of New York, had dreamed of a church that (as Charles Morris puts it) "would be *in* America, vehemently *for* America, but never *of* America."[53] By the Eisenhower era, they seemed to have succeeded beyond their wildest dreams. On the one hand, American Catholicism felt like a rich world unto itself—with its own educational system (half of all Catholic children attended Catholic schools), its own holidays and festivals, its own newspapers and professional associations, its own language and literature, its own kitsch. Catholic exceptionalism, visible in church attendance, birthrates, and other indicators, was one of the striking facts of midcentury life. The memoirs of the period—whether critical or nostalgic—invariably emphasize the *comprehensiveness* of Catholic culture, the sense of Catholicism as "primal identity that absorbed and conditioned all the others,"[54] in Kenneth Woodward's words, and of the Church as an institution that "judged things not out of a deeper antiquity," as Garry Wills put it, "but from outside time altogether."[55]

Yet, for all its internal strength, the Catholicism of midcentury wasn't ghettoized and marginalized, as the immigrant church had often been in the nineteenth century, and as Evangelical Protestantism had recently become. Instead, both American politics and pop culture bore a distinctively Catholic stamp. Campaigning for the presidency in 1932, Franklin Roosevelt had linked Pope Pius XI's social encyclical *Quadragesimo Anno* ("one of the greatest documents of modern times,"[56] the future president declared) to his own economic agenda, and over the course of the next decade the papal vision of a third way between laissez-faire capitalism and socialism seemed to find expression in the Democratic Party's New Deal. (Monsignor John Ryan, head of the D.C.-based National Catholic Welfare Conference, earned the nickname "the Right Reverend New Dealer" for his vigorous efforts on behalf of Roosevelt's programs.) By the 1950s the political economy of the United States looked remarkably like the vision of the good society outlined by Pius and his predecessors, complete with labor-industry cooperation and a pro-family welfare state.

The entire media-entertainment complex, meanwhile, was almost shamelessly pro-Catholic. If a stranger to American life had only the movies, television, and popular journalism from which to draw inferences, he probably would have concluded that midcentury America was a Catholic-majority country—its military populated by the sturdy Irishmen of *The Fighting 69th* (1948) and *The Fighting Sullivans* (1944); its children educated and its orphans rescued by the heroic priests and nuns celebrated in *Boys Town* (1938), *The Bells of Saint Mary's* (1945), and *Fighting Father Dunne* (1948); its civic life dominated by urban potentates like Francis Cardinal Spellman of New York and Denis Dougherty of Philadelphia; its everyday life infused with Catholic kitsch, from the 1950s hit single "Our Lady of Fatima" to the "win one for the Gipper" cult of Notre Dame football.

No figure embodied the double life of Catholic culture—its simultaneously self-enclosed otherness and intense all-Americanism—more than the bishop and religious broadcaster Fulton Sheen. Like Niebuhr and Graham, Sheen was a Middle American who made good. Descended from Irish immigrants who fled the Great Famine, he was raised in Peoria, Illinois, by a farmer father and educated exclusively within the network of American parochial schools, rising through Catholic grammar school and high school to St. Viator College in Bourbonnais, Illinois (a school run by French priests in a town founded by Quebecois immigrants), and thence to the seminary in St. Paul, Minnesota. After his ordination, in 1919, he completed his education in Europe, earning a Ph.D. in philosophy from the Catholic University of Louvain before returning to a tenured position at the Catholic University of America in Washington, D.C., where his academic work was soon eclipsed by a stream of apologetics and polemics and then by a career in radio and television.

In an earlier era, this biography could have made Sheen seem like an exotic and even threatening character—the suave and sinister papist, subverting Protestant America from within. From his personal piety (the teenage intuition of his vocation to the priesthood, the particular devotion to the Virgin Mary) to his style of dress (in the full old-world regalia of the pre–Vatican II Catholic priest) to his unembarrassed interest in winning converts (he was associated with numerous high-profile conversions, including those of Henry Ford Jr. and Clare Boothe Luce), Sheen offered skeptics enough material to weave an entire web of anti-Catholic suspicion. And yet he was instead embraced as an American icon—a highbrow televangelist without a hint of scandal, a courtly and more intellectual version of Billy Graham. Like Graham, he had flair for turning the new mass media to Christian ends, and a talent for disarming and charming viewers who didn't share his theological commitments. Like Graham, he understood his era perfectly, using first World War II and later the Cold War to sell an ecumenical audience on the idea of a Christian civilization imperiled by secularism and Communism alike.

Sheen honed his skills as a radio broadcaster on the *Catholic Hour* in the 1930s and 1940s: a *Time* magazine profile in 1946 described him as "the golden-voiced Msgr. Fulton J. Sheen, U.S. Catholicism's famed proselytizer."[57] He was consecrated as an auxiliary bishop for New York in 1951, and offered the Tuesday-night slot on ABC that same year. The 8 p.m. hour had been a ratings graveyard, but within a few years Bishop Sheen could claim 30 million viewers. I will not attempt to improve on Morris's description of his television persona:

> Sheen may have been the finest popular lecturer ever to appear on television . . . he was elegant, elevated, relaxed, often very funny. Only Jack Benny could top Sheen's ability to hold back a punch line—for ten seconds, sometimes even longer—gazing calmly at the camera for the entire time. The shows had a precise formula. Sheen, wearing his bishop's cross, crimson cape, and skullcap, would stride into a parlor-like studio, pause, tell a humorous story, and then pose the problem for the evening: Are we more neurotic today? How to deal with the rat race? with temptation? with teenagers? What is the nature of love? the meaning of intimacy? About ten minutes would be devoted to analyzing the problem, always with diagrams on a blackboard . . . and a stock joke about the off-camera angel who cleaned the board. He had a knack for flattering his audiences. The lectures invariably introduced a technical term or two, usually from psychology or philosophy, which he wrote carefully on the board as if they were the key to wisdom. Every few minutes there would be another story, always on point, always seemingly impromptu. The problem analysis inevitably pointed in one direction—to humanity's need for God, for Truth, for Divine Love. Then the informal delivery would give way to a dramatic peroration, arms flung out, the cape spread wide, the voice suddenly husky with emotion, that would end, with a rhetorical shake of the fine head, exactly twenty-seven minutes and thirty seconds from the moment he had first walked on stage.[58]

Most remarkably, Morris adds, while "the philosophy was very Catholic," Sheen "pulled it off without a hint of sectarianism," never mentioning Catholic doctrine or the Church itself. Like Graham (again), he somehow made a very particular form of Christian thought seem like the natural common ground for a pious but deeply pluralistic society.

Not every viewer was persuaded. The assumption that the Catholic Church was fundamentally an enemy of democracy was deeply ingrained in the psyche of American Protestants, and the Church's midcentury strength prompted a last spasm of anti-Catholic anxieties. Just before Sheen began his prime-time career, Paul Blanshard's surprise bestseller *American Freedom and Catholic Power* (1949) warned non-Catholic Americans against the Church's "antidemocratic social policies" and accused Catholicism of being "intolerant," "separatist," and even "un-American."[59] Around the same time, Reinhold Niebuhr himself voiced similar concerns, fretting over the gulf between "the presuppositions of a free society and the inflexible authoritarianism of the Catholic religion."[60]

Sheen had an answer for this critique. Like many American Catholic apologists, he argued that the Church was actually a *better* custodian of American values than many of its secular critics, because of the way that Catholic natural-law philosophy overlapped with the Declaration of Independence's insistence on natural and inalienable rights. "The principle of democracy," Sheen argued, requires "a recognition of the sovereign, inalienable rights of man as a gift from God, the Source of law."[61] Because Catholics believed that rights were genuinely "endowed by our Creator," whereas many secular thinkers did not, Catholics were actually the natural heirs of the Founding Fathers. ("There is vastly more in common between the modern Catholic and the colonial Protestant," a typical Catholic polemic in this vein insisted, "than between the old colonial Protestant and the modern secularized product of public education."[62])

The argument had a surface plausibility, but in the 1930s and 1940s it was undercut by the example of the Vatican, which didn't merely frown on American ideas about religious liberty but seemed actively biased toward the Catholic authoritarianism of a Francisco Franco, an António Salazar, even a Marshal Pétain. By the postwar period, though, America's Catholic intellectuals were tugging the Church's political thought forward, out of the defensive antimodern crouch that the nineteenth-century papacy had assumed, and into a more mature appreciation of the benefits of democratic politics. The effort began with a group of European exiles, led by the French émigré Jacques Maritain, who reached America during the 1930s and found their new home remarkably congenial. Writing in the Eisenhower era, Maritain suggested that the United States, the secularism of its Constitution notwithstanding, possessed "a certain hidden disposition that is Christian in origin, and appears to me as a kind of humble and remote reminiscence of the Gospel."[63]

The American Jesuit John Courtney Murray took these ideas and ran with them. Active in ecumenical efforts from the 1940s onward, Murray produced a series of books and essays arguing not only that Catholicism blessed democracy but that it should bless American ideas about religious liberty as well. The long-running Catholic suspicion of the separation of church and state, he suggested, was rooted in a historical context—the chaos of the early Middle Ages, when the Church had no choice but to assume a civic and governmental role as well—that no longer obtained in the modern world. The true Catholic doctrine on church-state relations was suggested by Jesus' "render unto Caesar," not the contingencies of the barbarian invasions, and the best expression of Catholicism's original belief in the autonomy of civil government was to be found in (you guessed it) the American Constitution. In *We Hold These Truths: Catholic Reflections on the American Proposition* (1960), Murray ingeniously baptized Madison and Hamilton into an honorary Catholicism, suggesting that the Founding Fathers had been, in their understanding of church-state relations and of the rights of conscience, more Catholic than some popes.

Not all of this was greeted enthusiastically at the highest levels of the Church. A general acceptance of democracy was one thing, but the long-standing hope that the faith might retain some sort of privileged status in an idealized Catholic state died very hard. Maritain's views came under suspicion, and many of his fellow reformers were harassed or silenced. In 1950, Pius XII's encyclical *Humani Generis* echoed Pius X in rebuking certain "false opinions threatening to undermine the foundations of Catholic Doctrine."[64] In 1955, Murray's Jesuit superiors ordered him to temporarily cease writing on church-state questions.

In a sense, these conflicts anticipated the bloodier intellectual battles of the 1960s, pitting liberals seeking change against a Church hierarchy that resisted it. But what's striking, looking back, is how *Catholic* the reforming midcentury intellectuals were—how confident they seemed in their own tradition's intellectual resources, how naturally they framed their critiques of the present-day Church in the light of the Catholic past, how determined they were to find Catholic solutions for the problems they identified. The Church's own traditions, rather than the agenda of the secular world, were assumed to provide the natural patterns for reform. When liturgical reformers proposed changes to the Latin Mass, they looked back to medieval habits of worship for models to adapt and emulate. When

Murray wanted to persuade American theologians that Catholic doctrine could make room for religious liberty, he urged them to start by studying the Church Fathers. So too with Sheen himself: when the great apologist set out to bring the Catholic faith to a mass-market audience, he didn't doff his collar and throw on blue jeans; instead, his prime-time performances drew much of their power from the way his costume and style hinted at an authority that transcended the spirit of the age.

This style of Catholicism could have a touch of snobbery about it, and sometimes hints of self-deception as well. But it's telling that unlike a later generation of would-be reformers, the American Catholics of midcentury actually gained ground in Rome as well as in the United States—not least because the self-conscious Catholicity of their arguments ultimately brought their more conservative cobelievers around. All through the 1940s and 1950s, despite opposition and distrust, they pressed their argument and eventually won. At the Second Vatican Council, with both Sheen and Murray in attendance, what had once been distinctively American Catholic ideas about democracy and religious liberty were embraced as official teachings of the universal Church.

The trajectories of midcentury Evangelicalism and Catholicism were striking and surprising, but the developments in African-American religion were more remarkable still. The black church had spent a century as the darker brother of American religion, omnipresent within its own community—"the central organ of the organized life of the American Negro," wrote W. E. B. Du Bois, at once "a lyceum, library, and lecture bureau"[65]—and nearly invisible in the wider Christian world. Judged on the enthusiasm of its adherents and the institutional strength of its churches, no form of Christian belief was more vital, potent, and potentially transformative. But judged on its influence in the culture as a whole, no form of Christian belief was more marginal to the modern world's concerns.

"The most segregated hour in America," Martin Luther King Jr. was fond of saying, arrives at "11:00 on Sunday morning when we stand and sing that Christ has no east or west." But, unlike most other forms of segregation, the exile of the black churches had been partially self-imposed. Both the African Methodist Episcopal Church and the National Baptist

Convention, the two largest black religious bodies, had been formed by black ministers seeking refuge from the racism they encountered in white-led denominations. Their choice of exile had great advantages: it enabled blacks to do their own institution-building rather than waiting on white paternalism, and it turned the church into a source of pride, fellowship, and solidarity—"a refuge in a hostile white world,"[66] as E. Franklin Frazier writes in *The Negro Church in America* (1964), with none of the taint of second-classness that hung around many all-black institutions in the age of separate-but-equal.

But unity and solidarity came with a price. As Frazier notes, the self-sufficiency of black churches sometimes "aided the Negro to become accommodated to an inferior status,"[67] even as it deprived African-American religious leaders of the wider cultural influence that they deserved. For those with eyes to see, the black church's *indirect* impact on white culture was enormous. From Duke Ellington to James Baldwin, black music, novels, and poetry were all steeped in the cadences of gospel choirs and Sunday-morning services. But this was secondhand influence, passed along through African-American artists and intellectuals who had usually left the world of the black church behind. In the first half of the twentieth century, tellingly, black culture produced novelists, poets, musicians, essayists, actors, agitators, educators . . . but hardly any famous evangelists or public theologians. Indeed, tracing the life and work of pre-civil rights-era figures such as Du Bois, Paul Robeson, Marcus Garvey, and Richard Wright, one encounters a persistent sense that black Christianity is insufficient to the task of black uplift, that the answer must lie in secular ideology instead—in socialism, in pan-Africanism, in Marxism, or in some synthesis as yet undiscovered.

All of this changed with King's generation. In the decade between *Brown v. Board of Education of Topeka* and the passage of the Civil Rights Act of 1964, African-American religion—its churches, its ministers, its distinctive mix of conservative theology and prophetic social concern—moved to the center of national life with astounding speed. Beginning with the Montgomery bus boycott in 1955, a generation of younger preachers (led by King and Ralph Abernathy) recognized and then released the enormous political potential that was latent in African-American religion. Over the ensuing decade, the black church supplied the civil rights movement with most of its organizational muscle, and Christianity itself (supplemented with a dose of Mahatma Gandhi's methods of nonviolent protest) supplied the moral and theological capital.

"We must keep God in the forefront," King told the boycotters in Montgomery. "Let us be Christian in all our action." Two years later, his Southern Christian Leadership Conference invited civil rights activists "to accept Christian love in full knowledge of its power to defy evil."[68] Their cause had the tone of a crusade or a revival, shot through with doses of miracle and prophecy, and their political strategy was nothing less than the imitation of Christ, in the form of absolutist moral rhetoric joined to physical self-surrender. Fred Shuttlesworth, Birmingham's leading pastor-activist, described the cause of civil rights as Christianity's "greatest opportunity in centuries to make religion real in the lives of men,"[69] and the movement's progress seemed to vindicate his boast. In an age of general religious revival, the most powerful image of Christian love available to any midcentury believer was supplied by the black protesters who stood praying and singing while segregationist policemen loosed dogs and water cannons on them. Through their actions and activism, what had been the most marginal of American Christian traditions suddenly came to define Christian heroism and the gospel fully lived.

This change did not happen without considerable resistance from within the black church itself, many of whose leaders had grown comfortable preaching what Abernathy called "the Gospel of 'otherworldliness,'" whose "ultimate solution to Jim Crow was death—when you died you were equal in the eyes of God."[70] The leader of King's own National Baptist Convention, the Reverend Joseph Jackson, was one such figure. He "symbolized the old black establishment," Martin Marty writes, which had "settled for its place in segregated America and grown somewhat complacent in it, while serving seriously the needs of its members in their communities."[71] The needs of those members, Jackson had decided by the late 1950s, did not include risking their lives for integration, and he moved repeatedly to block King's efforts to consolidate the National Baptist Convention behind the civil rights movement. In 1957 and again in 1960, Jackson loyalists fended off civil rights activists in the Convention's leadership elections, and by the early 1960s it was clear that King's SCLC, not the older institutions of black Protestantism, would remain the locus of the movement. (Describing the contrast between the cautious older leaders and the bolder younger ones, one activist remarked that "for the first time, I can imagine what type of persons the pharisees must have been and I can imagine what type of persons the Disciples must have been—intense, devoted, earthy, erring, but still moving forwards."[72])

But if King sometimes failed to assuage the doubts of his co-religionists, he succeeded beyond all expectations in winning over white Christians to his cause. The moral witness of the marchers was the crucial element here, but the intellectual aspect of the civil rights movement deserves particular attention. King himself wasn't just an activist and preacher; he was a public theologian as well, whose intellectual journey followed the same path that many Mainline Protestants had taken in the 1930s and '40s, when they reconsidered modernism and liberalism and turned to neo-orthodoxy.

King's initial training for the ministry took place at Pennsylvania's Crozer Theological Seminary, where he studied under disciples of Social Gospel theorist Walter Rauschenbusch. But the future civil rights leader tempered the modernist influence of his academic environment with the pessimism of Reinhold Niebuhr, whose work he praised for refuting "the false optimism characteristic of a great segment of Protestant liberalism."[73] Studying for the theologate at Boston University, he began writing his dissertation on Paul Tillich, in many ways the least traditionally Christian of the great midcentury theologians. But he rejected the impersonal qualities of Tillich's God in favor of a more orthodox emphasis on the importance of personality, both human and divine. "I am convinced of the reality of a personal God," King wrote. "In Him there is feeling and will, responsive to the deepest yearnings of the human heart: this God both evokes and answers prayer."[74]

Calling King's worldview a kind of African-American neo-orthodoxy, though, is insufficient to describe its scope and reach. What he really did was to graft together the high-toned, sometimes overintellectualized Protestantism of figures like Niebuhr with the more visceral, prophetic Christian spirituality of the black church, creating an organic whole where many observers saw only contradiction. ("I was always amazed," the secular civil rights activist Bayard Rustin told an interviewer later, "at how it was possible to combine this intense, analytical philosophical mind with this more or less fundamental—well, I don't like to use the word 'fundamentalist'— but this abiding faith."[75]) In certain ways, King had more in common with

Billy Graham than with the Mainline intellectuals he studied under, since both men shared a sense of providence and the supernatural, a belief in tongues and prophecy, that many neo-orthodox thinkers probably found more than a little embarrassing. As David Chappell notes in *A Stone of Hope* (2007), his revisionist history of religion and the civil rights movement, "to Graham, belief in old-time concepts like Hell was just as natural as disbelief in modern concepts like racism," and King's "similar beliefs . . . generated uneasiness among his less pious advisers."[76]

But unlike Graham, King managed to successfully combine the emotional and intellectual sides of Christian faith, shifting easily from register to register depending on the forum and the audience, and suggesting— more than any other figure in that age, perhaps—the essential unity between the Christianity of Augustine and Aquinas and Luther and Barth and the Christianity of the revival tent. Meanwhile, the movement that he led hinted at another unity as well. The fact that it took a revivalist, prophetic, supernaturally inclined mass movement to fulfill the promise of American democracy seemed to vindicate those postwar Christians, from Auden onward, who had decided that the supposedly "secular" ideals of liberal civilization rested on a preliberal and essentially religious foundation.

Certainly the Christian character of the civil rights movement was crucial to winning over (or at least neutralizing) the most important constituency of all: the Protestant churches of the white South. As *The Atlantic*'s Ben Schwarz writes, distilling Chappell's argument from *A Stone of Hope*:

In the struggle over segregation white denizens of the Bible Belt, no less than black ones, needed the cultural depth, tradition, and moral authority of their churches. But . . . the segregationists got none of that. In the mid-1950s the Southern Baptists and the Southern Presbyterians each overwhelmingly passed resolutions endorsing desegregation, and appealing to all southerners to accept it peacefully (in the Southern Baptist Convention the vote was staggeringly lopsided—about 9,000 to 50). In a land that embraced literalist views of the Bible, nearly every important southern white conservative clergyman and theologian averred that there was no biblical sanction for segregation or for white supremacy. And the country's—and world's—best-known Southern Baptist, the North Carolinian Billy Graham, shared the pulpit with

Martin Luther King in 1957, [and] commended what he called the "social revolution" King was leading in the South.[77]

Southern clergymen were not the great heroes of the civil rights era, for the most part. Steeped in a racist culture and wary of alienating their parishioners, they opted for lukewarmness over zeal and circumspection over confrontation. Graham took some risks for integration, but he never went nearly as far as civil rights activists wanted him to go, and his friendship with King cooled as a result. The white evangelists stressed individual conversion over political change, supporting legal reform in cautious terms while insisting that only the Gospel could really improve race relations. Where King used eschatological language as a spur to political change, Graham regularly used eschatology to emphasize the limits of politics. "Only when Christ comes again," he reportedly said after the 1963 March on Washington, "will the lion lie down with the lamb and the little white children of Alabama walk hand in hand with the little black children."[78]

But even a grudging, ambivalent endorsement of King's cause from white Evangelicals was enough to fatally undermine support for segregation. Chappell writes, "King and others saw where the weak points were, and they drove in wedges. . . . The historically significant thing about white religion in the 1950s–60s is not its failure to join the civil rights movement. The significant thing . . . is that it failed in any meaningful way to join the anti–civil rights movement."[79]

Meanwhile, the rest of American Christianity was enthusiastically in King's corner. Mainline Protestantism's leadership had sometimes flirted with eugenics and racial science during the high tide of modernism, and Catholicism's record on race, slavery, and segregation had even more blemishes. (In one of the more grotesque moments, Pius IX sent a crown of thorns to the imprisoned Jefferson Davis as a gesture of solidarity.) But both branches of American Christendom embraced the civil rights movement well before the politicians did. The Catholic hierarchy was particularly proactive: urged on by Rome, bishops and archbishops moved to desegregate their own school systems, often employing threats of excommunication to overcome furious local opposition. (Sometimes it was more than a threat: In 1962, New Orleans Archbishop Joseph Rummel excommunicated three Catholics who had organized protests against his efforts to integrate the archdiocese.) In Washington, D.C., in 1956, Patrick Cardinal O'Boyle personally met with a delegation from southern Maryland, who insisted that their parishes wouldn't be ready for desegregation for ten years. "Well, gentlemen," the cardinal told them, "we're going to do it tomorrow."[80]

Thanks to these efforts, the civil rights movement became the place where the converging lines of the postwar revival intersected. The purely spiritual revivalism of Graham helped seed the ground where the more political revivalism of King and Abernathy bore fruit. The Catholic hierarchy's efforts on behalf of integration helped Catholics build bridges not only to black churches but to the Protestant Mainline as well. ("I don't prefer an authoritarian church to a democratic one," Niebuhr remarked to a friend in 1957, but Protestants needed to have "a measure of respect for what the Catholics are doing."[81]) From Rome and Manhattan to Atlanta and New Orleans, Christian churches seemed to speak with one voice. In Selma and Birmingham and Montgomery, their representatives—black preachers and white ministers, nuns and priests and seminarians—marched shoulder to shoulder for a single cause.

King's second greatest flight of rhetoric, his 1962 "Letter from Birmingham Jail," stands as a kind of literary monument to this convergence. In his famous apologia for Christian political activism, directed to precisely the kind of white southern clergymen whose support ultimately guaranteed the civil right movement's success, King marshaled all the intellectual resources of a "mere orthodoxy" on behalf of his cause. He quoted Jesus, Augustine, Aquinas, Martin Luther, John Bunyan, Reinhold Niebuhr, and T. S. Eliot; he drew analogies to Paul of Tarsus and the prophet Amos; he invoked the example of the early Christians; he wove together scholastic theology and Reformation polemic. Above all, he presented himself as a minister of a universal church that transcended both racial and denominational divisions, which made the same claims on every Christian—and whose universality was such that a black Baptist could cite the Catholic theory of natural law to persuade white Protestants of the merits of his case.

The "Letter" was a tour de force. It made Christianity seem vital, inexhaustible, and permanently relevant. And it could have only been written, as King's larger cause could only have succeeded, in the world that the postwar revival made.

*   *   *

The foregoing is an interpretation of an era, not a comprehensive history. A different set of emphases and shadings could yield a very different portrait of American Christianity at midcentury. Instead of highlighting the convergence between Protestants and Catholics, it could emphasize the continuing mistrust that defined their relationship—the persistence of bigotry on the Protestant side, down to the election of John F. Kennedy, and the mix of triumphalism and intellectual closed-mindedness that often characterized the Catholic response. Instead of dwelling on the sudden receptiveness to religious ideas in the secular intelligentsia and the mass media, it could dwell on the many figures in the same era who earned their celebrity by making open war on Christian ethics—think of Alfred Kinsey or Wilhelm Reich, Ayn Rand or Hugh Hefner, plus all the various Freudians and B. F. Skinner acolytes who cluttered up the culture in those days. Instead of placing figures like Barth and Niebuhr at the heart of its portrait of Mainline Protestantism's last hurrah, it could focus on the many suburban parishes that were more interested in putting a Christian gloss on middle-class striving than in preaching the stark gospel of Barth's *Epistle to the Romans*. Instead of highlighting the positive political contributions of many religious leaders, it could emphasize the negative—from white preachers who did their utmost to thwart the civil rights movement to Catholic prelates who waxed enthusiastic for Joseph McCarthy's witch hunts.

True golden ages do not exist. Martin Luther King was a Christian hero, but he was also a reckless adulterer whose academic work was partially ghostwritten. The neo-orthodox theologians did a brilliant job of making the Christian intellectual framework intelligible to a secular audience, but they also frequently seemed to purposefully dance around some of the most important—and necessarily controversial—issues of Christian faith. (Martin Gardner's 1971 novel-of-ideas, *The Flight of Peter Fromm*, features a young seminarian driven mad by Reinhold Niebuhr's evasiveness on supernatural questions: "He tapped his finger on the book's brown cloth cover and said angrily: 'Can you imagine this? There are six hundred pages here. It's a full statement of the theology of America's most famous Protestant thinker. How many references do you suppose there are to the Resurrection of Christ? . . . Not one! Not a single one!'"[82]) John Courtney Murray's marriage of Catholic faith and American democracy was an ingenious shotgun wedding, but its emphasis on rendering unto Caesar made it rather unclear what Catholics should do when Caesar's policies were at odds with the Church's teaching—a problem that would present itself to both left-wing and conservative Catholics soon enough. The neo-evangelical escape from the fundamentalist ghetto was intellectually significant, but in terms of raw numbers of congregants, a harder-core fundamentalism probably saw the most growth in the 1940s and 1950s. And the entire Christian cultural renaissance, from the box office to the bestseller list, was made possible by a middlebrow mass media whose dominance was as much an accident of technological progress as an expression of the culture's deepest values. (More than a few of Fulton Sheen's 30 million viewers would presumably have been happy to turn their television dials to *The Real Housewives of Levittown* if that option had been available.)

At the same time, many of the heresies that have flourished amid institutional Christianity's decline were very much present at midcentury as well. Contemporary preachers of self-help and self-love such as Oprah Winfrey owe an enormous debt to Norman Vincent Peale's *The Power of Positive Thinking,* which debuted on the *New York Times* bestseller list in 1952 and stayed there for 180 weeks. The prosperity gospel, mainstreamed in our own era by smooth televangelists like Joel Osteen, has its roots in the ministry of proto-Osteens (Oral Roberts, Kenneth Hagin, and others) who already loomed large among American Evangelicals in the 1940s and 1950s. The "spiritual but not religious" mentality, embodied today by figures as diverse as Deepak Chopra and Elizabeth Gilbert, animated Anne Morrow Lindbergh's *Gift from the Sea,* a huge bestseller in 1955. The perfervid blend of religion, paranoia, and American nationalism that made Glenn Beck a phenomenon in the last few years owes an immense debt to the midcentury conspiracy theorist W. Cleon Skousen, whose tract *The Naked Communist* debuted in 1958.

In the Eisenhower era, as in our own, frequent churchgoing and public professions of piety often coexisted with scriptural ignorance and spiritual self-satisfaction; "American" values often trumped genuinely Christian ones when the two threatened to conflict; and Eisenhower's famous remark that American democracy depended on "a deeply felt religious faith, and I don't care what it is" seemed to be the first and greatest commandment for many believers. As apostles for a revived orthodoxy, figures like Niebuhr and

Graham and Sheen and even King often tended to succeed only insofar as they met the American Way of Life halfway, making the Christian message seem nonsectarian, forward-looking, and obviously relevant to the questions of the age.

Nevertheless, there were still great differences between their era and our own, and the continuities should not obscure the dramatic changes that overtook the nation's religious culture after the postwar revival ran its course. Of course there were limits to the midcentury Christian renaissance, and compromises with the spirit of the age. But Reinhold Niebuhr's quest to make orthodox theology relevant in the academy and the halls of power alike was undertaken from a far stronger position than any of his Mainline Protestant successors have enjoyed. Fulton Sheen's genial confidence in the underlying theological coherence of the Catholic faith contrasts sharply with the posture of preemptive surrender or the hunched defensiveness that too many Catholics have adopted in the decades since. No subsequent evangelist has managed to strike Billy Graham's delicate balance between Evangelical rigor and openhanded ecumenism, between a Christian particularism and a universal Americanism, between warnings about God's justice and promises of God's all-encompassing love. And no subsequent marriage of Christian faith and political activism has come close to matching Martin Luther King's ability to use the language of Scripture to break down ideological barriers and transcend partisan divides.

The crucial element, in each of these cases, was a deep and abiding *confidence*: Not just faith alone, but a kind of faith in Christian faith, and a sense that after decades of marginalization and division, orthodox Christians might actually be on the winning side of history. Both institutionally and intellectually, American Christianity at midcentury offered believers a relatively secure position from which to engage with society as a whole—a foundation that had been rebuilt, as we have seen, rather than simply inherited, and that seemed the stronger for it. At its best, this culture enjoyed the mix of openness and well-defendedness that any religious tradition should seek in its dealings with the world, supplying believers with both "a place to stand and look outward on the world," as Jody Bottum put it in a 2008 essay on the era, and a "system of truth by which other things could be judged."[83]

For a fleeting historical moment, it seemed as though the Christian churches might not have to choose between becoming religious hermit kingdoms or the spiritual equivalents of Vichy France. Instead, they might become something more like what the Gospels suggested they should be: the salt of the earth, a light to the nations, and a place where even modern man could find a home.

TWO

THE LOCUST YEARS

The end of the midcentury revival was also its culmination. In 1957—the same summer that Billy Graham staged his famous Manhattan crusade—Martin Luther King addressed 15,000 people on the National Mall, in a precursor of the 1963 March on Washington. Eighteen months later, the newly elected Pope John XXIII announced that he would be convening an ecumenical council in Rome, both to take up questions left unaddressed by the First Vatican Council seventy years before and also—as the Pope famously put it—"to throw open the windows of the Church so that we can see out and the people can see in." The following year, 1960, the number of American converts to Roman Catholicism hit an all-time peak.[1] By the time Vatican II began its sessions in 1962, a Roman Catholic had been elected president of the United States (with an assist from African-American voters after the Kennedy brothers helped secure King's release from prison) and John Courtney Murray had appeared on the cover of *Time*. Less than a year later, the "I Have a Dream" speech had electrified 200,000 marchers on the Washington Mall.

One could argue that the postwar moment ended that same summer and fall, with the death of the "two Johns"—JFK and John XXIII. But the next two years felt like a crescendo. By 1965, "Letter from Birmingham Jail" had secured King's reputation as a prophet, and Lyndon Johnson had secured the legal revolution that King's movement had marched and bled and suffered to attain. The same year, the Second Vatican Council swept away centuries of Roman sympathy for established churches and authoritarian regimes.

These events were the hinge into the social revolutions that ultimately defined the 1960s and '70s. But in the moment they felt like triumphs for the midcentury Christian consensus, vindications for the hope that orthodox Christianity and liberal modernity could harmonize rather than conflict.

In Rome, with an ecumenical cast of observers looking on and the secular press paying often breathless attention, the ideas of American Catholics carried the day completely. Murray was summoned to the Vatican as a *peritus,* or theological adviser (the ranks of reform-minded *periti* at the Council also included the young German theologian Joseph Ratzinger), and Murray played a crucial role in drafting the major document on religious freedom, *Dignitatis Humanae,* which the Council Fathers approved by a vote of 2,308 to 70. In the same session, the document *Nostra Aetate* formally repudiated the enduring "Christ killer" slur against the Jews. Both of these statements were strongly supported by the American bishops, Fulton Sheen included, and taken together they marked the end of the process that the Catholic émigrés of the 1930s had begun: the rapprochement between Rome and liberal democracy and the validation of American Catholicism as a model for the universal Church. And all of this had been accomplished—or so it temporarily seemed—without altering fundamental Catholic doctrine or calling into question anything essential to the faith.

Meanwhile, in Washington, the pan-Christian crusade for civil rights moved inexorably toward a comprehensive victory, in which the old-time religion fulfilled generations of unrequited liberal hope. In May 1963, the Kennedy administration summoned religious leaders to join civil rights activists for a strategy session at the White House, at which groups like the National Catholic Welfare Conference (the Right Reverend New Dealer's old outfit) and the National Council of Churches agreed, as Garry Wills puts it, to help "create a constituency" for civil rights legislation among churchgoers in Middle America. In August of the same year, King spoke to the marchers crowding the National Mall in the words of the prophet Isaiah: "I have a dream that one day every valley shall be exalted, every hill and mountain shall be made low, the rough places will be made plain and the crooked places will be made straight and the glory of the Lord shall be revealed and all flesh shall see it together."[2] Two months later, Kennedy was assassinated, and King's dream became Lyndon Johnson's sacred cause.

"By the time the bill reached a vote," Wills notes, "bishops and priests and rabbis were openly lobbying in the halls of Congress," and "no important Senator lacked a visit" from the religious delegation. One old D.C. hand remarked that "he had never witnessed such a powerful lobbying effort." Richard Russell, the arch-segregationist senator, made the same point rather more bitterly. The Civil Rights Act only passed, he groused, because "those damn preachers got the idea that it was a moral issue."[3]

With those words, and their foretaste of culture wars to come, we can leave the lost world of American Christianity behind. The postwar revival had been forged in a mood of pessimism, by men and women who turned to biblical religion in the wake of a world-historical disaster, seeking harder truths and older forms of wisdom than the modern world could easily supply. But by the early 1960s, the revival's remarkable achievements had convinced many Christians that all good things might go together after all: prophetic mysticism and political reform, ancient faith and modern liberalism, Roman Catholicism and the American experiment.

In this best of all possible worlds, politicians could learn from preachers, theologians could take instruction from the secular world, and there need be no contradiction between Christianity and progress, between dogma and democracy, between the vox populi and the voice of God. What had begun with a poet brooding over Spain's shuttered churches ended two decades later with churchmen lobbying presidents and a pope throwing open the windows of the Catholic Church—confident that the era of convergence was only the beginning, and that the City of God had far more to offer the City of Man than it had to fear from it.

Less than a decade had passed since this apparent apotheosis when a Methodist vestryman named Dean Kelley published a slim work of religious sociology. The title of his 1973 book was *Why Conservative Churches Are Growing*, but the real revelation involved tidings of sudden decline. "In the latter years of the 1960s something remarkable happened in the United States," ran Kelley's opening lines. "For the first time in the nation's history most of the major church groups stopped growing and began to shrink."[4]

To twenty-first-century Americans, accustomed to the waning influ-

ence of what were once the country's leading denominations, the idea
that "major church groups" might dwindle rather than expand seems as
natural as humidity in Georgia. So it's worth pausing to consider how
momentous the shift that Kelley spotted really was. From the Revolutionary War to the Eisenhower era, the story of religion in America had
involved steady, seemingly inexorable growth. Year upon year, decade
upon decade, the rate of religious adherence expanded, and the country
as a whole grew steadily more "churched." In every generation, there
were Christian Cassandras who argued that the golden age of American
churchgoing lay somewhere in the past. In every generation, they were
proven wrong.

Not that this growth was constant across every church and sect and denomination. Some churches leapfrogged over others; some sects rose swiftly
to prominence and then slowly went into decline. The established Protes-
tantisms of the colonial age—Congregationalist and Episcopalian—found
themselves eclipsed by Methodists and Baptists soon after independence.
"I trust that there is not a young man now living in the United States who
will not die an Unitarian," Thomas Jefferson wrote in 1822, unaware that
his favored denomination had already passed its demographic peak.[5] The
early twentieth century was better for Pentecostalists than Presbyterians;
the 1950s were better for Southern Baptists than Methodists. And parallel
to all these ups and downs within American Protestantism ran the Catholic
Church's slow but steady expansion, from a marginal and persecuted minority to America's largest Christian body.

But even as churches gained or lost ground relative to one another, the
basic pattern held. At worst, most established denominations could hope
to keep up with population growth; at best, they could expect to grow
much faster than the country as whole. Small wonder that church leaders
confidently expected more of the same. In 1955, the dean of Yale Divinity
School told *Newsweek* that "in the next twenty years, American Protestantism will enlarge its numbers by one third."[6] That same decade, Boston's
Cardinal Cushing declared that he hoped to someday ordain a hundred
new priests in a single year—a number that no Catholic archdiocese in the
world had ever achieved.

These hopes soon turned to ashes. The Protestant Mainline's membership stopped growing abruptly in the mid-1960s and then just as swiftly

plunged. Of the eleven Protestant churches that claimed more than a million members in the early 1970s, eight had fewer members in 1973 than in 1965. There were 10.6 million United Methodists in 1960, more than 11 million at mid-decade, and 10.6 million again by 1970—and it was down, down, down thereafter. The Lutherans peaked in 1968, the Episcopalians in 1966, and the United Church of Christ in 1965; by the middle of the following decade, they were all in steep decline.[7] The Presbyterian Church (U.S.A.) lost about 1.5 million members between the mid-1960s and the late 1980s.[8] By the early 1990s, 60 percent of Methodist parishioners were over fifty,[9] and there were more Muslims in America than Episcopalians.[10]

Of course, membership numbers don't tell the whole story. A religious tradition is more than the raw number of people in the pews; it's a network, a culture, a complex web of communities and institutions. Here, too, starting in the 1960s, the culture of Mainline Protestantism simply disintegrated. Church school enrollment plunged. Seminary enrollment declined. Donations dried up, budgets were cut, and churches ran enormous deficits. Foreign missionary work—once the glory of American Protestants—all but disappeared. The great church-building campaign of the 1950s ended, and churches began to close. The flood of denominational magazines and newspapers—all those *Lutheran Herald*s and *Gideon*s and *Presbyterian Outlook*s—became a stream, and then a trickle, as publications merged and shrank and closed up shop.

Roman Catholicism's crisis was no less striking. The absolute number of American Catholics stayed steady for decades after the 1960s, thanks in large part to Latino immigration. But the institutional life of the church began a long bleed. Weekly attendance at mass plummeted from 70 percent to 50 percent in just ten years.[11] In 1964, Catholics were twice as likely as Protestants to be in church on Sunday. By 1974, this gap had narrowed dramatically—and not because Protestants suddenly became more diligent in their churchgoing.[12] Donations, church-building, and religious school enrollment traced the same descending arc as in the Mainline churches. The thick culture that had defined and sustained the pre–Vatican II Church—the round of confessions and novenas, pilgrimages and Stations of the Cross—dissipated like a cloud of incense in a sudden breeze.

Meanwhile, religious vocations, the heart of the church's sacramental life, went into steep decline. In 1966, at the close of the Second Vatican Council, the American Catholic Church boasted roughly 60,000 priests, 12,000 religious brothers, and an astonishing 180,000 nuns. At the time this seemed not a high-water mark but a jumping-off point for future growth. The present appeared stable: during the Kennedy presidency, only one priest in a thousand requested to be released from his vows in a given year. The future was apparently secure: some 48,000 seminarians were studying for the priesthood in the mid-1960s. This meant there were ten priests-in-training for every thousand American Catholics.[13]

Then came the locust years. The rate at which priests left clerical life rose *twentyfold* in the 1960s, peaking in 1969, when 2 percent of the American Church's priests renounced their vows. That rate held throughout the next decade. The seminaries emptied (enrollment had fallen by two-thirds by 1980), and religious orders dwindled. Whereas in 1950 there had been a priest for every 600 American Catholics, by the time of Ronald Reagan's election there was only one for every thousand—and that pool of priests was aging fast. Nuns also abandoned the religious life, and the rate at which women entered religious communities fell by 88 percent from 1965 to 1971 alone. The ratio of American nuns to American Catholics stood at four per thousand in 1965; by 1985 it was two per thousand and still falling.[14]

Among Catholics and Protestants alike, this institutional collapse didn't affect just the millions of Americans who stopped identifying with the major Christian denominations during this era. It affected the tens of millions who didn't leave—who kept going to Sunday services (albeit perhaps less frequently), kept baptizing their children, kept calling themselves Lutherans and Methodists and Catholics, but who found themselves participating in institutions that no longer had the manpower, the financial resources, or the intellectual confidence to make orthodox faith seem as credible as it had been at midcentury.

Only what Dean Kelley described as the "conservative churches" bucked these trends. Kelley's broad category included the major Evangelical bodies, from the Southern Baptists to the Assemblies of God, as well as the more theologically traditional wings of the major Protestant denominations, which had broken off from the Mainline during the modernist-fundamentalist wars earlier in the century—the Missouri Synod Lutherans, the Wesleyan Church Methodists, and others like them. It included older sects like the Seventh-day Adventists, the Jehovah's Witnesses, and the Latter-day Saints. And it included the many charismatic and Pentecostal communities that embraced certain aspects of the counterculture—rock music, ecstatic services, informality and spontaneity and shaggy hair—while retaining a biblical and Christian core.

These were the institutional winners of the 1960s and 1970s. Their schools and charities and missionary efforts thrived; their seminaries remained full; their record labels and television stations and publishing houses reached larger audiences. And their numbers increased as well. There were almost a million more United Methodists than Southern Baptists in 1960; ten years later it was the Baptists who enjoyed a million-member edge. The Pentecostal Holiness Church grew by 4 percent in the 1960s, Jehovah's Witnesses by 5 percent, Mormons by almost 6 percent. The Assemblies of God saw their share of the churchgoing population nearly double between 1960 and 1980; the Church of God in Christ's share rose eightfold in the same period. The conservative branches of Lutheranism and Presbyterianism grew twice as fast as their more liberal competitors.[15] The Vineyard Fellowship, a Pentecostal sect founded by a group of counterculture-influenced preachers in the late 1970s, blossomed from a small group of California churches to a movement with 1,500 congregations around the world.

But, while these winners prospered, their expansion didn't offset the overall decline in American Christian practice, membership, influence, and belief. Demographically, the conservative churches started from a low threshold. The Southern Baptists were the largest of the expanding denominations, but as a percentage of the American population they were smaller in 1980 than the United Methodists had been in 1940. Mormons, Jehovah's Witnesses, and Assemblies of God between them had fewer congregants in 1970 than the Episcopal Church claimed in 1960.[16] Culturally, for reasons we will consider in more detail later, these churches struggled to claim the kind of influential role that Mainline Protestantism had taken for granted throughout most of American history and that the Catholicism of midcentury had joined in for a time.

Moreover, many of them remained doubtful custodians of Christian orthodoxy. They were havens for *political* conservatives, overall, and they tended to be more supernaturalist and stringent about sexual morality than some of their competitors. But the successes of the neo-evangelical project notwithstanding, their theological conservatism was often still the apocalyptism of the fundamentalist cul-de-sac, or else a mix of prosperity preaching and the gospel of self-help—the Evangelicalism of the Left Behind novels and Joel Osteen, one might say, rather than of Billy Graham or C. S. Lewis. Some of America's Evangelical churches provided a rallying point for orthodox Christians in the difficult post-1960s landscape. But others provided fertile ground for the heresies that increasingly dominated American religion.

For these reasons and more, the crisis of traditional Christianity, not the rise of the conservative churches, remains the major religious story of the 1960s and '70s. The gains of certain denominations notwithstanding, the era witnessed an extraordinary weakening of organized Christianity in the United States and a fundamental shift in America's spiritual ecology— away from institutional religion and toward a more do-it-yourself and consumer-oriented spirituality—that endures to the present day. In sub- sequent decades, traditional believers would hopefully cite various revivals or awakenings as evidence that their faith might be regaining the ground that it lost between 1965 and 1980. But nothing that's happened since, whether in small prayer groups or booming megachurches, has made up for the losses that institutional Christianity sustained during America's cultural revolution.

These losses led many observers to assume that the United States was becoming an increasingly secular country, in which atheism and indiffer- ence would predominate, and spiritual beliefs of every sort would gradually disappear. (As we shall see, both progressive and conservative Christians shared this assumption, with the progressives regarding secularization as an opportunity and the conservatives regarding it as a threat.) But this expec- tation turned out to be misplaced. America didn't actually become more secular in the 1960s and '70s. Instead, the crisis of Christianity occurred at a time when overall public interest in religious ideas and experiences was arguably still *increasing*. Belief in God, an afterlife, and intercessory prayer remained constant or even rose during these years (Americans were slightly more likely to believe in life after death in the 1990s than in the 1940s[17]), and the percentage of Americans who reported a personal encounter with the divine rose sharply. The influence of bishops and pastors ebbed, but there was a glut of gurus and sages, new prophets and rediscovered holy men—Timothy Leary and George Gurdjieff, Charles Reich and Kahlil Gibran, and many more.

"We're searching for more immediate, ecstatic, and penetrating modes of living," Hillary Clinton declared of her generation at Wellesley's 1969 commencement exercises, and this quest was religious as often as it was political or sexual or pharmacological.[18] For millions of Americans, Robert Ellwood would write in *The Sixties Spiritual Awakening*, "the crucial current event" of the 1960s "was not the campus conflicts or the Pentagon sieges . . . but the emergence of a wholly new culture, based on a new spirituality. A new world was gestating in the Haight-Ashbury, or the nurseries of scattered remote communes, or an East-West lamasery."[19]

In this sense, at least, the ecclesiastical optimists of the Kennedy era weren't wrong to predict that the new decade would be a still more fertile epoch for religion than the postwar revival had been. Viewed from a certain angle, the 1960s and 1970s even resemble earlier Great Awakening periods, in which a surge of social activism coexisted with a burst of supernatural enthusiasms and eschatological passions. The hippie movement, the turn to hallucinogen-assisted mysticism, the vogue for astrology and millenarianism and communal living—all of this was familiar stuff, redolent of the revivalist mood that in the previous century inspired Shakers and Millerites and the Oneida Community.

These echoes of earlier revivals would help inspire the argument (popular among panglossian religious conservatives in subsequent decades) that American Christianity hadn't *really* declined in the 1960s. Citing the growth of some Evangelical churches and the persistence of belief in God, Christian optimists would argue that their faith's center of gravity had simply shifted. What looked like decline was just the latest chapter in a classic American story, in which fervent start-ups outhustle and outconvert the more established churches. It happened in the awakenings of colonial America, they pointed out, it happened in the tent meetings of the nineteenth century—and now it had happened again in the ferment of the 1960s and '70s.

Except that this time was different. For all the short-term chaos they inspired, the awakenings of the eighteenth and nineteenth centuries had ultimately strengthened institutional Christianity rather than weakened it. They injected new energy into moribund churches, inspired existing denominations to imititate the tactics of start-up sects, and swelled the ranks of orthodox believers even as they inspired a dizzying array of heretical experiments. The First Great Awakening in the mid-eighteenth century essentially midwifed the Methodist Church into existence. The Presbyterians and Baptists gained far more new adherents in the turbulent aftermath of the Second Great Awakening than did the Mormons and Millerites. Even the Catholic Church found a way, during the revivals of the late nineteenth century, to borrow techniques from tent meetings for its immensely popular missions. The emblematic figures in a given awakening were usually religious freelancers with unusual theological ideas—a Joseph Smith, a Mary Baker Eddy, an Ellen G. White. But more orthodox churches nearly always managed to profit from the mood of spiritual enthusiasm as well.

In the 1960s and '70s, though, the heretics carried the day completely. America in those years became more religious but less traditionally Christian; more supernaturally minded but less churched; more spiritual in its sentiments but less pious in its practices. It was a golden age if you wanted to talk about UFOs or crystals, the Kama Sutra or the I Ching. It was a fertile period if you said "Christianity" but meant fundamentalism or Marxism or the New Age, the gospel of the flower children or the gospel of health and wealth. But amid all of this enthusiasm, all of this hunger for the numinous and transcendent and revolutionary, the message of Christianity itself seemed to have suddenly lost its credibility.

For observers seeking to explain this unexpected turn of events, it was easy to claim that the whole structure of American Christianity had simply been rotten to begin with—one of Jesus' whitened sepulchres, or a hollowed-out oak awaiting the hurricane. From the perspective of hindsight, this became the simplest argument to make. In *Vanishing Boundaries* (1994), a Clinton-era look back over three decades of Mainline Protestant decline, three Presbyterian sociologists asserted that the supposed revival of the 1940s and 1950s was just a lot of Norman Vincent Peale and suburban conformity with no authentic Christian core:

The mainline churches made few demands on those who flocked into its ranks during the 1950s. In effect, many members acquired only a thin gloss or a "veneer" of religiosity. . . . To some of their children, even the weak requirements of church membership seemed too burdensome or too pointless to assume. The church "boom" of the 1950s was an ephemeral one.[20]

Similar claims would be made about midcentury Roman Catholicism—that its apparent ruddy health had been the vitality of a hothouse flower. Thus Wills, a child of the Catholic 1950s, would look back on the pre–Vatican II Church of his youth from the vantage point of 1972 and see an institution whose doom was foreordained:

The church was enclosed, perfected in circular inner logic, strength distributed through all its interlocking aspects; turned in on itself, giving a good account of itself to itself—but so vulnerable, so fragile, if one looked outward, away from it. It had a crystalline ahistoricity; one touch of change or time could shatter it—and did.[21]

But this kind of hindsight logic is too simple. The weaknesses of midcentury religion were manifold, no doubt, but so are the weaknesses of religious culture in any time and place. Judged by the exacting standards of the Gospels, most Christians in the sixth and tenth and sixteenth centuries probably enjoyed only a "veneer" of true religion, and Wills's critique of American Catholicism on the eve of Vatican II could be applied to the Church of 1880 or 1910 or 1935. It's easy to recognize the fault lines in an institution after it's been shattered, easy to declare that a particular dissolution was inevitable once it's taken place. The more important question isn't "why?" but "why *then*?" Why did the churches have a bigger credibility problem in 1978 than in 1958? What were the proximate causes of Christianity's decline, and why did they kick in when they did?

Five major catalysts suggest themselves. First, *political polarization*. Midcentury Christianity had been political without appearing overtly partisan: Sometimes its leaders spoke for the American consensus and sometimes they critiqued it, but in either case they tended to transcend (or at least seemed to transcend) the liberal-conservative, Democrat-Republican divide. This approach bore impressive fruit with the civil rights movement, as we have seen. Across the 1950s and early 1960s, Martin Luther King's movement found a way to transform itself from a countercultural cause into a consensus position without ever being associated with a single party or faction. This was possible, in part, because it was perceived as a moral and religious movement first and foremost, with a politics rooted in theology rather than the other way around.

But with success came Christian hubris. In the heady aftermath of the Civil Rights Act, believers went looking for the next great cause, the next place where an essentially theological vision could transform the secular realm. What they found instead were issues that were swiftly turned to partisan ends by politicians in both parties and that divided churches against one another as no controversies had since slavery. And so convergence gave way to strife and division, and the age of consensus to a Christian civil war.

The first flashpoint was the war in Vietnam. The united anti-Communist front of the 1950s had sanctioned and even sanctified American involvement in Indochina, but the grinding stalemate of the mid-1960s quickly summoned up a religious protest movement, and the carnage created by Lyndon Johnson's bombing campaigns lent the protests a growing moral force. Clergy Concerned About Vietnam was founded in 1965, under ecumenical leadership: the Lutheran pastor Richard John Neuhaus, a veteran of Martin Luther King's marches, was joined by Rabbi Abraham Heschel and the charismatic Jesuit Daniel Berrigan, whose flair for theatrical acts of civil disobedience would make him a fugitive from justice soon enough. Their efforts had the backing of the Mainline establishment—the president of Union Theological Seminary hosted the inaugural meeting and the Interchurch Center lent them office space. The antiwar leadership even gained the support of Reinhold Niebuhr, now seventy-three, who went public in 1967 with his opinion that "the policy of restraining Asian communism by sheer military might is fantastic."[22] (He also privately deplored the way that Lyndon Johnson's administration was claiming his foreign-policy theories—the emphasis on the great responsibilities that came with America's unprecedented power and the moral complexities of political action in a fallen world—as justification for escalation.)

By 1967, the movement also had the backing of Martin Luther King, who denounced the war at a Clergy Concerned About Vietnam rally held in New York's Riverside Church in April. King's sermon drew analogies between the cause of African-American civil rights and the national liberation movements of the Third World, and it reflected a broader shift in the movement that he led. In the aftermath of the Civil Rights Act's passage, African-American leaders began to embrace increasingly ambitious and even revolutionary goals, attacking militarism and imperialism along with Jim Crow and promising to overthrow not only racism but every kind of poverty and exploitation.

There was a strong generational element in this shift: King's anguish over Vietnam was real, but he was also being tugged leftward by an impatient younger cohort of activists eager for more confrontational tactics, more revolutionary programs, and more immediate results. After his assassination, these trends would only accelerate. Amid competition from the Nation of Islam and other radical groups, many black churches migrated in a more Marxist and Afrocentric direction, embracing the kind of "liberation theologies" that would influence (among many other figures) a Chicago pastor named Jeremiah Wright.

A few months after King's Riverside sermon, the aging Fulton Sheen joined the antiwar cause as well, startling parishioners at Rochester's Sacred Heart Cathedral with a midsummer sermon calling for an immediate withdrawal of American forces from Southeast Asia. But Sheen, the embodiment of the Catholic center in the 1950s, was out on a limb this time. The Mainline and the black churches might be rallying against the war, but Catholicism was divided. The identity of the midcentury Catholic Church had revolved around the compatibility of American patriotism and Catholic faith. Its great intellectual project—reconciling Catholicism and liberal democracy—had insisted on the importance of rendering unto Caesar, even when Caesar didn't live up to the standards of the one true Church. A generation of bishops had come of age knowing that the best way to establish their faith's American bona fides was to outdo Protestants in patriotic fervor. A generation of intellectuals had labored to explain why Catholics should respect the authority of democratic leaders. And a generation of laypeople had thrown themselves into their country's service: from the military to the prosecutor's office to the FBI, Catholics were overrepresented in the public institutions of 1960s America at precisely the moment when those institutions found themselves under siege.

Inevitably, then, for every (usually younger) Catholic who saw the antiwar movement of the 1960s as a natural continuation of the Church's Eisenhower-era support for the cause of civil rights, there was another (usually older) Catholic who saw it as a mad betrayal of the hard-won rapprochement between their religion and their country. Many Catholic theologians and journalists denounced the war even as their bishops prayed publicly for victory. (It was "a war for civilization," New York's Cardinal Spellman insisted in his Christmas Eve sermon in 1966, in which "less than victory was inconceivable.") Young priests led protests while their older parishioners voted for Richard Nixon—or even George Wallace. Bobby Kennedy publicly turned against a conflict that his sainted brother had escalated. Even within the community of pacifist Catholics, there was a generational divide. Dorothy Day, the ur-radical of the pre–Vatican II Church, expressed public misgivings over the more confrontational approach of Daniel Berrigan and his imitators.

There were echoes of these disputes within American Evangelicalism as well. Some younger believers took the neo-evangelical call for a reengagement with social and political issues in directions more left-leaning than Billy Graham and Carl Henry's generation had anticipated. One of the leading antiwar voices in Washington, D.C., was Mark Hatfield, an Oregon Republican who was also the country's highest-profile Evangelical politician. But overall, the Evangelical left of the late 1960s was much weaker than its Catholic counterpart. The most common Evangelical complaint about Vietnam was still that the conflict wasn't being waged firmly enough. *Christianity Today* kept up its steady drumbeat of support for the war deep into the Nixon administration. (Henry was eased out of the editorship for not being hawkish enough.) Billy Graham offered more explicit support to his great friend Nixon than he offered to any president before or since. Certainly there was no Evangelical equivalent of the antiwar Catholic chorus denouncing first Lyndon Johnson and then Richard Nixon, to say nothing of the institutionalized antiwar activism of Mainline Protestant denominations and black churches.

For a time, the religious divisions over Vietnam were generational and ideological without being strikingly partisan. The antiwar movement pitted Democrat against Democrat, and as the example of Hatfield suggests, the Republican Party was divided in unpredictable ways as well. (The same was true of other emerging issues in that era: Ronald Reagan, a future pro-life stalwart, signed a sweeping abortion legalization bill as governor of California, and the most pro-life politician on a national ticket in the 1970s was probably George McGovern's running mate, Sargent Shriver.) But the polarization turned partisan soon enough. Beginning with the antiwar movement's takeover of the Democratic Party in the 1972 election, and continuing through the Republican Party's deliberate courtship of religious conservatives under Richard Nixon and Reagan, the religious divisions of the Vietnam era were frozen into amber by the growing ideological polarization of the two national parties.

The result was a divide that would endure across a generation of political debates, from the controversies of the 1980s down to the struggle over the Iraq War. Whether the issue was immigration or the nuclear freeze, school busing or global warming, you could count on how the nation's Christian bodies would line up. The leaders of the Mainline denominations and the black churches, who tended to see every new controversy through the lens of the civil rights struggle, were on the leftward side, the side of peace and social justice. The majority of Evangelicals tilted rightward, their identification with the Republican Party magnifying their political strength even as it often compromised their moral credibility. And somewhere in between, divided and agonized like the country, were the bishops and clergy and laypeople of the Catholic Church.

These divisions and debates were often driven by idealism and high principle. But they had mostly negative consequences for Christianity's spiritual witness. Religious leaders took too many positions on too many issues, indulged in Manichean rhetoric that overheated public policy debates, and generally behaved like would-be legislators or party activists instead of men of God. They even ran for president: two of Martin Luther King's would-be heirs, Jesse Jackson and Al Sharpton, both decided that the work of Christian ministry required them to occupy the Oval Office, as did a would-be Billy Graham, Pat Robertson, in 1988. Whether it was conservative Evangelicals hinting that the Holy Spirit had a strong position on the proper rate of marginal taxation, or liberal clergymen insisting that loving your neighbor as yourself required supporting higher levels of social spending, two generations of Christian spokesmen steadily undercut the credibility of their religious message by wedding it to the doctrines of the Democratic Party, or the platform of the GOP.

But, to be fair, from the later 1960s onward the churches were also confronting a set of issues that simply hadn't been on their radar screen at midcentury—issues where the personal and the political were so intertwined that no serious Christian body could refuse to take them up. The generational division that drove the controversies over Vietnam was cultural as well as ideological, reflecting not only an intellectual shift but also a broader revolution in social mores. This revolution forced the Christian churches to adapt to a wide variety of new and unexpected phenomena, from the electric guitar to blue denim to the drug culture. Most important, it forced them to deal with the debates surrounding *the sexual revolution*, the second great development in American life that diminished orthodox Christianity's credibility, and probably the most direct blow to the faith's appeal since the publication of *On the Origin of Species* a century earlier.

That blow had been delivered by a book; this one was delivered by a prophylactic. At first, the development of a safe, reliable birth control pill seemed like a theological and moral problem only for the Catholic Church, since most Protestant bodies already approved of contraceptive use by married couples. This assumption proved to be naive: while Catholics spent the 1960s publicly debating their church's teaching on contraception, the pill's promise was inspiring a far more sweeping private revolution, one that extended well beyond the narrow issue of birth control to encompass the entirety of sexual ethics. Over the course of a decade or so, a large swath of America decided that two millennia of Christian teaching on marriage and sexuality were simply out of date.

This leap came first; the rationalizations trailed behind. As a purely intellectual matter, nothing was suddenly discovered in the 1960s that contradicted the biblical witness on fornication, adultery, and homosexuality, or that established that Jesus hadn't *really* meant what he said about the indissolubility of marriage. Arguments along these lines had been made, of course, but they were no more inherently persuasive in 1970 than they had been in 1950. (Despite what some religious conservatives have suggested, Hugh Hefner and Erica Jong didn't suddenly bewitch the country with their case for the joys of promiscuity.) The difference was that in 1970 many more people wanted to believe these arguments because of the new sexual possibilities associated with the birth control pill.

Before the sexual revolution, a rigorous ethic of chastity and monogamy had seemed self-evidently commonsensical even to many non-Christians. What was moral was also practical, and vice versa; so long as sex made babies, it made sense that the only truly safe sex was married sex. Scripture and tradition supplied the Christian view of marriage, but it was the fear of illegitimacy, abandonment, and disease that made the position nearly universally respected.

This respect was granted in the breach as often as in the observance. In 1940 as in 2000, most Americans—male and female alike—didn't go virginal to their marriage beds. But the web of prohibitions rooted in Christian teaching had a real impact nonetheless. Before the sexual revolution, Americans waited longer to have sex, had fewer sexual partners across the course of a lifetime (less than half as many, by some estimates),[23] and were much more likely to see premarital lovemaking as a way station on the road to wedlock rather than an end unto itself. (According to one survey, 45 percent of Americans born around 1940 married the first person they slept with, compared to just 9 percent of Americans born around 1965.[24]) The same pattern held once the marriage bond was forged: infidelity and divorce were hardly unknown, but in pre-1960s America more married couples made a sustained attempt—and faced sustained social pressure, obviously—to live up to the demanding precepts of the Gospel.

By separating sex from procreation more completely than any previous technology (though not nearly as completely as was initially suggested), the birth control pill also severed the cultural connection between Christian ethics and American common sense. For the first time in human history, it was possible for the poor and middle class as well as the rich to imagine being *safely* promiscuous. In this atmosphere, the Christian emphasis on the necessary link between sex and procreation weakened significantly: In 1960, more than 85 percent of American women agreed that "almost all parents who can *ought* to have children," but by 1980 only 40 percent agreed.[25] As that domino fell, others went down with it. As late as 1969, more than half of Americans agreed with the traditional Christian prohibition on sex outside of marriage, and only 21 percent told Gallup's pollsters that premarital sex was "not wrong at all." In just four years, the latter figure had climbed to 43 percent; by the mid-1980s, it had reached 57 percent.[26] Public approval of divorce climbed swiftly as well. While in 1962 American women were evenly divided on whether parents in an unhappy marriage should stay together for the sake of their children, by 1980 more than 80 percent of women thought such parents should split up.[27] And there was a sudden spike in the acceptance of adultery and open marriages in the early 1970s—though there the numbers leveled off quickly, as fantasy gave way, presumably, to bitter experience.[28]

These changing attitudes led to the redefinition of the private sphere, in the courts and the culture alike, and a widespread sense that issues like contraception, premarital cohabitation, and divorce—and then, much more controversially, abortion—were private matters where the government had no business interfering. The very idea of "morals legislation" became suspect, and Christian arguments about family law and public policy that might have been accepted even by secular audiences in the 1940s came to be regarded with suspicion as potential violations of the separation of church and state.

At the same time, a more sweeping idea gained ground as well—the conceit that many of Christianity's stringent sexual prohibitions were not only unnecessary but actively perverse. Again, this was not a new concept; it was as old as paganism, and as young as Alfred Kinsey. But the social revolution of the 1960s made it vastly more attractive.

When a culture cuts itself loose from a set of precepts that it had taken for granted just a few short years ago, there's a natural instinct to cast the shift as a triumph for civilization, rather than just a change in mores—an evolutionary leap forward, a sudden step from darkness into light. Looking backward, it's never hard to identify particular cruelties that made the ancien régime worth abandoning—and worth deploring, loudly, with it safely in the rearview mirror.

Such cruelties abounded in the sexual order of midcentury America: couples forced into unhappy shotgun marriages, young women shunned and stigmatized for a single sexual mistake, homosexuals forced to pass as straight and persecuted when they didn't. The critics were right that the Christian sexual ethic had become intertwined, across the centuries, with a host of patriarchal assumptions that foreclosed opportunities for women and dismissed their legitimate aspirations and desires. So in the early years of the sexual revolution it was easy for many Americans, most of whom still considered themselves good Christians, to decide that their faith's sexual ethic wasn't just outdated—it was repressive, cruel, and pernicious, a stumbling block to female advancement and a blight on healthy eroticism. This meant, in turn, that anyone who defended it must be either nostalgic for an age of sexual repression or else a helpless victim of false consciousness, unable to escape the burden of shame and guilt a religious upbringing had imposed.

Over time, this premise would become perhaps the biggest drag on Christianity's public credibility. It created a presumptive bias against the Christian position on sexual ethics, no matter what arguments were deployed on its behalf. (If you opposed abortion, you wanted to control women. If you were against gay marriage, you were probably a pathetic closet case yourself. If you held up monogamy and fidelity as high ideals, it was just because you couldn't get laid.) At the same time, it became an all-purpose excuse whenever the revolution generated less than congenial results: if out-of-wedlock birthrates were climbing, or STD rates were going up, it was obviously just because the dead hand of patriarchy and repression was preventing young Americans from getting the sex education and birth control they really needed.

And not just young Americans. By the late 1960s, Christian teaching on sexuality was being held up as a scapegoat on the international stage as well, attacked by scientists and statesman as one of the many fuses lighting the supposed "population bomb." By resisting birth control, abortion, and sterilization campaigns in the Third World, intellectuals and activists repeatedly suggested, Christian leaders weren't just standing in the way of economic development and social progress—they were putting the entire world at risk of being swamped by population growth. Domestically, Christianity could be held responsible only for neurosis, repression, and bigotry. But widen your perspective to include Africa and Asia, and suddenly Christian teaching—particularly its emphasis on fecundity and familial integrity—could be blamed for precipitating what many authorities predicted would be the greatest catastrophe civilization had ever faced.

Here the sexual revolution overlapped with the third trend undercutting Christianity's credibility in the 1960s and 1970s: the dawn of late-twentieth-century globalization. This gave rise to a *global perspective* as the lens through which more and more Americans viewed the world. The America of midcentury hadn't been provincial, but it had been distinctly

Western in its cultural outlook and concerns. From architecture and poetry to education and philosophy, Eisenhower's America had drawn on
Europe's example, even as the country profited from an ongoing infusion
of European émigré talent into its salons and universities. Throughout
the era's religious renaissance, Hilaire Belloc's aphorism that "Europe is
the faith, and the faith Europe" found a kind of vindication in the way
that the New World's Catholics and Protestants drew inspiration from
intensely old-world figures such as W. H. Auden and Karl Barth and
Jacques Maritain.

What with British rock, Italian cinema, and French philosophizing,
Europe's cultural influence hardly disappeared in 1960s America. But
American horizons widened as well. The spread of air travel brought the
world closer. The spread of television thrust its wild diversity into millions
of American living rooms. The Peace Corps sent young Americans out
to experience it in the flesh. Every new development, from the terrors of
the Cuban Missile Crisis to the triumph of the moon landing, seemed to
hammer home the smallness of the earth and the interconnectedness of its
inhabitants. The Vietnam conflict turned American eyes to Asia in a more
profound way than either World War II or the Korean War had done. Decolonization did the same for Africa, providing an international analogue
to the domestic civil rights struggle. As a generation of African political
celebrities rose to prominence—from Kwame Nkrumah to Jomo Kenyatta
to Patrice Lumumba—their exotic charisma won them wave upon wave of
admiring coverage in the Western press.

Admiring, and also masochistic. To celebrate the new global civilization
was to celebrate the eclipse of European dominance. It was to cast a cold
eye across the many sins of Western civilization—America's included. This
had obvious political implications, especially for members of the boomer
generation, many of whom found themselves drawn to the United Nations
rather than to the Department of Defense, to Dag Hammarskjöld rather
than to Lyndon Johnson, to Fidel Castro rather than to William West-
moreland. But the new global perspective had significant religious implications as well. It wasn't just that the Second Vatican Council made Catholics
more aware of their faith's global footprint, or that the World Council of
Churches aspired to perform a similar feat for Mainline Protestants. For
millions of young Americans, Christianity suddenly felt like just one spiri-

tual option among many—and an option tainted by its long association with white chauvinism and Western imperialism. If you wanted a religion that lacked any such associations, there was suddenly Buddhism as a viable alternative to Methodism, Transcendental Meditation instead of the Our Father, the monasteries of Tibet as a rival to the Union Theological Seminary, the Maharishi as a more exotic guru than the Pope.

America had passed through Orientalist crazes before, during earlier religious awakenings, earlier ages of religious ferment. The Transcendentalists had been obsessed with Buddhism and Hinduism, and Asian holy men had knocked elbows with Spiritualists and Christian Scientists during the Victorian revivals. But this time Eastern religion gained a stronger foothold. Not as a comprehensive alternative to Christianity, necessarily; the overall number of self-described Buddhists and Hindus and Taoists remained relatively small, and many practitioners self-consciously emptied their newfound faith of anything that deviated too dramatically from the mores of the modern West. (The Fourteenth Dalai Lama's Western publishers, mindful of their likely audience, were careful to excise his criticisms of homosexuality from the American versions of his books.) But as *influences* on religion in America, Eastern faiths would become increasingly important in the post-1960s landscape. So would other exotic-seeming alternatives to Christianity, from Native American rituals and Sufi spirituality to the Nation of Islam's Afrocentric take on the religion of Mohammed and the faux-ancient fraud of Wicca.

So would Judaism, albeit in a somewhat different fashion. Jewish mysticism made inroads among Gentiles in much the same way that Buddhism did, complete with similar celebrity endorsers. But it was the memory of Jewish suffering that had the more significant impact on post-1960s religious culture. The Christian center of the 1950s had been philo-Semitic, but sometimes in a patronizing way: The spread of the term *Judeo-Christianity,* in particular, substituted a rhetorical nod for a more thoroughgoing examination of conscience about how cruelly Christian civilization had often treated the Jews.

This would change as the barriers to Jewish advancement in America continued to fall, and as the Holocaust—which had been downplayed in the immediate aftermath of World War II, by Jews as well as Gentiles—loomed ever larger in the West's intellectual consciousness. From the 1960s onward, Christians were forced to wrestle more directly with their faith's history of anti-Semitism, and treat Jews as equals rather than condescend to them as junior partners in American religion.

This process bore morally impressive fruit. The Second Vatican Council's renunciation of anti-Semitism, the swift integration of Jews into the great institutions of the WASP episcopacy, American Evangelicalism's love affair with Israel—these were all enormous advances for a relationship defined for centuries by polemics and persecution.

But along with this necessary purgation came a turn to self-flagellation and self-doubt, as the shame of Christian anti-Semitism generated not only an understandable disgust at the crimes of the Christian past but also a persistent sense of embarrassment about Christianity itself. In this atmosphere there was a tendency to find anti-Semitism lurking in every era and every institution, in every saint and every school of thought. All of Christian history was suddenly suspect: the Crusades were just an excuse for pogroms and genocide; Martin Luther was an eliminationist anti-Semite *avant la lettre*; Pius XII was "Hitler's Pope." All you needed to know about the fathers of the Church was that John Chrysostom preached vituperously against the Jews; all you needed to know about the Catholic Church was that it backed the Spanish Inquisition.

Indeed, the basic doctrines of the faith were suspect as well, for the role they had played in fomenting bigotry and persecution. The Gospels were anti-Semitic because they blamed the Jewish authorities for killing Jesus. Saint Paul was anti-Semitic because he argued that Christianity had superseded Judaism. The Nicene Creed was anti-Semitic because it emphasized Christ's suffering and death and implicitly reminded Christians of the role the Jews had played in both. The theology of divine atonement was anti-Semitic for the same reason. Indeed, the edifice of orthodox Christology, with its insistence on Christ's blood, pain, suffering, and death, had been exposed by the Holocaust as a terrible mistake.

You didn't have to follow this logic all the way to partake of the Christian crisis of confidence, this sense that the faith as a whole was tainted and tarnished by two thousand years' worth of Christian sins. Thus the sudden appeal of religious syncretism, which mixed and matched elements from various traditions, and the mounting wariness about exclusive truth claims. (Especially truth claims that had been used, as Christianity's often were, to justify exploitation and cultural chauvinism.) The more the newfound global perspective exposed Americans to non-Western realms and cultures, the more skeptical they became about the idea that their particular faith (whether Catholic or Protestant) could claim to speak distinctively for God and truth. The more that the world was swept up in the drama of decolonization and Third World empowerment, the more tainted Christianity seemed by its centuries of association with the now-discredited imperial projects of the European West. The more the Holocaust emerged as Western civilization's moral touchstone (the one "culturally available icon of absolute evil," in Richard John Neuhaus's phrase), the easier it became to regard the Christian past through the darkened glass of Auschwitz.

A broad trend toward "relativism, individualism and pluralism," as the authors of *Vanishing Boundaries* put it, had been at work in American religion for some time, but the combination of globalization and Christian guilt accelerated it sharply.[29] Religious certainty ebbed, even if belief did not: the proportion of Americans who stated they believed in God "without doubt" dropped from 77 percent to 65 percent between 1964 and the 1990s, and there was a concurrent rise in the percentage who believed more uncertainly. Belief in denominational distinctiveness also waned. This shift was visible in rising rates of intermarriage and declining interest, even among active churchgoers, in what their particular confession believed. (The authors of *Vanishing Boundaries* wrote in 1992 that "Our in-depth interviews suggest that the great majority of active Baby Boom Presbyterians subscribe to neither the traditional Presbyterian standards contained in the Westminster Confession of Faith and the Shorter Catechism, nor to any of the more contemporary theological formulations" espoused by their church.[30]) Faith in religious authorities weakened as well: Support for the bedrock Reformation belief that the Bible was "the actual word of God" fell by nine percentage points between the 1960s and the 1990s, and a 1997 study found that whereas 58 percent of Catholics born before 1941 agreed that theirs was "the one true Church," only 34 percent of those born in the 1940s and 1950s shared that conviction.[31]

On the question of Christianity's relationship to other religions, meanwhile, a spirit of universalism carried the day. The Baby Boom generation was significantly more likely than their parents to agree that all religions were "basically true," to agree that people of any faith could go to heaven, and to say that one could be a good Christian without attending church. This turn occurred first among the college-educated, but it spread to the rest of the country soon enough. When researchers returned to Muncie, Indiana, in the 1970s, fifty years after the original version of the famous "Middletown" study on middle-American values, one of the biggest changes they noted was a massive decline in the proportion of Muncie youth who agreed that "Christianity is the one true religion and everyone should be converted to it."[32]

As with the sexual revolution, these shifts were intuitive without being intellectually necessary. A more global perspective on politics and culture required giving more serious consideration to non-Western traditions and theologies. But it did not require, as a logical consequence, the thoroughgoing relativism about religious truth that many Americans came to embrace. Nor did the repudiation of imperialism require repudiating the faith of the imperialists, as Europe's former subjects swiftly demonstrated. The collapse of colonial regimes in Africa coincided with an era of explosive *growth* for the Christian churches that the now-departed occupiers had planted, and conversion rates ticked up sharply in many Asian countries as well. Even as Western Christians were wrestling with their faith's complicity in racism, imperialism, and anti-Semitism, actual Third Worlders were embracing exactly the kind of dogmas that their former colonial masters were suddenly desperate to be rid of.

But of course more than just guilt and cosmopolitanism separated the religious experiences of America and Africa. Here we come to the fourth great trend undercutting Christianity in the 1960s: the changing economic landscape and *the religious consequences of America's ever-growing wealth*.

One need not subscribe to a vulgar Marxism to recognize the impact of economic changes on patterns of belief. It was John Wesley, no prophet of secularization, who remarked that "wherever riches have increased, the essence of religion has decreased in the same proportion." His insight foreshadowed the story of Christianity in late-twentieth-century America, where the riches piled up by decades of unprecedented economic growth played an important role in the decline of traditional belief.

Christianity has never been a religion that appealed exclusively to the poor. Even in its earliest centuries, it won as many converts among the

Roman Empire's urban middle classes as it did among the dispossessed and marginalized. But there is no escaping the Gospels' critique of greed and acquisition, and an emphasis on renunciation and asceticism has always been part of both the theology and the practice of Christian orthodoxy. Inevitably, such emphases had less resonance for a generation that came of age amid the cornucopian abundance of postwar American life than for the generation that passed through the Great Depression.

One major consequence was institutional. The growing wealth available to the professional classes is an underrated factor in the decline of religious vocations. Entering the ministry had always involved sacrifice, but the scale of that sacrifice grew considerably steeper during the 1960s and '70s. Swiftly rising salaries in every nonclerical career almost certainly depleted the ranks of would-be priests and ministers, depriving the established churches of youthful leadership at precisely the moment when it was needed most. (A representative statistic: the average salary for a married Protestant minister with a graduate degree rose just 11 percent between the 1970s and the 1990s; for a doctor or lawyer, it rose 37 percent.[33])

These economic realities probably contributed as much to the collapse of vocations as the Catholic Church's refusal to lift its ban on married priests. The baby boomers believed in *fighting* poverty, but a generation "bred in at least modest comfort" (as the 1962 Port Huron Statement famously put it, in a crashing understatement) found the idea of sharing that poverty considerably less attractive. Embracing policies that promised to eradicate misery and want was one thing; embracing the vows of poverty that traditionally demonstrated Christianity's solidarity with the poor was quite another. Or at least embracing them permanently: there was a rush to self-conscious simplicity among the 1960s generation, certainly, but with some exceptions it tended to be just a phase. The Haight-Ashbury street people grew up and went to business school or law school; the communes closed up shop once their inhabitants turned thirty. The young men who quit the priesthood because they supposedly wanted to work with the poor directly had a habit of turning up as accountants or advertising executives a few years down the line.

The results were felt across denominations. Assessing the quality of America's clerical class for the *Atlantic* in 1990, Paul Wilkes painted a bleak picture:

There is little doubt that the quality of seminarians has declined. Dean after dean admits that seminaries are getting precious few of those ranked in the top reaches of their undergraduate classes. In 1947 some ten percent of college graduates nominated to Phi Beta Kappa went into the ministry. A Phi Beta Kappa member today who evinced an interest in the ministry would be recruited by seminaries with unholy zeal. The ministry these days must compete for the best and the brightest not only with the ill-paid and too-often thankless helping professions, such as social work and counseling, but also with the high-profile and well-paid professions of law, business, and medicine.[34]

In this climate, it wasn't surprising that the churches that had the most success attracting high-powered and well-adjusted candidates for ministry consciously encouraged their pastors to double as entrepreneurs. Nor was it surprising that the gospel such ministers preached tended to smile on Mammon and materialism in ways that were antithetical to the New Testament's hard ascetic core.

But wealth for wealth's sake wasn't the only economic factor undercutting orthodoxy. America in the 1960s and 1970s was becoming a steadily more suburban society, and after the initial wave of church-building subsided, religious community proved harder to sustain in the new commuter society than it had been in an America of small towns and urban neighborhoods. Examining a representative sample of baby boomer Protestants, Hoge and his coauthors found that 50 percent lived more than one hundred miles from the church where they'd been confirmed, and 15 percent had moved at least three times in the past five years.[35] This was a recipe for confessional decline. A Lutheran might remain a Lutheran when moving from his urban birthplace to a nearby suburb, but would he stick to his confession when he moved again, and yet again, shedding the ties of family and community along the way? The answer, often, was no: our hypothetical Protestant was more likely to find himself drawn to nondenominational churches and do-it-yourself religion.

Likewise, the increasing returns to college and graduate degrees, the rise of the information sector, and the decline of an industrial economy that had offered a certain permanence for many families changed how Americans lived and loved and worked in ways that cut against traditional

Christian practice and belief. For the well educated, in particular, a long "adultescence" suddenly yawned between childhood and the assumption of full adult responsibilities. This was a period in which active churchgoing tended to lapse and the Christian sexual ethic seemed particularly onerous.

Indeed, almost all the trends just discussed were felt most intensely among the American upper class. They were the wealthiest, of course, and the most mobile and well educated and worldly, and thus the most likely to prefer theologies that emphasized the divinity of the self rather than the demands of a jealous God. They had gained the most from the new sexual freedoms and had suffered the least from their darker repercussions. They therefore quickly came to regard even a whisper of the old ideals of chastity and continence as a threat to the liberation they enjoyed. Because they were better informed about national affairs, they tended to be more politically savvy than most Americans, and thus more likely to be dismissive, if not openly contemptuous, when religious leaders pretended to special wisdom on public policy questions. And they were the most cosmopolitan, moving in an increasingly multicultural and libertine milieu in which there were no greater sins than the anti-Semitism, racism, and sexism— and later, homophobia—that historic Christianity now stood accused of fostering.

And so, a final, crucial element entered the story of orthodox decline: the element of *class*. The old East Coast establishment weakened in parallel with the churches where its members worshipped, and the elite that displaced the WASPs soon exceeded every other stratum of American society in its rejection of traditional Christian practice and belief. Except that *rejection* was too strong a word. After a certain interval had passed, orthodoxy was less rejected than dismissed, reflexively, as something unworthy of an educated person's intellect and interest. Religion qua religion was acceptable (the more exotic the better, of course) and "spirituality" was welcome. But All Serious People understood that the only reason to pay attention to traditional Christianity was to subject it to a withering critique. Before long even that exercise grew stale, confined to Ivy League divinity schools whose relevance declined with every passing year.

This dismissive attitude held sway in every institution where the new meritocratic elite predominated—the great universities and law schools, the major newspapers and networks, the powerful New York founda-

tions and the upper reaches of the federal bureaucracy. In these exalted
precincts, it wasn't just that the faith of Peter and Paul, Charlemagne and
Aquinas, Luther and Erasmus, John Winthrop and George Washington
suddenly seemed anachronistic. It was something more devastating than
this. Among the tastemakers and power brokers and intellectual agenda
setters of late-twentieth-century America, orthodox Christianity was completely déclassé.

THREE

ACCOMMODATION

Amid such sweeping challenges to their faith, there were two obvious paths that the Christian churches could take: accommodation or resistance. The first approach would seek to forge a new Christianity more consonant with the spirit of the age, one better adapted to the trends that were undercutting orthodoxy. The latter would follow William F. Buckley's maxim and stand athwart religious history yelling "Stop!" The first approach would attempt to sustain Christianity's midcentury reconciliation with Western liberalism by adapting itself to the changing cultural circumstances. The second would break decisively with the revolutionary mood in American society and identify Christianity with cultural conservatism.

Both approaches were invoked as solutions to Christianity's struggles, and both were blamed for Christianity's eclipse. With every drop in church attendance, vocations, or donations, accommodationists would blame the forces of reaction for preventing necessary adaptations, alienating the changing population of a changing country by refusing to change themselves. Resisters would retort that the collapse of Christian culture was a direct consequence of accommodationists' surrender to contemporary fashions.

In the end, neither approach reaped the fruits that its adherents promised. But the forces of accommodation gained the upper hand first. They had the cultural wind at their back in ways the resisters never did. In terms of intellectual clout and institutional power, the 1960s and '70s were their decades. Yet these were precisely the years of Christianity's most dramatic decline. And while that decline may not have been the fault of the accommodationists, in the most immediate sense it was their problem.

The age of accommodation was heralded by *Time* magazine's famous cover story "Is God Dead?," which ran in April 1966, just six months after the Second Vatican Council closed its final session in Rome. Half-remembered as a brief for atheism, the story was actually an example of a kind of long-form journalism that was soon to vanish from the American scene: a sustained engagement, in a mass-market periodical, with just-emerging trends in Christian theology. Modern Christianity, *Time* informed its readers, was in a sense as vibrant as ever: in "a country where public faith in God seems to be as secure as it was in medieval France," the Christian faith was "now confidently renewing itself in spirit as well as form." But this renewal pointed away from the neo-orthodoxy of the 1940s and '50s, and toward what the magazine intimated was a more sophisticated and mature understanding of religion—one that might "formulate a new image and concept of God using contemporary thought categories" while requiring the revision of certain "Christian truths" and other "God-related issues."[1]

Nearly all of the "new concepts" of God considered in the article had a big idea in common: the notion that henceforward Christianity could flourish only by transforming itself into a more secular enterprise, dedicated to building the kingdom of God in this life rather than preparing believers for the hereafter. In this secularized faith, Christ would be invoked "as a spiritual hero whom even non-believers can admire," while God and transcendence would be associated with the modern hope for a better future—a hope that would be achieved through progressive politics and enjoyed by a human race that has "taken responsibility for the world." Religious institutions would need to "become more secular themselves," *Time* suggested, "recognizing that God is not the property of the church, and is acting in history as he wills, in encounters for which man is forever unprepared." Along the way, those same churches "might well need to take a position of reverent agnosticism regarding some doctrines that it had previously proclaimed with excessive conviction"—doctrines, for instance, like personal immortality and the resurrection of the dead.

This accommodationist Christianity drew on various influences from the 1940s and '50s, including the Catholic theologian Karl Rahner, with his doctrine of the "anonymous Christian" saved by works and good intentions rather than explicit faith in Jesus Christ, and Dietrich Bonhoeffer, the great Protestant martyr of Hitler's Germany, whose prison letters, published for the first time in 1960, meditated provocatively on a "religionless Christianity" for a "world come of age." But at heart the new theology was a revival of the modernism of the prewar era, a gospel of social progress like the one that Karl Barth and Reinhold Niebuhr had rejected as ultimately antithetical to Christianity, updated and reformulated for the age of the United Nations and the moon race.

The realism about original sin fostered by two world wars and an economic depression might have undercut this creed, but now the political aspirations and technological achievements of the 1960s made it possible to unite religious faith and secular ambition again. So did the turn of generations. The men who had fashioned the neo-orthodox epoch were dying: C. S. Lewis died on the same day as John F. Kennedy; Niebuhr and John Courtney Murray passed in 1967; Barth followed in 1968, the same year that Martin Luther King was assassinated, and Jacques Maritain in 1973. (Fulton Sheen would linger till 1979, but as a cultural figure he was an anachronism.) Their successors could see that the times were changing, and that Christianity faced new challenges that were too powerful to easily master or dismiss. Understandably, they wanted something bold and fresh with which to meet them. "Neo-orthodoxy doesn't work," the young theologian William Hamilton wrote in 1966, and "pessimism doesn't persuade anymore."[2] Half tongue-in-cheek, he cited January 4, 1965, as the date when the neo-orthodox era officially ended: the Anglo-Catholic poet T. S. Eliot passed away that day, even as Lyndon Johnson was delivering a triumphant State of the Union address committing his country to the Great Society and "revolutionary change."

Hamilton was just one of many tribunes for this renewal of the modernist gospel. In *The Gospel of Christian Atheism* (1966), Thomas J. J. Altizer framed it in the Nietzschean language of the "death of God" (which had given *Time* magazine its cover line), reinterpreting Christ's incarnation as a sign that God had entered history and been subsumed by it, leaving mankind the master of his own fate. Similar ideas were floated in Gabriel

Vahanian's more bluntly titled *The Death of God* (1961), and in books like Paul van Buren's *The Secular Meaning of the Gospel* (1966) and Ronald Gregor Smith's *Secular Christianity* (1966). (The era's titles tend to run together.) All of these authors offered variations on the same basic premise—that it was time for Christianity to turn from the supernatural to the natural, from theology to anthropology, and from the Kingdom of God to the City of Man.

Then there was Teilhard de Chardin, the brilliant Jesuit paleontologist-philosopher who died in relative obscurity in 1960, only to become a kind of posthumous court theologian to the New Frontier and the Great Society. His intellectual system was a shotgun marriage of Darwinism and Christianity, floated on a cloud of buzzwords—hominization! excentration! Christogenesis! Pleromization!—and perfectly tailored for a moment in which the cautious and disillusioned leaders of the World War II generation were giving way to John F. Kennedy's whiz kids. (De Chardin was reportedly Robert McNamara's favorite theologian.) The Jesuit was orthodox in his personal piety, but his arguments were easily turned to more heterodox ends. His admirers interpreted them as divinizing science and technology, capitalism and globalization: These were all signs of humanity's progress toward the second coming of Christ, which was implicitly redefined to mean the moment when God, mankind, and the cosmos all merged into one universal consciousness. There was no room for a Fall of Man in this narrative, and no original sin—just the steady upward ascent of an ever-improving, ever-evolving species, converging toward the "Omega Point" of unity and harmony with every passing year.

But the defining theologian of the age of accommodation, the Niebuhr (or, more properly, the anti-Niebuhr) of the 1960s, was probably the young Harvard professor Harvey Cox. His treatise *The Secular City* (1965) was a publishing phenomenon, selling more than a million copies despite containing sentences like this one: "The ruling figures who stand at the fountainhead of existentialist thought still breathe the air of the presecular *Bildungsschicht.*"[3] The abstruse language mattered less to Cox's eager readership than did his reassuring message, which suggested that all of the trends considered in the previous section, all of the forces then emerging to undercut Christian practice and belief, were actually opportunities for Christianity's growth and maturity and true fulfillment.

Was the Gospel in danger of being overpoliticized in the wake of the civil rights movement's successes? Not possible, Cox wrote: "What God is doing in the world is politics, which means making and keeping life human. Politics also describes man's role in response to God. . . . Theology today must be that reflection-action by which the church finds out what this politician-God is up to and moves to work along with him." Indeed, "in the epoch of the secular city, politics replaces metaphysics as the language of theology."

What about the rapidly accelerating sexual revolution, with its apparent threat to Christian sexual ethics? No such threat existed: The new sexual freedoms offered a chance for believers to transcend "dead-end arguments about virginity and chastity," with their "cheap attempt to oversimplify" complicated questions and "reduce all the intricacies" of sexuality "to one decision." Indeed, the new freedoms represented the true fulfillment of the New Testament, whose sexual teachings were actually far more open-ended that a cramped and narrow reading would suggest. "Instead of registering an answer [on sexuality], the Gospel poses a question of its own. . . . It asks how I can best nourish the maturity of those with whom I share the torments and transports of human existence." The "traditional Christian sexual norms" were all well and good, but "like all human codes they stand in continuous need of revision so that they will help rather than hinder God's maturation of man."[4]

What of the rise of moral and theological relativism, which threatened to recast Christianity as just one of many essentially equivalent religions? It was anticipated in the Old Testament, Cox assured his readers, where God's revelation from Sinai "relativizes" rival gods and values, revealing them "as human projections" rather than absolute truths. (In this sense, Cox suggested in a characteristic aside, the Bible "is very close to the modern social sciences.") Contemporary relativism is merely "the nonreligious expression of what Jews have expressed in their consistent opposition to idols, and Christians in their sporadic attacks on icons." Thus relativism actually fulfills "the work of the God of Creation, Exodus, and Sinai," by placing "the responsibility for the forging of human values, like the fashioning of political systems, in man's own hands."[5]

When it came to the economic forces undercutting orthodoxy, Cox did manage a few tepid criticisms of consumerism and commercialism. But mostly he followed Teilhard de Chardin's acolytes in heaping theological praise upon "technopolitan" man's quest for mastery, and the urbanizing, globalizing world's capacity for "vastly enlarging the range of human communication and widening the scope of individual choice."[6] What others saw as rootlessness and anomie, Cox ingeniously recast as the fulfillment, once again, of the Old Testament's warnings against idolatry. "By and large the mobile man is less tempted than the immobile man to demote Yahweh into a Baal," he wrote, and so "there is no reason that Christians should deplore the accelerating mobility of the modern metropolis." After all, "the Bible does not call man to renounce mobility, but 'to go to a place that I will show unto you.'"[7]

In a remarkable peroration, Cox distilled this accommodationist message to its essence—not just an affirmation of the modern world and modern man exactly as they were (or were becoming), but the bolder claim that all the biblical writers would agree with him:

> We have affirmed technopolitan man in his pragmatism and in his profanity. To do so we have not abandoned the Bible; we have found, on the contrary that its views of truth and of creation display important areas of similarity with the style of the secular city. . . . There is no pathos in this. Theology is a living enterprise. The Gospel does not call man to return to a previous stage of his development. It does not summon man back to dependence, awe and religiousness. Rather it is a call to imaginative urbanity and mature secularity. It is not a call to man to abandon his interest in the problems of this world, but an invitation to accept the full weight of this world's problems as the gift of its Maker. It is a call to be a man of this technical age, with all that means, seeking to make a human habitation for all who live in it.[8]

Cox's only worry was that the established Christian churches wouldn't be able to keep up. "God's reconciling work *may* be going on in them. It may not. Most likely it is and it isn't. Most likely it is occurring within them and also at many places outside them." In such times, "the real job of those in the churches . . . is to discern where God's reconciliation is breaking in and identify themselves with this action." And the great danger facing the established denominations was that their "intrinsic conservatism" would prevent them "from leaving their palaces behind and stepping into God's permanent revolution in history."[9]

Cox needn't have been so anxious. The churches were eager to embrace the revolution. There was generational change in the pulpit and pews as well as in the academy. For every accommodationist theologian eager to refashion Christian theology for an age of secular ambition, there were countless accommodationist clerics and laypeople eager to put this new Christianity into practice.

None was more famous, for a time at least, than the Episcopal bishop James Pike. Pike was already a minor celebrity in the Eisenhower years, when he served as the dean of Saint John the Divine Cathedral in New York and the host of a Fulton Sheen–esque hour of prime-time apologetics. By the late 1950s, he had been installed as the Bishop of California, in the long-unfinished Grace Episcopal Cathedral on San Francisco's Nob Hill. Perhaps inspired by the symbolism, he began fund-raising to bring that project to completion, even as he set out to renovate Christianity as well.

In New York, Pike had been politically liberal but otherwise High Church—activist in his politics but relatively traditional on matters of liturgy and doctrine. (In 1956, he edited a collection of essays by notable Episcopalians that included W. H. Auden's conversion memoir.) But once installed in California, he began easing his way toward a more thoroughgoing Coxian Christianity. His liturgical conservatism melted away: he told his parishioners that too many candles on the altar were a sign of "Zoroastrian light worship," and dismissed the idea of genuflecting toward the tabernacle with a terse "I don't think God cares."[10] He dismissed, as well, the ecclesiastical divides between Protestant denominations, ordaining a Methodist minister as an Episcopal priest on All Saints' Day in 1959—a move that earned him write-ups in *Time* and *Newsweek* along with the predictable criticism from conservative believers. Five years later, he ordained a woman as a "transitional deacon," the first step toward ordination to the Episcopal priesthood. And he effaced, with a bright flourish, the distinction between secular heroes and sacred ones: as the cathedral neared completion, he added Albert Einstein, Thurgood Marshall, and John Glenn to the church's stained-glass windows.

Pike soon became a theological revisionist as well. In December 1960, the Christmas issue of *Christian Century* invited contributors to discuss an issue on which their minds had recently changed. Pike picked the virgin birth, which he had once accepted but now regarded as a pious myth. That was just the warm-up act; over the next five years, operating on the conviction that Christians needed "more belief, fewer beliefs," Pike proceeded to jettison a slew of major Christian teachings, from the divinity of Christ to the doctrine of the Trinity to most of the moral traditions of the faith. (The revision of Christianity's sexual code was somewhat convenient, since Pike was a serial adulterer then in the process of moving on to wife number three.)

In the early 1960s, all of this was still controversial enough in Episcopalian circles to generate abortive attempts at a heresy trial for Bishop Pike. Over the next two decades, though, the San Franciscan prelate's vision would become essentially mainstream, in his own church and in the Protestant Mainline generally. By the late 1970s, women's ordination was universal among Mainline denominations. By the 1990s, the Episcopal Church, the American Methodist Church, and the Evangelical Lutheran Church of America all recognized one another's rites and holy orders. When Pike was elevated to the California bishopric, he claimed (falsely, it appears) that his first marriage had been annulled; otherwise his divorce and remarriage would have barred him from the office. Within two decades, that kind of difficulty was no longer an issue for Episcopalians, or indeed for the members of any Mainline Protestant denomination, nearly all of whom had passed from accepting divorce but forbidding remarriage (at least so long as the original spouse lived) to permitting remarriage in any case where the would-be remarryer displayed (in a passage from a 1982 Lutheran document) "a willingness to acknowledge one's own failures in a spirit of forgiveness toward all involved, and to work at correcting whatever personal characteristics may be detrimental to a marital relationship."[11]

Over the same period, the prohibition on premarital sex lapsed into irrelevance in some denominations; in others it was actually abandoned, replaced by a more palatable-seeming opposition to "promiscuity," hazily defined. By the early 1970s, too, nearly every Mainline denomination had endorsed some kind of legal abortion—a striking concession to contemporary trends, given how far back the traditional Christian opposition to the practice ran. (The Didache, arguably the earliest surviving Christian catechism, explicitly analogizes abortion to infanticide, admonishing readers,

"You shall not murder a child by abortion nor kill that which is born."[12])
Indeed, by the time the controversies over gay ordination and gay marriage
began in earnest in the 1980s, Mainline churches had moved so far from
traditional Christian sexual ethics that their approval of homosexuality
often felt more inevitable than wrenching.

Where traditional theology was concerned, the Mainline churches *as
churches* rarely offered anything quite so explicit as Pike's deliberate denial
of the Trinity and the Nicene Creed. They merely tolerated such denials, as
well as others that went further still—John Shelby Spong, Episcopal Bishop
of Newark in the 1980s, moved from denying the virgin birth to denying
the very existence of a personal God without facing any sanction—while
gradually purging the specifics of Christian theology from their public
language. In seminaries and ecclesiastical bureaucracies, where pastors
were trained and policy was set, politics rather than theology was increasingly regarded as the central mission of the church. Orthodox belief wasn't
officially abandoned; it was merely downgraded, declared optional, and
generally ignored. "Creeds divide, deeds unite," ran the refrain, and so the
distinctive theological traditions that had once distinguished Presbyterians
from Methodists and Lutherans from Congregationalists were steadily effaced, and the Protestant Mainline rebuilt itself along exactly the lines that
Cox and Pike had envisioned.

The idea behind all of these moves was inclusion. Inclusion of women,
through the ordination of female ministers and priests and then through
the gradual recasting of liturgies along more gender-neutral lines. Inclusion of racial minorities and immigrants, who would be drawn (or so the
theory went) by the churches' emphasis on social justice. Inclusion of the
young cohabiting couple and the older divorcée, the gay man and the
lesbian. Inclusion of the counterculture, through folk music services and
rock-and-roll liturgies. Inclusion of the seeker, the doubter, the lukewarm
believer and the agnostic. Inclusion even of the explicitly non-Christian:
the Manhattan headquarters of the National Council of Churches, originally conceived as a meeting place for the "scattered sheep" of Christianity,
eventually became an inter*faith* center instead—"a richly diverse community of many faiths," the head of the NCC boasted at its semicentennial,
"Protestant, Orthodox, Catholic, Jewish, Muslim, and more . . . a perfect
microcosm of God's world."[13]

Christianity's problem, the leaders of the Mainline decided somewhere in the tumult of the 1960s, was that it turned too many people off; it was too rigid in its moral teachings, too exclusive in its truth claims, too remote from the problems of this world, this life, this moment on the earth. Only a more inclusive faith, they assumed, could succeed where orthodoxy was failing and sustain a version of Christianity amid the various forces undercutting the older dogmas and traditions.

For many people in the Mainline churches, these shifts generated a tremendous amount of excitement. Some of this was the enthusiasm that always accompanies novelty and revolution, joined to the natural human desire to sprinkle this or that appealing innovation with the baptismal water of one's childhood faith. Some of it was inspired by the latest trends in scriptural scholarship: just as early-twentieth-century modernism drew on the German Higher Criticism of the Bible, the accommodationists of the 1960s and '70s often claimed to find the Christianity they were looking for in the lost scriptures and secret gospels that archaeologists and textual critics had recently uncovered.

More importantly, though, there was a widespread and understandable belief that a more inclusive Christianity would ultimately achieve a deeper fidelity to the message of Christ. By tearing down the walls of dogma and tradition that separated the various Protestant communions, accommodationists saw themselves as acting in obedience to Jesus' precrucifixion prayer that his followers would "all be one, just as you, Father, are in me and I in you." By destigmatizing homosexuality and cohabitation and divorce, they understood themselves to be following the example of the Jesus who had dined with prostitutes and publicans and ignored the purity codes of Temple Judaism. By opening their hearts and minds to the wisdom of non-Christian traditions, they meant to imitate the Jesus who had conversed freely with Samaritans and Romans. Through all these efforts and more, they hoped to correct institutional Christianity's persistent tendency toward many of the very faults that Jesus had so furiously condemned—a dead ritualism, an unforgiving legalism, and a Pharisaical focus on forms over realities.

This last theme recurred throughout the era of accommodation. In December 1973, a group of would-be female priests presented themselves to the progressive Episcopal Bishop of New York, Paul Moore, during an ordination ceremony. They knew that his sympathies were with their cause, but also that his position would be at risk if he followed Bishop Pike's example and laid his hands upon them. When he refused to do so, they read the following statement aloud in the cathedral, explicitly linking their opponents to the Jewish establishment of Jesus' day:

> We are . . . aware of the uncomfortable position in which our pastor and friend, Bishop Paul Moore, finds himself. There are precedents in church history for this uncomfortable position. James himself was no stranger to the snarls of Pharisaic law. Paul, we cannot spare you the discomfort of your position.[14]

Three years later, this discomfort was removed when the Episcopal House of Bishops voted to admit women to holy orders. One of the newly ordained, Peggy Boysmer, received a heroine's welcome when she returned from the convention to her hometown of Little Rock: "A huge crowd of people were there with iced champagne," she recalled later, "and a huge sign, ALLELUIA, that went all across the front of the terminal. . . . Everybody in the airplane was going, 'Wow, look at that! What's happening?' And we said: 'The Episcopal Church just voted to ordain women.'"[15]

Not everyone was quite so enthusiastic about accommodation's progress. The gradual disappearance of denominational differences had dispiriting consequences for those believers who were invested in *being* distinctively Methodist or Presbyterian or Lutheran. In the first decade of the twenty-first century, after the accommodationist project had been in motion for decades, the aging Lutheran theologian Carl Braaten penned a letter to Mark Hanson, presiding bishop of the Evangelical Lutheran Church of America, bemoaning where this trend had left his own tradition:

> The kind of Lutheranism that I learned—from Nygren, Aulen, Bring, Pinomaa, Schlink, P. Brunner, Bonhoeffer, Pannenberg, Piepkorn, Quanbeck, Preus, and Lindbeck, not to mention the pious missionary teachers from whom I learned the Bible, the Catechism, and the Christian faith—and taught in a Lutheran parish and seminary for many years is now marginalized to the point of near extinction. In looking for evidence that could convincingly contradict the charge that the ELCA

has become just another liberal Protestant denomination, it would seem reasonable to examine what is produced by its publishing house, theological schools, magazines, publications, church council resolutions, commission statements, task force recommendations, statements and actions by its bishops. The end result is an embarrassment. . . . I must tell you that I read all your episcopal letters that come across my desk. But I must also tell you that your stated convictions, punctuated by many pious sentiments, are not significantly distinguishable from those that come from the liberal Protestant leaders of other American denominations.[16]

But of course for the accommodationists this was exactly the point. Everyone had to subsume their theological particularities in an ecumenical and tolerant Protestantism, because an ecumenical and tolerant faith was what the times demanded. Only such a faith could hope to hold the allegiance of modern man, who was too sophisticated and cosmopolitan to accept archaic dogma, too invested in the affairs of this world to look expectantly to the life to come. Only such a faith could hope to satisfy the God who presided over Harvey Cox's secular city, and who had no time for either abstruse theology or "fasting and cultic adoration," because He "wants man to be interested not in Him but in his fellow man."[17]

This logic wasn't confined to the Protestant Mainline. In the wake of the Second Vatican Council, it swiftly prevailed in much of American Catholicism as well. In the previous chapter, we considered Vatican II as the marriage of orthodoxy and American liberalism, and as the fulfillment of the work of Sheen, Jacques Maritain, and John Courtney Murray. But there were also other forces at work in the council's sessions. Vatican II looked back to the achievements of the midcentury Christian renaissance, but it also partook of the accommodationist spirit of the 1960s, and its documents hinted at sympathy for the theological currents that would inspire Pike and Cox and their peers.

One peer in particular seemed to enjoy a distinctive influence over the Council's work. "Few wanted to be associated with him publicly," Richard John Neuhaus would note in a late-1980s assessment, but "the work of

Teilhard de Chardin was a powerful presence in background conversation surrounding Council deliberations." From De Chardin's oeuvre, Neuhaus pointed out, some of the Council's documents seemed to take the idea of a "unified, developmental, and evolutionary cosmos; new things are happening with ever-accelerating speed, and it is all going somewhere, though it is impossible to say quite where." In contrast to traditional Christian teaching, the Council sometimes appeared to locate God and the transcendent "not above us but ahead of us, the future toward which we are rapidly rushing . . . only rarely in the Council's hundred thousand words is the distinction between natural and supernatural even implied." Again and again, Neuhaus pointed out, the documents of Vatican II—and especially *Gaudium et Spes,* the Constitution on the Church in the Modern World—described "the Christian hope . . . in remarkably this-worldly terms," as though John F. Kennedy rather than John XXIII had been the inspiration for the Council.[18]

Alongside this secular, political turn, the Council also seemed to ease Catholicism toward a somewhat more democratic understanding of religious authority—one that insisted on the authority of bishops as well as the power of the Pope, the vocations of laymen as well as those of priests, and the Church as the "people of God" as well as the Church as a hierarchy of ecclesiastics. This "decentralization of decision-making" on certain matters (as the young Joseph Ratzinger would put it—favorably—in his notes on the Council)[19] represented an ambitious attempt to correct Catholicism's tendency to clericalism and papolatry, and it opened possibilities for ecumenical dialogue with Protestants that hadn't existed since the Reformation. At the same time, though, it blurred distinctions that had historically been crucial to Catholicism—between the Roman Church and other Christian churches, between priestly and lay vocations, between what constituted disagreement and what constituted dissent.

None of this amounted to a formal shift away from Catholic orthodoxy. However, a generation of Catholic leaders wasn't entirely mistaken in claiming that there was a "spirit of Vatican II" easing the Church toward ever greater accommodation with the modern world. Nor were they mistaken in seeing an opportunity, as the Council's decrees passed from theory into practice, to push the Church much further in this direction than the Council had been willing to go.

This push didn't come from the hierarchy, and it didn't instantly bubble upward from the pews. (Indeed, the reformers of the 1960s and '70s devoted a great deal of time to griping about the backwardness not only of Catholic bishops but of Catholic parishioners as well.) The accommodationist spirit was strongest, instead, in the intermediate institutions of Catholicism: the religious orders and the universities, the seminaries and diocesan bureaucracies and liturgical committees. It was there that the greatest efforts were expended to keep Catholic Christianity relevant in a changing world. It was there that the transformation of the American Church was attempted—and, often, successfully achieved.

For the religious orders, nuns and monks and priestly fraternities, accommodation meant straightforward secularization. The Jesuits, for instance, moved their training centers from rural and suburban facilities (many of them designed for the larger seminary classes of an earlier era) to urban settings—in one case, spread across apartment buildings—in which Jesuits-to-be could experience Harvey Cox's secular city more directly. ("Experimentation wth different life-styles is indispensible for our Jesuit studies, if we are to prepare . . . for a contemporary ministry," wrote the editor of *Jesuit Theological Review*.[20]) Other orders adopted similar approaches, shedding habits and priestly collars for pantsuits and turtlenecks, and the rhythms of communal life for the hurly-burly of the world. The theory behind these innovations was captured by Brother Gabriel Moran, author of *The New Community* (1970). In the modern age, he suggested, "a distinction between people who live in community and those who do not is no longer meaningful. Everyone needs to live in a community, but no one should live in *one* community." (The distinction between religious and secular communities, he added, was particularly "obsolete.")[21]

Some orders had to fight for the right to put these ideas into practice. The Sisters of the Immaculate Heart of Mary engaged in a long public battle with Los Angeles's aging Cardinal McIntyre, which earned them a *Newsweek* cover and finally ended with their transformation into a religious community only tangentially connected to the institutional Church. There were similar high-profile conflicts in New York, Milwaukee, and other cities. But mostly the changes met with only limited opposition from the hierarchy and received the enthusiastic endorsement of immediate authorities. (When the Vatican tried to reinforce the older rule that every order needed some distinctive habit, the president of America's Leadership Conference of Women Religious responded that if "a woman is not to be trusted with a decision as to how, when, and where she is to wear a particular form of dress, she can hardly be entrusted with the really serious matters of conscience which absorption in today's apostolate requires."[22])

For the universities, accommodation meant a swift march away from their former deference to the Vatican's authority. In 1967, a group of twenty-six educators, led by Notre Dame president Fr. Theodore Hesburgh, signed the "Land O'Lakes" statement, which declared that "the Catholic university must have a true autonomy and academic freedom in the face of authority of whatever kind, lay or clerical, external to the academic community itself." While Catholicism must be "perceptibly present and effectively operative" within a Catholic university, the authors allowed, such schools' primary obligation must be to carry out "a continual examination of all aspects and all activities of the Church and . . . objectively evaluate them," rather than simply seeking to transmit the Catholic tradition intact to their students.[23] Not surprisingly, given the temper of the times, this "objective evaluation" tended to favor the accommodationist position in nearly every controversy.

In the seminaries, accommodation meant that this "reinterpretation of the transcendent" was taught as the coming thing and assumed to be the only dogma that a priest needed to carry with him into the ministry. And it meant extreme laxness, as well, on sexual discipline—particularly on issues related to homosexuality. The priesthood had always enjoyed an obvious attraction for gay Catholics, but the atmosphere of the sexual revolution encouraged a wink-and-a-nod approach to homosexual relationships—a tendency reinforced by the collapse in clerical vocations in the 1970s. With more and more straight men leaving the priesthood to marry, seminaries became known for their gay subcultures (Notre Dame Seminary in New Orleans was dubbed "Notre Flame," Baltimore's Mount Saint Mary's Seminary was known as the "Pink Palace," and so on), which in turn tended to turn off heterosexual candidates for holy orders. The idea that the priesthood was dominated by a kind of "lavender mafia" became a staple of traditionalist critiques of the Second Vatican Council and its aftermath. But the issue was also raised by accommodationist Catholics, who cited it as another reason to allow priests to marry. Notre Dame's Richard P. McBrien, a leading liberal theologian, told PBS that men who may "have a genuine vocation for priesthood go into a seminary and feel very alienated by the gay culture. I don't say this in any homophobic sense. It's just the reality."[24]

In Catholic liturgy, accommodation meant experimentation and upheaval. Prior to the Second Vatican Council, many liturgical reformers insisted that their cause was less about "modernization" than about reengaging with the wisdom of the Christian past. The shift from Latin to the vernacular, in particular, was framed as a means of more effectively immersing the congregation in ancient prayers and Scripture readings. Once the baroque excesses of the Tridentine Mass were stripped away, the theory went, there would be a revival of medieval and patristic piety, and with it would come a deeper encounter with the core of Christian faith. But by the mid-1960s, with the battle over the vernacular won and Latin banished to the fringes of Catholic life, reformers soured on the idea of looking backward for inspiration. That way lay ossification; only by leaning forward, into secularization and modernity, could the Catholic liturgy hope to engage the rising generation.

So liturgical experts like Rembert Weakland, then Abbot Primate of the Benedictines and later Archbishop of Milwaukee, dismissed the quest for "a feeling of infinity or eternity or the world beyond" as "a new archaism," insisting that modern worship needed instead to promote "the communal sensitivity that I am one with my brother next to me and that our song is our common twentieth-century situation."[25] In the conferences and journals where liturgists debated the future of the Mass, there were similar attacks on the "magic superstitious character" of the older Christian way of worship and demands for rituals that spoke more directly to Harvey Cox's technopolitan man. The liturgy needed to be relevant: there were calls to model services on presidential inaugurations, on antiwar protests, on bullfights and skating parties and film festivals. It needed to be hip: a successful mass would generate "the fun of a successful cocktail party," an enthusiastic Benedictine declared in 1966.[26] And it needed, of course, to be political: By 1968, the Liturgical Conference's annual Liturgical Week was being held on the theme of "Revolution," and the following year, Garry Wills noted drily, "the best-known speakers were some Black Panthers, Dr. Benjamin Spock, Wayne Morse (former Senator from Oregon), and the SCLC's Andrew Young."[27]

The wilder experiments—a "Christmas mass" that opened with a Yuletide-themed reading from Henry Miller's *Tropic of Capricorn*; a "divorce mass" that reversed the wedding service, with a soloist playing "It's Too Late, Baby"—rarely penetrated all the way to the parish level. There, renewal mainly meant a kind of unpredictable Protestantization, in which the rhythms of Latin gave way to a theoretically more accessible vernacular, and local leaders often took it upon themselves to strip away the material culture of preconciliar Catholicism—incense and icons, prayer cards and rosaries—in the name of renewal and modernization. But since nobody could quite agree on exactly what form this renewal ought to take, every pastor became a liturgical reformer unto himself, and the mass came to vary markedly from church to church and service to service. As Philip Lawler put it, in *The Faithful Departed*, his history of Catholicism's Bostonian decline:

> Up until the 1960s, when a new pastor was appointed to a Catholic parish, he might introduce a different style of preaching and a different method of conducting parish meetings, but the essentials of parish life—the Sunday mass, the teaching in the parochial school, the advice given in confessions, the requirements for Baptism, and the programs for marriage preparation—would be unchanged. By the 1970s, the introduction of a new pastor could bring a complete transformation in all these areas. . . . Different parishes developed their own distinctive personalities, emphasizing more "high" or "low" liturgy . . . traditional hymns or rock music. "Parish shopping" became commonplace, with devoted families driving past several Catholic churches every Sunday to reach the one where they felt most comfortable.[28]

If there was confusion in the pews, some of it probably flowed from the fact that while everything was changing, the reality of the change wasn't always publicly acknowledged. As in Mainline Protestantism, the Catholic accommodationists didn't always engage in a frontal assault on orthodox Christian belief. Catholicism had its outspoken radicals, including dissident priests James Kavanagh and Matthew Fox, feminist theologians Rosemary Ruether and Mary Daly, and others who seemed to want to burn the Church to the ground and then stage a successful cocktail party amid the ashes. But the turn away from traditional theology happened just as often through gradual transformations rather than revolutionary shifts, and manifested itself in subtle substitutions rather than open critiques. From seminaries to parishes, theology departments to church bureaucracies, accommodationism became ubiquitous without always being made explicit.

Still, it *was* ubiquitous. By 1984, Thomas Sheehan could survey the state of Catholic intellectual life and announce, in a *New York Review of Books* essay entitled "The Revolution in the Church," that "the dismantling of traditional Roman Catholic theology, by Catholics themselves, is by now a *fait accompli*. . . . In Roman Catholic seminaries, for example, it is now common teaching that Jesus of Nazareth did not assert any of the divine or messianic claims the Gospels attribute to him and that he died without believing he was Christ or the Son of God, not to mention the founder of a new religion."[29] Of all the dogmas of Catholic faith, Sheehan's essay suggested, only a "purified" (that is, largely symbolic) belief in the resurrection endured among the present generation of scholars and theologians; the rest had been quietly dismissed, through what was rather credulously described as a "scientific" process of biblical criticism, as encrustrations created by popular piety and Vatican self-aggrandizement.

As went the university, so went catechism class. A typical religious education textbook from the post–Vatican II period wouldn't deny basic Christian teachings like the Resurrection and the Atonement, or specifically Catholic concepts like purgatory and the intercession of the saints—but it would often ignore or minimize them, substituting the language of self-actualization and personal growth, until it became hard to distinguish a religious education manual from a typical handbook for building self-esteem. (An eighth-grade Catholic religion text from the late 1970s, entitled *Seek*, began as follows: *I sit at my desk, head cupped in my hands, staring into space. What do I see? I see me. I see myself as doing my own thing, the master of my destiny. . . .*[30])

Another case study: In 1970, the Catholic Theological Society released a text called *Human Sexuality: New Directions in American Catholic Thought*, which aimed to provide a guide for Catholics (and seminarians, in particular) interested in the most au courant Catholic thinking on matters of sexuality. Its findings were very au courant indeed. "At this time the behavioral sciences have not identified any sexual expression that can be empirically demonstrated to be of itself, in a culture-free way, detrimental to the full human existence," the authors assured their readers. The best theological thinking, they suggested, indicated that Catholic teachings on sexuality were best understood as rough guidelines, to be applied creatively and charitably to the necessarily complicated realities of human sexual desire. Eventually, the institutional Church would grow up and recognize this reality. "Until that day arrives, enlightened and well-integrated individuals might well free themselves of conflicts by simply reflecting on the relativity of their society's sexual ethic and proceed discreetly with their sexual project."[31] (These recommendations were issued at the height of the priestly sexual abuse epidemic, though it would be decades before anyone realized that fact.)

Sometimes the accommodationists proceeded less "discreetly" and admitted publicly to the scope of their reforming efforts. Thus Robert Hoyt, editor of the liberal *National Catholic Reporter*, would write in 1970:

> It is simply true that the religion texts of today are vastly different from those of yesteryear, that progressive views dominate most Catholic religious and theological training, that in consequence the Catholicism of tomorrow will be something new on earth—and that all of this has been accomplished in something less than democratic fashion, by ways and means that eluded standard ecclesiastical safeguards. . . . Liberal theologians dominate the public prints, the catechetical training seminars, the publishing houses, the professional associations, much of Catholic bureaucracy; they praise each other's books, award each other contracts, jobs, awards and perquisites. There wasn't anything sinister in all this; it wasn't planned, it just happened.[32]

Hoyt's reference to "standard ecclesiastical safeguards" was a reminder that this progressive dominance remained de facto rather than de jure. Whereas in Mainline Protestantism the bishops and the bureaucracies were more or less on the same accommodationist page (at least in those denominations that had bishops at all), in Catholicism the hierarchy often strove to restrain and revise the work of its subordinates when they seemed to take accommodationism too far. In Rome, certainly, there were no moves to revise Catholic teaching on any of the suddenly contested subjects, from sexual ethics to biblical interpretation, where accommodationists were convinced that only further, swifter change could keep Catholicism relevant. Indeed, Pope Paul VI's only explicit response to the accommodationist moment was the encyclical *Humanae Vitae,* which shocked the world by reaffirming what most people considered the most extreme Catholic teaching on human sexuality, the ban on artificial birth control.

But even a de facto triumph was enough to transform the life of the American Catholic Church. Catholicism might not officially approve of divorce, but the diocesan bureaucracies granted annulments in the hundreds of thousands. (By 1980, 90 percent of the world's annulments took place in the United States.) The Pope might not have blessed contraception, but you would be hard-pressed to find a theologian interested in defending that position, or a pastor willing to expound upon it. Priestly celibacy was still mandatory, but you wouldn't know that from observing social life in many seminaries. In a swift march, the accommodationists had come to dominate faculties, bureaucracies, and liturgical committees. They picked the hymns, wrote the religious-education textbooks, issued the press releases, and most important, perhaps, educated the next generation of Catholics. "In ten years people will believe only what they experience; anything else they will not believe," a Jesuit told readers of *U.S. Catholic* in 1968.[33] He was describing the new philosophy of religious education, but his words expressed the assumptions of the entire accommodationist project.

As the 1970s rolled onward, the changes that had transformed seminaries and Catholic universities seemed poised to transform the hierarchy as well. Indeed, this transformation was already happening, under the supervision of the Belgian Archbishop Jean Jadot, Apostolic Delegate to the United States from 1973 to 1980 and a progressive's progressive. His advice on episcopal appointments created a generation of like-minded bishops, nicknamed the "Jadot boys" by admirers and critics alike, who began to steer the U.S. bishops' conference away from theological line-drawing and toward the political activism that accommodationists saw as the proper mission of the modern church.

The same sense of inevitability was captured by Sheehan's *New York Review* essay, which suggested that the Church had engaged in "a quiet but momentous shift of emphasis" from dogma to politics, abstract belief to worldly action. Aware that its doctrines were fundamentally untenable,

Catholicism would henceforward become an institution geared toward personal improvement and social reform:

> The Church's gradual shift of concern away from theoretical questions and toward social, political, and moral issues . . . is, I believe, one of the major consequences of the undoing of traditional theology. Perhaps the current regime in Rome will slap a few more wrists in a futile effort to stop the liberal movements launched by the Second Vatican Council. But it is more likely that, as the Church approaches the beginning of its third millennium, things will continue to follow the trajectory of the last two decades: an entrenchment of conservative forces in their shrinking pockets of power; the vigorous advancement of liberal exegesis and theology in scholarly circles; and the equally vigorous pursuit of the social gospel where issues of politics and morality are concerned.[34]

There was only one difficulty. By the time Sheehan was writing these words, it was increasingly clear that the brave new world of the accommodationists had fewer and fewer people in it.

In fact, this had been clear almost from the beginning; it just took some time for the anecdotal evidence to harden into data. Before the collapse in churchgoing began, accommodation was represented as the only way to forestall Christianity's decline. Once that decline began in earnest, accommodation was hailed as the obvious way to stanch the bleeding and revive the patient's health. But the collapse was often swiftest in the churches and orders and dioceses where accommodationism had triumphed most completely. The more a Protestant body pressed forward down the path blazed by Harvey Cox and James Pike, the more its seminaries emptied and its congregations shrank. The more a given Catholic order reframed its way of life along more secular lines, the fewer new members it attracted.

This pattern wasn't universal. Sometimes the initial burst of excitement created something lasting and significant. Sometimes accommodationist congregations flourished; sometimes their leaders won converts from less-adaptable churches. Nor were all forms of accommodation identical, since a church or pastor or theologian might go only a certain distance with the reformers and then stop. It was possible to ordain women without rewriting the Nicene Creed, to embrace left-wing political activism while remaining doctrinally conservative, to reread Scripture through a feminist lens without demanding that the Bible be rewritten in gender-neutral language, to dissent from the Catholic Church's position on homosexuality without abandoning its position on abortion, and so forth.

But in a great many cases, one form of accommodation tended to lead inexorably to another (and another, and another), and after many waves of accommodationist enthusiasm the tide of faith went rushing out. No sooner had a liberalizing faction won a great victory over what it perceived as the forces of reaction, it often seemed, than the next phase in its life was decay and dissolution. The Sisters of the Immaculate Heart of Mary barely survived doffing their habits and breaking with the Archdiocese of Los Angeles. The Liturgical Conference didn't survive its renovation of the liturgy. (The chaotic, politicized "Liturgy Week" of 1969 was the last one ever held.) In Mainline Protestantism, churches merged triumphantly—another victory for ecumenism!—and then went on shrinking. The National Council of Churches headquarters on Riverside Drive, erected as a monument to Mainline power, soon became a half-empty monument to the Mainline's swift decline.

The Catholic accommodationists, at least, had someone to blame for their failures to keep people in the pews: their Church's hidebound hierarchy, with its blinkered refusal to let Catholicism's reformation go as far as they believed it needed to go. As the crisis in religious vocations mounted, they suggested that all the good priests were being driven out—by the slow pace of reform, by the resistance of bishops, by the intransigence of the Pope. As attendance at mass plummeted, they blamed Paul VI's birth control encyclical for alienating believers. The Pope "did to his reign what Lyndon Johnson did [to his presidency] with the Vietnam war," Garry Wills wrote,[35] and the Catholic sociologist Andrew Greeley argued that 70 percent of the drop in Catholic churchgoing was explained by lay revulsion against *Humanae Vitae*. And they wrapped the two arguments together, arguing that priests as well as laymen were leaving because they could not abide the sexual repression preached from Rome: "Even a priest who feels called to celibacy," Wills argued, "must be reluctant to identify his own way of life with church authorities' views on sex; must feel his own witness cheapened and distorted by the imbalance and ignorance displayed at the very top rungs of the hierarchy; and must fear that he will end up resembling the obsessive old men who have risked all credibility, order and good will within the church to uphold their animus against human intercourse."[36]

But there were two problems with this theory. The first was that Rome was distant, whereas the accommodationists were increasingly the ones running American Catholicism in the day-to-day. The more power they obtained within the American Church, the harder it became to claim that their ideas weren't being put into practice, or that they were being held back by the Vatican's medieval instincts. Yes, the formal strictures remained in place, but by the late 1970s you could pass from a Catholic grade school to a Catholic university to a Catholic seminary and finally a Catholic diocesan bureaucracy—all while faithfully attending Sunday mass—without hearing much of anything that deviated from the accommodationist line. The accommodationists had built their own church-within-a-church in many cases. Yet they had reaped none of the victories (floods of new members, a generation of activist priests and nuns) that their theories predicted.

Instead, the opposite was happening. What growth there was in American Catholicism was appearing in precisely those orders and dioceses that had refused to yield to the spirit of the age. By the 1990s, ordination rates in prominent "traditional" dioceses were more than four times higher than ordination rates in "progressive" dioceses, and the same held true in religious orders. A 1993 survey found that nuns who rated traditional modes of living (either communal life or close proximity to a motherhouse) as "extremely important" had five times as many novices as those who had more thoroughly secularized. Similarly, orders that had officially "changed their spirituality" since Vatican II had only half as many novices as those that hadn't.[37]

All of this could be explained away, perhaps, as the last spasms of a dead tradition, just before rigor mortis finally set in. The deeper problem for Catholic accommodationists was the struggling Protestant Mainline, which was providing a perfect test case for their theories of how religion ought to be renewed. There were no Vaticans bestriding the Mainline, no reactionary popes, no onerous celibacy requirements or bans on contraception. Women were being ordained, politics was given pride of place, sexual strictures were being downplayed, and traditional theology was being dismissed. The Episcopal Church, in particular, was fast becoming the Catholicism that reformers so earnestly desired—democratic, egalitarian, politicized, and sexually liberated, but with the outward forms of liturgy and hierarchy still intact, and the Eucharist still offered every Sunday. Yet Episcopalianism's slide, like that of its sister churches in the Mainline, was more precipitous than anything the Catholic Church experienced. Liberal Protestants were selling exactly what the accommodationists claimed the public desperately wanted from religion, and nobody was buying it.

So what was going wrong? In part, the reformers had overestimated the potential for sustaining religious practices by marrying them to secular causes. "He who marries the spirit of the age is soon left a widower," the Anglican Ralph Inge remarked, and so it was with the accommodationists. Their theories about what the God of the secular city desired had been forged in the brief and optimistic window that gave America the New Frontier, the Great Society, and the triumph of the Civil Rights Act—and when the optimism of the early 1960s collapsed into polarization and pessimism, this faith in progressive politics suddenly looked less prophetic and more partisan. There were still causes to embrace and crusades to champion—environmentalism and the Equal Rights Amendment, the campaign for nuclear disarmament and the movement for gay rights. But fewer and fewer people believed that these causes added up to some kind of Chardin-esque "Omega Point" rather than representing the usual political give-and-take. The more firmly accommodationist Christianity defined itself by taking sides in this give-and-take, the more it came to be seen as just another faction, just another interest group, with nothing particularly transcendent to offer anyone.

And transcendence, it turned out, was still what people wanted from religion. Here, too, the early accommodationists went astray. They mistakenly associated sexual liberation, theological relativism, and growing prosperity with straightforward secularization, and assumed that what post-1960s America wanted from religion was something rational, nonmystical, antisupernatural. But it turned out that while a single twentysomething might have no time for Christianity's sexual taboos, and a prosperous suburbanite might not want to ponder its critique of wealth and acquisition, they were both still interested—more interested than ever, perhaps—in a religion that promised encounters with the mysterious and numinous, one that promised to make the universe responsive to their prayers and rituals and spiritual gestures. Thus the irony that James Hitchcock noted in the early 1970s:

> Progressive clergy shed their vestments on the sacristy floor, threw their incense in the trash, and sold their golden vessels to antique dealers, only to discover that somehow the puritanical young men and women who had marched with them on the picket line had got hold of all these discards and more besides—tarot cards, Ouija boards, Tibetan prayer wheels, and temple gongs. The Latin had been eliminated from the Mass so that the young could comprehend it, but they preferred instead to chant in Sanskrit. Campus chaplains had ceased trying to sell prayer and were selling social action instead, but their former constituents were hunting up Hindu gurus and undertaking systematic regimens of meditation and fasting.[38]

The accommodationists could try to adapt, and often did. Just five years after the publication of *The Secular City,* the flexible Harvey Cox produced *Feast of Fools,* a "theological essay on festivity and fantasy" that celebrated "neomysticism" and urged readers to move beyond the austerity of death-of-God theology to something more playful, ritualistic, and spiritually rich.[39] (Cox's tract was timed to coincide with Woodstock, and it was cited as an inspiration for Broadway's *Godspell.*) Other accommodationists followed his example, looking for ways to reunite the sacred and the secular that would fulfill, rather than betray, the broader liberal Christian project.

Ways weren't hard to find, as it turned out. Churches committed to interfaith dialogue could integrate Buddhist meditation techniques or Hindu oblations into traditional Christian prayer and liturgy. Churches committed to feminist theology could invite their members to dabble in goddess worship, borrowing rituals from Wicca and other modern pseudo-paganisms. (The Episcopal Cathedral of St. John the Divine, once James Pike's home parish, became a center of such efforts, displaying a female "Christa" in lieu of crucifixes and hosting "Solstice services" at Christmastime, complete with ritual howling from the audience.) Churches devoted to the politics of environmentalism could embrace the kind of eco-spirituality that inspired Matthew Fox, the Catholic dissident turned Episcopal priest, to create what he called the Techno-Cosmic Mass, a mix of Christian liturgy, paeans to Gaia, and rave-style music that briefly excited liberal Protestant enthusiasm in the 1990s.

But genuine mysticism ultimately depends on genuine belief, and it often seemed that all of these efforts were just so much "play"—in Cox's telling phrase—with little connection to actual conviction. It was this conviction deficit, above all, that explains the failure of accommodationist churches to keep believers in the pews. Their pastors and theologians had recognized, correctly, that the old foundations of Christianity were being undercut by the social revolutions of their era. Yet they had failed to identify any new foundation that could inspire real piety, real allegiance, real belief.

Here their emulation of Jesus proved fatally incomplete. In their quest to be inclusive and tolerant and up-to-date, the accommodationists imitated his scandalously comprehensive love, while ignoring his scandalously comprehensive judgments. They used his friendship with prostitutes as an excuse to ignore his explicit condemnations of fornication and divorce. They turned his disdain for the religious authorities of his day and his fondness for tax collectors and Roman soldiers into a thin excuse for privileging the secular realm over the sacred. While recognizing his willingness to dine with outcasts and converse with nonbelievers, they deemphasized the crucial fact that he had done so in order to heal them and convert them—ridding the leper of his sickness, telling the Samaritans that soon they would *worship in spirit and truth,* urging the woman taken in adultery to *go, and from now on sin no more.*

Given the climate of the 1960s and '70s, these choices were understandable. But the more the accommodationists emptied Christianity of anything that might offend the sensibilities of a changing country, the more they lost any sense that what they were engaged in really mattered, or was really, truly *true*. In the process, they burned their candle at both ends, losing their more dogmatic parishioners to more fervent congregations and their doubters to the lure of sleeping in on Sundays.

Any institution that calls human beings to devotion and self-sacrifice needs to justify that call. The accommodationist churches had no such institutional justification—or at least, they had no justification that explained why Americans should be involved with their church *in particular*. Political activism wasn't enough: Why would you need to wash down your left-wing convictions with a draft of Communion wine, when you could take the activism straight and do something else with your weekends? Nor was their belated rediscovery of the numinous element in religion enough to stem the tide of defections: Why would you get your mysticism from somebody who was just play-acting, when you could get it instead from someone who really believed it—whether that someone was a swami or a Pentecostalist?

Even a triumphalist like Sheehan, hailing the accommodationist influence within Catholicism, could see the inherent contradiction in the project. The accommodationist theologians, he suggested, have "pushed Catholic theology to the limits of its own language," and raised the question of what makes liberal Catholicism "essentially different from non-Catholic religions and non-religious humanism."[40] And if the answer is "nothing," then why should anyone be Catholic at all?

The ecumenical efforts that increasingly consumed progressive leaders only added to these difficulties by contributing to the impression that liberal Christianity had no distinctive theological convictions, no principles that couldn't be compromised in the name of conciliation and unity. Already in 1973, the author of *Why Conservative Churches Are Growing* saw this problem taking shape. Whatever the advantages of ecumenism, Dean Kelley wrote, the ecumenical personality is ill suited to institutional leadership and incapable of creating the sense of shared purpose that successful religious institutions require:

> The balanced, mature person with an awareness of the wide range of values and interests open to modern man is not going to sacrifice all (or much) for any single set of values or any sole area of fulfillment. Rather he will try to find an equilibrium among them. . . . He will recognize the validity of conflicting views, the complexity of countervailing forces. . . . He will be a balancer, a temporizer, an equivocator, and organizations composed of his ilk will be correspondingly ambivalent and immobilized.[41]

It wasn't just that such leaders failed to attract parishioners to their churches or inspire would-be clergymen to join their seminaries. It was that *they themselves* often drifted away from the organizations that they headed, looking for something less constraining and restrictive, less dogmatic and demanding. In Catholicism and Protestantism alike, many of the most vocal and active reformers of the 1960s had left organized Christianity entirely by the 1970s and '80s. The explanation (especially among departing Catholic priests) was almost always that change wasn't coming as fast as they had hoped, and sometimes this seemed plausible. But more often these defectors seemed to be in the position of a general who has fought and won a series of battles, only to decide that the territory wasn't worth ruling after all.

This pattern was captured by the liberal Wills, in a sympathetic *Esquire* profile of the Jesuits' fateful leap from rural seminaries to the secular city of New York: "Standing under the El," he wrote, "talking in the rain . . . I asked about the two priests who, more than any others, performed the herculean labor of lifting the whole dead weight out of its slumber and flinging it into this sewery living city—but Sponga and Cardena are, neither of them, Jesuits any more."[42] And the pattern was analyzed, perceptively, by the more conservative Hitchcock:

> The chief dishonesty of the reformers was their studious concealment, even from themselves, of the problem of belief, until almost the end of [the 1960s]. Theological language, liturgical forms, vigorous social action, the uses of authority . . . all were seen and discussed as problems. But never faith. . . . In retrospect it is possible to see the preoccupation of the progressives with changes of various kinds as a way of avoiding the ultimate question of their own faith.

When "the problem of faith finally comes to the surface," Hitchcock concluded, in what could serve as an epitaph for the era of accommodation, "many progressives found little fundamental belief on which they could rest."[43]

Many, but not all. The accommodationist churches lost members faster than any other Christian bodies, but they didn't simply disappear. Eventually the declines leveled off, and in their much-reduced state they gained something like stability. There *was* a market niche for accommodationism, it turned out, even if it was vastly smaller than Harvey Cox had imagined, and there was a swath of America who found its appeals comforting and even inspiring. To the extent that religion endured among the nation's intelligentsia, it was usually in the form that Cox and James Pike had championed, which meant that accommodationist Christians retained a cultural clout disproportionate to their numbers. To the extent that more orthodox Christian attempts to resist cultural change ended in defeat or disillusionment, too, accommodationism was always there as an appealing fallback option. It was forever failing—but forever being rediscovered. And it remains potent enough today to justify returning to the heirs of Cox and Pike later in this book, and considering their most enduring contemporary project—the quest for a "real Jesus" who would supposedly vindicate their theological premises.

For now, though, it's fitting to conclude with Pike's own bizarre exit from the American scene. Always ahead of the curve, he was one of the first accommodationists to abandon secularism for a kind of postmodern mysticism, which in his case took the form of a sudden interest, following his son's suicide, in parapsychology and spiritualism. He reported polter-geist activities and psychokinetic episodes, befriended various mediums who promised to put him in touch with his departed child, and eventually participated in a filmed séance, broadcast on Canadian television, with a professional psychic named Arthur Ford. These experiences inspired a 1968 book, *The Other Side,* coauthored with his soon-to-be third wife, in which Pike reported on his otherworldly encounters with not only his son's spirit but with other shades as well—including the recently deceased Paul Tillich, whose spirit supposedly thanked Pike for dedicating a book to him.

That same year—and again anticipating many of his fellow accommo-dationists—the Californian bishop gave up on institutional Christianity entirely. Amid the round of controversy that followed his second divorce and third marriage, he turned in his bishop's miter and left the Episcopal Church. (There would have been even more controversy, no doubt, had there been greater publicity surrounding the 1967 suicide of his mistress and Pike's apparent role in erasing evidence of their affair before the police arrived.) Pike justified his departure with typical bravado, taking to the pages of *Look* to dismiss the organized Church as a "sick—even dying—institution."[44] And he swiftly proceeded to found a Center for Religious

Transition to minister to other souls who might follow him out of organized religion into what he insisted would be a deeper spiritual quest.

It was this spirit of pilgrimage that carried the ex-bishop and his new wife, Diane, to Israel in August 1969. Pike had become fascinated by the Dead Sea Scrolls, first-century texts uncovered near the ancient settlement of Qumran in the late 1940s and early 1950s, because they seemed to open a window into alternative Christianities—Gnostic Christianities, in particular—that dated back to the earliest decades after Christ's death. (Once again, he was blazing the trail that others would follow.) Hoping to experience the atmosphere around Qumran directly, as a first-century mystic might have—"to drink it all in, as Jim said so many times," his wife would later put it[45]—the couple rented a Ford Cortina, stopped to buy two Cokes near the Church of the Nativity, and drove out into the desert.

The third Mrs. Pike reappeared a day later, dazed and bloody and on foot. They had taken several wrong turns, their car had stalled in the wilderness, and her husband had sent her back to find help. A frantic search ensued, complete with various interventions from the psychics Pike had cultivated. By the time the searchers found him, in a dry riverbed seventy miles from Jerusalem, the era's most celebrated heretic had perished of exposure.

FOUR

RESISTANCE

In the spring of 1994, a once-unimaginable rapprochement was consummated in the pages of the religious journal *First Things*.

For hundreds of years, the gulf between Evangelical Protestants and the Catholic Church had been the widest in Christendom. On the major questions dividing Christians, from theology to liturgy to church governance, Catholics and Evangelicals seemed to occupy opposite poles. To Rome, Evangelicals were the most dangerous and pernicious sort of schismatics; in the Evangelical world, the Vatican was Babylon and most Catholics as hell-bound as any nonbeliever. For most of American history, Evangelicals were the most zealous guardians of the United States's Protestant character and the most vigorous critics of Catholicism's growing influence. American Catholics, for their part, often behaved as if Evangelical Christianity didn't merit notice at all. Even during the years of convergence that followed World War II, the Church's idea of ecumenical dialogue involved debating the role of the papacy with Anglicans and Lutherans, not sitting down with Baptists to argue over whether there should be a bishop of Rome at all.

But now here were twenty of America's leading Catholic intellectuals, theologians, and bishops signing their name to a public statement with the heretofore-unlikely title "Evangelicals and Catholics Together." And if the roster of Catholic signatories (headed by Richard John Neuhaus, once a founder of Clergy Concerned About Vietnam, and now editor of *First*

Things and a Lutheran convert to the Church) was impressive, the Evangelical names were even bigger. They were led by Charles Colson, Richard Nixon's Watergate–era hatchet man and then, following his jailhouse conversion, the born-again founder of America's most famous prison ministry. He was joined by Bill Bright, the head of Campus Crusade for Christ; Pat Robertson, then probably America's most famous religious broadcaster; Richard Land, president of the Southern Baptist Convention's public policy arm; Richard Mouw, president of Fuller Theological Seminary; J. I. Packer, the leading Evangelical theologian of the 1970s and '80s; Wheaton College's Mark Noll, a prominent Evangelical scholar who was then emerging as the finest historian, period, of American religion; and many more.

The document they were signing, subtitled "The Christian Mission in the Third Millennium," made no pretense of resolving the knottier theological questions dividing the two parties. But it emphasized their common ground and common faith. "Evangelicals and Catholics are brothers and sisters in Christ," the statement declared, and "however imperfect our communion with one another . . . we recognize that there is but one church of Christ." Its theological passages placed a particular emphasis on the bedrock of a "mere orthodoxy"—defined, in particular, by "the canon of the Scriptures" and "the orthodox response to the great Christological and Trinitarian controversies of the early centuries." And it condemned "the practice of recruiting people from another community for purposes of denominational or institutional aggrandizement"—a remarkable step toward a kind of truce between once-irreconcilable opponents.[1]

The unity that the document promoted, though, was ultimately unity against a common threat. "In our so-called developed societies," the document declared, "a widespread secularization increasingly descends into a moral, intellectual, and spiritual nihilism." To combat this enemy, the cosignatories pledged themselves to spiritual witness, but also to political engagement. Denouncing the conceit that the separation of church and state requires "the separation of religion from public life," they argued that America's constitutional order is "essentially a moral experiment," premised from the beginning on the assumption that "only a virtuous people can be free and just, and that virtue is secured by religion." And they proceeded to delineate a common political and cultural agenda, which would seek "the legal protection of the unborn" and defend the connection between "marriage, parenthood, and family" while resisting euthanasia, eugenics, pornography, and other perceived threats to the American moral fabric.

Indeed, it was their joint political engagement on questions like abortion, the document suggested, that had made an Evangelical-Catholic rapprochement possible in the first place. By contending together for Christian principles in the public square, they had rediscovered how much theology they had in common.

This was not, to put it mildly, the kind of ecumenical cooperation that the leading lights of 1960s religion had expected. The Evangelicals and Catholics signing their names to the *First Things* statement were theological conservatives rather than accommodationist liberals. They hadn't bridged the gap between their traditions by abandoning the spiky paradoxes of Christian dogma for an inclusive message of secular improvement. Instead, they had achieved an unlooked-for unity in their common *resistance* to many of the same trends that an earlier generation of ecumenists had eagerly embraced. In the process, they had undercut a host of 1960s-era assumptions about the quest for Christian unity—that fervor and orthodoxy were stumbling blocks to dialogue and cooperation, that only theological modernists could be genuinely ecumenical, and that accommodation and accommodation alone could keep Christianity viable in the modern world.

Instead, as the crisis of the 1960s and 1970s gave way to the age of Ronald Reagan and John Paul II, it became increasingly clear that what vitality remained in American Christendom was being sustained by the unexpected alliance between Evangelicals and Catholics. Amid their faith's increasing weakness, Christians from both traditions found in their rediscovered brotherhood an unexpected source of strength—a partial healing of the Reformation's wounds, which united long-divided brethren in the cause of culture war.

This unity was made possible by intellectual pilgrimages on both sides. For Catholics it involved the gradually dawning conviction, often among figures who had considered themselves liberals, that the age of accommodation had gone too far and that their Church was in danger of being reformed into something unrecognizable.

At first, this spirit of resistance was confined to yesterday's voices—conservative bishops clinging to their power and prerogatives, Latin Mass diehards and reactionary mystics, and a grumbling older generation in the pews. They were joined, here and there, by some of the aging Catholic luminaries of midcentury, whose synthesis of orthodoxy and liberalism had been overtaken by events. Washington's Cardinal Patrick O'Boyle, a great desegregator in the 1950s, made the only significant attempt to discipline priests who publicly dissented from Paul VI's birth control encyclical and found that even the Vatican wasn't prepared to push too hard against the tide. Two years before his death, Jacques Maritain disappointed many of his admirers when he used his final book, *The Peasant of the Garonne* (1966), to issue a querulous critique of the accommodationists' "Christian tomfoolery."[2] Even the Jesuit theologian Karl Rahner, an icon for Catholic progressives, eventually griped waspishly about the way so many accommodationists "behave as if they're especially wise and holy, and suffer the most from the Church's defects and failings, to which they haven't contributed in any way."[3]

To the 1960s generation, all of this could be dismissed—for a time—as old people's doubts and incomprehensions. Reviewing Maritain's polemic in the pages of *Commentary,* a young ex-seminarian named Michael Novak gave the great Thomist a condescending send-off. Calling the book "a testament to the immense progress made by Catholics in these last ten years," he concluded regretfully that "Maritain, who was once a leader, has fallen back. . . . And what good are giants if we do not mount their shoulders and see what they did not?"[4] What Novak glimpsed, predictably, was what Harvey Cox had claimed to see—a more secular Christianity, focused on the natural rather than the supernatural, on the needs of this world rather than the life to come.

But as the utopianism of the middle 1960s faded into disillusionment, younger believers also began to lose their optimism about where accommodationism was taking the faith. While some, as we have seen, gave up on institutional Christianity altogether, an influential minority of Catholic intellectuals gradually turned back toward a more traditional piety, distinguishing the reforms of the Second Vatican Council (which, as loyal Catholics, they were obliged to support) from the reinventions that had followed in its wake.

No one executed this turn more sharply than Novak himself. He was the most progressive of progressive Catholics in the 1960s, when his books had titles like *The Open Church* (1964) and *A Theology for Radical Politics* (1969). But by the Reagan era he had become one of the Church's leading neoconservatives, championing papal authority with the same cheerful optimism that he had once employed in the service of the counterculture. In his *Commentary* review, he had emphasized the intellectually stifling climate of a pre–Vatican II boyhood. With time, though, he would redis-cover some of the virtues of that world, and so would other Catholics of his generation.

A crucial hinge moment was the Supreme Court's announcement in 1972 of a nearly unlimited right to an abortion. Many progressive-minded Catholics had come to terms with some sort of abortion license: as early as 1964, a group of liberal theologians had huddled with Robert F. Kennedy in Hyannisport, mapping out the "personally opposed, but . . ." style of argument that would be rehearsed by a generation of Catholic Democrats. But even some accommodationists were surprised by the scope of *Roe v. Wade* (1973), and the decisive turn it seemed to represent away from the solidarity-oriented and Catholic-friendly Democratic politics of the New Deal era to a liberal politics of autonomy, privacy, and choice. The divide between an ethic of autonomy and traditional Catholic teachings could be bridged on some questions—with the expansion of annulment-granting, for instance, as a kind of Catholic answer to no-fault divorce. But on abor-tion the chasm was too wide to cross and the clash of values too explicit to finesse.

Tellingly, whereas many Catholics felt comfortable simply taking sides against the Vatican in the debate over contraception, dissent on abortion was more anguished, and the nascent pro-life movement was supported by a number of figures who had been vocal in their criticisms of *Humanae Vitae*. But the antiabortion cause found few allies in the Mainline Protes-tant churches that post–Vatican II Catholics had expected to supply their natural peers and conversation partners. For many Catholic intellectuals and activists, this was the second shock associated with the abortion de-bate—not just how far the Supreme Court were willing to take the sexual revolution but also how many Mainline churches were willing to go along for the ride. As late as the early 1960s, the Second Vatican Council's denunciation of the practice as an "abominable" offense still found an echo, if an uncertain one, in the National Council of Churches' promise that "Protestant Christians are agreed" in opposing most abortions.[5] But by the time *Roe v. Wade* was decided, Mainline Protestantism had essentially switched sides on the issue.

So the abortion debate undercut some of the basic premises of Catholic accommodationism. It suggested, *pace* Harvey Cox, that progressive politics wasn't necessarily a God-given conduit for translating Christian ethics into social and political action. After *Roe* and its consequences, it became harder to imagine that the Catholic Church would advance, through comfortable and high-minded ecumenical dialogue, toward ever greater unity with accommodationist Episcopalians and Methodists and Lutherans. Instead the decision cracked opened the door to an era of dialogue with Evangelicals—a genuinely startling development.

It also opened the door to a broader reconsideration of the social revolution of the 1960s, and particularly the assumption that the Church needed to take instruction from the secular world on thorny questions like divorce, premarital sex, and priestly celibacy. Even the case against contraception began to receive a more respectful hearing from at least some members of the Vatican II generation. Pope Paul VI's theological arguments had not necessarily grown more persuasive with time, but as divorce rates and out-of-wedlock births rose along with the abortion rate, his prediction that a contraceptive culture could encourage "marital infidelity and a general lowering of moral standards" looked considerably more prophetic. So did his political fears: "Public authorities . . . may even impose [contraceptive] use on everyone," *Humanae Vitae* had predicted, just a few short years before China's one-child policy and India's mass sterilization campaign put a brutal face on the population control movement.[6]

It was against the backdrop of these reconsiderations that John Paul II was elected Pope in 1978. As George Weigel has pointed out, the former Karol Wojtyla was exactly the kind of pontiff accommodationists had hoped for: "A modern European intellectual, widely traveled, multilingual, happy and confident, with extensive pastoral experience and terrific public presence . . . the first truly modern pope, in the sense of a pope with a thoroughly modern intellectual formation."[7] Moreover, the Polish cardinal had been one of the young reformers at the Second Vatican Council, pressing the Council fathers in a liberal direction on issues of religious freedom and papal authority—as had the man who swiftly became his aide-de-camp, the German prelate Joseph Ratzinger.

However, in the intervening decade Wojtyla had come to the same view of Christianity's situation as had Novak and other American Catholic neo-conservatives. Instead of ratifying accommodationism's advance through Catholic institutions, the new pope was determined to resist and reverse it. Instead of embracing the "spirit" of Vatican II, he set out to rescue the Council from its more radical interpreters. Instead of assuming, like many of his contemporaries, that traditional Christian belief was essentially incompatible with twentieth-century life, he sought to present a face for Catholicism that was intensely modern and strongly orthodox all at once.

The result was a pontificate dedicated to a robust and unexpected reassertion of Catholic dogma. Oceans of ink were spilled on the supposed "paradoxes" of John Paul—his deftness at using the tools provided by technological progress (air travel, television) to advance a conservative religious message; the fact that he was both an intellectual's intellectual and a mystic with an abiding belief in the supernatural; his affinity for young people and his insistence on an absolute sexual idealism; and so on. But all these were paradoxes only if you accepted the mid-1960s premise that Christianity needed to be completely renovated in order to provide an attractive home for modern man. As Weigel put it, the new pope "did not propose to surrender to modernity. He proposed to convert it."[8]

In part, this project required a confrontation with the accommodationist church-within-the-Church. To this end, Jean Jadot was recalled from the United States, and the appointments to the American episcopacy took a more traditional cast. Paul VI's policy of allowing almost any priest who asked to be liberated from his vows was reversed. On his first visit to America, the new pope told a gathering of priests that "the priesthood is forever—*Tu es sacerdos in aeternum*—we do not return the gift once given."[9] (This policy could be taken too far; in several scandalous cases, it led to a long delay in laicizing abusive priests.) Then came the high-profile battles with accommodationist figures and factions within Catholicism, in which Ratzinger, as the head of the Congregation for the Doctrine of the Faith, earned his reputation as "God's rottweiler."

But the most significant work that John Paul and Ratzinger did was intellectual rather than institutional. Through sermons and speeches, encyclicals and letters, they set out to reestablish what Catholicism stood for—essentially to teach the faith anew, a conservative notion that seemed almost radical after the free-for-all of the 1960s and '70s.

Some of this teaching was genuinely innovative. The Pope's lectures on the "theology of the body," for instance, represented an ambitious attempt to link the arguments for chastity and continence to an essentially pro-sex vision, rather than a crabbed list of dos and (mostly) don'ts. Some of it expanded on the Second Vatican Council's work: the championing of democracy, religious freedom and human rights; the celebration of modern science's potential (the Pope was at pains to suggest that the theory of evolution was compatible with Catholic doctrine); the pursuit of dialogue with other world religions; the slow work of improving Catholic relations with the Jews.

Yet much of what John Paul wrote and said, with Ratzinger's influence and help, was simply a reaffirmation that the Church still believed in itself, and that the definition of Catholicism wasn't nearly as up for grabs as it had seemed. The most controversial Vatican documents of his pontificate were controversial not because they said something new but because they reiterated something old—and in reiterating it, implied that the Church would not continue moving in the direction that so many accommodationists had confidently mapped out for it.

In effect, John Paul made his pontificate a rallying point for resistance to the redefinition of Christianity. And rally many Catholics did. This resistance movement wasn't large enough to reconquer theology departments or diocesan bureacracies, or to arrest the liberal drift of influential religious orders. But thinkers like Novak and Weigel, Harvard's Mary Ann Glendon and Princeton's Robert George, and the Jesuit theologian Avery Dulles (another Vatican II liberal turned *First Things* contributor) were high-powered enough to seize the initiative from tenured accommodationists. Schools like the University of Dallas and the Franciscan University at Steubenville and orthodox start-ups like Christendom College and Thomas Aquinas lacked the prestige and history of the colleges that had taken the "Land O'Lakes" path, but their graduates were far more likely to actually stay Catholic than the graduates of a Georgetown or even a Notre Dame. New orders and lay movements like Opus Dei, Communion and Liberation, and the Legionaries of Christ weren't as famous as the Jesuits (though that would later change for Opus Dei, thanks to a novelist named Dan Brown), but they had growth and vitality and vocations, whereas many of the more established orders were gradually aging into museums of 1960s Catholicism. The newer orders were populated by what their admirers described as the "John Paul II generation" of priests—a more orthodox group (albeit also a much smaller one) than the class of priests that had filled seminaries and then abandoned rectories in the 1960s and '70s.

At the same time, under John Paul, the Church became a magnet for Mainline Protestants alienated by the changes at work within their declining denominations. Neuhaus, the anti–Vietnam War Lutheran who became the Catholic editor of *First Things,* was the most prominent of these intellectual converts. The archetypal accommodationist-turned-resister, he seemed poised in the late 1960s (as his friend Robert George would later put it) "to become the nation's next great liberal public intellectual."[10] But then came the abortion issue, and Neuhaus "threw it all away"—breaking ranks with his fellow Mainline Protestants, choosing Christian tradition over accommodation and putting himself on the path toward resistance, neoconservatism, and, eventually, Rome.

Others followed Neuhaus across the Tiber—Episcopalians, Presbyterians, Lutherans, Methodists. But you didn't have to become a Catholic outright to admire John Paul and Ratzinger, or to draw inspiration from papal encyclicals and the *Catechism of the Catholic Church.* The Church of John Paul II won some of its most influential converts from the Mainline Protestant intelligentsia. But the Polish pope's resistance movement found its most important friends and allies in America's Evangelical churches.

While Catholics reconsidered accommodationism, Evangelicals were continuing the process of reengagement that Billy Graham's generation had begun. Politically, they were passing from obscurity to influence. Intellectually, there was an opening of the Evangelical mind, as churches that had retreated into a narrow and ahistorical understanding of Christian orthodoxy gradually rediscovered their half-forgotten patrimony. Culturally and economically, Evangelicals were moving from the margins of American life toward something like the center, and their successes seemed to provide a case study in how Christian churches could thrive while resisting the trends of the 1960s and '70s.

The political turn attracted the most attention. In the Vietnam era, as we have seen, Evangelicals tilted right-wing and Republican, but they weren't yet *mobilized*. There was no Moral Majority or Christian Coalition; pundits didn't talk about "values voters" or the "Evangelical vote." There were no Evangelical activists with the profile of a James Dobson or a Pat Robertson and few Evangelical politicians with a brand like Mike Huckabee or Sarah Palin.

That changed across the 1970s, as more and more Evangelicals rallied to socially conservative causes: the fights against public-school sex education, against pornography, against gay-rights initiatives (led, famously, by pop singer Anita Bryant), and eventually against the Equal Rights Amendment. Still, the decade also saw the emergence of a stronger Evangelical left: *Sojourners* magazine, the home of the writer-activist Jim Wallis, was founded in 1971, and younger Evangelicals turned John Howard Yoder's *The Politics of Jesus* (1972) and Ronald Sider's *Rich Christians in an Age of Hunger* (1977) into countercultural bestsellers. In national politics, the loose alliance between Evangelicals and the GOP foundered amid the corruption of Watergate, and in what was dubbed "the year of the evangelical" by *Newsweek,* a religious groundswell helped elect a pious Southern Baptist named Jimmy Carter as president of the United States.

Ultimately, though, the same issues that inspired many Catholics to turn against accommodationism—specifically abortion, and more broadly the social costs of the sexual revolution—drew many Evangelicals who had voted for Carter back toward the political right. Here a crucial figure was Francis Schaeffer, a Pennsylvania native who moved to Switzerland with his wife in the 1950s to found a Christian community called L'Abri. Schaeffer's theology was grimly sectarian ("neo-orthodoxy is not Christianity,"[11] he insisted amid the Christian renaissance of the late 1940s), but his persona—worlds away from the Dixie-accented dourness of a stereotypical fundamentalist preacher—made a bridge between pre-1960s Evangelicals and the younger generation. As a PBS special put it: "With his long hair, goatee, knickers and knee socks, he appeared the embodiment of the counterculture, a man equally at ease quoting the songs of Bob Dylan or passages from Scripture."[12]

More than any figure after Carl Henry and Billy Graham, it was Schaeffer who pushed Evangelicals toward greater engagement with the secular culture. (God's mandate to care for creation, he argued, included a "cultural commission" to influence human society as a whole, rather than simply withdrawing into the purity of separatism.) It was Schaeffer who prodded his fellow believers toward dialogue with Catholics, by arguing for what he termed "co-belligerency" in political struggles. And it was Schaeffer who pushed the abortion issue to the center of Evangelical social thought. In 1977, in the wake of *Roe v. Wade,* Schaeffer teamed with C. Everett Koop, the future Reagan surgeon general, to produce an antiabortion documentary series entitled *Whatever Happened to the Human Race?,* which he tirelessly promoted in American churches. In the early 1970s, channeling their centuries-old suspicion of papist aggrandizement, some Evangelicals had regarded abortion as a largely "Catholic" issue. But by the time Schaeffer died, in 1984, the fate of the unborn had become perhaps *the* animating issue driving Evangelical political mobilization.

This mobilization had mixed results. It brought Evangelicals into the halls of power for the first time in generations, but it swiftly exposed them to the compromises of partisanship as well. From the Reagan era onward, Evangelical voters became the Republican Party's loyal foot soldiers, delivering votes even when the politicians weren't delivering much for them in return. In a polarized country, this tight association with a single political party probably turned off many people who might have been attracted to Evangelical religion on its own terms. So did the fact that the early leaders of the religious right often kept one foot in a fundamentalist past, which led them to read Cold War brinksmanship and Middle Eastern adventures through the lens of the *Scofield Study Bible* and the book of Revelation. For many Reagan-era Americans, a Pat Robertson or a Tim LaHaye was the off-putting face of the Evangelical revival—unless it was the hucksters of the prosperity gospel, the Jim Bakkers and Jimmy Swaggarts and their fellow grotesques, who burst onto the scene around the same time.

But Evangelical political engagement also had positive consequences. While the bigotry and bluster of Robertson and Jerry Falwell earned the headlines, many Evangelical leaders gradually moved beyond the binaries of fundamentalism toward a more sophisticated approach to politics. The pro-life movement failed to overturn *Roe v. Wade,* but its mix of legal activism, public protest, and moral suasion succeeded in creating a stigma around abortion that even pro-choice politicians needed to reckon with.

At the same time, many Evangelicals began fashioning a kind of socially conservative social-justice agenda, focused on charity work and public-private partnerships rather than on the sweeping government programs of the Great Society era. Young Evangelicals went abroad on missions and returned as champions of foreign aid and Third World debt relief. Even as they remained reliable Republicans, Evangelical politicians often emerged as critics of the American prison system, or as foes of human trafficking, or as champions of efforts to fight AIDS in Africa.

Behind the broadening of Evangelical concern lay a rediscovery of the nineteenth century's great Evangelical reformers, from the English antislavery crusader William Wilberforce (who became an icon for many antiabortion Christians) to William Jennings Bryan. This rediscovery, in turn, was part of a broader intellectual renewal within Evangelical Protestant circles, which simultaneously reconnected believers to their own past and opened their eyes to the broader world of Christian orthodoxy, Catholic and Protestant alike.

There was no surer sign of this renewal than the growing willingness to reexamine fundamentalism's approach to the interpretation of the Bible. At Fuller Theological Seminary, ground zero for the neo-evangelical movement in the 1940s and '50s, the first generation of scholars and students had pledged themselves to the fundamentalist view that the inspiration of the Bible made it as exact a guide to geology and biology as it was to the history of salvation. But by the 1960s, much of the faculty and a majority of the student body had shifted toward what was termed "limited inerrancy"—the view that *what God intends to convey* in Scripture is without error, but that this inerrancy might not apply to every historical, scientific, or geographic detail. The following decade, two Fuller professors, Jack Rogers and Donald McKim, produced *The Authority and Interpretation of the Bible: A Historical Approach* (1979), which mounted a sustained case that the rigid fundamentalist understanding of inerrancy was a seventeenth-century innovation rather than an essential aspect of Christian orthodoxy—and, more important, that it had been rejected by the very figures (Calvin, Augustine) whose theology Evangelical Christians generally regarded as authoritative.

These arguments met with a great deal of opposition, beginning with the so-called Battle for the Bible—a 1975 controversy in which Harold

Lindsell, one of Fuller's original founders, lambasted both the seminary and its scholars for betraying "the fundamentals of the faith." The counter-attack reached its intellectual culmination with the International Council on Biblical Inerrancy, in which a group of Evangelical luminaries produced a ringing defense of the strict inerrantist position.

But even the inerrantists were willing to offer qualifiers. Consider how one of the members of the Council—James Innell Packer, an English theo-logian whose influence over American Evangelicalism proved more signifi-cant, perhaps, than that of any figure apart from C. S. Lewis—addressed the vexed question of evolution and the book of Genesis:

> I believe in the inerrancy of Scripture . . . but exegetically I cannot see that anything Scripture says, in the first chapters of Genesis or elsewhere, bears on the biological theory of evolution one way or an-other. . . . Scripture was given to reveal God, not to address scientific issues in scientific terms, and . . . as it does not use the language of modern science, so it does not require scientific knowledge about the internal processes of God's creation for the understanding of its essen-tial message about God and ourselves.[13]

These sensible words pointed to the way that many Evangelical thinkers ultimately resolved the Battle for the Bible—not by officially breaking with the concept of "inerrancy" but by reinterpreting its implications, and by allowing that an inerrant Bible might express its truths through figurative and allegorical language as well as through strictly factual narratives. In this fashion fundamentalism was not so much repudiated as transcended, and a more plausible approach to Scripture gradually came to predominate in many Evangelical circles.

The process of reengagement proceeded in fits and starts, of course. What the Evangelical historian Mark Noll called the "disaster of funda-mentalism" was still an anchor pulling American Evangelicals downward and backward.[14] But even as he was diagnosing the problem, Noll embod-ied at least part of the solution. He belonged to a growing coterie of Evan-gelical scholars who could compete as equals with the best and brightest in the wider academic world. Institutions such as Calvin College and Whea-ton College, Billy Graham's alma mater and Noll's employer, were attracting a more impressive pool of students and faculty (and moving steadily up in the college rankings, no doubt to the delight of their trustees) without jettisoning their Evangelical identity. Baylor University, the flagship school of Southern Baptists, was gradually emerging as the first significant Evangelical research university. Colleges were springing up to cater to the growing ranks of high-SAT Evangelical homeschoolers, led by Virginia's Patrick Henry College (dubbed "God's Harvard" by journalist Hanna Rosin). And Evangelical initiatives were established at topflight universities—sometimes as institutions-within-institutions (like the University of Virginia's Institute for Advanced Studies, which became the home of the prolific Christian sociologist James Davison Hunter), and sometimes as more provisional efforts, with titles like Spiritual Vistas (at Dartmouth) or the Veritas Forum (at Harvard).

By the 1990s, one could make a strong case that Evangelicalism had displaced the Mainline as the most important force in American Protestantism. Evangelical churches and "parachurch" organizations had taken up the missionary activity that the Mainline had abandoned. Evangelical institutions were home to Protestant Christianity's most significant debates. Intellectuals who once would have spoken at Union Theological Seminary now came to address audiences at Wheaton or Calvin. A theological movement knew it had arrived when it received a favorable write-up in *Christianity Today*—or in its highbrow spin-off, *Books and Culture,* which aimed to be an Evangelical answer to the *New York Review of Books*—rather than when it was deemed worthy of notice by editors of the *Christian Century.* Accommodationist theology still predominated in Ivy League divinity schools, but its pool of thinkers was increasingly isolated from the ocean of actual American belief.

All of this took place against a backdrop of Evangelical upward mobility. In earlier eras of American history, Protestants (and some Catholics) had changed churches as they climbed the socioeconomic ladder. A poor Baptist or Pentecostalist might rise to become a middle-class Methodist, and his successful sons would end up as well-to-do Episcopalians. But the crisis of the Mainline and the growing confidence of Evangelicalism put an end to this pattern. By 1991, when the *Washington Post* earned itself eternal right-wing opprobrium by describing the Christian Coalition's activists as "poor, uneducated, and easily led," Evangelicals were actually better off and better educated than the American average. A Southern religious tradition had migrated to the boomtowns of the Sun Belt and the Mountain West. A rural, agrarian faith had become suburban, exurban, and even occasionally urban. The well-appointed megachurch rather than the tent revival had become the stereotypical Evangelical temple. A tradition defined in the 1920s and 1930s by emotionalism, anti-intellectualism, and social marginalization—the "religion of the disinherited," in Richard Niebuhr's words—had become a faith for solid middle-class professionals.

And not only the middle class. Late in the Bush presidency, a Rice sociologist named D. Michael Lindsay penned *Faith in the Halls of Power: How Evangelicals Joined the American Elite* (2007). His title and thesis would have been implausible two generations earlier, but no longer. Ranging across politics, entertainment, business, and academia, Lindsay filled three hundred pages with case study after case study: the Evangelical officials scattered throughout the Bush administration, from the speechwriting office to the National Security Council; the Evangelical executives at companies ranging from Intel to Coca-Cola; the Evangelical movie tycoon responsible for adapting C. S. Lewis's Narnia cycle for the screen; the Evangelical Manhattanites holding events for young Christian professionals at the Algonquin Club—even the Evangelical collegian who was elected student body president at Dartmouth and proceeded to court controversy by citing "Jesus' message of redemption" in his speech to incoming freshmen.

That bold Ivy Leaguer wasn't alone. By the early 2000s, there were enough Evangelical students in the upper echelons of the American meritocracy to prompt a long trend story in the *New York Times,* which used the born-again presence at Brown University, of all places, as a window onto the broader landscape of Evangelical advancement. Even the most liberal of the Ivies, the reporters noted, was now home to roughly four hundred Evangelical undergraduates—part of a "beachhead" that had inspired campus Bible studies, Evangelical a capella groups, and a growing pan-Ivy alumni network that aimed to "reclaim the Ivy League for Christ."

Evangelicals were still a small minority in Brown's student body. But they had won at least one telling victory: their numbers made them a larger presence than "active mainline Protestants, the campus chaplain says."[15]

*　　*　　*

Nothing, though, was more indicative of Evangelicals' changing position and perspective than their rapidly improving relationship with Roman Catholicism. The Catholic-Evangelical rapprochement was at once intellectual and populist, elite-driven and grassroots. It was made possible by the "high" ecumenism of the Second Vatican Council and the "low" ecumenism of Billy Graham's crusades. It was furthered by the official dialogues between theologians and by the local Bible studies and prayer meetings that increasingly brought together believers from both branches of Christendom. It was visible in the intellectual "co-belligerency" of a statement like "Evangelicals and Catholics Together," and the spectacle of the annual March for Life in Washington, when Baptists and Pentecostalists stood shoulder to shoulder with nuns and priests and Knights of Columbus.

By easing into the vacuum left by the Mainline's decline, Evangelicals were in a sense reclaiming territory that they had forfeited relatively recently, in the fundamentalist-modernist wars of the 1920s. But by pursuing conversations and even alliances with Catholics, they were entering terrain that had been left largely uncharted since the Council of Trent.

For the most part, they liked what they found. This was particularly true in politics, where aspects of Catholic thought provided an intellectual architecture for what Evangelicals, historically suspicious of centralized power, already intuitively believed about the welfare state—namely, that a "preferential option for the poor" (in the language of the Church) should coexist with the principle of "subsidiarity," which held that activism should take place on the most local level possible. Catholicism's emphasis on a natural law that was accessible (in theory, at least) to nonbelievers supplied Evangelicals with a nonsectarian language for the escalating public controversies over abortion and euthanasia and, later, gay marriage. And because nobody could be more lawyerly than a good Roman Catholic, the world of Catholic legal scholarship increasingly supplied both the framework that many Evangelicals employed in their critiques of the Supreme Court's rulings and the men (from Antonin Scalia to Samuel Alito) whose appointment to the highest court they assiduously sought.

Particular American Catholic intellectuals, too, became heroes and inspirations in the Evangelical world. Of these, Neuhaus was the most influential. In his landmark book, *The Naked Public Square* (1984), and then for two decades in the pages of *First Things,* the Lutheran-turned-Catholic offered a theory of religion's role in American life (essentially an updated version of John Courtney Murray's midcentury argument) that was more sophisticated and persuasive than the fundamentalist insistence that the United States had been founded as a "Christian nation." At the same time, Neuhaus's experience marching alongside Martin Luther King lent credibility to his frequent portrayal of the pro-life cause as the continuation of both the antislavery and civil rights movements—a portrayal that Evangelicals eagerly embraced.

No Catholic, though, was more admired by Evangelicals than John Paul II. He was the most ecumenical of popes, his tireless proselytization made him a model of evangelistic virtues, and his moral arguments on issues like abortion and euthanasia were hailed even by Christians who doubted his authority. It was with a touch of hyperbole that the Evangelical writer Ian Hunter suggested that "the very first place every serious Protestant that I know turns today for guidance on Christian doctrine is the Catechism of the Catholic Church; failing that, the encyclicals of Pope John Paul II."[16] But there was more truth in his claim than any previous generation could have imagined.

Less high-profile intellectual borrowing happened on the Catholic side of the rapprochement. Still, the new generation of Evangelical scholars found readers and patrons in unlikely places, a reality that was illustrated in 2003, when the Evangelical editors of the InterVarsity Press's Ancient Christian Commentary Series were warmly received in Rome, with a papal audience held to celebrate their series. An even more instructive case occurred three years later, when Mark Noll himself left Wheaton College, after twenty-seven years of teaching, to accept a prominent post at Notre Dame, confirming the Catholic university's burgeoning reputation as a center for Evangelical scholarship.

But Evangelicalism's deepest influence on Catholicism was in the practice of Christian faith, where the zeal of Evangelicals could put even the most intellectually confident Catholic to shame. The desire for a personal encounter with the God they worshipped, the emphasis on individual conversion and salvation, the willingness to tithe and proselytize and go on missions and even sing in church—in all of this and more, Evangelicalism at its best offered a rebuke not only to accommodationist Catholicism's diffidence about the basic truth of the Gospel message, but to some of conservative Catholicism's characteristic faults (clericalism, legalism, ritual as a substitute for faith) as well.

In this sense, the most significant fruits of the Evangelical-Catholic encounter weren't found in academies or seminaries or in the pages of religious journals—or in the halls of Congress, for that matter. They were found in the church halls and basements where a Catholic charismatic movement was flowering, marrying Pentecostalist enthusiasm to the Church's own mystical tradition; in the mission fields where Catholics and Protestants shared resources and made common cause; and in Catholic youth ministries that borrowed Evangelical materials and hosted Evangelical speakers, and vice versa. They were found anywhere that Evangelicals and Catholics prayed and worked together, as brothers and sisters at a common task.

So Evangelicals rose, and Catholics reconsidered, and by the late 1990s their unexpected convergence was being spun by optimists in both camps into a kind of broader comeback narrative for Christianity as a whole. Yes, these optimists acknowledged, their common faith had suffered losses during the 1960s and '70s. But liberal theology and secularism alike had failed to satisfy the heart of modern man, and the rising generation, coming of age amid the moral and spiritual anarchy that their parents had unleashed, would eventually turn back to the Christianity the baby boomers had abandoned.

In this spirit, Catholics pointed to the crowds of teens and twentysomethings who thronged to the Pope's World Youth Days, while Evangelicals looked at their post-1960s gains and talked hopefully about a Fourth Great Awakening. Books were written with titles like *"The New Faithful," "The Twilight of Atheism,"* and *"The End of Secularism,"* which touted the younger generation's receptivity to orthodox religion and the weakness of the accommodationist and secular alternatives. Global developments were invoked to disprove secularization theory: conservative Christians pointed out that the developing world seemed to be growing more religious, not less, defying the prognostications of an earlier generation. Just as the accommodationists of the 1970s and early '80s had read the signs of the times and confidently predicted their theology's inevitable victory, by the turn of the millennium it was the resisters' turn to claim that theirs would soon be the only Christianity left standing.

Whether this optimism was justified, though, depended on one's definition of success. In the 1970s and '80s, figures like Neuhaus and Schaeffer had feared that secularization would carry all before it—that religious arguments would be banished from the public square altogether, and that believers might be stigmatized and even persecuted. None of this happened. Instead, the influence of the Christian right kept religious issues and concerns front and center in national politics, the Supreme Court often took a less aggressively secularizing line on church-state issues, and the space for public religious expression arguably widened somewhat in the 1980s and 1990s. Meanwhile, the public rhetoric of American life remained intensely theological, with presidential God-talk as common under Bill Clinton and even Barack Obama as it was under George W. Bush.

But the fact that America wasn't rapidly secularizing didn't mean that it was returning to Christian orthodoxy. Like the accommodationists before them, the resistance project assumed that Christianity's chief peril was growing unbelief, when the greater peril was really the *rival* religious beliefs—pseudo-Christian and heretical—whose influence we will consider in more detail later in this book. And in the struggle to win the wider religious culture back to Christian orthodoxy, the resisters' optimism seemed less warranted.

An unexpected endurance and even vibrancy, yes—that much the Evangelical-Catholic alliance had achieved, especially in comparison with Christian churches where accommodationism held sway. But the growth and momentum and confidence of post–World War II Christianity was still a distant memory. The institutional power of the midcentury churches seemed gone beyond recovery, and the intellectual climate of that era seemed irrecoverable as well. The awakening that some believers claimed was happening around them was often more evident in their particular subcultures than in the culture as a whole. And, like accommodationism before it, the resistance project had a host of weaknesses—weaknesses that the first decade of the twenty-first century would ruthlessly expose.

For American Catholics, a millennium that John Paul II had hailed as a "new springtime" for Christianity began instead with a wave of revelations about priestly sex abuse. There had been intimations of this crisis in the 1980s, when several high-profile instances of priestly pedophilia had surfaced in the media. But nothing prepared Catholic America for the flood of 2003, which began in New England but ultimately left no diocese or community untouched, reaching even to the doors of the Vatican itself. Horror upon horror, cover-up upon cover-up, and sacrilege piled on sacrilege—it was like an anti-Catholic polemic from the nineteenth century, except that it was all too terribly true. No atheist or anticlericalist, no Voltaire or Ingersoll or Twain could have invented a story so perfectly calculated to discredit the message of the Gospel as the depredations of Thomas Geoghan and the legalistic indifference of Bernard Cardinal Law. No external enemy of the faith, no Attila or Barbarossa or Hitler, could have sown so much confusion and dismay among the faithful as Catholicism's own bishops managed to do.

The crisis did more than expose the crimes of specific priests and the failings of individual prelates. It laid bare the deeper challenges facing American Catholicism, which the charisma of John Paul and the optimism of his admirers had sometimes managed to gloss over. The fact that so many bishops had shuttled abusive priests from parish to parish instead of removing them from ministry was a horrific moral failing, but also an all-too-human response to an increasingly dire shortage of priests. The post-1960s plunge in vocations stopped during John Paul's pontificate. But there had been no significant upward momentum. Instead, the numbers had flatlined at a level far too low to sustain sacramental life in a church of fifty million. The new religious orders mentioned earlier in this chapter were the exception to this trend, but they were not exceptional enough. They drew hundreds of new priests, but Catholicism needed thousands.

Likewise, in Boston and other traditional centers of Catholic life, the drop in mass attendance and participation that followed the worst revelations only accelerated an existing decline. After an initial falloff in Catholic churchgoing after Vatican II, Hispanic immigration kept overall mass attendance reasonably high. But if you looked at "Anglos" alone, it was obvious that the slow bleed begun in the 1970s had continued apace throughout John Paul's pontificate. Among white Catholics, mass attendance dropped by 30 percent between his 1978 election and the millennium.[17] By the early 2000s, cradle Catholics were as likely to switch faiths, or lapse from churchgoing entirely, as Mainline Protestants.[18] "If these ex-Catholics were to form a single church," Peter Steinfels noted in *Commonweal,* "they would constitute the second largest church in the nation."[19]

These trends reflected the extent to which the robust Catholic exceptionalism of the pre–Vatican II Church had dissolved into an unexceptional Americanism. Pundits still talked about the "Catholic vote," but by the time of Clinton's presidency, no such bloc existed. The average Catholic voted like the average American, shifting from left to right with the country rather than marching to a different drummer. On "values" questions like divorce, abortion, and eventually gay marriage, polls showed no discernible differences between Catholics and non-Catholics.[20] Some neoconservative intellectuals might feel that *Humanae Vitae* had been vindicated, but just 20 percent of American Catholics agreed with the ban on artificial birth control,[21] and the Catholic birthrate had fallen into line with the American average. John Paul II's rapport with young people notwithstanding, a major survey of religious teenagers conducted across the 1990s and 2000s found that young Catholics scored distressingly low on basic metrics of belief, knowledge, and engagement.[22]

Culturally, too, the Catholic difference all but disappeared. There were still plenty of novelists and filmmakers and poets in the Roman fold, but it was harder and harder to discern the kind of particularly Catholic artistic sensibility that had once bound Flannery O'Connor and Thomas Merton, Walker Percy and Walter Miller, even Frank Capra and John Ford. (This sensibility had endured into the cinema of the 1970s, influencing filmmakers such as Martin Scorsese, Francis Ford Coppola, and Paul Schrader, but their tormented blend of Catholic guilt and countercultural transgression inspired no significant heirs.) Intellectually, the struggle between accommodation and resistance seemed to have taken a toll on Catholic witness. The great Catholic writers of midcentury had been ambassadors for Christian faith to the secular world, explaining the Church's ideas and illuminating its culture to readers who did not share the faith. Their successors were more likely to expend the greater part of their energy on intra-Catholic disputes over liturgy and doctrine and the legacy of Vatican II.

In this landscape, it was rare to hear a pundit or theologian (or even an architect or novelist or screenwriter) described as a Catholic without the appellation *liberal* or *conservative* attached. The same was true of magazines and newspapers, colleges and publishing houses. Instead of the Church against the world, it was *Commonweal* against *First Things,* the *National Catholic Reporter* against the *National Catholic Register,* liberal colleges "in the Jesuit tradition" against more traditionalist schools. Instead of Fulton Sheen witnessing to secular audiences, it was Neuhaus and Garry Wills locked in battle over the future direction of the Church. Instead of *The Bells of Saint Mary's* or *Going My Way,* it was the revisionist theology of *The Last Temptation of Christ* pitted against the pre–Vatican II theology of *The Passion of the Christ.*

These divisions defined the way Catholicism reckoned with the sex abuse crisis as well. Sensing an opportunity amid the horror, the Church's aging accommodationists roused themselves to another round of combat. Repression, hierarchy, and a blind adherence to tradition were responsible for the scandal, they insisted. It was the cruelty of celibacy, the warping influence of an all-male clerical culture, and (for gay priests) the torture of the closet that had led so many men to act out their darker impulses in so many terrible ways. A church that had explicitly adapted to the sexual revolution, as they had so often urged—ordaining women, permitting priests to marry, and blessing nonprocreative sex—would never have undergone this trauma.

The resisters, needless to say, had a different interpretation. Citing the John Jay Report, an exhaustive accounting of the scandal commissioned by the Catholic bishops in 2004, they noted that the rate of abuse had risen sharply in the 1960s and crested in the accommodationist-dominated 1970s, before falling in the years following John Paul II's election. They also pointed out that while a few horrific pedophiles earned the headlines, the lion's share of the abuse cases involved misconduct with teenage boys, not prepubescents.[23] Whereas the accommodationists blamed repression, in other words, the resisters blamed liberation: the chaos of the sexual revolution, the anything-goes climate of seminary life in the wake of Vatican II, the theological confusion that had produced justifications for any kind of "life-style choice."

Both sides had valid points to make. There was little evidence to indicate that celibate priests were more likely to be abusers than married men,[24] and the historical data did suggest some kind of link between the sexual revolution and the wave of sexual misbehavior. (The rate of reported clerical abuse rose and then declined in tandem with similar patterns of disorder in American society as a whole, from sexual assaults to teen pregnancies to STD transmission.) Resisters could also find plenty of instances where accommodation and abuse went hand in hand: Paul Shanley, for instance, the most egregious of the Bostonian abusers, had been a celebrity in some progressive Catholic circles in the 1970s—a "street priest" who publicly championed gay rights even as he secretly preyed on teenage acolytes.

But whether it was Bernard Law protecting pedophiles or Marcel Macial—the charismatic founder of the Legionaries of Christ and a personal friend of John Paul—being exposed as a secret bigamist who molested his order's seminarians, the champions of orthodoxy had plenty of evils to account for. Meanwhile, the cover-ups represented Catholic conservatism at its worst—hierarchical and high-handed, demanding obedience at the expense of justice, and putting the supposed good of the faith above the actual good of the faithful. As Leon Podles put it in *Sacrilege* (2007), his magisterial and sickening history of clerical sexual abuse, both "new errors" and "old errors" were at work in the Church's scandal—relativism and clericalism, permissiveness and authoritarianism, the worst impulses of liberalizers and traditionalists intertwining in an awful tangle of corruption.[25]

From the ordinary Catholic's perspective, and indeed the ordinary American's, the question of whether accommodationists or resisters were more to blame for the scandal mattered relatively little. Wherever the fault lay, it clearly lay *somewhere* in the Church—and that knowledge alone was enough to undercut even the most fervent Catholic's loyalty, to damn the Church in the eyes of many people who might otherwise have been sympathetic to its message, and to provide endless ammunition to its critics. The sex abuse scandals did not finish off American Catholicism, but they dealt a deadly blow to the Church's prestige in many quarters, undercut its potential witness to the questing and the unconverted, and weakened its already weakened influence over many Catholic hearts. And they ensured that the American Church experienced the first decade of the third Christian millennium not as an Easter or a Pentecost, but as a limping agony, a long and bitter Lent.

For Evangelicals, the presidency of George W. Bush had a similarly chastening effect. In a sense, the Bush era represented the high tide of the

Evangelical-Catholic alliance. In the person of Bush, America had an Evangelical president who was comfortable with the language of Catholic social teaching and who drew inspiration from figures as diverse as Billy Graham and John Paul II. In the president's "compassionate conservatism," with its emphasis on fighting poverty at home and AIDS abroad, the Republican Party had the beginnings of a public philosophy that felt more completely Christian than the apocalyptic partisanship of the Jerry Falwell era. In the trauma of 9/11 and its aftermath, the nation seemed to be experiencing exactly the kind of period of moral and religious renewal that many conservative Christians had spent decades pining for.

Instead, the Bush administration ultimately became a case study in the limits of winning elections as a means to achieving religious and cultural change. Many of the culture-war controversies of the early 2000s—the debate over embryo-destroying stem cell research, the arguments over abstinence eduction, the tragic case of Terri Schiavo—demonstrated the extent to which orthodox Christian views on matters of life and death had become a distinctly minority persuasion, easily dismissed as sectarian by the press and the wider public alike. Even more strikingly, the debate over gay wedlock was moving in the same direction. In the 1970s and '80s, many Americans who accepted no-fault divorce, premarital cohabitation, and even abortion-on-demand had drawn a line at gay rights and (especially) gay marriage. But by 2004, when the Bush White House rallied religious conservatives with a notional and soon-abandoned commitment to a constitutional amendment codifying the traditional definition of marriage, it was increasingly clear that what had looked like a stronghold was actually a weak point. Ultimately, the Christian sexual ethic asks *more* of people with same-sex attraction than it does of straights—a far greater self-denial, a more heroic chastity. And as gays left the closet behind and entered the mainstream of American life, they ceased to be convenient scapegoats for the moral revolution that heterosexual desire had wrought. Instead, they became just sons and daughters, friends and siblings whose aspirations seemed no more radical than the sexual freedoms that straight Americans had already embraced.

Having a conservative Evangelical in the White House, it turned out, didn't necessarily make it easier for conservative Christians to win converts or to gain ground in moral and cultural debates. Indeed, in certain ways it seemed to make it harder. The president's very public piety made it easy for his detractors to lay the blame for his administration's policy failures at the door of Evangelical Christianity itself, so that the more things soured for the Bush administration, the more they soured for Evangelicals as well. And the extent to which Bush's religious style ultimately polarized the country rather than uniting it hinted at deeper problems facing the Evangelical community—problems that limited their ability to fill the space that the Mainline had once occupied and that placed sharp constraints on their influence and growth.

Unlike the American Catholic Church, Evangelicalism didn't lack for internal vigor. It was "the strongest of the major Christian traditions in the United States today," Christian Smith concluded in his 1998 assessment, *American Evangelicalism: Embattled and Thriving.*[26] Evangelicals were more zealous, more biblically literate, and more engaged with their religious communities than either Catholics or Mainline Protestants. Their churches were more likely to retain their younger members and more likely to seek out and welcome converts from other Christian denominations. They exhibited "the highest degree of adherence to many of the traditionally orthodox Christian beliefs," Smith wrote,[27] and displayed the most optimism about the likelihood of a Christian revival in the United States. Many of the qualities that Catholicism had lost since the Second Vatican Council, Evangelicalism had either retained or gained—a sense of mission, purpose, and cohesion, an intense spirit of in-group loyalty joined to a desire to win the world. (Indeed, in the 1970s and '80s and then again after the sex abuse scandals, many undercatechized and disaffected Catholics ended up in Evangelical pews.[28])

At the same time, however, there seemed to be a demographic ceiling on Evangelicals' expansion and a limit to their message's appeal. Even before Bush assumed the presidency, the Evangelical share of the American population was beginning to level off or even fall. In 1970 on a typical Sunday, 12 out of every 100 American adults could be found in Evangelical churches. By the late 1980s, that number was up to around 15 out of every 100, but it hit a plateau thereafter and dipped throughout the Clinton era.[29] Among young people, in particular, Evangelicalism's appeal waxed among Generation X—the teens and twentysomethings who came of age in the Carter and Reagan years—but then waned as the Xers gave way to the Millennial Generation. A quarter of Americans under thirty identified as Evangelical in the middle 1980s, but by the election of Barack Obama in 2008, that number was below 20 percent and dropping.[30]

This was not for want of proselytization. Indeed, after noting that Evangelicals were more misunderstood, mistrusted, and disliked than members of other American religious traditions, Smith suggested that the way they sought converts was often part of the problem:

> Evangelicals . . . do not appear to be slackening off the task of evangelizing outsiders. For every one (self-identified) evangelical in America, between five and seven nonconservative-Protestants had been proselytized by an evangelical. But the evidence from there becomes somewhat less heartening for evangelicals. . . . According to those who say an evangelical had at some time tried to convert them to their faith, only between ten and twenty percent said that it was a positive experience. About one-half said it was a negative experience.[31]

Not surprisingly, given this hostile reaction, there seemed to be a kind of ceiling on evangelical cultural influence as well. "Although evangelicalism does sustain a thriving religious tradition for itself," Smith's analysis concluded, "it does not fare so well when it comes to achieving its goal of transforming the world for Christ."[32] Evangelicals had entered the halls of power, but they hadn't even begun to remake them in a Christian image. From the Ivy League to Hollywood, the Evangelicals' presence was accepted but not necessarily welcomed, and their influence rarely extended beyond the narrow footholds they had carved out for themselves.

In part, the problem seemed to be one of talent. Either Evangelicals still weren't sufficiently successful at nurturing intellectual and artistic gifts in their churches and communities, or else the most creative young believers tended to drift away from the fold. The roster of Evangelical theologians and Bible scholars was impressive, but the ranks of Evangelical novelists, filmmakers, poets, and public intellectuals were strikingly thin, especially compared to the Christian flowering of midcentury. There was no real Evangelical analogue to W. H. Auden or T. S. Eliot, no impressive Evangelical literary school to match the Catholic novelists of the 1940s and '50s, no Evangelical public intellectual who enjoyed the kind of respect from non-Christians that Reinhold Niebuhr and other golden-age figures had commanded. (You couldn't imagine a secular writer joking about founding "Atheists for J. I. Packer.") Evangelical apologetics leaned heavily on long-dead figures such as Lewis; Evangelical political thought depended on contemporary Catholics such as Neuhaus and Novak; Evangelical art and architecture were generally middlebrow, garish, and naive. The best attempts of Christian hipsters and Bono acolytes notwithstanding, Evangelical pop culture still felt ingenuous and tacky—the stuff of Kirk Cameron movies and Christian rock music, geared to an undemanding audience and easily dismissed by anyone outside the circle of the devout. Much of it was theologically embarrassing as well: the old mistakes of fundamentalism pervaded millennarian kitsch like the Left Behind novels, while a pseudo-Christian prosperity theology suffused the world of cable televangelism.

These cultural deficits reflected a failure of strategic vision as well as a talent deficit—an unwillingness or inability on the part of Evangelicals to build the kind of institutions necessary to a vibrant Christian culture. A certain kind of anti-institutionalism is inherent in Protestant theology, going back to Luther's break with Rome. But the neo-evangelical project may have pushed the tendency too far, strengthening Evangelical faith in the short term but weakening its churches in the longer run.

In an effort to escape the mad accretions and endless civil wars of fundamentalism, Billy Graham and others had preached a more stripped-down Gospel, emphasizing the core tenets of orthodoxy and downplaying the application of strict litmus tests in secondary matters. Figures like Carl Henry had downgraded older denominational differences in favor of "parachurch" umbrella groups (from Fuller and *Christianity Today* to the National Association of Evangelicals and Campus Crusade for Christ) that effectively straddled theological divides. Leaders such as Schaeffer had urged believers to unite around certain core moral truths and fight for them in the public square, choosing a common political activism over a private doctrinal purity.

Each of these choices led to cultural successes and theological breakthroughs. But as in the parable, in chasing out one set of devils, the neo-evangelical reformers allowed a different set to enter in their place. While Graham's stripped-down gospel weaned its audience away from sectarianism and separatism, his example—the charismatic, inclusive figure who didn't sweat every doctrinal detail—often left his followers vulnerable to the appeals of charlatans and opportunists. Likewise, the emphasis on para-church ministries increased cooperation across denominations, but once unleashed, the "para" mentality was difficult to contain, and among too many believers, it eventually threatened to supplant the idea of an institutional church entirely. "In the early postwar years," writes David F. Wells, one of the most perceptive critics of contemporary Evangelicalism, "evangelicals began to think of the whole of evangelical faith in para terms. . . . Past traditions of believing, distinctive church architecture, doctrinal language, and the formalities of traditional church life all seemed like baggage that needed to be shed as rapidly as possible."[33]

This turn boded ill for Evangelicalism's long-term future, because although the "para" groups were immensely successful at religious mobilization, they weren't as effective at sustaining commitment across a life span or across generations. They were institutions for an anti-institutional faith, you might say, which meant that they were organized around personalities and causes and rarely created the sense of comprehensive, intergenerational community that both the Mainline churches and Catholicism had traditionally offered. You couldn't spend your whole life in Campus Crusade for Christ, or raise your daughter as a Promise Keeper, or count on groups like the Moral Majority or the Christian Coalition to sustain your belief system beyond the next election cycle. For that kind of staying power you needed a confessional tradition, a church, an institution capable of outlasting its charismatic founders. Instead, Evangelicalism became dominated by empire-building megachurch pastors whose ministries often burned brightly and then just as quickly burned out.

These problems reproduced themselves in the political realm. As James Davison Hunter notes, the emphasis on potent individuals over enduring institutions tends to incline Evangelicals to a great man theory of political engagement, in which all that's required for good to triumph over evil is for the right Christian politician to "stand at the crossroads and change things for good."[34] The widespread sense that George W. Bush was such a figure helps explain why Evangelicals, more than any other constituency or cohort, remained intensely loyal to him long after the rest of the country had given up on him.

Saints may deserve such loyalty, but politicians rarely do. The urge to rally around "their" president robbed many conservative Christians of the capacity for prophetic witness and left them captive to a team player mentality that was fatal to religious credibility. The ease with which Evangelicals (and many conservative Catholics as well) fell in line behind the invasion of Iraq was understandable, if unfortunate in hindsight. The vigor with which they sealed themselves off from bad news from the front was much more depressing. The polls showing that frequent churchgoers were the most fervent supporters of waterboarding detainees, among other seemingly un-Christian practices, were more depressing still. And the fact that, amid egregious financial chicanery and frantic speculation, so many conservative Christians served as boosters for the virtues of the Bush economy—well, that was a scandal, and a shame.

Worse, no sooner had Barack Obama succeeded Bush in the White House than there was an immediate search for the next political hero or heroine, the next godly Evangelical come to save the republic from itself. Many of the candidates for this role (including Sarah Palin, Michele Bachmann, and Rick Perry) embodied Evangelical politics at its worst: the tendency toward purely sectarian appeals, the reliance on the language of outrage and resentment, the conflation of partisanship with Christian principle and the confusion of the American political system with the Church itself.

Resentment, partisanship, hero worship, martial language . . . these were unattractive features for a movement whose primary goal was supposed to be winning converts, not elections. In the 1970s and '80s, the liberal Christianity of Harvey Cox and James Pike had been fatally compromised by the perception that it was elevating ideology over theology. In much the same way, in the 1990s and 2000s the witness of Evangelicals was undercut by the association of Christianity with ideological conservatism, and by the widespread sense that the Evangelical communion was really just the Republican Party at prayer.

Indeed, this proved to be the Achilles' heel not only of Evangelicalism but of the entire ecumenical resistance project. The Evangelical-Catholic alliance had benefited from a backlash against the excesses of America's cultural revolution, but its association with partisan causes inspired a backlash of its own. Even before George W. Bush took office, surveys began to show a mounting anxiety about the conflation of religion and politics.

More and more Americans told pollsters that churches should stay out of political activism and fretted that Republican candidates were too close to religious leaders (and vice versa). In a 2002 paper in the *American Sociological Review,* Michael Hout and Claude S. Fischer announced the startling fact that the percentage of Americans who said they had "no religious preference" had doubled in less than ten years, rising from 7 percent to 14 percent of the population.[35] In the Bush presidency, this trend accelerated, becoming particularly pronounced among the young. By the late 2000s, more than 25 percent of twentysomethings declined to affiliate themselves explicitly with any religious body.[36]

These developments, crucially, didn't reflect a Richard Dawkins–esque rejection of religion itself. The rise of the New Atheists notwithstanding, true unbelief remained a rare thing in American life. The majority of the "nones" (as Robert Putnam and David Campbell called the "no religious preference" demographic) declared their faith in some kind of divinity; most professed to believe in some kind of afterlife; and many took a strong interest in religious practices, broadly understood. They seemed to be distancing themselves from institutional religion less out of theological conviction than as a way to make a "a symbolic statement" (in the words of Hout and Fischer) against the religious right.

Over the same period, similar impulses were driving the growth of what the pollster George Barna called the "unchurched Christian" demographic—those Americans who gave Christian answers to at least some questions (claiming faith in Jesus Christ, expressing hope that they would go to heaven when they died) but who rarely if ever actually found themselves in church.[37] Most strikingly, perhaps, both of these trends were more pronounced among downscale and blue-collar Americans than they had been in the past. Whereas in the locust years of the 1960s and '70s institutional Christianity had weakened most swiftly among the well-off and well educated, by the early twenty-first century both religious affiliation and observance were dropping precipitously among the less educated as well. (Indeed, by the mid-2000s, college graduates were actually more likely to be in church on Sunday than Americans who had only a high school diploma.) Evangelical Christians might have succeeded in following Catholics up the income and educational ladder, but the nation's churches seemed to be having trouble reaching the people left below.

Taken together, the "nones" and the "unchurched Christians" provided crucial constituencies for the alternative theologies that we will take up in Part II. And their growth points to the real legacy of Christianity's Bush-era struggles—not the end of faith itself, but the continued rise of heresy.

None of this means that the Evangelical-Catholic rapprochement was a failure. At the very least, the energy and common purpose instilled by the culture war lent American Christianity a resilience that was largely absent in Canada and Western Europe, where the cultural revolution of the 1960s carried all before it, and Christian orthodoxy was reduced to an anachronistic hobby, or else consigned to the cultural catacombs.

But there was only so much that the project could ultimately achieve. The theological gulf between Evangelicals and Catholics could be bridged but not completely filled in, and all the ecumenical cooperation in the world wasn't a substitute for vigor on both sides of the Protestant-Catholic divide. The two strongest branches of American Christendom had found a way to work together, learn from each other, and recognize how much they had in common. But the more pressing issue was still whether they could thrive and grow *as* Evangelical Protestants and as the Roman Catholic Church, rather than just surviving as two slightly different forms of a weakened Mere Christianity—or, worse, as two interchangeable vehicles for the identity politics of Red America.

As the third millennium dawned, this was very much an open question. In *To Change the World* (2010), James Davison Hunter distinguishes between "strong cultures" and "weak cultures" in American life. A strong culture exerts influence commensurate with its demographic strength—or, better, punches above its weight. It instills a strong sense of esprit de corps among its members and inspires admiration, imitation, and respectful engagement from those outside its confines. It establishes parameters for debate, supplies a common moral language for many of the great questions of the day, and influences millions of people's ways of thinking without their even necessarily knowing it.

A weak culture, by contrast, tends to "have institutional strength and vitality exactly in the lower and peripheral areas of cultural production,"[38] while enjoying only marginal leverage over the institutions with the greatest power to shape the culture as a whole. A weak culture is always embattled, always back on its heels, always resentful of its enemies and uncertain of its friends. It imitates but doesn't influence, alienates rather than seduces, and looks backward toward a better past instead of forward to a vibrant future. This is true even if a majority or a plurality of Americans seems to share the culture's values, because looking at numbers alone tends to overstate its potency: in a weak culture, "the whole . . . is significantly less than the sum of its parts."[39]

By Hunter's standard, both the Protestant Mainline and the Catholic Church were strong cultures in 1950s America—capable of making their presence felt in the commanding heights of American life, from the media and the academy to the film and television industries, even as they provided a powerful spiritual and ethical vocabulary for everyday life down below. Together, these two traditions supplied a common religious story and a common moral framework for a vast and complicated nation, influencing even where they did not predominate, and sowing seeds in fields where they did not reap the harvest.

A half-century later, the picture looks very different. The Mainline has drifted to the sidelines of American life, Catholicism's cultural capital has been reduced by decades of civil war, and Evangelicalism still has the air of an embattled subculture rather than the confidence of an ascendant force. Thus Hunter's pessimistic verdict on American Christianity:

The vitality of its cultural capital today is a vitality that resides almost exclusively among average people in the pew rather than those in leadership, on the periphery not the center of cultural production, in tastes that run to the popular rather than the exceptional, the middle brow rather than the high brow, and almost always to the practical as opposed to the theoretical or the imaginative. . . . The main reason why Christian believers today (from various communities) have not had the influence in the culture to which they have aspired is not that they don't believe enough, or try hard enough, or care enough, or think Christianly enough, and have the right worldview, but rather because they have been absent from the arenas in which the greatest influence in the culture is exerted.[40]

Those who took note of this absence in the late 2000s often assumed, like accommodationists and resisters before them, that Christian orthodoxy's weakness would open the door to the growth of outright unbelief. In this vein, the liberal Catholic Andrew Sullivan, writing in early 2009, suggested that if Christianity continued to marginalize itself, "the new atheist wave . . . will continue to pick up that slack."[41] Likewise Daniel Dennett, the philosopher and atheist polemicist, announced in 2007 that he expected "to live to see the evaporation of the powerful mystique of religion. . . . Cults will rise and fall, as they do today and have done for millennia, but only those that can metamorphose into socially benign organizations will be able to flourish."[42]

But again, the requiem for faith was premature. America at the close of the Bush presidency was in many ways still as religious as ever, and the spiritual instincts of most Americans were still heavily influenced, overtly or covertly, by two millennia of Christian faith. Culture abhors a metaphysical vacuum, and there was no materialist ideology capable of supplying the kind of holistic account of human life that the great "isms" of the nineteenth and early twentieth century had attempted to provide. Marxism and fascism had been ground into fertilizer by the wheels of history, and Freudianism was increasingly regarded as a superstition—or, at best, a kind of literary conceit—rather than a science. Darwinism supplied explanations but not meaning: the attempts of evolutionists to answer the ultimate questions were either thin and unpersuasive or else led swiftly into Nietzschean abysses that only a few safely tenured academics still felt comfortable plumbing.

So the waning of Christian orthodoxy has led to the spread of Christian heresy rather than to the disappearance of religion altogether. And it is by no means clear, Dennett's optimism notwithstanding, that these heresies are actually more "benign" and beneficial than the beliefs they have displaced.

II

The Age of Heresy

FIVE

LOST IN THE GOSPELS

Just before Palm Sunday in 2006, the National Geographic Society held a press conference in Washington, D.C., to announce the publication of an ancient document that promised to turn the Easter story on its head. Styled "The Lost Gospel of Judas" in the Society's publicity materials, the text in question had been uncovered in a Middle Eastern burial cave in 1978, only to spend a quarter century hopscotching from dealer to dealer and library to library, suffering untold physical abuse along the way. By the time National Geographic acquired the document, a full restoration and translation were impossible, but, after years of labor, some 85 percent of it was salvaged. That was enough to establish (or so the Society's team of scholars claimed) the startling fact that the gospel of Judas retold the Passion narrative from the perspective of its villain and made a hero of him. Rather than portraying Judas Iscariot as the worst of traitors, the newly translated gospel suggested that he had been Jesus' most intimate companion and the recipient of secret wisdom withheld from Peter, John, and the rest of the disciples. And, instead of blaming Judas for handing his master over to the Sanhedrin and the Romans, the text insisted that his famous "betrayal" had taken place at Jesus' own request.

In the popular press, this was treated as very big news for Christianity—and very bad news for orthodox belief. Having dropped a modest fortune on the project ($1 million to acquire the document, plus the cost of restoration), the National Geographic Society was at pains to tout the newfound gospel's revolutionary potential. A magazine cover story, a prime-time television documentary on the text, and multiple critical editions of the gospel soon followed, all of which were shot through with what *The New Yorker*'s Joan Acocella called "sensationalist formulas" about what the discovery meant for Christian faith.[1] The sensationalism paid off: the Gospel of Judas made front-page news around the world, the documentary earned some of the highest ratings in the history of National Geographic television, and the Society's official translation swiftly climbed the bestseller lists. Within the year, it was joined by glosses on the text from the University of North Carolina's Bart Ehrman and Princeton University's Elaine Pagels, two of the most prominent popularizers of early Christianity's "lost gospels." Both had been consultants on the project, and both found it easy to fold the new document into the revisionist story they'd already been telling.

True, historians might need years to discern "what in the Gospel of Judas . . . goes back to Jesus' actual teaching," Pagels wrote in the *New York Times*. But the lost gospel had already "joined the other spectacular discoveries that are exploding the myth of a monolithic Christianity and showing how diverse and fascinating the early Christian movement really was."[2]

Yet how "spectacular" was this discovery, really? Analyzing the Judas media blitz two years later, the *Chronicle of Higher Education*'s Thomas Bartlett noted that "one of the questions the National Geographic team was asked most frequently was 'is it the real thing?'" The answer, he pointed out, "depends on what you mean by 'real' and 'thing.'"[3] Yes, the Gospel of Judas was a legitimately ancient text, rather than a forgery; yes, its subversive theological message was a genuine example of the Gnostic teachings that flourished during the early history of the Christian Church. The Gnostic worldview, in outline, held that the material world is not fallen but irredeemably corrupt. We have all been imprisoned in flesh and time by the machinations of a foolish or wicked demigod (usually associated with the Yahweh of the Old Testament), and Jesus is not a man of any sort but a pure spirit in disguise, come to liberate a small elect and lead them out of bondage to a higher, more unsullied realm. In the Gospel of Judas, this is the secret wisdom—the "mysteries of the kingdom"—that Jesus shares with Judas and withholds from his other disciples, whose simpler piety he seems to regard with something like contempt.

But if, by "real" and "thing," one meant that the Gospel of Judas shed light on the actual origins of Christianity, then the answer was a resounding no. The newfound text's connections to the historical Judas and the historical Jesus of Nazareth were tenuous to nonexistent. Notwithstanding news reports that read (in Bartlett's words) "as if the gospel came straight from Judas' pen," the text could be dated, at the earliest, to the middle of the second century A.D., and there was no evidence that any of its distinctive sayings boasted an earlier provenance. This meant that using the most generous estimates, the Gospel of Judas antedated the New Testament canon by at least fifty years; more likely, it was penned more than a century later. To claim that it threw "new light on the historical relationship between Jesus and Judas," as one early press account put it,[4] was an extraordinary stretch—the equivalent of suggesting that Civil War historians should conduct a critical rereading of Ulysses S. Grant's memoirs in the light of Michael Shaara's 1974 novel of Gettysburg, *The Killer Angels*.

The problems with the way the Gospel of Judas was presented to the world ran deeper than exaggerated claims about its historical significance. Six months after the gospel's Easter launch, with the story off the front pages, a Rice University professor named April DeConick announced that she had retranslated the gospel and found that "several of the translation choices made by the society's scholars fall well outside the commonly accepted practices in the field."[5] This was a dry and academic way of saying that the National Geographic team members had botched their work. In their eagerness to set the religious world abuzz, they had effectively rewritten the lost gospel to make Judas come out looking like a hero. Their translation had Jesus saying that his betrayer was set apart "for" salvation, when the text actually said that Judas would be separated "from" it. They had eliminated a crucial negative, so that a passage stating that Judas would "not ascend to the holy generation" seemed to say that he *would* be counted among the saved. They had translated a reference to Judas as a "spirit" when the more appropriate translation would have been "demon." In the real Gospel of Judas, it turned out, the Iscariot was worse than the corrupted human being of the canonical gospels: he was the mortal incarnation of the Gnostic cosmology's prince of demons.

By the time the *Chronicle of Higher Education* took up the story, DeConick's interpretation had largely carried the day, and most of the academic conversation on the subject revolved around how and why the original team of translators had gotten things so wrong. But that conversation was carried out among a narrow circle of professors, making only a ripple in the popular consciousness where the initial, erroneous, interpretation had made a wave. And it was a conversation that focused almost exclusively on the particulars of the case—the challenges of the text, the personalities involved in interpreting it, and the pressures created by the National Geographic Society's desire to justify an expensive investment.

What was missing from the discussion was a recognition of how the selling of the Gospel of Judas fit into broader trends in American religion. This was more than a cautionary tale about scholarship and sensationalism. It was a moment when the prejudices of an entire spiritual culture were laid bare.

Every argument about Christianity is at bottom an argument about the character of Christ himself, and every interpretation of Christian faith begins with an answer to the question Jesus posed to his disciples: "Who do you say that I am?" From Thomas Jefferson and Ralph Waldo Emerson to Joseph Smith and Mary Baker Eddy, America's famous heretics have always offered their own answers to that question, drawing on a mix of scholarship and supposition to craft alternatives to the Christ of orthodoxy. But amid the post-1960s decline of institutional Christian faith, the question has taken on a new urgency, and the various answers have won an ever-wider audience. So there's no better way to turn from the first part of this book to the second—from the story of orthodoxy's decline to a portrait of heresy's newfound dominance—than with an exploration of the current debate over Christian origins.

From highbrow scholarship to middlebrow entertainments, from academic figures like Pagels and Ehrman to popularizers like *The Da Vinci Code*'s Dan Brown, this debate is dominated by the symbiosis that made the Gospel of Judas such a cultural phenomenon. On the one hand you have the American public, disillusioned with traditional Christianity but still religious enough to be eager for alternative portrayals of Jesus. On the other you have a host of scholars, journalists, novelists, and provocateurs eager to supply them—even to the point of fantasy and folly.

Christianity is a paradoxical religion because the Jew of Nazareth is a paradoxical character. No figure in history or fiction contains as many multitudes as the New Testament's Jesus. He's a celibate ascetic who enjoys dining with publicans and changing water into wine at weddings. He's an apocalyptic prophet one moment, a wise ethicist the next. He's a fierce critic of Jewish religious law who insists that he's actually fulfilling rather than subverting it. He preaches a reversal of every social hierarchy while deliberately avoiding explicitly political claims. He promises to set parents against children and then disallows divorce; he consorts with prostitutes while denouncing even lustful thoughts. He makes wild claims about his own relationship to God, and perhaps his own divinity, without displaying any of the usual signs of megalomania or madness. He can be egalitarian and hierarchical, gentle and impatient, extraordinarily charitable and extraordinarily judgmental. He sets impossible standards and then forgives the worst of sinners. He blesses the peacemakers and then promises that he's brought not peace but the sword. He's superhuman one moment; the next he's weeping. And of course the accounts of his resurrection only heighten these paradoxes, by introducing a post-crucifixion Jesus who is somehow neither a resuscitated body nor a flitting ghost but something even stranger still—a being at once fleshly and supernatural, recognizable and transfigured, bearing the wounds of the crucifixion even as he passes easily through walls.

The boast of Christian orthodoxy, as codified by the councils of the early Church and expounded in the Creeds, has always been its fidelity to *the whole of Jesus.* Its dogmas and definitions seek to encompass the seeming contradictions in the gospel narratives rather than evading them. Was he God or was he man? *Both,* says orthodoxy. Is the kingdom he preached something to be lived out in this world or something to be expected in the next? *Both.* Did he offer a blueprint for moral conduct or a call to spiritual enlightenment? *Both.* Did he mean to fulfill Judaism among the Jews, or to convert the Gentile world? *Both.* Was he the bloodied Man of Sorrows of Mel Gibson; the hippie, lilies-of-the-field Jesus of *Godspell;* or the wise moralist beloved by Victorian liberals? *All of them and more. . . .*

The goal of the great heresies, on the other hand, has often been to extract from the tensions of the gospel narratives a more consistent, streamlined, and noncontradictory Jesus. For the Marcionites in the second century, this meant a merciful Jesus with no connection to the vengeful Hebrew God; for their rivals the Ebionites, it meant a Jesus whose Judaism required would-be followers to become observant Jews themselves. For the various apocalyptic sects that have dotted Christian history, this has meant a Jesus whose only real concern was the imminent end-times; for modern

Christians seeking a more secular, this-worldly religion, it's meant a Jesus who was mainly a moralist and social critic, with no real interest in eschatology.

These simplifications have usually required telling a somewhat different story about Jesus than the one told across the books of the New Testament. Sometimes this retelling has involved thinning out the Christian canon, eliminating tensions by subtracting them. Sometimes it's been achieved by combining the four gospels into one, smoothing out their seeming contradictions in the process. More often, though, it's been achieved by straightforwardly rewriting or even inventing crucial portions of the New Testament account, as the Gospel of Judas' authors did, to make them offer up a smoother, more palatable, and more straightforward theology.

America's heretics have taken all of these approaches. In our founding generation, Thomas Jefferson edited the gospel accounts to remove everything supernatural and apocalyptic—producing a gospel fit for Deists and a Nazarene tailored to the Age of Enlightenment. Here is how Jefferson described his *Life and Morals of Jesus Christ,* in a letter to John Adams:

> In extracting the pure principles which [Jesus] taught, we should have
> to strip off the artificial vestments in which they have been muffled by
> priests, who have travestied them into various forms, as instruments
> of riches and power to themselves. We must dismiss the Platonists and
> Plotinists, the Stagyrites and Gamalielites, the Eclectics, the Gnostics
> and Scholastics, their essences and emanations, their logos and demi-
> urges, aeons and daemons, male and female, with a long train of . . .
> or, shall I say at once, of nonsense. We must reduce our volume to the
> simple evangelists, select, even from them, the very words only of Jesus.
> There will be found remaining the most sublime and benevolent code
> of morals which has ever been offered to man. I have performed this
> operation for my own use, by cutting verse by verse out of the printed
> book, and arranging the matter which is evidently his, and which is as
> easily distinguishable as diamonds in a dunghill.[6]

Later Americans sought a similar authenticity, but they were more likely to make additions than to prune. Nearly all our famous start-up faiths have kept the New Testament and then added an extra scripture or two, either as a supplement to the gospels or as a key to interpreting the originals. Joseph Smith's Book of Mormon gave his Saints a more American and family-friendly Jesus; Ellen Gould White's *The Great Controversy Between Christ and Satan* gave Seventh-day Adventists a Christ who vindicated their faith's apocalyptic origins; Mary Baker Eddy's *Science and Health with a Key to the Scriptures* reimagined Jesus as the original Christian Scientist. Lesser-known spiritualists multiplied gospels prodigiously, as divine voices murmured further revelations in their ears. Even fundamentalism, for all its official emphasis on "the Bible alone," owes its end-time obsessions to the extracanonical innovations that Cyrus Scofield's influential *Study Bible* wove into the scriptures it was supposedly dispassionately interpreting. "Unlike most commentators," Paul Boyer points out in his history of end-times beliefs, *When Time Shall Be No More* (1994), "Scofield combined his notes and the biblical text on the same page, so the former took on much the same authority as the latter."[7]

Both Jefferson and Scofield claimed to be reworking the New Testament based on pure reason and simple common sense, while Smith and White and Eddy and all the various spiritualists claimed to be taking divine dictation. To these tools for recovering the real Jesus, nineteenth-century European academics added a third, the historical-critical method. Their First Quest of the Historical Jesus, as it was later called, flowered in Germany and then spread across the Western world, promising to use the tools of scholarship to excavate the biblical narratives, reveal the layers of invention that lay atop the Jesus of history, and recover the truth about his life. To this end, the First Quest pioneered the use of textual analysis to probe the gospels' underlying source material, forging the plausible hypothesis that both Matthew and Luke draw on a common proto-gospel—eventually labeled *Q,* from the German *Quelle,* or "source"—whose text has been lost to history. It pioneered, as well, the use of apocryphal literature to reinterpret the early history of the Church. The highly influential "Tübingen School" of biblical criticism propagated an extraordinarily complicated theory, based on noncanonical epistles and forgotten gospels, in which nearly all of the New Testament was composed late in the second century to paper over the dispute between Pauline and Petrine Christianity and to unify the faith under the leadership of Rome. (Subsequent research has not been kind to this hypothesis.) And the First Quest inspired a raft of revisionist biographies of Christ, which offered differing interpretations of their subject but shared the view that the New Testament accounts were largely mythological, piling on miracle stories to make their merely mortal hero seem superhuman.

These claims were mildly controversial, of course. The English translation of Friedrich Strauss's *The Life of Jesus, Critically Examined* (1835) was denounced by a British peer as "the most pestilential book ever vomited out of the jaws of hell." However, subsequent generations of liberal-minded religious believers came to accept them as practically dispositive. The whole edifice of Protestant modernism in America was founded, in part, on the assumption that biblical scholarship required a new understanding not only of Genesis and Exodus but of Jesus' life and ministry as well. In his landmark 1922 sermon, "Shall the Fundamentalists Win?," the modernist minister Henry Emerson Fosdick cited the "new knowledge about human history and in particular about the ways in which the ancient peoples used to think in matters of religion" as his basis for dismissing much of the New Testament's supernatural passages as little more than pious myth.[8]

From an intellectual perspective, though, what Fosdick and his co-religionists took as dispositive had actually been decisively debunked two decades before, with the 1906 publication of Albert Schweitzer's *The Quest of the Historical Jesus,* which subjected a century's worth of "real Jesus" scholarship to a critique that still resonates today. In almost every instance, Schweitzer pointed out, the biographies of Christ penned by Victorian scholars read almost like *auto*biographies, revealing more about their authors than about their purported subject. Moreover, Schweitzer suggested, the historical Jesus scholarship deliberately ignored the apocalyptic dimension of the New Testament, which fit badly with the nineteenth century's liberal and rationalistic prejudices but was crucial to comprehending who Jesus was and what he was about.

These insights provided ammunition for the neo-orthodox response to modernism, and they also set the tone for the next fifty-odd years of New Testament scholarship, which tended to emphasize the difficulty of somehow piercing through the gospel accounts to attain a more perfect vision of Jesus's life and times.

In the aftermath of World War II, though, there was a certain embarrassment about the ends to which this agnosticism had been turned. (Dehistoricizing Jesus made it all too easy to reinvent him as the Aryan Christ of Nazi propaganda, for instance.) There was also a renewed optimism about what historical methods could reveal. A new wave of textual criticism led the way in this "New Quest," but the most important development was archaeological—the 1945 discovery, at Nag Hammadi in Egypt, of a trove of alternative gospels from the third and fourth centuries A.D. These documents seemed to provide precisely the kind of credible, noncanonical sources for Jesus' life and times that earlier generations of questers had conspicuously lacked.

For Christians of the Harvey Cox/James Pike school, especially, these discoveries couldn't have arrived at a more propitious time. The idea of a reconstructed Jesus seemed to dovetail neatly with the accommodationism they were promoting. Their new Christianity needed a new Christ, surely, and so much the better if he turned out to be the original Jesus as well, obscured for two millennia but now finally ready for his close-up.

As the optimism of the 1960s curdled and liberal churches suffered setback after setback, one might have expected this enthusiasm to wane. But, in an unexpected way, the "real Jesus" project would become even *more* important for liberal Protestantism in the years after Bishop Pike met his maker in the Israeli desert. (Recall that Pike's fatal journey was inspired by the Dead Sea Scrolls, which were discovered around the same time as the Nag Hammadi trove but turned out to have little connection to early Christianity.) The quest for the historical Jesus became accommodationism's trump card, in a sense, drawing on the resources of the one institution where liberal Christianity was thriving—the secular academy—and offering proofs that supposedly vindicated liberal religion and exposed the folly of its rivals. The New Quest was the swift sword of the intelligentsia, forged in history departments and divinity schools to cleave through biblical literalism and fundamentalist superstition. It promised to ground a thoroughly modern faith in ancient soil, to justify all of liberal Christianity's seeming surrenders to the spirit of the age, and—perhaps above all—to exact a kind of revenge on the Evangelical churches that gained ground at accommodationism's expense.

Not all the post-1960s scholarship on the historical Jesus has this kind of polemical edge. Much of it has been careful, well grounded, self-critical, and realistic about the limitations of its methods. But, inevitably, the scholars with the most influence outside the academy—the ones who show up on television to talk about their findings, the ones who earn newspaper headlines and magazine profiles, the ones whose books climb the bestseller lists—have been the ones who make the most shocking and attention-grabbing claims. And all of these efforts, in turn, have inspired a slew of less-credentialed authors—novelists and clerics, journalists and armchair theologians—who have borrowed the revisionists' ideas, aped their methods, and touted the same kind of conclusions.

These arguments have had two great purposes in common. The first has been to establish that the orthodox story of Christian origins is largely mythical and self-serving, that the followers of Jesus were divided from the beginning, that one man's heretic was always another man's true Christian. The so-called "proto-orthodox" won out over their heretical rivals by force and fraud, and the Christian canon was history rewritten by the winners, with competing arguments denigrated or effaced.

The outline of this argument was neatly summarized by Bart Ehrman in one of his many books popularizing the thesis:

> Virtually all forms of modern Christianity, whether they acknowledge it or not, go back to one form of Christianity that emerged victorious from the conflicts of the second and third centuries. This one form of Christianity decided what was the "correct" Christian perspective; it decided who could exercise authority of Christian belief and practice; and it determined what forms of Christianity would be marginalized, set aside, destroyed. It also decided which books to canonize into Scripture and which books to set aside as "heretical," teaching false ideas. . . . And then, as a coup de grace, this victorious party rewrote the history of the controversy, making it appear that there had not been much of a conflict at all, claiming that its own views had always been those of the majority of Christians at all times, back to the time of Jesus and his apostles, that its perspective, in effect, had always been "orthodox."[9]

It's easy to see why accommodationist Christians have found this framework so appealing. What better way to reimagine their religion for an age of diversity and multiculturalism and "cafeteria" spirituality than to assert that diversity was in the faith's very DNA—that in the time of the apostles as in the 1970s, Christianity was a do-it-yourself religion, and that the details have always been in flux and up for grabs?

But establishing the diversity of early Christianity—or rather, early Christianit*ies*—is only the first step. The other important purpose of the project has been to sift through that diversity to find a Jesus for the third millennium—a Jesus at once more historical *and* more modern than the orthodox man-God, a Jesus whose life and works and message could serve as the basis for a new religious synthesis. There's a certain element of hucksterism in the modern Jesus quest, embodied by figures like the late Robert Funk, who seized the media spotlight in the 1980s and 1990s by assembling a group of revisionist historians and theologians—which he dubbed the Jesus Seminar—to vote on the authentic words of Jesus. ("If we are to survive as scholars of the Humanities, as well as Theologians," Funk told the initial meeting of the Seminar, "we must quit the academic closet. . . . We must begin to sell a product that has some utilitarian value to somebody."[10]) But there's also a side that's entirely earnest and high-minded, dedicated not only to deconstructing orthodoxy but to forging a newer and more vital Christianity from the wreckage. In this sense, most of the "real Jesus" popularizers are religious idealists rather than pure skeptics, convinced that God himself (or herself) would smile upon their work.

"These remarkable texts," Elaine Pagels wrote hopefully of the Nag Hammadi documents, which she has explored in books like *The Gnostic Gospels* (1979) and *Beyond Belief: The Secret Gospel of Thomas* (2003), are capable of "transforming what we know as Christianity."[11] The vision of Christ "emerging" from the "historical-metaphorical paradigm," declared Marcus Borg, author of more than a dozen popular works on the historical Jesus, goes "hand in hand" with "an emerging vision of Christianity" that's capable of supplanting the traditional portrait.[12] The Jesus "reconstructed in the dialogues, debates, controversies and conclusions of contemporary scholarship," suggested John Dominic Crossan—whose own reconstructions, in works like *The Historical Jesus: The Life of a Mediterranean Jewish Peasant* (1991), have been fearlessly inventive—should shape the way that contemporary believers understand "for now" the concepts of "the Christ, the Lord, the Son of God."[13] The deep goal of modern Jesus scholarship, according to Funk, should be to supplant the old myth of orthodoxy with a "new fiction that takes as its starting point the central event in the Judaeo-

Christian drama and reconciles that middle with a new story that reaches beyond old beginnings and endings."[14]

There is no agreement among these writers on the exact details of the "new story." Pagels promotes a Gnostic Jesus, who preaches a God Within rather than a Heavenly Father and "speaks of illusion and enlightenment, not of sin and repentance."[15] Burton Mack, like Borg a member of the Jesus Seminar, has focused on the "Q" proto-gospel, imagining an original "Q" community that meditated on Jesus' words without believing that he rose from the dead. Elisabeth Schüssler Fiorenza, the author of *In Memory of Her* (1983), has sought to recover a Jesus who embodied a "feminist impulse"[16] within Judaism that was gradually suppressed as the early Church adapted to "patriarchal society and religion."[17] In Borg's writings, Jesus is a Jewish mystic, a "spirit person" primarily interested in critiquing the political theology of first-century Judaism.[18] For Crossan, he is a "peasant Jewish cynic," preaching a "brokerless kingdom" that challenges the hierarchies of the Roman Mediterranean.[19] To other writers, Ehrman chief among them, he is nothing if not an apocalyptic prophet.

And this is only a partial list of the diverse conclusions that revisionist writers have reached. Sometimes Jesus' Jewishness is insisted on; sometimes it's deemphasized in favor of a Jesus who seems more concerned with a very modern kind of social criticism than with the particular controversies of first-century Judaism. Sometimes the miraculous element in the gospels is deemed crucial to grasping Jesus' popular appeal; sometimes the miracles are dismissed as after-the-fact mythologizing. Sometimes the real Jesus is portrayed as being much more political than the Jesus of the gospels; sometimes he's cast as a hippie naïf—"a sort of flower child," in one of Funk's many quotable assessments.[20] Often Paul emerges as the villain of the Christian story, for having imposed a hateful dogmatism on Jesus' message of peace and love and kindness. Occasionally, Paul is cast as the real hero of the Christian story, as in Robert Wright's *The Evolution of God* (2009), hailed for taking a message of brotherhood that Jesus meant to apply only to his fellow Jews and universalizing it to include the Gentile world as well.

But for all the superficial diversity of these portraits, their intellectual method and their theological conclusions are remarkably similar. The method is almost always heresy's either/or, rejecting any attempt to resolve contradictions or honor paradoxes in favor of a ruthless narrowing designed to make the character of Jesus more consistent, even if this achievement comes at the expense of the tensions that make him fascinating. Either Jesus was divine or he was human. Either he was compassionate toward sinners or he preached a rigorous sexual morality. Either he preached in parables or he engaged in longer theological discourses. Either "all apocalyptic elements should be expunged from the Christian agenda," as Funk puts it, or else Jesus should be understood exclusively as an end-times prophet.[21]

In the revisionist mind-set, synthesis is always suspect. We have to choose between Mark's Jesus or John's Christ, between the aphoristic Jesus and the messianic Jesus, between Jesus the Jew and Jesus the light to the Gentiles. There's no possibility that the original Jesus married eschatology to everyday ethics, or that he seemed both divine and human, in different ways and at different times, even to the first apostles. There's no chance that he actually contained multitudes, or that this quality was recognized and recounted by the people who knew him best.

Meanwhile, wherever this narrowing takes us—whether we end up with Jesus the Gnostic mystic, the Cynic philosopher, the proto-feminist, or the apocalyptic prophet—the present-day theological implications of his "real" identity usually turn out to look a lot like the accommodationist Christianity of the Protestant Mainline. And they almost always represent a rebuke to Evangelical Christianity, conservative politics, and the combination thereof.

Sometimes this is made clear through the authors' personal flourishes. Ehrman recounts his own "up from fundamentalism" story in most of his bestselling books, returning again and again to the way the biblical literalism of his childhood was shattered by a collegiate encounter with New Testament scholarship. Pagels writes about her teenage flirtation with Evangelicalism—which ended "after a close friend was killed in an automobile accident at the age of sixteen, [and] my fellow evangelicals commiserated but declared that, since he was Jewish and not 'born again,' he was eternally damned."[22]

Sometimes it's apparent in their political polemics. Both Borg and Crossan explicitly analogize the Roman Empire to a Republican-governed United States, deploring the way (as Crossan puts it) the "Bible-fed Christian violence" of the religious right is "supporting or even instigating our imperial violence,"[23] and envisioning a renewed Christianity that could "disrupt the temple" (as Borg puts it) and shatter "the unholy alliance between religion and empire."[24]

But mostly it's clear in the kind of Christian church that nearly all these authors envision. The postmodern ecclesia should be nonjudgmental about sex (in a reformed Christianity, Funk suggests, there should be "neither Jew nor Greek, male nor female, slave nor free, homosexual nor heterosexual . . .")[25], open-minded about doctrine (to create space for those, like Pagels, who cannot subscribe to a "single, authorized set of beliefs")[26], and equipped with a canon that makes room for apocryphal texts while policing the existing New Testament to (as Ehrman puts it) "encourage interpretations . . . that don't lead to sexism, racism, bigotry, and all kinds of oppression."[27] In its intervention into public affairs, this Christianity would line up with the left of the Democratic Party; in its communal life, it would emphasize experience above all. It's less about replacing orthodoxy with "a different 'system of doctrines,'" Pagels writes, and more about rejecting doctrinal religion entirely, in favor of the quest for "insights or intimations of the divine that validate themselves in experience."[28]

This is a decent summary of the commitments of what remains of Mainline Protestantism in the early years of the third millennium. No matter who the real Jesus was in Palestine two thousand years ago, his modern popularizers always come around to the idea that he would want his followers to be accommodationist Christians today.

Over the last three decades, the idea of a "real Jesus," hidden for millennia and only now revealed, has probably been the religious intelligentsia's greatest contribution to the culture of American Christianity. From its academic core the quest has rippled outward, influencing high art and lowbrow entertainment, novelists and nonfiction writers, believers and atheists and everyone in between. It doesn't matter whether you take instruction from credentialed theologians or Hollywood producers, the works of Harold Bloom or paperback thrillers like *The Templar Legacy*. If you believe what's on television, in the paper, and on the front table at Barnes & Noble, a historical Jesus *has* to mean a revisionist Jesus—and a heretical Jesus, ultimately, rather than the orthodox Christ.

Along with Mainline Protestants seeking a blessing for accommodationist theology, two other groups have shown a particular enthusiasm for the "real Jesus" project. One consists of lapsed and doubting Catholics—particularly Catholics who came of age in the pre–Vatican II Church, and whose initial experience of the Bible was largely secondhand, filtered through a religious culture that sometimes seemed to imply that Jesus himself had written the Latin Mass and forbidden meat on Friday. The other consists of former fundamentalists, or people who grew up in the fundamentalist orbit, who were taught that there was no possible middle ground between an entirely literal reading of Scripture and outright apostasy. For both groups the idea of reinterpreting Christian origins in the light of modern scholarship has an understandable appeal.

But, as with the nineteenth century's "real Jesus" quest, most of these reinterpretations turn out to be built on sand. As a critique of naive beliefs about the New Testament and the early Church, the "real Jesus" project has no trouble scoring points. Early Christianity really was contentious and diverse, and many basic Christian dogmas did develop gradually rather than being handed down in pristine form directly from the apostles. When a writer like Ehrman describes Christian orthodoxy as an "invention," he's being tendentious, but he isn't exactly wrong. The Christianity of the Nicene Creed isn't a set of self-evident statements that follow inexorably from a quick read of Matthew, Mark, Luke, and John. It's the fruit of an intellectual effort that spanned generations—an effort that took one of religious history's most striking stories, as told and retold in a multiplicity of styles and voices, and tried to tease out its implications for ritual, theology, and belief. The project may have been guided by the Holy Spirit, as orthodox Christianity insists, but it clearly was a *project* rather than a simple matter of reading the gospels and believing what they said. And, like any other complicated intellectual undertaking, its conclusions can certainly be doubted or dismissed.

The "real Jesus" campaign has earned so much attention and won so much influence, though, because it goes much further than this. It doesn't just argue with orthodoxy's conclusions, it denies its premises. To read Pagels and Ehrman, the Jesus Seminarians, and many others, the reader would think that orthodox interpretation of the Christian story has *no* claim to greater antiquity, and *no* stronger connection to the first followers of Christ, than the many and various heretical interpretations. In their view, the New Testament reflects only the theological-ideological biases of the "proto-orthodox" party, and the canon as we know it was imposed retrospectively, rather than developing organically in the early Church.

These claims are enormously appealing to the modern religious mind, but they aren't particularly tenable. The inconvenient truth is that nearly all scholars identify the letters of Saint Paul as the oldest extant Christian documents, the earliest dating from the 50s A.D., two decades after the crucifixion. It's possible to draw different conclusions from Paul's Christology than later Church fathers did. But what would become basic premises of orthodoxy are clearly affirmed, while the basic premises of, say, the Gnostics or the Marcionites or the Ebionites or the hypothetical "Q Community" are implicitly or explicitly ruled out.

For Paul, Christian faith means worshipping Jesus Christ rather than just emulating him. It means regarding the crucifixion as an atonement for human sins. It means believing in a physical resurrection rather than some sort of "spiritual" or psychological event. It means seeing Jesus' life and death as the fulfillment of Jewish prophecy as well as a witness to the Gentiles. It means celebrating the Eucharist as a memorial of Christ's passion. It means . . . well, let Paul himself tell it:

> Now I would remind you, brothers, of the gospel I preached to you, which you received, in which you stand, and by which you are being saved, if you hold fast to the word I preached to you—unless you believed in vain. For I delivered to you as of first importance what I also received: that Christ died for our sins in accordance with the Scriptures, that he was buried, that he was raised on the third day in accordance with the Scriptures, and that he appeared to Cephas, then to the twelve.

The chronological priority of this message is often obscured by "real Jesus" popularizers. As Luke Timothy Johnson notes, they tend to write as though the New Testament consists only of the four gospels, shaping "their portrait of Jesus and their account of Christian origins without reference to other canonical sources" and dismissing Paul's epistles as "irrelevant for historical knowledge."[29] But chronologically speaking, the Pauline letters are the most historically relevant texts we know of. There's no need to reconstruct hypothetical documents and even more hypothetical communities in order to open a window into the mind-set of the first Christians. In Corinthians and Romans and Galatians, we have direct evidence of what it meant to be a follower of Jesus just a few years after his crucifixion. And what it meant, at least to Paul and his communities, looks more like the Christianity of the Nicene Creed than does any heretical alternative.

In other words, the popular revisionist conceit that the early Christians initially meditated on Jesus' sayings and only gradually mythologized their way toward the idea of his divinity finds no support whatsoever in the oldest surviving stratum of Christian writing. As Adam Gopnik, no believer himself, put it in a *New Yorker* essay: "If one thing seems clear from all the scholarship . . . it's that Paul's divine Christ came first, and Jesus the wise rabbi came later. This fixed, steady twoness at the heart of the Christian story can't be wished away by liberal hope. . . . Its intractability is part of the intoxication of belief."[30]

Moreover, just as Paul's portrait of Christ predates the heretical alternatives, so too the canonical portraits of Jesus generally predate their more heterodox rivals. Mark is generally dated to the 60s A.D., Matthew and Luke to the 70s, and John to the 90s, and "real Jesus" enthusiasts make much of the gulf of years separating the events recounted in the gospels from their estimated dates of composition. But even if we accept these (provisional and arguably tendentious) datings, the four canonical gospels are the only narratives of Jesus' life and death that definitely survive from the first century, whereas all of the apocryphal gospels that we have probably date from the middle of the second century at the earliest. The only possible exception to this pattern is the Gnostic Gospel of Thomas—a collection of Jesus' sayings, with no narrative spine, that sometimes echoes the synoptic gospels and sometimes diverges markedly from them. A minority of scholars date Thomas to the early decades of Christianity, which explains why "real Jesus" enthusiasts lean heavily on it. (The Jesus Seminar's *The Five Gospels* places it on an equal footing with Matthew, Mark, Luke, and John, as does Pagels's bestselling *Beyond Belief: The Secret Gospel of Thomas*.) But it's more likely that Thomas's gospel, too, is a second-century document, at least in the form that's come down to us today.

Presumably there were other first-century documents that the gospel writers drew on, proto-gospels like Q, passion narratives, and the like. But what has reached us intact is the canon as we know it. It's only later, long after the last eyewitnesses to Jesus' life and death were dead and buried, that we have definitive evidence of radically different narratives circulating in the Christian world.

As with Paul's letters, when you contrast Matthew, Mark, Luke, and John with their apocryphal rivals, it's hard to miss their essential theological unity. This unity doesn't preclude divergent factual claims and theological emphases. Within the broad framework of Christian orthodoxy, the New Testament obviously contains what Timothy Beal calls "a tense diversity of perspectives and voices, difference and argument"[31]—a diversity that has given rise to the great theological debates of Christendom, dividing Catholicism from Orthodoxy, Luther from the Pope, Armininians from Calvinists, and so on. But the broad framework still exists. Here Andreas Kostenburger and Michael Kruger have it right:

> The New Testament bears credible and early witness to the unified doc-trinal core, in particular with regard to Christology, centered on Jesus and his apostles, a core that is, in turn, grounded in Old Testament messianic prophecy. This Christological core, for its part, is in essential continuity with the gospel Paul and the early Christians preached, a gospel that centered on Jesus crucified, buried, and risen according to the Scriptures.[32]

What's more, there's good reason to think that the early heretics were aware of this continuity and the challenge it posed to their interpretations of Christianity. In his invaluable work *Who Chose the Gospels?* (2010), the New Testament scholar C. E. Hill points out that noncanonical gospels make a "persistent appeal to secret teachings of Jesus given to one or another of the apostles," which seems like "a tacit admission that not very much support could be gained from his acknowledged public teachings."[33] He also points out that if you look at the range of Christian writings from the early centuries of the Church, there's far more unanimity about the basic contours of the canon than the "lost gospel" enthusiasts would lead one to expect. While this or that alternative gospel may make an appearance in the writing of a given Church Father, the citations from noncanonical works are usually swamped by citations from Matthew, Mark, Luke, and John. It's clear from early Christian sources that the canon was up for grabs around the edges—with debates over whether to include certain non-Pauline epistles, devotional texts like the Shepherd of Hermas, and so forth. But the basic core shows up, implicitly or explicitly, in nearly every pre-fourth-century version of the New Testament that we have.

If you read the revisionist scholars closely, they implicitly acknowledge these points. Ehrman's *Lost Christianities,* for instance, opens with a list of the documents that he considers evidence of Christian roads not taken, with a probable date attached to each. He lists thirty-four texts, and only *one*—the First Letter of Clement, itself clearly proto-orthodox—is believed to date from the first century A.D.

This might lead the reader to suspect that the Christians who formalized the canon placed as much weight on a document's historical credibility as they did on theological power politics. Indeed, Ehrman basically admits as much: "Almost all of the lost Scriptures of the early Christians were forgeries,"[34] he allows—and then here is his explanation, in *Jesus, Interrupted,* of the criteria (besides doctrine) that the orthodox canon shapers used:

> By the second and third centuries it was clear to many of the proto-orthodox that even if a recently penned writing was important, useful, and trustworthy, it could not be seen as sacred Scripture. Scriptural books had to be ancient, going back to the original decades of the Christian church. . . . Only those books that were widely used throughout the proto-orthodox church could be accepted as Scripture. Books that had only local appeal might be valuable, but they could not be considered part of the canon. . . . For a book to be considered Scripture it had to have been written by an apostle or a companion of an apostle. That's why the Gospels were attributed to particular people: Scripture was not acceptable if it was anonymous.[35]

In other words, in an age that lacked the tools of modern historical scholarship and textual analysis, the canon makers did their best to be faithful to the actual historical record of their faith. All things considered, they did a remarkably impressive job: every surviving Christian text that has a strong claim to having been written within fifty years of Jesus' crucifixion is in the New Testament, and almost everything from later eras—including "lost gospels" that were perfectly proto-orthodox, it should be noted, as well as those that leaned toward heresy—was successfully screened out.

"Through the course of our study," Ehrman writes in the introduction to *Lost Christianities,* "I will be asking the question: What if it had been otherwise? What if some other form of Christianity had become dominant, instead of the one that did?"[36] Relying on Ehrman's own work, we can venture at least one conclusion. If it had been otherwise, the Christian story would have *much* less historical credibility than the narrative that was actually handed down to us.

What's more, even if you accept the theological premises of accommodationist Christianity—that Christian belief needs to modernize and secularize to survive, that tolerance needs to trump dogmatism and the sins of the Christian past need to be repudiated, and so on—it isn't clear that the early Christian heresies have as much to recommend them as their popularizers often imply. Pagels, for instance, spends an entire book (1996's *The Origin of Satan*) deploring orthodox Christianity's literal demonization of its opponents—pagan, Jewish, and heretical alike. There is much to deplore, certainly, in the uses to which the New Testament has been turned over the centuries. But are we really supposed to believe that opening more theological space for Pagels's Gnosticism, with its rejection of the entire Old Testament as the work of a malignant demigod, would have made Christianity *better* disposed to the Jews?

So too with gender politics. The early Christian community does seem to have taken a gradually more patriarchal line on female participation and leadership as its influence in the Roman world increased, accommodating itself to existing social structures rather than transforming them entirely. But the heretical roads not taken hardly seem likely to have led to a more female-friendly faith. As in Greek and Roman paganism, their gestures toward a sacred feminine often coexisted with barely concealed misogyny. To take only the most famous example, some later versions of the Gospel of Thomas include the following passage, which has no parallel whatsoever in the canonical New Testament:

Simon Peter said to them, "Make Mary leave us, for females don't deserve life."

Jesus said, "Look, I will guide her to make her male, so that she too may become a living spirit resembling you males. For every female who makes herself male will enter the kingdom of Heaven."[37]

Finally, there's the question of miracles and metaphysics. It's understandable that some modern readers might want a Christianity with fewer miracle stories and tamer metaphysical claims. But it's utterly baffling that they would cite the lost gospels and early Christian heresies as a plausible source for such a faith. Many of the apocryphal gospels *add* miracles, piling on childhood wonders and post-resurrection pyrotechnics to create a Jesus who seems more like a magician than a savior. The cosmology of the early heresies, likewise, was often far more tangled and mythological than that of orthodoxy. Having proposed a divine realm that's completely separate from our own fleshly plane, the Gnostics decided to make it feel completely different as well—and the next thing you know, they were piling on a pantheon of supernatural beings (archons and demiurges, pleromas and syzygies), in a vision that seems much weirder in hindsight than the Trinitarian Christianity with which they competed for adherents.

Perhaps weirdness is simply in the eye of the beholder. In Jorge Luis Borges's vision of a world where Gnostic Christianity triumphed, Dante ended up penning a hymnody to the mystic realm of Barbelo (Jesus' point of origin in the Gospel of Judas) instead of Heaven, Hell, and Purgatory. But I suspect that a reader unprejudiced by the contemporary culture wars would be more inclined to agree with the New Testament scholar Bruce Metzger, who answered the eternal question "Who chose the gospels?" by suggesting that they effectively chose themselves. "Neither individuals nor councils created the canon," Metzger concluded. "Instead, they came to recognize and acknowledge the self-authenticating quality of these writings, which imposed themselves as canonical upon the church."[38] Compared with the alternatives, they were more credible as eyewitness testimony, more persuasive as religious apologia, and simply more interesting as narratives than any of the competition.

Indeed, given how much attention has been lavished on the supposed revelatory content of the lost gospels, it's remarkable just how shabby and second-rate many of them turn out to be. To read them all back to back to back, in a collection like Ehrman's *Lost Christianities,* is to feel curiosity give way to disappointment, and then to boredom. There are flashes of eloquence and insight, but as a general rule, the rival gospels are derivative in their substance, inferior in their art, and tedious in their embellishments. Some of their Jesuses are clearly just fairy-tale heroes, and the rest either make Jesus a flatter character than the Christ of the canonical gospels, or else (in the case of certain Gnostic texts) portray him as irritating and even repellent, dripping with smug disdain and spiritual elitism—"like the ruler of a dubious planet in *Star Trek,*" as Gopnik memorably put it.[39]

If the gospels and the letters of Saint Paul didn't make such extraordinary claims about Jesus' miracles, his resurrection, and his divinity, it's hard to imagine that many modern historians would spend much time parsing second-century apocrypha for clues about the "real" Jesus. The gospel of Thomas might attract some modest attention, but the later "lost gospels," very little. For the most part, the argument over how the Nazarene lived and died would revolve around competing interpretations of the existing Christian canon, and the rough accuracy of the synoptic narrative would be accepted by the vast majority of scholars.

In the event, the synoptic gospels and Saint Paul's epistles do make extraordinary claims, and modern scholars have every right to read them with a skeptical eye, question their reliability, and parse them stringently for propaganda and mythologizing. But if you downgrade the earliest Christian documents or try to bracket them entirely, the documentary evidence that's left is too intensely unreliable (dated, fragmentary, obviously mythological) to serve as the basis for anything save interesting fictions and speculative forays. In this landscape, historical analysis can only deconstruct; it cannot successfully rebuild.

There's nothing necessarily wrong with deconstruction. But if we're honest with ourselves, we need to acknowledge where it leads—not to the beginning of a fruitful quest for the Jesus of history but to its end.

Understandably, few of the thinkers invested in the quest for a "real Jesus" want to admit that their journey backward through the Christian past dead-ends somewhere in the early second century, generations shy of

Nazareth and Calvary. But this refusal has led the whole project inexorably downward—from scholarship into speculation, and from history into conspiracy theory.

Like Elizabethan buffs in search of the "real" Shakespeare, the questers for the historical Jesus turn out to be masters of detection and geniuses at code breaking, capable of seeing through every cover-up and unpacking every con. Is there a dearth of evidence for alternative Christianities in the earliest history of the church? Why, then that very absence is itself evidence that these Christianities existed—and then were cruelly suppressed. Indeed, the whole of the New Testament must represent a pure propaganda campaign against these lost communities—and, happily, we can recover their teachings and beliefs through the simple expedient of taking every claim made in the canonical texts and treating it as a polemic against a group, or groups, that held roughly the opposite beliefs.

Alternatively, if New Testament books aren't read as straightforward propaganda, they're treated as palimpsests and pastiches, in whose complexities and inconsistencies the adept reader can discern earlier traditions and older, purer ways of being Christian, obscured by the propaganda mills of the early Church but visible in the stitchwork and legible between the lines. This licenses scholars to pore over centuries' worth of early Christian texts, yanking out bits and pieces that fit a particular thesis and moving them forward or backward in time to prove whatever point they want.

As for factual and theological consistencies within the earliest Christian texts—why, that's just evidence that the various writers were all in on the conspiracy, all agents of the cover-up. The theological commonalities between Paul's epistles and Matthew or John only prove that the gospel writers did violence to the facts in order to vindicate a Pauline theology. The consistency of the Passion narratives across the four gospels is proof that their authors colluded in a triumphalist fantasy.

Here is Crossan, for instance, explaining how we should really read the resurrection narratives:

> The stories . . . tell us nothing whatsoever about the origins of Christian *faith* but quite a lot about the origins of Christian *authority*. They tell us about power and leadership in the earliest Christian communities. They tell us about the establishment of leadership groups over general

communities and they tell us very clearly about competing specific leaders within and among these groups. [The portrayal of Mary Magdalene in John's Gospel], for instance, tells us that, at least for the community of the Beloved Disciple, Mary Magdalene's authority needed to be opposed just as much as did that of Peter or Thomas. . . .

These stories were not, in other words, about events that first Easter Sunday. Or, if you prefer, Easter Sunday lasted quite a few years.[40]

Note the brave certainty of the paranoid style. The gospel narrative tells us "nothing" about the history it claims to be recounting, but it tells us everything that we need to know about the secret motivations of its authors. This claim becomes all the braver when you realize exactly which New Testament detail Crossan claims as slam-dunk evidence for his vision of a power struggle between John and Mary Magdalene. He takes Jesus' post-resurrection encounter with Mary outside the empty tomb—which portrays the Magdalene as the first person to see the resurrected Christ, before John or Peter or anyone—and argues that the Johannine author actually "denigrated" Mary by making her not recognize the risen Jesus "until he addresses her."[41] (We should all be so denigrated.)

This kind of bravado is typical of the field. Here is Pagels, explaining the real reason why the leaders of the early Church preached that Christ had risen bodily from the dead:

When we examine its practical effect on the Christian movement, we can see . . . that the doctrine of bodily resurrection also serves an essential political function: it legitimizes the authority of certain men who claim to exercise exclusive leadership over the churches as the successors of the apostle Peter. From the second century, the doctrine has served to validate the apostolic succession of bishops, the basis of papal authority to this day.

Whatever we think of the historicity of the orthodox account, we can admire its ingenuity.[42]

Following this cui bono style of reasoning, "we" soon discover a darkly political motive behind Christianity's insistence on monotheism as well: "The doctrine of the 'one God' confirms, for orthodox Christians, the emerging institution of the 'one bishop' as monarch ('sole ruler') of the church."[43] (As though there were no other reason for a faith founded by a *Jewish* messiah to insist on monotheism.) And then "we" can trace this consolidation of apostolic power backward to its likely source—none other than Simon Peter himself, whom Pagels insinuates invented both the resurrection story itself and the idea that he was to lead the disciples after Christ's departure.

A somewhat less paranoid reader might wonder why, if the gospel accounts were really written to consolidate Petrine authority, Peter comes off as such an epic bumbler—and at the crucial hour even a kind of betrayer—throughout all four canonical texts. But Pagels is convinced that her reading of the gospels has delivered the true story of orthodoxy's origins—a story which reveals that the leaders of first-century Christianity, while shepherding a persecuted and despised sect that courted martyrdom and expected the apocalypse, somehow found time to carefully construct their theology with an eye toward the day when their heirs would sit in the Vatican issuing anathemas.

To say that these kinds of briefs are unpersuasive is to understate the case. They speak the language of the conspiratorial pamphlet, the paranoid chain e-mail—or the paperback thriller. Which is why it's only fitting that the greatest popularizer by far of lost gospels and alternative Christianities isn't Pagels or Ehrman—or any of the Jesus Seminar's academics. It's the bestselling novelist Dan Brown.

In fairness, the term *bestselling novelist* seems too modest to do justice to an author who has outsold almost every other English-language scribbler for the last decade and counting. Certainly it doesn't do justice to Dan Brown's intellectual ambitions, which have been crucial to his extraordinary success. If you want to sell a million copies of a potboiler, you need to know how to hook the reader and keep the pages turning. But if you want to sell the nearly 100 million copies that Brown's *The Da Vinci Code* has sold, you need to preach as well as entertain—to present fiction that can be read as fact and that promises to unlock the secrets of history, the universe, and God along the way.

Brown is explicit about this mission. He isn't a serious novelist, but he's a deadly serious writer. His thrilling plots, he's told interviewers, are there to make his books' didacticism go down easy, so that readers don't realize till the end "how much they are learning along the way."[44] What they learn, of course, is the "real truth" about Jesus of Nazareth, concealed for centuries but finally brought to light by the conspiracy-exploding hero of *The Da Vinci Code,* the brilliant Harvard scholar Robert Langdon.

Brown's real Jesus is a thoroughly modern messiah: political and feminist, sexy and worldly, with a wife and kids, a house in the Galilean suburbs, and no delusions about his own divinity. He worships the sacred feminine rather than the patriarchal Hebrew god, and marries the supposedly aristocratic Mary Magdalene, creating a "potent political union with the potential of making a legitimate claim to the throne."[45] After this claim is foiled by the crucifixion, Jesus' "merely mortal" career is memorialized in the Gnostic Gospels (which Brown falsely claims are far older than their canonical rivals), while his heirs get spirited away to Merovingian France, where their existence is concealed by a secret society and encoded in the West's great artistic masterpieces. The cover-up is necessitated, presumably, because Jesus' true legacy was tragically betrayed by Emperor Constantine, who invents the concept of a divine Jesus out of whole cloth, pushes the idea through a supposedly "close vote" at the First Council of Nicaea, and then has the New Testament rewritten and the Gnostic gospels burned so that nobody can ever discover the truth. Nobody, that is, except the indefatigable Langdon . . .

Even by the loosey-goosey standards of New Testament revisionism, this "history" is the purest hogwash. Yet even as he makes free with the facts, there's a sense in which Brown is remarkably faithful to the spirit of the "real Jesus" enterprise. Like many of the project's more intellectually serious enthusiasts, he's convinced that his exertions will ultimately help to save Western religion rather than undermine or discredit it. This becomes clear when you read *The Da Vinci Code* alongside *Angels and Demons* and *The Lost Symbol,* respectively its bestselling predecessor and sequel. In *Angels and Demons,* Brown rhapsodizes about a potential marriage of science and spirituality—which will become possible, he suggests, once Western Christianity stops thinking that it holds any kind of exclusive claim to truth. In *The Lost Symbol,* he slobbers all over the Masons, whose nonsectarian theism he has called a "beautiful blueprint for human spirituality."[46] In the Brownian worldview, faith isn't the enemy, and all religions have the potential to be wonderful, so long as we can get over the idea that any one of them might be particularly true. Only then can they be turned to their deepest purpose—not the worship of a particular God but the unlocking of the awesome potential of the human soul.

If Brown's sense of mission mirrors the ethos of the historical Jesus project, his mix of conspiracy theories and pseudo-historical excursions bears a telling resemblance to the supposedly scholarly treatments of the same material. It's ridiculous, for instance, for Brown to claim that the Gnostic Gospels offer a "merely mortal" Jesus, when in fact their Christ is arguably more superhuman—in the sense of being the purest spirit, rather than actual flesh and blood—than the Jesus of the gospels. But is it that much more implausible than the attempt to sell the baroque cosmology of second-century Gnosticism as a kind of forerunner of contemporary liberal Protestantism? It's ludicrous to suggest that the idea of a divine Jesus was fabricated by Constantine three centuries after the crucifixion. But is it so much more ludicrous than the more commonplace claim that the same idea was imposed on the early Christian community by a power-hungry apostle?

Meanwhile, the fact that Brown's fantasies have enjoyed such wild commercial success suggests that rather than being an unfortunate flaw in an otherwise sound effort, the historical Jesus project's tendency toward conspiracy theorizing is in fact crucial to its mass-market appeal. Indeed, one suspects that for many of the general public's lost-gospel enthusiasts, conspiracy-mongering is an end unto itself. The point is the journey, not the destination, and any too specific answer to "Who was Jesus?" would probably only disappoint. (Brown's answer especially: as Gopnik notes, if *The Da Vinci Code* has it right, "Jesus is reduced from the Cosmic Overlord to the founder of a minor line of Merovingian despots."[47]) Better by far to leave the question open—to posit a hidden truth so astonishing that it makes orthodoxy seem thin and pathetic by comparison, without ever answering the question of what that hidden truth might mean. Better to read Pagels and Ehrman and Brown for their theories about who Jesus wasn't rather than who he really was. Better to send all the various gospels (lost, canonical, hypothetical) fluttering skyward together, and then leave them hanging in the air. . . .

*   *   *

But while this may be an appealing spirituality for a postmodern age, it's a rather poor foundation on which to build a Church. Conspiracy theories and promises of secret revelations can feed a powerful *interest* in religion, but they tend to discourage real commitment. They promote a hermeneutics of suspicion instead—a way of looking at faith that inspires searching rather than settling, a highly individualistic theology rather than submission to authority, and a skepticism that makes any sort of enthusiastic joining seem like a mug's game.

It shouldn't be surprising, then, that for all its popular appeal, the "real Jesus" project has done next to nothing to revive the accommodationist churches where many of its promoters worship. The bestselling works of Elaine Pagels haven't reversed the fortunes of her beloved Episcopalianism. The "coming radical reformation" prophesied by Robert Funk has shown little evidence of revitalizing the most liberal Reformed denominations. Dan Brown's potboilers have probably been a greater boon to Opus Dei than to accommodationist Catholicism.

However superficially appealing, the idea that a religious tradition could be saved from crisis because a group of intellectuals radically reinterpreted its sacred texts is the kind of conceit that only, well, an intellectual could possibly believe. Recovering a more heterodox and political and postmodern Jesus was supposed to answer the "why go to church at all?" question that hit accommodationist congregations so hard from the 1960s onward. But deconstructing the orthodox Jesus has the same institutional consequences as deconstructing orthodox doctrine and orthodox morality. The acid of the "real Jesus" dissolves the Book of Common Prayer and the Methodist Hymnal as completely as it does resurrection narratives.

"Liberal religion is adept at releasing energy," James Hitchcock wrote in a 1977 essay, "freeing people from established obligations and prohibitions, but not at refocusing it."[48] This turns out to be as true when the "establishment" in question is Jesus of Nazareth himself, rather than this doctrine or that sexual taboo. The rush is exciting, but the hangover is a killer.

In fairness, the theological perspectives that the real-Jesus enthusiasts are promoting often do find a wider American audience. Certainly the Gnostic heresy, or at least the spin that a writer like Pagels puts on it, has a mass following that far exceeds the Sunday attendance at every Mainline denomination. The idea that "self-knowledge is knowledge of God" and "the self and the divine are identical"[49] (to quote her reformulations of what the Gnostic Gospels taught) has enormous currency in American culture, and there are echoes of this vision of a God Within everywhere, from *Eat, Pray, Love* to *The Oprah Winfrey Show*. (These trends will be discussed in greater detail two chapters hence.) But the accommodationist churches are not the main vehicle for this theology's steady expansion, nor are they the place where most Americans encounter it. Their leaders and thinkers contribute to its cultural power without benefiting from its potency.

Instead, the style of the historical Jesus project—the emphasis on secret and esoteric knowledge, the suggestion that credentialed historians should have a license to rewrite traditional theology—has ultimately hardened liberal Christianity's contemporary identification as a religion for the intelligentsia and *only* the intelligentsia, for people at once embarrassed by the dogmatism of the Christian past and self-congratulatory about their rejection of "simple" piety and "ordinary" belief. And the greatest tragedy of today's religious intellectuals, perhaps, is their refusal to recognize that this combination represents an abdication of their responsibilities to their fellow believers. Consider the following lament from Mark Lilla, a lapsed Catholic and one of America's leading scholars of religion:

> A half-century ago, an American Christian seeking assistance could have turned to the popularizing works of serious religious thinkers like Reinhold Niebuhr, Paul Tillich, John Courtney Murray, Thomas Merton, Jacques Maritain and even Martin Buber and Will Herberg. Those writers were steeped in philosophy and the theological traditions of their faiths, which they brought to bear on the vital spiritual concerns of ordinary believers. . . . But intellectual figures like these have disappeared from the American landscape and have been replaced by half-educated evangelical gurus who either publish vacant, cheery self-help books or are politically motivated.[50]

The shift that Lilla is describing is one of the themes of this book. But he's wrong to suggest that highbrow religious thinkers have disappeared from the American scene. It's just that they're far more likely than their midcentury predecessors to see themselves as critics of Christianity first, and explicators of the "philosophy and the theological traditions of their faith" a distant second. Lilla's plaint is a common one: the number of religiously minded intellectuals who have pined for the days of Reinhold Niebuhr would fill a small cathedral. But what few of them seem to recognize is that Niebuhr's greatness and influence lay in his willingness to *defend* Christian orthodoxy in an often-hostile world, rather than perpetually currying favor with its cultured despisers.

This failure of vision hasn't been a tragedy just for the Mainline Protestant denominations. It's a tragedy for American Christianity as a whole. For a generation or more, many of the writers who might have busied themselves exploring and explaining the Christian tradition—to the benefit of the secular world and ordinary believers alike—have been engaged instead in a project that has undercut historic Christianity while building nothing lasting in its place. The cultural impact of figures like Pagels and Ehrman and Borg and Crossan has been almost entirely destabilizing. Rather than propagating an understanding of Jesus' identity that's more intellectually compelling than the orthodox portrait, all they've succeeded in doing is validating the idea that Jesus' identity is entirely up for grabs, and that one can be a follower of Christ without having to accept any constraints on what that "following" might mean.

The consequences of this destabilization have rippled far and wide, influencing American religious culture in ways that liberal Christians never intended. The way orthodoxy synthesizes the New Testament's complexities has forced churchgoers of every prejudice and persuasion to confront a side of Jesus that cuts against their own assumptions. A rationalist has to confront the supernatural Christ, and a pure mystic the worldly, eat-drink-and-be-merry Jesus, with his wedding feasts and fish fries. A Reaganite conservative has to confront the Jesus who railed against the rich; a post–sexual revolution liberal, the Jesus who forbade divorce. There is something to please almost everyone in the orthodox approach to the gospels, but something to challenge them as well.

A choose-your-own Jesus mentality, by contrast, encourages spiritual seekers to screen out discomfiting parts of the New Testament and focus only on whichever Christ they find most congenial. And our religious culture is now dominated by figures who flatter this impulse, in all its myriad forms—conservative and liberal, conspiratorial and mystical, eco-friendly and consumerist, and everything in between.

Lilla's "gurus" and their "vacant, cheery self-help books" have benefited, in this sense, from the work of the Jesus Seminar and the efforts of Dan Brown. So have prosperity preachers, from the Bakkers and Swaggarts of the 1980s to their smoother modern heirs. So have the politicizers of the gospel, on the right and left alike.

So have fundamentalists, in a great irony—indeed, fundamentalists perhaps above all. The real-Jesus project, though intended as a rebuke to biblical literalism, has ended up vindicating modern fundamentalism twice over. On the one hand, the self-understanding of fundamental-ists depends on the assumption that once you depart even an iota from a literal-factual-commonsensical reading of Scripture you're on a slippery slope to denying basic Christian dogmas—which of course is exactly what most of the historical Jesus popularizers believe as well! (The example of a figure like Ehrman, who lost his faith completely when he went to gradu-ate school and realized that actual human beings might have been involved in the composition of the gospels, is almost a parody of a fundamentalist cautionary tale.) At the same time, the way that many fundamentalists actually interpret the Bible—through Cyrus Scofield's dispensationalist framework—is precisely the sort of do-it-yourself Christianity that real-Jesus "scholarship" implicitly encourages. What are the Left Behind novels if not a "new fiction that takes as its starting point the central event in the Judaeo-Christian drama and reconciles that middle with a new story that reaches beyond old beginnings and endings"? Like Funk and Pagels and so many others, fundamentalists have fashioned a Jesus in their own image, and declared that he is good.

For a more specific example of how this works—how the work of "real Jesus" intellectuals influences American religious culture in ways that they would probably find horrifying—consider the following excerpt from an episode of Glenn Beck's radio show. This is the last place, in a sense, that one would expect to find echoes of accommodationist Christianity, since Beck is a right-wing Mormon who rather famously urged his Christian listeners to quit their denomination or congregation if it used the leftward-tilting term "social justice" in its literature. (Beck's broader theological commitments will be discussed in the last chapter.) And yet there it is:

Glenn: The Dead Sea Scrolls, you know what they are? Stu, do you
    know what the Dead Sea Scrolls are?

Stu: Well, of course I do . . .

Glenn: Now, c'mon, most people don't.

Stu: Well, I heard of them, I don't really know.

Glenn: You don't really know. You have no idea why they were there. . . . Even though I've explained this on this program a couple of times, I'm glad to see that even the people that work with me don't even listen. So here's what happened. When Constantine decided that he was going to cobble together an army, he did the Council of Nicea [*sic*], right, Pat?

Pat: Yea.

Glenn: The Council of Nicea, and what they did is brought all of the religious figures together, all the Christians and then they said, "OK, let's put together the Apostles' Creed, let's you know, you guys do it." So they brought all their religious scripture together, that's when the Bible was first bound and everything else. And then they said, "Anybody that disagrees with this is a heretic and off with their head!"

Well, that's what the Dead Sea Scrolls are. The Dead Sea Scrolls are those scriptures that people had at the time that they said, "They are destroying all of this truth." *Whether it's truth or not is up to the individual* [emphasis mine—RD], but at that time those people thought that this was something that needed to be preserved and so they rolled up the scrolls and put them in clay pots and they put them in the back of caves where no one could find them. They were hidden scripture because everything was being destroyed that disagreed with the Council of Nicea and Constantine. That's what those things are.[51]

As history, this is Dan Brown-esque stuff. (Beck is confusing the Dead Sea Scrolls with the Nag Hammadi documents and the Apostles' Creed with the Nicene Creed, and his description of the emperor Constantine's role in the formation of the canon is a *Da Vinci Code*–influenced fantasy.) As an example of the real Jesus project's cultural reach, it's genuinely remarkable. And if there is a purgatory, the members of the Jesus Seminar will probably spend their sojourn there listening to this monologue on an endless loop.

Such unlikely convergences explain why it makes sense to begin a discussion of heresy in America with the quest for the historical Jesus. Institutionally, liberal Christianity is as weak as it's ever been, and certainly less influential than the heresies we will turn to next. But in their attempts to distill a thoroughly modern Jesus from the challenging paradoxes of the New Testament, the leading lights of liberal faith have set the tone not only for the religious intelligentsia but for the broader religious culture as well— highbrow and lowbrow and everybrow in between. Their conclusions haven't carried the day, but their premises dominate American religion: No account of Christian origins is more authoritative than any other, "cafeteria" Christianity is more intellectually serious than the orthodox attempt to grapple with the entire New Testament buffet, and the only Jesus who really matters is the one you invent for yourself.

SIX

PRAY AND GROW RICH

The most influential work of popular theology published this century comes with a glossy gold dust jacket and a slew of celebrity blurbs on the back. Celebrity Texan blurbs, mostly: Chuck Norris loved the book; so did the former NBA coach Rudy Tomjanovich; so did the then-owner of the Houston Astros, Drayton McLane; so did David Carr, the Houston Texans' quarterback. The author himself gazes out from the front cover: his black hair is piled up and slick with gel; his hands are extended and touching at the fingertips; his smile is enormous, front teeth like piano keys or filed-down tusks. The book's title hovers like an angel above his left shoulder, promising *Your Best Life Now: 7 Steps to Living at Your Full Potential.*

This is Joel Osteen, a Houston-based preacher who inherited a 7,500-seat megachurch from his late father, John Osteen, in 1999, and parlayed his pastorship into the highest-rated religious television show in America, a trio of #1 *New York Times* bestsellers, and a home for his congregation, Lakewood Church, in Houston's 18,000-seat Compaq Center. In the fragmented landscape of American religion, Osteen comes as close to Billy Graham's level of popularity and influence as any contemporary evangelist—and his cultural empire is arguably larger than Graham's ever was. *Your Best Life Now* sold more than 4 million copies in the five years following its 2004 release, and it spawned a host of spin-offs—from *Daily Readings from Your Best Life Now* to a *Your Best Life Now 2006 Journal and Daily*

Calendar. Its 2007 sequel, *Become a Better You,* followed a similar trajectory, in sales and spin-offs alike. Osteen's weekly television show runs constantly on Daystar and the Trinity Broadcasting Network, both Christian channels—but also on network affiliates in all of the top thirty markets. (On a typical Sunday in Washington, D.C., in the mid-2000s, you could catch ten different showings of an Osteen service, on eight different channels.) Like Graham, Osteen courts a worldwide audience: More than 200 million people around the globe tune in to his broadcasts. And like Graham, he's been known to sell out Madison Square Garden.

But there the similarities end. Graham's persona was warm and inclusive, but theologically he preached a stark, stripped-down gospel—a series of altar calls, with eternity hanging in the balance and Christianity distilled to a yes or no for Christ. Osteen's message is considerably more upbeat. His God gives without demanding, forgives without threatening to judge, and hands out His rewards in this life rather than in the next. Where Graham was inclined to comments like "we're all on death row . . . the only way out of death row is Jesus," Osteen prefers cheerier formulations. "Too many times we get stuck in a rut, thinking we've reached our limits," he writes in *Your Best Life Now.* "But God wants us to constantly be increasing, to be rising to new heights. He wants to increase you in his wisdom and help you make better decisions. God wants to increase you financially, by giving you promotions, fresh ideas, and creativity."[1] And whereas Graham embodied evangelical Christianity's shift back toward the Christian mainstream, and the beginning of its disassociation from fundamentalist separatism, Osteen embodies a shift of a very different sort—the refashioning of Christianity to suit an age of abundance, in which the old war between monotheism and money seems to have ended, for many believers, in a marriage of God and Mammon.

In the 1980s, this marriage was associated with hucksters and charlatans—preachers who robbed their followers, slept with prostitutes, and sobbed on camera. But in twenty-first-century America, the gospel of wealth has come of age. By linking the spread of the gospel to the habits and mores of entrepreneurial capitalism, and by explicitly baptizing the pursuit of worldly gain, prosperity theology has helped millions of believers reconcile their religious faith with their nation's seemingly unbiblical wealth and un-Christian consumer culture.

As much as any trend in contemporary belief, the success of this message suggests that modernity and religious faith cannot only coexist but actually reinforce each other—so long as modernity means American capitalism, and religion means the Christian heresy that has made Joel Osteen famous, and also rich.

This message that God wants nothing more than to shower riches on believers has deep roots in American soil. Already in 1831, Alexis de Tocqueville noted the difficulty of ascertaining from American sermons "whether the principal object of religion is to procure eternal felicity in the other world or prosperity in this."[2] Victorian Social Darwinists like Russell Conwell, a Baptist minister and the founder of Temple University, chose the latter: Conwell's famous "Acres of Diamonds" sermon proclaimed that "it is your duty to get rich" and that "to make money honestly is to preach the gospel."[3] So did bestselling self-help books like *The Man Nobody Knows,* published amid the boom of the 1920s, which recast Christ as a savvy salesman and the twelve apostles as his smooth-running management team—an idea so compelling that it persists to the present day in business books like *The Leadership Lessons of Jesus* and *Jesus, CEO.*

But Osteen and his imitators are the heirs to a particular strain of prosperity preaching, which has its origin in the late-nineteenth-century movement known as New Thought. This was a loosely affiliated collection of ministers, authors, activists, and organizations, united by their belief in the extraordinary potential of the human mind. New Thought's practitioners argued that mental and spiritual realities shaped material events, that God (or "Infinite Intelligence," to the more secular-minded) pervaded the universe, and that the physical realities that human beings experienced—good health and bad, bankruptcy and success—had their origins in the mental and metaphysical spheres. Thus, prayer could lead to healing, and positive thinking to worldly wealth. The key was to recognize the spark of divinity within yourself and bring it into alignment with the divine spirit of the universe.

The ranks of New Thought practitioners were large, and the movement's heirs were numerous. (More of them will appear in the next chapter, which considers the contemporary cult of self-love and self-help.) Some New Thinkers prided themselves on having left religion behind entirely, insisting strenuously that theirs was an essentially scientific practice, with empirical methods, provable results, and no need for theology of any sort. (The claims of L. Ron Hubbard's Church of Scientology owe an obvious debt to this strain of New Thought.) Others favored an ecumenical spirituality that was "open at the top" to almost any sort of god, a tradition carried on today by figures like megaselling author Rhonda Byrne, whose mind-over-matter promises in books like *The Secret* ("You can have whatever you want in your life, no limits. But there's one catch: You have to feel good. And when you think about it, isn't that all you ever want?")[4] are punctuated by quotations from long-forgotten New Thought gurus.

But many more followers of New Thought believed that their system represented a fulfillment of the Christian gospel. After all, what did Jesus' career represent if not the triumph of the spiritual over the physical, of divine mind over earthly matter? What was Christian prayer, in the end, but a quest to bring the individual soul into alignment with God's purposes? "If you had faith like a grain of mustard seed," Jesus told his disciples, "you could say to this mulberry tree, 'Be uprooted and planted in the sea'; and it would obey you." Wasn't this a suggestion that true Christians should be able to bend the universe to their purposes through spiritual exertions alone?

This was the view of Mary Baker Eddy, whose Church of Christ, Scientist offered one of the more successful syntheses of Christianity and New Thought. Eddy was a classic New Thought figure: entrepreneurial, iron-willed, and prolific, with a story of personal healing to back up her claims of a supernatural mandate. As medical science advanced, however, Christian Science's emphasis on prayer-driven healing—and its rejection of nonspiritual medical treatments—cost Eddy's church prestige and membership. In the long run, New Thought's emphasis on the *financial* possibilities of prayer and positivity had a more profound impact on American Christianity than did Eddy's insistence on prayer as the highest form of medicine.

It was one of her fellow New Englanders, an obscure late-Victorian minister named E. W. Kenyon, whose theology enjoys the widest influence on contemporary faith. Like many of his contemporaries, Kenyon blurred the distinction between God and man, emphasizing God's immanence and man's perfectability, and going so far as to suggest "the believer is as much an Incarnation as Jesus of Nazareth."[5] It followed, then, that the believer could potentially wield a near-omnipotent power through the act of prayer—which, Kenyon argued, wasn't a matter of supplication but a legal transaction. In the incarnation, death, and resurrection of Jesus Christ, he suggested, God had given believers "the power of attorney," and by calling on the name of Jesus and making a "positive confession" of belief, a Christian had the right not only to ask things of God but to "demand" them. So, faithful Christians need never experience poor health—or, more important, financial difficulty. "God never planned that we should live in poverty, either physical, mental or spiritual," Kenyon wrote in his *Advanced Bible Course*. "He made Israel go to the head of the nations financially. When we go into partnership with Him, and we learn his way of doing business, we cannot be failures."[6]

Kenyon died in 1948, neither a failure nor a great success, and his career would be a footnote to American religious history were it not for the efforts of a preacher named Kenneth W. Hagin. Born in Texas in 1917, Hagin suffered from a congenital heart defect that at the age of fifteen left him partially paralyzed and confined to bed for sixteen months. Delirious and near death, he experienced a series of descents into hell and received a pair of revelations: "Here is the principle of faith: believe in your heart, say it with your mouth, and 'he shall have whatsoever he saith.'"[7] What he wanted was healing, and it came. Hagin's crisis passed, and he lived to be eighty-six.

By then he was famous in the world of evangelical Christianity, widely revered (and sometimes vilified) as the founder and "grand-daddy" of the "Word-Faith" movement—a widespread network of churches, schools, and other ministries bound together by a common belief in a "name it and claim it" theology, in which believers can exercise the same world-changing power as God, so long as they "think God's thoughts after him and speak his words after him." It's a theology best summed up by the title of a Hagin pamphlet: *Write Your Own Ticket with God*.

Though Hagin attributed this message to divine revelation, he actually plagiarized huge chunks of E. W. Kenyon's writing over the years. Nearly all of the Word-Faith theology has obvious roots in Kenyon's work, from the contractual nature of prayer and the near-divinization of the individual believer to the conviction that Christians who suffered failure and privation

PRAY AND GROW RICH 187

had only themselves to blame. But whereas Kenyon's newsletter had twenty thousand subscribers, Hagin reached an audience of millions and lived to see a generation of preachers seize his appealing, intensely American theology and run with it—Joel Osteen's father among them.

You can watch many of these preachers at work every week on Osteen *fils*'s broadcast home, Trinity Broadcast Network, the largest Christian network in the country, which is carried on six thousand television stations and reaches 5 million households every week in the United States alone. TBN was founded in 1973 by Paul Crouch and his wife, Jan, in a partnership with Jim and Tammy Faye Bakker. Since then the Crouches have successfully weathered various controversies—the Bakker scandals in the 1980s, the hush money paid to a former employee who alleged a gay encounter with Paul Crouch—while shepherding a ministry that takes in over $170 million a year, two-thirds of it from viewer contributions.[8]

Their network provides a home to Kenneth and Gloria Copeland, a husband-wife team who were mentored by Hagin; the website for the Copelands' program, *Believer's Voice of Victory*, once called for donations to purchase his-and-her Cessna Citation X jets, so that "when God tells Kenneth to travel to South Africa and hold a three-day Victory Campaign, he won't have to wait to make commercial travel arrangements."[9] It broadcasts Creflo Augustus Dollar Jr., the flamboyant African-American pastor of Atlanta's World Changers megachurch; he's the author of *Total Life Prosperity: 14 Practical Steps to Receiving God's Full Blessing,* and his own full blessing includes Rolls-Royces, bespoke suits, and (again) a private jet. It showcases Frederick K. C. Price, another black preacher, who once told an audience that Jesus Christ must have been rich, because why else would he have needed Judas as his treasurer? It airs the preaching of the endlessly fascinating Benny Hinn, with his bouffant hair and his Nehru jacket, his huge overseas rallies, his team of bodyguards and the multimillion-dollar Southern California mansion. Hinn, though, has reportedly expressed skepticism about the Word-Faith formula, preferring to speculate instead about whether there might actually be nine persons in the Trinity and whether Adam possessed supernatural powers and flew to the Moon.

Evangelists like Hinn and the Copelands represent an older generation of prosperity preachers—enthusiastic to a fault, crassly materialistic, lachrymose, and tacky. The newer generation is cut from a much more mainstream cloth. Gone are the garish outfits, the naked appeals for cash, and the extraordinary, ripe-for-debunking claims of healing. As Hanna Rosin put it, in an *Atlantic* essay on the prosperity gospel's expanding influence: "Instead of shiny robes or gaudy jewelry, these preachers wear Italian suits and modest wedding bands. Instead of screaming and sweating, they smile broadly and speak in soothing, therapeutic terms."[10]

This is a good description of Joyce Meyer, who has emerged as perhaps the most popular and mainstream of TBN's preachers apart from Osteen. An ex-housewife with a twelfth-grade education, as she often describes herself, Meyer endured childhood sexual abuse and a failed marriage before finding her calling as the author of more than fifty inspirational books, and as the face of the *Life in the Word* television show, which airs in forty-three states and seventy countries. Her goal, according to a recent slogan, is "Every nation, every city, every day." On the page and in person, she seems less like a celebrity preacherette in the Tammy Faye Bakker or Gloria Copeland mode, and more like the sensible Christian housewife next door. She dresses simply and talks bluntly, offering earthy, self-deprecating pep talks that emphasize emotional well-being and then slip the promise of financial success in between the lines.

That promise is still crucial to Meyer's appeal. "The whole Bible really has one message: 'Obey me and do what I tell you to do, and you'll be blessed,'" she told the *St. Lous Post-Dispatch* in 2004, when it ran a series of stories revealing just how blessed she has been.[11] (These blessings include, yes, a private jet.) But she's careful not to flaunt her wealth, and she's more restrained in her pray-and-grow-rich preaching than the earlier generation of prosperity apostles.

The same is true of Osteen. Since taking over his father's church, he has refused to identify explicitly with the Word-Faith movement, and distanced himself from the more extreme claims of its preachers. "I never preach that whatever you say, you can get," he told a reporter in 2005.[12] Instead, he offers a more careful and conditional version of the Kenyon-Hagin gospel, in which the idea that believers can pray and grow rich is constantly implied but rarely stated baldly.

Osteen doesn't claim, for instance, that God wants you to be promoted; he says instead that "When God wants you to be promoted, it doesn't matter whether your boss likes you or not. . . . God is in control."[13] He doesn't exactly tell his readers to say "I want a Cadillac"; he tells them to "quit complaining about poverty and lack and start declaring, 'God supplies all my needs in abundance.'"[14] He doesn't necessarily promise his readers that God will give them a big house and then help them get full market value when it's time to sell it; he just tells stories about how God has blessed *him* with a big house and then blessed him with a buyer who happened to pay the whole sticker price.

The message is still clear. Osteen's God may not necessarily be contractually obligated to supply his faithful with everything they ask for, as Kenyon's original theology would have it. But He still seems less like a savior than like a college buddy with really good stock tips, which are more or less guaranteed to pay off for any Christian bold enough to act on them. "Ask and ye shall receive" is the central tenet of Osteen's Christianity—not money alone, but all the accoutrements of the modern good life: the big house and the beautiful children, the new Lexus and the successful real estate investments. And where Christ told his disciples not to worry about material possessions—because *the lilies of the field neither toil nor spin, and yet I tell you, even Solomon in all his glory was not arrayed like one of these*—Osteen is slightly more crass: "If somebody cheats you out of some money," he advises, your response should be: "No big deal. God's promised me double."[15]

The crudeness of this rhetoric can obscure the subtlety of its appeal. There's an assumption that Christianity's traditional critique of Mammon worship is aimed primarily at the richest of the rich—the people who are most likely to resemble the camel struggling to nose its way through the needle's eye, as the gospel image has it. But there's a reason that the disciples responded to Jesus' famous simile with a shocked "Who then can be saved?" They understood, as many of today's casual readers might not, that the image implies a broader condemnation of acquisitiveness in all its forms. In Christian teaching, the pursuit of money can be as morally dangerous as the possession of great wealth, and the middle-class striver may be as steeped in sinfulness as an Andrew Carnegie or a Donald Trump. In the story of the camel and the needle's eye, the disciples recognized, all men stand condemned—not because we are all rich, but because almost all of us desire to be so and too often organize our lives around that desire.

This is a hard teaching in any society, but especially in one as steeped in capitalist competition as our own. It feels like a monk's creed, and yet most churches insist that the average Christian isn't necessarily called to be a monk. Instead, believers are expected to be active participants in society, to be breadwinners and home owners and business proprietors, to be fruitful and multiply and then support their kids, all without succumbing to the siren song of greed, acquisitiveness, and wealth-worship. *In the world but not of it,* the admonition runs, but that's an awfully difficult balance to strike when you're angling for a promotion or hoping for a bonus, or just hunting for a job to pay the bills. The stringency of Christianity's sexual teachings gets most of the press, but the commandment against avarice, if taken seriously, can be the faith's most difficult by far. You can wall yourself off from pornography and avoid people who tempt you into adultery, but everybody has to work—and every day in the workplace is a potential occasion of sin.

The prosperity gospel does away with this anxiety. Like most heresies, it resolves one of orthodoxy's tensions by emphasizing one part of Christian doctrine—in this case, the idea that the things of this life are gifts from the Creator, rather than simply snares to be avoided, and that Christians are expected to participate in the world rather than withdraw from it. Then it effaces the harder teachings that traditionally balance it out. The result is a message that's tailored less to the very rich than to the middle and working classes—to people who are hardworking but financially insecure, who feel that they have to think about money all the time because they're trying to make more of it, and who want to be reassured that their striving is in accordance with God's plan rather than a threat to their salvation. The stereotype of the prosperity gospel involves a rich preacher fleecing the gullible poor, growing fat off their donations while promising God-given blessings that never materialize. But the reality is just as likely to involve ministers who prosper by flattering their upwardly mobile, American Dreaming congregations, telling them to keep on striving and praying, because God wants them to keep up with the Joneses next door.

Of course, some of them won't keep up, the promises of their pastors notwithstanding. But the "name it and claim it" school of prosperity theology resolves this difficulty as well, solving the problem of suffering by recasting it as a simple failure of piety and willpower. It's a brilliant solution to the riddle of theodicy: while orthodox Christianity suggests that evil is a mystery to be endured, the Word-Faith gospel suggests that evil is something that can be mastered, through a combination of spiritual exertion and the divine intervention it summons up. If you fail to master everyday events, and fall into struggles and suffering, it's a sign that you just haven't prayed hard enough, or trusted faithfully enough, or thought big enough, or otherwise behaved the way a child of God really should. The fault where any evil is concerned, in other words, lies not with God, the devil, or the fallen-ness of creation but with you—so stop whining about your troubles, get down on your knees, and do something about it!

Such a message may sound cruel. But it can also be strangely comforting, since it makes sense of one of Christianity's more difficult dilemmas, and then suggests, in fine American style, that there's always something you can do about your troubles. (Pray harder! Trust more! Widen your horizons!) And it has a further appeal in our disenchanted age, because it simultaneously preserves orthodox Christianity's emphasis on prayers, miracles, and divine actions—on a God who loves and cares and intervenes—while avoiding anything too medieval or visceral-seeming. In prosperity theology, there's no need for bleeding statues or levitating saints to prove that God acts in history or that He answers individual prayers. Everyday blessings and ordinary triumphs are the miracles, if you're seeing things "in the supernatural." That promotion, that new car, that long-awaited child or family reconciliation—they're all instances of divine providence responding to your petitions, and holding up heaven's end of the bargain Jesus made.

When you ask God for help, in other words, He doesn't need to send an angel or an apparition to prove His love for you and prove your prayer's power over earthly powers and principalities. He can just send you a raise.

Trinity Broadcasting Network is ground zero for this message, and Joel Osteen its most popular proponent. But the prosperity gospel influences a much broader swath of American Christianity as well. It thrives in the Sun Belt and in megachurches. In her *Atlantic* essay, Rosin cites research suggesting that 50 of the 260 largest churches in America now preach prosperity theology. It's immensely popular among recent immigrants, whose ambitions it validates and whose aspirations it supports. According to a 2008 Pew survey, among Hispanics who described themselves as religious, 73 percent agreed that "God will grant financial success to all believers who have enough faith."[16]

In African-American Christianity, too, prosperity theology has become steadily more mainstream in recent decades. The black church's "pray and grow rich" tradition dates back to flamboyant Depression-era evangelists like Sweet Daddy Grace (born Marcelino Manoel de Graça) and Father Divine (born George Baker), as well as midcentury figures like the pioneering radio preacher Reverend Ike (born Frederick J. Eikerenkoetter II), who preached a New Thought–style gospel of mind over matter from a renovated Harlem movie theater. But as denominational ties have weakened, more and more authority has passed to a generation of superstar pastors who either flirt with prosperity theology or else embrace it outright—figures like Dollar and Price, Houston's Kirbyjon Caldwell (who delivered the benediction at both of George W. Bush's inaugurations), Atlanta's Bishop Eddie Long, and many others.

Prior to the civil rights era, the African-American prosperity churches' explicit materialism often made a deliberate contrast with the "the Gospel of 'otherworldliness'"—to borrow Ralph Abernathy's exasperated phrase—preached in many more traditional black congregations. "Don't wait for pie in the sky by-and-by when you die!" Reverend Ike was known to shout. "Get yours now with ice cream on top!"[17] Since the 1960s, though, the prosperity gospel has increasingly filled a different sort of void—the one created by "official" African-American theology's hyperpolitical turn. Amid the country's Vietnam-era convulsions, the black church's intelligentsia followed the same trajectory as many Mainline liberals, abandoning the neo-orthodox sensibility that informed Martin Luther King Jr.'s early thought in favor of more explicitly political interpretations of gospel—revolutionary, quasi-Marxist, Afrocentric, et cetera. But as the radical mood burned itself out and a black middle class began to gain its footing, the black clergy's preoccupation with structural critiques of the white man's "isms" (capitalism, imperialism, and so on) became less and less obviously relevant to the everyday lives of their potential parishioners.

Prosperity preachers stepped into this breach, ministering to a growing black bourgeoisie that doesn't see its own struggles reflected in the kind of Vietnam-vintage theology urged on them by a Cornel West or a Jeremiah Wright.

In his thoughtful book on black televangelists, *Watch This!,* Jonathan L. Walton takes note of this disconnect. Emerging from seminary steeped in radical theology, he writes, he was ready to preach a God who "offered liberation from racial and gender injustice and capitalist exploitation." But "I soon discovered that my academic experience of the God of the 'freedom-fighting black church' did not necessarily jibe with the Jesus that the black people in suburban Atlanta desired to know firsthand."[18] This was something that many of his fellow theology students had already realized:

> I have noticed that many African American students embrace [the superstar pastor] phenomenon as a guilty pleasure. Influenced by the social pressures and sense of shame imposed on students by the academic environment, they stash away Bishop Noel Jones and Reverend Jamal Harrison-Bryant videos in dorm rooms like some sort of spiritual porn collection that can be viewed in privacy. The videos offer a fantasy (of mass appeal, public acclaim, luxurious living) that many who have received a "call" to ministry privately indulge but refuse to admit that they will probably never experience. All the while, both professors and students contribute to the resounding silence, particularly in African American theological education, where the black liberal Protestant theologies and a black theology of liberation make a poor fit with the sensibilities of the increasing number of students informed by Trinity Broadcasting Network.[19]

For many of these celebrity preachers, white as well as black, prosperity theology turns out to be natural fit with Pentecostalist and charismatic styles of worship. When students of religion analyze the rise of Pentecostalism, they usually focus on the ecstastic prayer services, the reports of physical healing, and the insistence that the spiritual gifts of the early Church (such as speaking in tongues and prophecy) are available to present-day believers. But from the moment of its birth, in a famous 1906 outbreak of glossolalia in Los Angeles's Azusa Street Church, Pentecostalism has been a fertile field for prosperity theology as well. The movement's emphasis on the extraordinary power of prayer dovetails neatly with the tenets of New Thought. Its demographic base—blacks, immigrants, the white petite bourgeoisie—has an understandable interest in a gospel of upward mobility. Its distance from the institutions and traditions of both Catholicism and Reformation-era Protestantism creates a theological vacuum that the prosperity gospel's boosters are more than eager to fill. And Pentecostalism's entrepreneurial structure, in which every church is effectively a start-up, has always attracted ministers prone to the kind of self-aggrandizement that's more easily justified by prosperity theology than by more orthodox strands of Christian faith.

Small wonder, then, that from the Jazz Age evangelist Aimee Semple McPherson down to TBN's nightly lineup of televangelists, Pentecostalist worship and prosperity preaching have been consistently intertwined. Indeed, prosperity theology may actually be eclipsing ecstatic prayer as the defining attribute of modern charismatic Christianity. As *Christianity Today*'s Ted Olsen noted in 2006, only half of American Pentecostalists report having spoken in tongues—but 66 percent agreed with the premise that "God grants believers wealth."[20]

Crucially, though, it isn't just Pentecostalists who think this way. The same survey found that 43 percent of "other Christians"—white and black, Catholic, Mainline, and Evangelical alike—concurred that the Almighty showers riches on believers.[21] While the prosperity gospel's proselytizers have been moving steadily into the Christian mainstream, in other words, the mainstream has been moving to meet them.

Three years before Osteen's *Your Best Life Now* hit shelves, the break-out evangelical Christian book of the moment—complete with its own line of spin-offs and study guides—was *The Prayer of Jabez,* a ninety-page pamphlet by an evangelical pastor named Bruce Wilkinson. Jabez is a minor Old Testament figure, part of the genealogy of Judah; his story takes up two verses in the Book of Chronicles:

> Now Jabez was more honorable than his brothers, and his mother called his name Jabez, saying, "Because I bore him in pain." And Jabez

called upon the God of Israel saying, "Oh, that you would bless me indeed, and enlarge my territory, that your hand might be with me, and that you would keep me from evil, that I may not cause pain!" So God granted what he requested.

From this modest thread, Wilkinson weaves a theological tapestry in which the prayer of Jabez is the key to "breaking through to the blessed life," the realm in which countless "unclaimed blessings" are just waiting to be handed out to believers.[22] But where Osteen and the "name it and claim it" crowd tend to define these blessings in material terms—good health, a raise, a suburban McMansion—Wilkinson's pamphlet conflates personal success with Christian missionary work. When God "enlarges your territory," he's also enlarging his own. While Osteen speckles his text with examples of all the material comfort God has doled out to him, Wilkinson speaks the language of evangelization. He describes addressing the student body at a Christian college and telling them to pray "for more blessing and greater influence"—and offers this example of what "influence" might mean:

> "Why not look at a globe and pick an island," I suggested. "When you
> have picked it out, put together a team of students, charter an airliner,
> and take over the island for God . . .
>   "You should ask God for Trinidad," I said. "And a DC-10."[23]

Of course, not everyone is called to claim Third World countries for Christ. "If Jabez had worked on Wall Street," Wilkinson writes, "he might have prayed, 'Lord, increase the value of my investment portfolios.'" Any worldly success can be sanctified, so long as it's approached as a form of missionary work. "Your business," *The Prayer of Jabez* explains, "is the territory God has entrusted to you. He wants you to accept it as a significant opportunity to touch individual lives, the business community, and the larger world for His glory."[24]

The theology of Jabez is a feel-good distillation of the way that many Evangelicals reconcile their Christian faith with the demands and temptations of late modern capitalism. The Evangelical compromise with Mammon is more complex and indirect than the Word-Faith movement's almost childlike delight in material abundance, but it's an accommodation nonetheless—in which piety mixes with middle-class anxiety and aspiration, and it's difficult to tell where the missionary spirit ends and the entrepreneurial spirit begins.

Consider a figure like T. D. Jakes, who is probably America's most successful African-American pastor, with thousands of worshippers thronging his Potter's House megachurch and millions of readers snapping up his books. Jakes's ministry's emphasis on upward mobility and his Pentecostalist background (along with his own personal fortune) often prompt critics to lump him in with the Creflo Dollars and Joyce Meyers of the world. But Jakes is a critic of the Word-Faith movement, and his theology of wealth is somewhat more complex than "ask and ye shall receive." In *The Great Investment: Balancing Faith, Family, and Finance to Build a Rich Spiritual Life* (2000), he argues that there are two mistakes a Christian can make—becoming a "monk" and becoming a "prosperity preacher." Both have an "extreme" view of wealth, he argues; the key for Christians is to pursue a middle way, seeking financial success without becoming "controlled" by their ambitions—like the apostle Paul, say, who "was both a preacher and a businessman."[25]

Or consider a more obscure but equally significant figure: The late Larry Burkett, whose career almost perfectly encapsulates the mainstream Evangelical accommodation with moneymaking. Burkett was the managing vice-president of a small electronics firm in Titusville, Florida, when he converted to Christianity in 1971, under the influence of his wife, the local Southern Baptist congregation, and the Gospel of John. "I knew I was not going to stay in the electronics field," Burkett wrote years later, but he had the soul of a businessman, and it wasn't long before he found himself taking a highlighter and marking every passage in the Bible that deals with personal finance—seven hundred verses all told, which he eventually organized into a "financial concordance" of Scripture, the better to rebut those members of his Bible study who claimed that the Almighty wasn't that concerned with how His people managed their money.[26]

Over the next two decades, Burkett built one of the most successful "financial ministries" in the history of American Christianity. (A biographer wrote that Burkett "almost single-handedly created 'money' and 'finance' sections in the nation's Christian bookstores.")[27] In the advice he offered, Burkett was always careful to dismiss "the prosperity peddlers" and to reject the notion that wealth was in any way a direct reward for good-ness or generosity. Yet, like Jakes, Burkett also dismissed those "stoics" who "believe that to follow Jesus a Christian must sell everything and become a pauper," insisting instead that "God wants us to lead a comfortable life."[28] He preached a doctrine of "radical" financial surrender, but this surrender turned out to be entirely spiritual: the money "belongs" to the Almighty, but it stays safely in the individual Christian's bank account or investment portfolio.

Even more than the pure prosperity gospel, this turns out to be a re-ligious path ideally suited to an upwardly mobile society. It disciplines believers against excess and folly by insisting that they always tithe, think of the poor, and keep God uppermost in their minds. At the same time, it frees them to be as ambitious and acquisitive as their secular neighbors, so long as they put their ambitions in the service of Christian faith. ("How much more impact these good Christians could have had," Jakes writes of his less financially savvy Pentecostalist forebears, "if they availed them-selves of the riches the world offered?"[29]) And it's particularly well suited to successful church-building, where it translates into what the sociologist Michael Hamilton has memorably described as a theology of "more money, more ministry."[30]

Early in the twentieth century, Evangelical Christians tended to take a lilies-of-the-field attitude to financing their ministries, following what the president of the Dallas Theological Seminary described in 1945 as the theory that "if we were worthy and were faithful in prayer, no fund-raising activity would be necessary."[31] But from the post–World War II era onward, this model was replaced by a more entrepreneurial approach. As Hamilton writes, "leaders of evangelical organizations scrambled to lay claim to as much of the new American wealth as they could"—not for their own enrichment (or not always), but for the sake of spreading the Gospel.[32]

This "more money, more ministry" logic underlies not only the growth of big-budget megachurches and parachurch organizations like Campus Crusade for Christ and Promise Keepers, but also the vast, multibillion-dollar Evangelical culture industry that has sprung up to peddle Christian pop music and Left Behind–style page-turners, biblical action figurines, and Scripture mints. Its success is part of the larger story of Evangelical suc-cess and Mainline Protestant decline. Earlier, we considered the Mainline's collapse primarily in terms of theology and belief, but there's an economic component as well. Religion is about the search for God, but it's also about the search for a community, which means different things to different searchers—or shoppers, to be a bit more cynical about it. Some believers are looking for a day care center, concession stands, an upbeat sermon and a kick-ass choir—hence the megachurch explosion. Others want the comfort of a small group and kitchen table—hence the boom in "mini-churches" and house churches. Still others want both—a network of small "cells" woven into a huge congregation. Whatever a given Christian is looking for, in the competition for congregants, the older denominations are like command economies—centralized, inflexible, and inefficient. Whereas the more freewheeling Evangelical world, in which pastors compete to "enlarge their territory," tends to be more dynamic, more adaptable, and capable of leaving its more static rivals in the dust.

So the entrepreneurial churches attract more customers—and they also attract a more entrepreneurial crop of would-be leaders, by offering men of the cloth the chance to be empire-building CEOs. Leaders like Rick Warren, for instance, the bestselling author of *The Purpose-Driven Life,* who shot to the top of the Evangelical food chain by applying the insights of management guru Peter Drucker to church-building. Or James Dobson, the child psychologist turned political kingmaker, who presided over Focus on the Family, a (not-for-profit) organization so large that its headquarters, on an eighty-one-acre campus in Colorado, requires its own ZIP code. Or Pat Robertson, whose Regent University became one of the country's largest for-profit schools and who sold his International Family Entertainment Inc. to Fox in 1997 for $1.9 billion. Or nearly every nationally known evangelical pastor, all of whom are busy building their own media kingdoms.

Many of these figures would be horrified to hear themselves associated with prosperity theology, of course. Warren, who donates his royalties to charity, has been particularly eloquent in his critique of the Word-Faith movement's theology: "This idea that God wants everybody to be wealthy?" he said to *Time* magazine in 2006. "There is a word for that: baloney. It's creating a false idol. You don't measure your self-worth by your net worth. I can show you millions of faithful followers of Christ who live in poverty. Why isn't everyone in the church a millionaire?"[33]

But Warren's wisdom (and personal generosity) notwithstanding, the line between his model of Christian witness—the pastor as businessman, the spiritual leader as entrepreneur—and Joel Osteen's straightforward pray-and-grow-rich theology can get blurry. The "more money, more ministry" ethos isn't necessarily heretical. At its best (and purest), it can feel like a fulfillment of Jesus' admonition to believers to be as wise as serpents, and not just as innocent as doves, and to use the ways of the world to convert the world when necessary. But it also carries a whiff of late medieval Catholicism's blithe and foolhardy assumption that even the most worldly ways of living and thinking can be turned to Christian ends, so long as they supply the funding for the propagation of the gospel. Amid all the stewardship and the investing, the careful philanthropy and the fast-growing congregations, the "more money, more ministry" attitude doesn't always leave much space for more radical religious gestures and more ascetic ways of faith, for aspirations at once grander and more humble, or for a sustained Christian critique of capitalism's excesses as well as an accommodation to its benefits and perks.

It was American Catholicism, with its emphasis on personal asceticism and social solidarity, that long offered the most prominent alternative to the marriage of God and Mammon. In part, this critique was explicitly political. *Rerum Novarum,* Pope Leo XIII's 1891 encyclical, rejected Marxist calls to abolish private property and tried to steer a middle ground between the errors of collectivism and the evils of unfettered capitalism. Yet the Pope's insistence that the state should pursue "distributive justice" and "the benefit of the working classes" suggested a strong Catholic affinity for significant wealth redistribution.[34] This developed into a long-standing consensus that, as Pope Benedict XVI put it recently, "democratic socialism was and is close[r] to Catholic social doctrine" than the Anglo-Saxon capitalist alternative.[35]

At the same time, poverty and renunciation were woven into the fabric of everyday American Catholic life. Catholicism was an immigrant's faith and the Church's abundance of vocations meant that a life of vowed poverty occupied a place of honor in Catholic communities, even if most believers didn't share in it. No matter how mainstream or prosperous

Catholics became, the heroes of the American Church were nearly always figures who had renounced the world—from nineteenth-century saints like Elizabeth Ann Seton and Frances Cabrini down through Eisenhower-era religious celebrities like Thomas Merton and Dorothy Day. The pre–Vatican II Church was freighted with more than its share of pomp and circumstance, of course. But it also offered near-constant contact with examples of asceticism, and it placed such examples at the heart of Catholic identity.

Since the collapse in vocations in the 1960s and 1970s, such contact is no longer available to most American Catholics. Fewer and fewer Catholics have Fathers for brothers or Sisters for sisters; fewer and fewer Catholic schools can staff their classrooms with the nuns and priests who once educated most of America's Catholic youth; fewer and fewer parishes have more than one overstressed, overworked, spread-too-thin priest to personally embody Catholicism's solidarity with the poor. The institutional Church is still theoretically committed to such solidarity, but it lacks the numbers necessary to make that commitment manifest in a comprehensive, culturally significant way.

It lacks, as well, the easy confidence with which the New Deal generation of American Catholics embraced welfare-state liberalism and the Democratic Party. That confidence was shaken, like so many things, in the upheavals of the sexual revolution, when American liberalism gradually adopted a social agenda that was explicitly at odds with Catholic teaching. Over the ensuing decades, as the country as a whole tilted rightward and the Republican Party began to seem like an attractive home, some Catholics began to consider the possibility that the older understanding of capitalism had been mistaken. Far from being a threat to Christianity, the free market might be a positive good—the economic system best suited to mankind's fallen nature.

This case was made with particular eloquence by the Catholic neoconservative Michael Novak. In 1982, early in Ronald Reagan's presidency, he published *The Spirit of Democratic Capitalism,* the most impressive attempt to reconcile Catholic theology to the market-driven society. Like John Courtney Murray criticizing the Vatican's hostility to liberal democracy a generation earlier, Novak argued that the traditional Catholic presumption against market capitalism—which the Church associated with Anglo-

America, Protestantism, individualism, and atomized modernity—was inherited from a static, medieval world that no longer existed. The modern free-market system is actually perfectly compatible with Christian doctrine, even if many Catholics have failed to realize it.

In their "due recognition of the errant human heart, whose liberty they respect," Novak argued, capitalist societies "follow the example of the Creator who knows what is in humans—who hates sin but permits it for the sake of liberty, who suffers from it but remains faithful to his sinful children." The realization, by Adam Smith and others, that permitting sin for liberty's sake and "putting less stress on moral purposes" might actually lead to greater good—"the abolition of famine, the raising up of the poor, and the banishment of material suffering"—represented not only a moral breakthrough, but "even, if you please, a theological breakthrough."[36]

This breakthrough trades on the ambitions of an acquisitive, competitive humanity, Novak allowed, but then again competition is an integral part of Christianity as well: the "critics who sometimes suggest that competitiveness is foreign to a religion of love, meekness and peace . . . have no idea how hard it is to be meeker than one's neighbor."[37] Therefore, he concluded:

> It is wrong to imagine that the spirit of competition is foreign to the gospels, and that, in particular, competition for money is humankind's most mortal spiritual danger. Under God, a wealthy nation faces an especially harsh judgment, but that judgment will not be aimed so much at the existence of wealth as at the character of the uses made of it. On Judgment Day, the rich may find it especially hard to get through the eye of the needle, but this will not be because they had money but because their use of it will be subjected to an accounting on different ledgers from those scrutinized by the Internal Revenue Service. The rich have reason to tremble. If their wealth has been productive for others, though, the world has reason to be merciful to them even if God's standards are higher.[38]

Over the decade that followed, Novak expanded on these arguments, in books like *The Catholic Ethic and the Spirit of Capitalism* and *Business*

As a Calling, and his rightward turn mirrored the journey that many of his co-religionists made—from diehard Democrats to staunch Republicans, and from instinctive statists to supporters, reluctant or enthusiastic, of free-market capitalism.

Meanwhile, the events and trends that followed its publication seemed largely to vindicate *The Spirit of Democratic Capitalism.* Communism collapsed less than a decade after Novak's book was published. Welfare states the world over began renovating themselves in a more free-market direction. Pope John Paul II even seemed to partially endorse Novak's argument a decade later, in the encyclical *Centesimus Annus* (published on the anniversary of *Rerum Novarum*). Meanwhile, the fate of Western Europe seemed to offer a cautionary tale for Catholic social democrats. The post–World War II architects of Europe's welfare states were often devout Catholics—Jean Monnet and Konrad Adenauer, Robert Schuman and Alcide De Gasperi—and their efforts represented a far more comprehensive attempt than even the Catholic-backed New Deal to weave the Church's social doctrine into politics. Yet, fifty years after the seeming triumph of Catholicism's preferred approach to political economy, the declining birthrates and empty churches of Italy and France and Germany suggested that large-scale efforts to impose God's justice on a fallen world may erode the very religious beliefs that motivated the efforts in the first place. Indeed, they may even undercut the very demographic foundation of civilization, by making it too easy to live in a comfortable and childless present and let the future take care of itself.

By contrast, the risks and shocks of commerce and competition may help explain why Americans remain more religious and more fecund than our continental cousins. Perhaps the uncertainties of a capitalist economy make us cling more tightly to the promises of God; perhaps the absence of a cradle-to-the-grave welfare state encourages us to rely on the networks of family and community instead. If so, then this suggests in turn that some kind of Christian compromise with Mammon—perhaps not the excesses of the prosperity gospel, but at the very least the understanding that capitalism is the economic system best suited to man's fallen nature—might be necessary to the faith's survival in the modern age.

*   *   *

But is faith that's made its peace with the free market, that prefers laissez-faire to government redistribution and finds theological justifications for the pursuit of worldly gain, really recognizably Christian? This is the critique often leveled by what remains of the religious left, Protestant and Catholic alike—that the marriage of God and Mammon is nothing more than Social Darwinism with a religious face. Joel Osteen and Company may be studiously apolitical, Michael Novak may urge believers to "make their wealth productive for others," and T. D. Jakes may insist on the importance of tithing—but in the real world, this argument goes, a gospel that blesses prosperity leads only to private selfishness and public squalor. It encourages believers to ignore the poor, keep the best of everything for themselves . . . and, worst of all, vote Republican.

"America," Bill McKibben complained in *Harper's* magazine in 2006, "is simultaneously the most professedly Christian of the developed nations and the least Christian in its behavior."[39] He went on to catalogue America's sins: we give less in foreign aid than any developed nation save Italy; we trail the developed world on a host of indicators, from infant mortality to child poverty to childhood nutrition; we keep our taxes low even as schools fail and people go hungry; we don't have (or didn't have) universal health care and we execute and imprison our citizens at unusually high clips; we reward Republican candidates who perform the "outrageous con" of "making Christ the front man for a program of tax cuts for the rich."[40]

But the picture is more complicated than this. Americans give more money to private charity, by far, than any other developed nation—donations totaled 2.3 percent of our GDP in 2007, more than twice as much as England, the next-most-generous Western country.[41] A study of giving in the year 2000 found that religious Americans gave almost four times much money to charity as their secular neighbors, and volunteered more than twice as often as well. (They were also more likely to give money to family and friends.)[42] And Evangelical Christians—who are the most compromised Christians of all, if you follow McKibben's line of reasoning, because they vote for the GOP and its tax-cutting policies in the greatest numbers—are also the most generous major religious group in the United States. True, much of this money goes to religious charities, but much of it doesn't: churchgoers are more likely than nonchurchgoers to give to nonreligious charities as well.[43]

Nor is there any evidence that the prosperity gospel's recent progress has made Americans notably less generous. As a percentage of GDP, philanthropy in the United States was as high in the Bush years as in any era since the 1960s.[44] Nor, as is often alleged, has the rise of the religious right produced a generation of Christians who worry more about sex than poverty: for every dollar American Evangelicals spend on political action, they spend $12 on foreign missions and international relief efforts.[45] If anything, increasing Christian involvement in conservative politics has coincided with a return of Evangelical dollars to social reform, reversing the early-twentieth-century Evangelical disengagement from the wider culture.

Consider the trajectory of Evangelicalism's overseas work. In the first half of the twentieth century, before the idea of "more money, more ministry" took hold, funds tended to be funneled exclusively into planting churches and winning converts. But by the late 1990s, six of the seven largest overseas parachurch organizations (all of them founded after 1945) were focused on development, health care, and education, with evangelization as a secondary concern. Africa, in particular, has benefited from an outpouring of evangelical generosity. Rick Warren made his name by fusing megachurch Christianity with the science of marketing, but his Purpose-Driven earnings were funneled into a crusade against AIDS in Africa, among other noble causes. T. D. Jakes's Potter's House ministers to a well-heeled congregation, but his church is also heavily invested in development work in Kenya. Bruce Wilkinson could have coasted into retirement on the royalties from *The Prayer of Jabez*, but instead his "enlarge-your-territory" theology carried him to Swaziland, where he announced plans to house and feed the children left homeless by HIV.

None of this is to say that McKibben and other left-wing critics are wrong to snipe at Evangelical Christians for identifying too strongly with the Republican Party. But the popularity of the prosperity gospel among blacks and Hispanics—neither exactly reliable Republican constituencies—suggests that it's too easy to assume that the marriage of God and Mammon leads inexorably toward conservative policy prescriptions. And while it's easy to get in digs at self-satisfied megachurchgoers, the idea that they aren't concerned about the less fortunate won't quite wash.

In reality, prosperity theology's greatest weaknesses are often qualities that it *shares* with the Christian socialism of its fiercest critics: an emphasis on the social utility of belief, an eagerness to define spiritual success in worldly terms, a hint of utopianism, and an abiding naïveté about human nature. At its best, the prosperity gospel can be well-meaning, openhanded, and personally empowering; and it thrives as few other forms of Christian faith do in the soil of modernity. But like many forms of liberal Christianity, the marriage of God and Mammon half-expects somehow to undo the Fall, through the beneficence of Providence and the magic of the free market. In its emphasis on the virtues of prosperity, it risks losing something essential to Christianity—skipping on to Easter, you might say, without lingering at the foot of the cross.

It's there that you find the pieces of Christian tradition that a gospel of prosperity leaves by the wayside. An understanding that there can be strength in weakness and defeat; an appreciation for the idea that there might be greater virtue in poverty and renunciation, suffering and purgation, than there is in abundance and "delight"; a hard-earned wisdom about the seductions and corruptions associated with worldliness, power, and wealth. Shorn of these aspects of the faith, Christianity risks becoming an appendage to Americanism—a useful metaphysical thread for a capitalist society's social fabric, but a faith that's bound, perhaps fatally, to the rise and fall of the gross domestic product.

It's not that the Jesus of the Gospels ordered everyone he met to give up everything they had. But he did ask such renunciation of some people, and strongly implied that it would be asked of many more before his return. Too much of contemporary American religion dismisses vows of poverty entirely, as monkish and self-righteous. Or it counsels believers enduring hard times that they should soldier on in faith, not because of any spiritual reward, but because God's promised them double, and like a good mutual fund He'll pay out eventually.

Sometimes He does—but sometimes He doesn't. Bruce Wilkinson, for instance, began his African effort with surpassing confidence: "We're going to see the largest humanitarian religious movement in the history of the world from the U.S. to Africa to help with this crisis," he announced in 2007, as he made plans to house 10,000 children left orphans by AIDS.[46] Their new home would consist of a series of orphanage-villages, in which they would live twenty to a house. Their room and board would be paid for, in Wilkinson's plan, by the tourists who would shell out $500 a week to stay at the mini-villages. And these tourists, in the true God-and-Mammon spirit, would be mixing charity with an exotic vacation—complete with an eighteen-hole golf course and nearby game reserves, where the orphans would be trained to work as guides and rodeo stars.

It was an ingenious plan—or it would have been, if Swaziland's king hadn't balked; if the plan hadn't attracted unfavorable attention in the Swazi press; if there had been a way to ensure that the orphans would have somewhere to go when they turned eighteen; if the U.S. government had done more to help Wilkinson push forward; if there wasn't so much resistance, in a land-poor country, to giving away prime parcels to a foreigner; and on and on. So the orphanage dream fell apart, and Wilkinson resigned from the charity he had founded, announcing that God had suggested that he leave Africa. He seemed baffled, in an interview with the *Wall Street Journal,* that things hadn't turned out better. "I asked hard enough," he insisted, as if he were in a business partnership with the Almighty, and God hadn't held up His end of the bargain.[47]

There is innocence at work here, but not a holy innocence. God-and-Mammon Christianity often seems determined to veil the possibility that God might desire something less than perfect success for all His faithful, that He might want small churches as well as thriving congregations, people who fail by the world's lights as well as those who succeed and thrive, Christians who embrace poverty as well as those who pay off the mortgage and live debt-free. Prosperity theology speaks a language of abundance and skates over the passages in the Bible that deal with the value of little things and hidden virtues—of salt in the earth and treasures buried in the field, of little flocks and narrow gates that few enter.

It veils, too, the idea that success often comes at a price, and that those who want to enlarge their territory are at greater risk than most of losing their souls. In *Business as a Calling,* Michael Novak offered portraits of well-off Christians and the way they integrate their faith with the pursuit of wealth. Here is one such snapshot:

> [The] chairman and chief executive of the largest natural gas company
> in the United States . . . some time ago announced publicly his compa-
> ny's vision: "To become . . . the most innovating and reliable provider

of clean energy worldwide." His greatest inward satisfaction, however, has a somewhat different focus.

"In my own case," [he] confided, "I grew up the son of a Baptist minister. From this background, I was fully exposed to not only legal behavior but moral and ethical behavior and what that means from the standpoint of leading organizations and people. I was, and am, a strong believer that one of the most satisfying things in life is to create a highly moral and ethical environment in which every individual is allowed and encouraged to realize their God-given potential."[48]

The natural gas company in question was Enron; its Christian chairman was Kenneth Lay.

This is where the union of God and Mammon goes astray, ultimately: it succumbs to a naïveté about how riches are often accumulated and about the dark pull that money can exert over the human heart. And its sunny boosterism leads believers into temptation, equipping them for success without preparing them for setbacks—which in turn makes failure all the more devastating when it finally, inevitably, arrives.

Americans have faced a great deal of devastation in the past few years. It would be far too simple to suggest that the advance of the prosperity gospel and the retreat of a more ascetic Christian faith caused the Bush-era housing bubble and the subsequent economic crisis. (I suspect that few people were reading Word-Faith literature in the cubicles and corner offices of Lehman Brothers or Goldman Sachs.)

But it's still striking to note that Joel Osteen seemed particularly fixated on real estate as a sign of God's favor. (*Your Best Life Now* opens with an anecdote about a Hawaiian vacationer who sees a beautiful home and thinks, "I can't even imagine living in a place like that"—a sentiment that Osteen holds up as an example of a Christian giving in to "mediocrity."[49]) It's still interesting to track the way mortgages and home ownership show up again and again in the stories and testimonies that crowd the rhetoric of prosperity preaching. ("I thought I'd never have enough money but God gave me my own home anyway." . . . "The Lord set me free from bad credit.") It's still interesting to note that the regions (the Sun Belt, the exurbs) and populations (blacks, Hispanics, the white working class) most affected by the housing bubble were also the places and people where prosperity preaching was most popular.

And it's depressing to contemplate the anecdotes in Hanna Rosin's *Atlantic* essay, which moves through the world of prosperity preaching in the aftermath of the housing crash. There's the Wells Fargo loan officer who recounts how her office developed the idea of reaching out to preachers, because they "figured pastors had a lot of influence with their parishioners and could give the loan officers credibility and new customers. . . . They would tell pastors that for every person who took out a mortgage, $350 would be donated to the church, or to a charity of the parishioner's choice." Describing the sales pitch, the loan officer explained to Rosin that "they wouldn't say, 'Hey, Mr. Minister. We want to give your people a bunch of subprime loans.' . . . They would say, 'Your congregants will be homeowners! They will be able to live the American dream!'"[50]

Rosin meets the parishioners at one of these churches, Casa del Padre in Charlottesville, Virginia—a largely Latino congregation, full of recent immigrants, whose preacher describes God as the "Owner of All the Silver and Gold," and punctuates his sermons by crying out, "We declare financial blessings! Financial miracles this week, NOW NOW NOW!" One churchgoer made a little money working as a handyman during the boom and quickly bought a $270,000 house, at which point "he threw a huge housewarming party and invited everyone from church. He gave a weepy testimony about the house God had given him, passing around the title for all to see. . . . Within three months he had three families living in the three-bedroom house, and he still could not keep up with the payments. After five months, he went into foreclosure and ducked out of the country."[51] Another, Billy Gonzales, lives with his wife and stepdaughters in a tiny, roach-infested apartment, and lacks the capital to even get his car repaired. But he has ambitions:

> "I want to buy a house," he confessed to me one evening this summer. It turned out his lease was almost up, and he needed to move in the fall. "Not a small one but a really huge one, a nice one. With six bedrooms and a kitchen and living room. I know, it's crazy! But nothing is impossible! God, you saved my life," he said, no longer speaking to me.

"You saved my life, and now you will give me a gift. Now I'm crazy!"
Last I heard, he and Garay were house-hunting together.[52]

Garay is Fernando Garay, the pastor of Casa del Padre—a self-made man whose self-making included a lengthy stint at two different mortgage companies, where he was tasked with doing outreach to the Hispanic community. In hindsight, "he makes astute criticisms of the risky loans," Rosin writes, but "like many former loan officers, he does so with a curious sense of distance, as if he had been just a cog in the machine." What's more, Garay resolutely refuses to acknowledge any connection between his preaching and the financial recklessness that it seemed to enable and endorse. ("'Look,'" he said, and rounded his hands as if to indicate a protective shield. 'The recession has not hit *my* church.'"[53])

And if things *have* gone bad—well, prosperity theology is always ready with the answer: "Ten Christians will say that God told them to buy a house," he tells Rosin. "In nine of the cases, it will go bad. The 10th one is the real Christian."

And the others? "For them, there's always another house."[54]

There's always another house turns out to be Joel Osteen's motto as well. In 2009, in the teeth of the Great Recession, he released his third book: *It's Your Time: Activate Your Faith, Achieve Your Dreams, and Increase in God's Favor.* "My desire," he wrote in the foreword, "is to speak faith into the lives of others, encouraging them when they are discouraged, calling forth the seeds of greatness God planted within them, assuring them that their best days are ahead."[55] To those who were surviving, he promised transformation: "You need a bigger vision, a bolder prayer: 'God, I'm asking to be debt-free—my home, my car, my business, my credit cards!'"[56] To those who were struggling, he promised liberation: "Somewhere in your path there's promotion, increase, good breaks, divine connections."[57] To those who might have lost everything, he promised recompense: "God always has another season. . . . [He] can make the rest of your life so rewarding and fulfilling that it makes up for lost opportunities in your past."[58]

In all this, there was no embarrassment, no hint that Osteen might be second-guessing his theology, no examination of conscience or anything like penance. Instead, the economic climate only inspired America's leading prosperity theologian to be more explicit in his message—more emphatic about the link between Christian hope and worldly success, more promiscuous in his get-rich-quick anecdotes, and more inclined than in his previous works to sound the Word-Faith notes first struck by E. W. Kenyon a hundred years before.

"Right now God is showering down blessings, healing, promotions, good ideas," Osteen promised his readers. "If you are not sharing in His favor, you might want to watch your words. Here's the key: If you don't unleash your words in the right direction, if you don't call in a favor, you will not experience those blessings. Nothing happens unless we speak."[59]

Name it, one might say, and claim it.

Did Osteen's vast audience turn on him? Did they compare his promises in this book with the promises in the last one, and the one before that, and decide that there might be some other force at work in their struggles than the simple failure to boldly ask God for His blessings on their lives? Did they contrast his perpetually sunny vision to their own grim financial straits and decide that now might be the time for the sort of Christianity that's willing to tell its faithful things they might not want to hear? Did they turn to their churches and their traditions for a set of Christian stories more applicable to troubled times than Osteen's parade of upbeat parables—the forty days in the desert, the agony in the garden, the suffering on the Cross? Did they open their Bibles and read, as if for the first time, that you cannot serve both God and Mammon?

They did not. The book sold. The ratings rose. The tours continued. In March 2009, with the unemployment rate at 8.5 percent and rising, Osteen sold out Yankee Stadium.

SEVEN

THE GOD WITHIN

If there is a representative religious pilgrim for our times, it's probably the blond, rangy magazine writer–turned–memoirist Elizabeth Gilbert. In 2001, at age thirty-two, Gilbert was a professional success story with a seemingly enviable private life. She had three books and a National Book Award nomination under her belt, a rewarding day job as a travel writer, an apartment in Manhattan, and a big new house in the Hudson Valley, as well as a devoted husband with whom she intended to start a family, and soon. But just five short years later, she was something else entirely, having traded in the marriage and the houses for a globe-trotting spiritual quest. This quest led to the publishing phenomenon known as *Eat, Pray, Love: One Woman's Search for Everything Across Italy, India and Indonesia*—a book that spent an extraordinary 187 weeks on the *New York Times* bestseller list and transformed Gilbert into the kind of woman who gets embodied by Julia Roberts and romanced by Javier Bardem in the big-screen version of her life story.

The spiritual odyssey that made all this possible began, like many similar odysseys before it, with a dark night of the soul—a literal 3 a.m. of misery that found Gilbert locked in the bathroom of her Hudson Valley home, weeping furiously over the life she thought she wanted but didn't want anymore, and then falling on her knees in prayer. "This was a first for me," she informs the reader: Culturally, she was some sort of Christian ("born a Protestant of the White Anglo-Saxon persuasion"), but theologically, she had always been unable to swallow "that one fixed rule of Christianity insisting that Christ is the only path to God." So she addressed the divine that night using Christian terminology—"God," "He"—but with a more open-ended attitude toward Whoever might be listening. ("The Universe, the Great Void, the Force, the Supreme Self, The Whole, The Creator, the Light, The Higher Power . . .") Her prayer was simple enough—a litany repeated deep into the night, pleading for deliverance from the vows she'd taken and the life she'd planned:

I don't want to be married anymore. I don't want to be married anymore. I don't want to live in this big house. I don't want to have this baby.

At long last, someone spoke back. "It was not an Old Testament Hollywood Charlton Heston voice," Gilbert writes, "nor was it a voice telling me I must build a baseball field in my backyard. It was merely my own voice, speaking from within my own self." And yet, and yet—"this was my voice as I had never heard it before. This was my voice, but perfectly wise, calm and compassionate. This was what my voice would sound like if I'd only ever experienced love and certainty in my life. How can I describe the warmth of affection in that voice, as it gave me the answer that would forever seal my faith in the divine?"

"Go back to bed, Liz," the voice told her. So she did. And eventually, fortified by what she describes as more of a "religious conversation" than a "typical Christian conversion experience," she left the husband and the house and the plans for having kids behind and set out into the unknown.[1]

At first, this leap led to only more misery—her husband fought her tooth and nail over a divorce he didn't want, and the boyfriend she "moved right in with" after leaving her spouse proved to be more emotionally withdrawn than she expected, and then more sexually withdrawn as well, which sent her into a tailspin of loneliness, alienation, and "meticulously detailed suicidal thoughts."[2]

But eventually, the God she'd met that fateful night began to make His presence felt. Her relationship with her boyfriend was miserable, but he also introduced her to his spiritual guru, who had an ashram in India and whose acolytes in New York City chanted together every Tuesday night. At the same time, on a magazine assignment in Indonesia, she met a "ninth-generation Balinese medicine man" who prophesied that she would lose all her money at least once in her life (which is basically what was happening in the divorce) but then "get it all right back again," and also that she would return to Bali "someday soon," stay for three or four months, and help him practice his English.[3] And she also found herself developing a sudden, unexpected fascination with Italy—the language, the culture, the food . . .

Then come the two miracles. First, her husband finally signed off on their divorce. It had taken a year and a half to bring him to the negotiating table, and even after a deal seemed to be hammered out, he kept her on tenterhooks for weeks and months. Amid this agony, a friend encouraged her to write a mental petition to God, asking Him to "help us end this conflict, so that two more people can have the chance to be free and healthy, and so there will be just a little bit less animosity and bitterness in a world that is already far too troubled by suffering."[4] Then, in an echo of Catholicism's invocations of the saints, her friend suggested that she mentally add other people's names to the petition—her mother and father and sister, her friends and coworkers, Bill and Hillary Clinton, Saint Francis of Assisi, Gandhi and Mandela and the Dalai Lama, all holy men and women and all the living and the dead.

Within an hour of performing this spiritual exercise, her cell phone buzzed. Her husband had signed.

The second miracle followed swiftly, in the form of an ample publisher's advance that allowed her to unite her three newfound "I" fascinations—Italy, India, Indonesia—into a world tour and then a travel book. Thus freed, fortified, and funded, Gilbert set out on the journey that became *Eat, Pray, Love*: a four-month Roman holiday, where she learned to love herself and life again; a sojourn in her (now ex-) boyfriend's guru's South Asian ashram, where she learned to commune with God; and finally the prophesied months in Bali, where she found a way to balance worldliness and godliness, by sitting at the medicine man's feet (and correcting his English) while gradually falling into the arms of a handsome Brazilian divorcé.

The Roman excursion supplies the travel porn, and the Balinese sojourn the requisite happy ending, but it's the ashram section that really distinguishes *Eat, Pray, Love* from the ordinary run of self-help books. Here Gilbert fulfills the promise of that first late-night encounter, with a frank, earthy, and entirely unembarrassed account of what it feels like for a late-modern, postfeminist, haute-bourgeoise American to search relentlessly for the direct, unmediated, and overwhelming experience of God. Her story captures the grittiness of spiritual exertion—the psychological agony involved in shutting off one's internal monologue, the cruel physicality of extended prayer and meditation, the boredom that so many rituals can inspire, the necessity of fighting your way through all these obstacles. Then it captures, humorously but also movingly, what so many mystics have found waiting on the other side: the sense of an overwhelming divine love, like a "lion roaring from within my chest"[5]; the sense of a God who "plays in my bloodstream the way sunlight amuses itself on water"[6]; and, above all, the sense that all of mortal life is a "kind of limited comic-strip world" compared with what it feels like to be "pulled through the wormhole of the Absolute."[7]

Through all these earth-shaking, all-enveloping encounters, though, Gilbert's theological views don't seem to change a whit. Despite meeting God in a Hindu ashram, she doesn't become a Hindu, but then again neither does she revert to the Christianity of her American upbringing. Her initial premises endured unchallenged to the end: All religious traditions offer equally valid paths to the divine; all religious teachings are just "transporting metaphors"[8] designed to bridge the gulf between the finite and the infinite; most religious institutions claim a monopoly on divinity that they don't really enjoy. To the plight of so many contemporary Americans, awash in spiritual choices but skeptical of every particular religious option, eager to worship and pray but uncertain where and how and to whom to do it, Gilbert offers a reassuring endorsement of do-it-yourself religion. "You have every right to cherry-pick when it comes to moving your spirit and finding peace in God," she insists. Not only a right, indeed, but a positive duty: "You take whatever works from wherever you can find it, and you keep moving toward the light."[9]

Her final theological epiphany is the same as her first one. A journey that began with God speaking to her in "my own voice from within my own self"—albeit "as I had never heard it before"—ends with the realization that the Elizabeth Gilbert-ness of that Voice is the key to understanding the nature of divinity itself. The highest spiritual wisdom, she writes, isn't just that God waits for us inside our own hearts and minds and souls. It's that "God dwells within you as you yourself, exactly the way you are."[10]

The best way to remedy our "heartbreaking inability to sustain contentment,"[11] then, isn't to remake ourselves in imitation of Christ (or Bud-
dha, or Krishna, or whomever), but rather to recognize that "somewhere
within us all, there does exist a supreme self who is eternally at peace. That
supreme Self is our true identity, universal and divine."[12] This is the highest religious dogma, and our highest religious obligation is like unto it: To
"honor the divinity that resides within me,"[13] and to worship at the feet of
the God Within.

Gilbert's voice is distinctive—warm and chatty, self-deprecating and sin-
cere—but her testimony isn't unique. The message of *Eat, Pray, Love* is the
same gospel preached by a cavalcade of contemporary gurus, teachers, and
would-be holy men and women: Deepak Chopra and Eckhart Tolle, Paulo
Coelho and James Redfield, Neale Donald Walsch and Marianne Wil-
liamson. It's the insight offered by just about every spiritual authority ever
given a platform in Oprah Winfrey's media empire. (Winfrey dedicated
two episodes of her show to Gilbert's book.) It's the theology that Elaine
Pagels claims to have rediscovered in the lost gospels of the early Christian
Church. It's the religious message with the most currency in American
popular culture—the truth that Kevin Costner discovered when he went
dancing with wolves, the metaphysic woven through Disney cartoons and
Discovery Channel specials, and the dogma of George Lucas's Jedi, whose
mystical Force, like Gilbert's God, "surrounds us, penetrates us, and binds
the galaxy together."

This creed is sometimes described as "spiritual, not religious"—
because some of its proponents are uncomfortable with the word *God* (a
term that "has become empty of meaning through thousands of years of
misuse,"[14] according to Tolle), and because all of them are critical of institutional religion and insistent that their spiritual vision is bigger than
any particular church or creed or faith. But this is perhaps a distinction
without a difference. Whether you drop *Eat, Pray, Love* into the "religion"
section or the "spirituality" section at your local bookseller, it still testi-
fies as explicitly as Augustine's *Confessions* or Thomas Merton's *The Seven
Storey Mountain* to the truth of a particular theology, a particular way of
thinking about God.

The theology's tenets can be summed up as follows. First, that all organized religions offer only partial glimpses of the God or light or Being that all of them pursue, and that the true spiritual adept must seek to experience God through feeling rather than reason, experience rather than dogma, a direct encounter rather than a hand-me-down revelation. "Being can be felt," writes Tolle, "but it can never be understood mentally."[15] "Listen to your feelings," the Deity counsels Walsch in his *Conversations with God.* "Listen to your Highest Thought. . . . Whenever any of these differ from what you've been told by your teachers, or read in your books, forget the words."[16]

Second, that God is everywhere and within everything, but at the same time the best way to encounter the divine is through the God within, the divinity that resides inside your very self and soul. "The boy reached through the Soul of the World," Coelho writes at the climax of his parable *The Alchemist,* "and saw that it was a part of the Soul of God. And he saw that the Soul of God was his own soul."[17] In *Beyond Belief: The Secret Gospel of Thomas,* Elaine Pagels praises the early Gnostics for "recognizing that one's affinity with God is the key to the kingdom of God."[18]

Third, that God's all-encompassing nature means that sin and death and evil—or what seem like sin and death and evil—will ultimately be reconciled rather than defeated. There is no hell save the one we make for ourselves on Earth, no final separation from the Being that all our beings rest within. "Consciousness is universal," writes Chopra, "and if there is a such a thing as God-consciousness, no one can be excluded from it."[19] "There is no such thing in this universe as hell," Gilbert assures her readers, "except maybe in our own terrified minds."[20]

Finally, that beatitude is constantly available. Heaven is on earth, "God is right here, right now," and eternity can be entered at any moment, by any person who understands how to let go, let God, and let themselves be washed away in love. "At some point everyone will vibrate highly enough so that we can walk into heaven, in our same form,"[21] writes Redfield. "I do believe in life after death," says Coelho, "but I also don't think that it's that important. What's important is to understand that we are also living this life after death now."[22]

This theology overlaps in some interesting respects with the prosperity gospel. Both propose an answer to the problem of theodicy; both blur the distinction between God and man; both open a path to numinous experience for people uncomfortable with the flesh-and-blood miracles of Christian orthodoxy; both insist on a tight link between spiritual health and physical well-being. The notes are somewhat different, but the rhythm of New Thought pulses underneath Chopra as well as Osteen, Tolle as well as Meyer. And many pop metaphysicians—Rhonda Byrne, for instance— move smoothly in between the two worldviews, mixing and matching as the spirit moves them. Both belong to what Sydney Ahlstrom calls the "harmonial" element in American religion, which "encompasses those forms of piety and belief in which spiritual composure, physical health, and even economic well-being are understood to flow from a person's rapport with the cosmos."[23]

But at the deepest level, the theology of the God Within ministers to a different set of spiritual needs, and tries to resolve a different set of contradictions, than the marriage of God and Mammon. Whereas the prosperity gospel suggests that material abundance is the main sign of God's activity in this world, the apostles of the God Within focus on internal harmony— mental, psychological, spiritual—as the chief evidence of things unseen. Whereas the prosperity gospel talks about prayer primarily in terms of supplication, the theology of the God Within talks about it primarily in terms of meditation and communion. And while the prosperity gospel insists that evil and suffering can be mastered by prayer, the God Within theology suggests that true spiritual enlightenment will expose both as illusions. The prosperity gospel is a theology of striving and reaching and demanding; the gospel of the God Within is a theology of letting go. The prosperity gospel makes the divine sound like your broker; the theology of the God Within makes him sound like your shrink.

This distinction is illustrated by Oprah Winfrey herself, arguably the greatest popularizer of God Within theology. ("Our mission," Winfrey has said of her ever-expanding cultural empire, "is to use television to transform people's lives. . . . I am talking about each individual coming to the awareness that, 'I am Creation's son. I am Creation's daughter . . . ultimately I am Spirit come from the greatest Spirit. I am Spirit.'"[24]) Yale University professor Kathryn Lofton, the author of *Oprah: The Gospel of an Icon* (2011), notes that Winfrey's message always has a strong consumerist bent. "At the end of an episode, once a couple has gotten control over their credit cards, there has to be some way of finding a reward for them. Peace of mind is one thing, but wow, much better if they get to take a road trip with their new Hyundai!"[25] But whereas it's clear with prosperity preachers that everything is subservient to the goal of upward mobility and wealth accumulation, for Oprah, consumption is just a means to a higher end. Instead of making everything secondary to the commercial, Lofton points out, in her ministry "all else becomes subservient to the *spirit*. The first question everyone should ask is, 'What is my spirit telling me to do?' How do you tap into your spirit? How do you re-enchant your spirit after being pulled upon, tugged upon, by the false pragmatism of men, family, work? The replies to that are frequently flattered by the commercial, but not solely comprised of it."[26]

At the same time, where the prosperity gospel's adherents insist, often noisily, that they're just as orthodox as the next Christian, the devotees of the God Within do something more sweeping but also more subtle. As Gilbert's eastward pilgrimage suggests, their theology is heavily indebted to Hindu and Buddhist concepts of divinity, and to the Eastern mystical tradition more broadly. But in the American context, the God Within represents itself as the truest form of *every* religion—Eastern and Western, monotheistic and polytheistic, and, yes, Christian above all. Rather than rejecting "the great teacher of peace who was called Jesus"[27] (as Gilbert describes him) or claiming to have found a more excellent way than Christianity, its exponents insist that they are being truer to Christ than many Christian churches. Chopra has written two books about Jesus, Tolle quotes him throughout his spiritual manuals, Coelho is constantly reworking New Testament parables for his own purposes. At the climax of Redfield's *The Celestine Prophecy,* one of the more enlightened characters explains that they've actually been pursuing "the path shown by the Christ," who "opened up to the energy until he was so light he could walk on water" and "was the first to cross over, to expand the physical world into the spiritual."[28]

Call a prosperity preacher a Christian heretic, and he'll angrily dispute the premise. Accuse Deepak Chopra or Paulo Coelho or Oprah of being a Christian heretic, and you'll get a tolerant smile and the suggestion that perhaps you just haven't opened your mind to a broad enough conception of what Christianity really is.

This tendency is connected, as I've already suggested, to the quest for the "real Jesus" and the contemporary fascination with the Gnostic strand in early Christianity. But while the church of the God Within welcomes the patina of Pagels-style scholarship, it doesn't require dusty archaeological troves or careful textual reinterpretations to claim Jesus of Nazareth as its own. Go all the way back to Ralph Waldo Emerson, in many ways the originator of American-style God Within theology, and you find this:

> Jesus Christ belongs to the true race of prophets. He saw with an open eye the mystery of the soul. Drawn by its severe harmony, ravished with its beauty, he lived in it, and had his being there. Alone in all history he estimated the greatness of man. One man was true to what is in you and me. He saw that God incarnates himself in man, and evermore goes forth to take possession of his World. He said, in this jubilee of sublime emotion, "I am divine. Through me, God acts; through me, speaks. Would you see God, see me, or see thee, when thou also thinkest as I think."[29]

The reader will search the canonical gospels in vain for the words Emerson places in quotation marks. But never mind—a genial confidence in its own intuitions, untrammeled by inconvenient factual roadblocks, is part of the God Within theology's appeal. Its universalism speaks to the characteristically modern assumption that no single tradition could possibly encompass the fullness of religious truth. Its eagerness to recruit Jesus to its cause reassures Americans that they are staying true, in some sense, to their childhood faith. (And not only Jesus: The apostles of the God Within are at pains to appropriate the great Christian mystics, and many Christian philosophers as well.) The result is a faith that's at once cosmopolitan and comforting, promising all the pleasures of exoticism— the mysteries of the Orient! the wisdom of the Maya!—without any of the pain of actually turning your back on anything you love.

But its attempt to reconcile the universal and the particular runs deeper than culture and geography. The appeal of God Within theology also rests in the way it addresses a more ancient dilemma: the problem of how to reconcile God's immanence with His transcendence, His activity in the world with the absolute gulf separating creator and creation, His seemingly

human attributes (love, compassion, mercy; justice, anger, vengeance) with
His impassable Otherness.

In Christian orthodoxy, characteristically, this dilemma has been left
unresolved—either audaciously or illogically, depending on your point of
view. The early Christians made bold to claim that the God of the Greek
philosophers—omnipotent and omniscient, beyond time and space and
change—was simultaneously the more personal, activist God of Abraham,
Isaac, and Jacob. Jehovah of the Hebrews was also the Prime Mover of the
universe; Jesus of Nazareth was somehow the Alpha and Omega as well. If
there was a contradiction between these two conceptions of God—between
the Bible's sometimes loving, sometimes wrathful father and philosophy's
unchanging Absolute—it was left to percolate as one of Christianity's many
mysteries. "If philosophers wanted to remain faithful to the traditional
teaching," the Polish philosopher Leszek Kolakowski writes, "and to believe
in a God who is simultaneously Plotinus's One, the Old Testament's Angry
Leader and Jesus's loving Father, they were bound to confess their helpless-
ness; no intellectual effort could pierce the ultimate mystery."[30]

America was founded, in part, by men who found the idea of an ultimate mystery offensive, and set out to rationalize this paradox away. This
was the great appeal of Deism, to Thomas Jefferson and many others. Deist
theology reconciled Christianity's contradictions by depersonalizing the
Christian God, making him a First Cause rather than a constant active
force in history—a clockmaker who stands forever outside the universe he's
built, unmoving and unmoved.

But while Deism was reasonably satisfying as a philosophical school, it
was sterile as a religion. A clockmaker God could provide no consolation,
little guidance, and no grace, and Deist theology had nothing of significance to say about the kind of numinous experiences that have nourished
and sustained the world's religions. The Deist God was forever inaccessible,
forever out of reach, and anyone claiming to have encountered Him was
either deluded or a fraud.

Small wonder that from Emerson and the Transcendentalists onward,
the Deists' American descendants have often been more attracted to the
opposite approach—to a faith rooted in mysticism, which starts with the
direct experience of an ultimate Reality and then tries to reason from this
unmediated experience to a coherent understanding of the Almighty.

THE GOD WITHIN 221

Like Deism, this understanding inevitably depersonalizes God. He is no longer Yahweh, no longer Jesus, no longer Father, Son, and Holy Ghost; instead, He's "Being," "the Soul of the World," "the Highest Thought," or "the experience of supreme love." But where the Deists' depersonalization pushed God into the empyrean and out of reach, the God Within's depersonalization makes him absolutely accessible. To quote Kolakowski again, this theology represents an "effort to bring God closer to human experience" by "depriving him of recognizable personal traits."[31] He's so absolute that He's immanent, so beyond time and space that He's available to everyone at every moment, so universal that He's in you as you.

In *The American Religion* (1993), Harold Bloom offers the following distillation of this message:

> The soul stands apart, and something deeper than the soul, the Real Me or self or spark, thus is made free to be utterly alone with a God who is also quite separate or solitary. . . . What makes it possible for the self and God to commune so freely is that the self already is of God; unlike body or even soul, the American self is no part of the creation, or of evolution through the ages. The American self is not the Adam of Genesis but a more primordial Adam, a Man before there were men and women. Higher and earlier than the angels, this true Adam is as old as God, older than the Bible, and is free of time, unstained by mortality.[32]

This is almost exact. But Bloom, himself a self-proclaimed Gnostic, is drawing too strong a connection between the contemporary religion of the self and ancient Gnosticism's disdain for the fleshly snares of the natural, created world. The cult of the God Within owes a debt to the ancient Gnostics, clearly, but it takes their impulse in a more democratic and optimistic direction, shedding both the spiritual elitism woven into texts like the Gospel of Judas and the idea that the physical universe itself is corrupt and needs to be escaped. It accepts the Gnostic premise that we should seek after our divine spark, but it locates this spark both inside and outside the self. The human soul has God within it, but so does the entirety of the natural world as well.

Thus Bloom's claim that "no American ultimately concedes that she is part of nature" is arguably false. Instead, from Emerson down to Elizabeth

Gilbert, American God Within theology blurs naturally into a kind of pantheism. "Being indivisible," Kolakowski writes of this conception of God, "He cannot be, of course, the raw stuff that things have been made of; His unspoiled plenitude is to be found in every fragment of the world and thus whatever is, is divine."[33] This idea would be anathema to many ancient Gnostics, but it's completely natural to the modern apostles of the God Within. When they aren't urging people to look within themselves for God, they're urging them to seek Him in the natural world instead. "I have built into all things an energy that transmits its signal throughout the universe," Walsch's God informs the reader. "Every person, animal, plant, rock, tree—every physical thing—sends out energy, like a radio transmitter."[34] One of Gilbert's visions culminates with her rushing into the midst of a meadow, throwing her arms around a clutch of eucalyptus trees, and kissing them ecstatically: "I looked around the darkened valley and I could see nothing that was not God."[35]

Here we see the vindication of another of Alexis de Tocqueville's predictions about America's religious future:

> When the conditions of society are becoming more equal and each individual man becomes more like all the rest . . . a habit grows up of ceasing to notice the citizens and considering only the people, of overlooking individuals to think only of their kind. At such times the human mind seeks to embrace a multitude of different objects at once, and it constantly strives to connect a variety of consequences with a single cause. The idea of unity so possesses man and is sought by him so generally that if he thinks he has found it, he readily yields himself to repose in that belief. Not content with the discovery that there is nothing in the world but a creation and a Creator, he is still embarrassed by this primary division of things and seeks to expand and simplify his conception by including God and the universe in one great whole.[36]

The appeal of this simplified conception has only been sharpened by the materialism and scientism of modern life. Our very alienation from nature makes us more likely to invest it with metaphysical significance. We pine for what we've left behind, and associating God with the natural world is an obvious way to express unease about our hypertechnological society.

The threat of global warming, in particular, has lent to mystical pantheism qualities that every successful religion needs—a crusading spirit, a rigorous set of "thou shalt nots," and a piping-hot apocalypse. (No recent cultural development captures this tension more than the immense box-office success of James Cameron's *Avatar,* a pantheistic-message movie that earned a billion dollars while lecturing its audience on the perils of precisely the kind of technological mastery that made its lavish visual effects possible in the first place.)

At the same time, a mystical pantheism, in which God is an experience rather than a person, turns out to represent a form of religion that even some of our more strident atheists can support. Richard Dawkins has called pantheism "a sexed-up atheism." (He means that as a compliment.) Citing Albert Einstein's expression of religious awe at the "beauty and sublimity" of the universe, Dawkins allows, "In this sense I too am religious."[37] Likewise, Sam Harris concluded his polemic *The End of Faith* by rhapsodizing about the numinous experiences available from immersion in "the roiling mystery of the world."[38]

With Harris's and Dawkins's endorsements, we seem to have come a long way from anything like traditional Christianity. Yet the most sophisticated exponents of God Within theology would beg to differ. What the New Atheists are responding to, they argue, is an insight about God that can also be found in the works of impeccably orthodox Christian metaphysicians. The apparent divide between Harris's "roiling mystery of the world" and the God of an Augustine or a Teresa of Ávila isn't actually that vast. The two conceptions of divinity are separated more by terminology and historical contingency than by anything truly essential.

This argument has been advanced most persuasively by Karen Armstrong, the former nun turned prolific popular historian. Like many others of her generation, Armstrong left both her convent and Catholicism behind in the 1970s, and eventually found her vocation elucidating the common themes that she sees running through all the great religious traditions.[39] The first is that a universal compassion is the highest moral good; the second, that the mystical pursuit of an essential unknowable Deity ultimately trumps the more superficial quest for theological correctness. Against the more strident antitheists, Armstrong insists that this religious mentality is entirely compatible with a liberal, scientific, technologically advanced society. But, more important, she insists that it's actually truer to the ancient traditions of Judaism, Islam, and (especially) Christianity than is much of what currently passes for conservative religion today.

Her argument is developed to its fullest in her 2009 book *The Case for God*, which sets out to rescue the idea of a Deity from its cultured despisers and its more literal-minded defenders alike. Both modern fundamentalists and modern atheists, Armstrong contends, have mistaken religion for a set of propositions to be assented to, or a catalogue of specific facts about the nature of God, the world, and human life. This approach to piety would be foreign to many premodern religious thinkers, including the greatest minds of the Christian past, from the early Fathers of the Church to medieval eminences like Thomas Aquinas. These and other thinkers, she writes, understood faith primarily as a practice, rather than as a system—not as "something that people thought but something they did."[40] Their God was not a being to be defined or a proposition to be tested but an ultimate reality to be approached through myth, ritual, and "apophatic" theology, which practices "a deliberate and principled reticence about God and/or the sacred"[41] and emphasizes what we can't know about the divine.

In other words, in the highest forms of Christian theology, the experience of God—which, inevitably, passeth all rational understanding—was always primary and dogmatic definitions strictly secondary. Here, for instance, is Armstrong limning the views of Gregory of Nyssa, the fourth-century saint and theologian: "[He argued that] we could not speak about God rationally, as we speak about ordinary beings, but that did not mean that we should give up thinking about God at all. We had to press on, pushing our minds to the limit of what we could know, descending ever deeper into the darkness of unknowing and acknowledging that there could be no final clarity."[42] Or, again, here's her gloss on Thomas Aquinas: "Whenever he made a statement about God, [Aquinas insisted that] the theologian must realize that it was inescapably inadequate. . . . By revealing the inherent limitation of words and concepts, theology should reduce both the speaker and his audience to silent awe. When reason was applied to faith, it must show that what we call 'God' was unknowable."[43]

Here, finally, is her summary of what the doctrine of the Trinity really meant to the more mystically inclined Fathers of the Church:

There is no selfhood in the Trinity. Instead there is silence and keno-
sis. The Father, the ground of being, empties itself of all that it is and
transmits it to the Son, giving up everything, even the possibility of
expressing itself in another Word. Once that Word, has been spoken,
the Father no longer has an "I" and remains forever silent and unknowable. There is nothing that we can say about the Father, since
the only God we know is the Son. At the very source of being is the
speechless "nothingness" of Brahman, Dao, and Nirvana, because the
Father is not another being and resembles nothing in our mundane
experience. The Father confounds all notions of personality and, since
the Father is presented in the New Testament as the end of the Christian quest, this becomes a journey to no place, no thing, and no one.
In the same way, the Son, our only access to the divine, is merely an
eikon of the ultimately reality. . . . Like any symbol, the Son points
beyond itself to the Father, while the Spirit is simply the atman of
the Father and the "we" between Father and Son. We cannot pray to
the Spirit, because the Spirit is the ultimate innerness of every being,
ourselves included.[44]

This is heady, high-level stuff. But note that it all brings us back to the
same place that Elizabeth Gilbert ended up—with a divine spirit who's in
you as you, a God of the Universe who turns out to be the God Within.

If we accept Armstrong's interpretation of the history of Western theology, then, today's mass-market spirituality doesn't really represent a rupture
with the deepest message of Christianity. Rather, it represents an attempt
to take an insight that was historically the property of the faith's greatest
spiritual adepts—theologians, philosophers, mystics—and democratize it,
popularize it, bring it to the masses. Instead of settling for inadequate attempts to intellectually circumscribe divinity, ordinary believers can finally
experience the ultimate reality directly. Instead of half-truths about God's
knowability, they'll get the whole truth about His transcendence of every
human concept and conceit. In the age of the God Within, the insights
that were once available only to cloistered Carmelites or the *Summa Theo-
logica*'s most sophisticated readers can be offered to everybody, everywhere.
And they'll reveal a God at once more transcendent and more immediately
available than anyone had dared to guess.

*   *   *

There are some difficulties with this appealing synthesis, however. Armstrong's story is provocative but frustratingly incomplete. Nothing she says is quite wrong: the great Christian sages did indeed insist on the limits of theological language in describing God (the whole of the *Summa,* Aquinas once suggested, was "mere straw" compared to the the insights of the mystics), and many Christian saints reported ecstatic experiences not unlike those that envelop Elizabeth Gilbert and her fellow travelers. But the casual reader of the *The Case for God* would be forgiven for thinking, from Armstrong's portraits of apophatic theology in action, that figures like Aquinas and Augustine were essentially Gilberts or Chopras or Tolles *avant la lettre,* preaching a universal and nonspecific deity rather than the God of Christian orthodoxy.

In reality, all of those figures were fiercely dogmatic by any modern standard. They were not fundamentalists, reading every line of scripture literally and worshipping an anthropomorphic God, and they were, as Armstrong says, "inventive, fearless and confident in their interpretation of faith." But their inventiveness was grounded in shared doctrines, and constrained by shared assumptions. Their theology was reticent in its claims about the ultimate nature of God, but it was very specific about how God had revealed Himself on Earth. Acknowledging that the mystical logic of the Trinity piled unknowability on unknowability did not permit a believer to dissent from the dogma entirely and invent one that "worked" for him instead. Accepting the bottomless mystery inherent in the Incarnation did not justify treating that doctrine as just one way among many to understand and worship God. The biblical revelation might ultimately suggest that Yahweh/Jehovah/Jesus was inherently ungraspable, but it was still the only revelation that Christians were licensed to accept. Many great Christian theologians would argue that human reason could never quite comprehend exactly what the resurrection meant, but none of them would deny that Jesus was physically resurrected—and they would have been pretty poor Christian theologians if they had.

The same respect for the specificity of revelation has defined the greatest Christian mystics. Christianity has certainly made room, as Armstrong suggests, for mystical encounters not unlike the kind that are celebrated by the apostles of the God Within—encounters that seem to transcend time and space, and that hint at divine realities that no creed or catechism can quite capture. But at the same time, as Kolakowski notes, the Christian churches imposed strict limits on their mystics as well. They were expected to maintain "the ontological distinction between God and the soul" and to refrain from suggesting that "the mystical union involves a total anni- hilation of personality." They were forbidden to use their experiences "as a pretext for disregarding the traditional rules of obedience, let alone the common moral duties." And their claims to divine favor were tested against their conduct: "A mystic's experience, if genuine, strengthens his common virtues of humility, charity, chastity; it proves to be a diabolic temptation, rather than God's gift, if it breeds hubris, indifference to others, or irregu- larities of conduct."[45]

To most modern writers, these kinds of restrictions just reflect the tyranny of religious institutions and their discomfort with the kind of free- dom that true visionaries deserve. "I am a Catholic," says Paulo Coelho, but "in between the light and us, sometimes there are too many rules."[46] Discussing Teresa of Ávila, Elizabeth Gilbert bemoans the way the saint veers from wild ecstasies ("it is a glorious bewilderment, a heavenly mad- ness, in which true wisdom is acquired") to swift and dutiful expressions of self-abnegation and humility. "Reading Saint Teresa today," Gilbert remarks, "you can almost feel her coming out of that delirious experience, then looking around at the political climate of medieval Spain (where she lived under one of the most repressive religious tyrannies of history) and soberly, dutifully, apologizing for her excitement."[47]

Yet there may be wisdom in the rules and limits that Christian institu- tions imposed on their visionaries. (Or, more often, attempted to impose, Gilbert's exaggerated portrait of medieval repression notwithstanding.) For one thing, it's more difficult than many modern spiritual writers suggest to separate ideas from actions, teaching from conduct, and dogma from prac- tice in religious history. The dogmas tend to sustain the practices, and vice versa; making a bricolage of different religious traditions is often just a way of guaranteeing that those same traditions die out within a generation. It's possible to gain some sort of "knack" for a religion without believing that all its dogmas are literally true. A spiritually inclined person can no doubt draw nourishment from the Roman Catholic Mass, for instance, without believing that the Eucharist literally becomes the body and blood of Christ. But without the doctrine of transubstantiation, the Mass would not exist to provide that nourishment. Not every churchgoer will share Flannery O'Connor's opinion that if the Eucharist is "a symbol, to hell with it." But Catholic faith has been sustained for two thousand years because of the Flannery O'Connors, not the Paulo Coelhos.

So God Within religion tends to be parasitic on more dogmatic forms of faith, which create and sustain the practices that the spiritual-but-not-religious seeker picks and chooses from, reads symbolically, and reinterprets for a more enlightened age. The breadth of God Within religion can represent a kind of shallowness, since real spiritual breakthroughs generally require a narrowing—the decision to pick a path and stick with it, rather than hopscotching around in search of a synthesis that "works for me." Without these kind of strictures and commitments, Luke Timothy Johnson has argued, mysticism drifts easily into a kind of solipsism: "Kabbalism apart from Torah-observance is playacting; Sufism disconnected from Shariah is vague theosophy; and Christian mysticism that finds no center in the Eucharist or the Passion of Christ drifts into a form of self-grooming."[48]

Such solipsism carries moral as well as spiritual dangers. For anyone familiar with the spiritual memoirs and manuals of earlier eras, it's startling how little moral exhortation there is in the pages of the God Within literature. There are frequent calls to "compassion" and "kindness," but little guidance for people facing actual dilemmas. And what guidance there is often amounts to "if it feels good, do it"—quite literally, in some cases. "I tell you this," Walsch's God insists: "No kind of evolution ever took place through denial. If you are to evolve, it will not be because you've been able to deny yourself the things that you know 'feel good,' but because you've granted yourself these pleasures—and found something even greater. For how can you know that something is 'greater' if you've never tasted the 'lesser'?"[49]

For a faith rooted in mystical experience alone, this is probably an inevitable problem. The sense of harmony, unity, and communion that so many mystics experience can provoke a somewhat blasé attitude toward sin and wickedness, and a dismissive attitude toward ordinary moral duties. ("He was fundamentally treacherous to civilization," a contemporary wrote of Emerson, because "he appeared to me utterly unconscious of himself as either good or evil.") If pushed too far, the quest for a "Supreme Self" can blur into the most ancient human temptation, the whisper in Eden that "ye shall be as gods." If pushed too far, Julian of Norwich's mystic's creed that "all will be well and all will be well and all manner of thing will be well" can become a blithe assumption that every choice and happening is divinely inspired. If God is beyond personality, perhaps He is beyond morality as well—and thus why should his beloved followers worry overmuch about petty questions like whom they happen to be sleeping with, or how best to dispose of their income? After all, all will be well and all will be well and all manner of thing will be well. . . .

In her provocative book on spiritual experience, *Fingerprints of God* (2009), Barbara Bradley Hagerty notes that "virtually every woman I interviewed, and several of the men, reported that their values and goals had veered so dramatically away from their spouses' [after a mystical encounter] that they eventually divorced." Usually "the transformed people felt a twinge of regret at losing their former life but found invariably that the spiritual adventure more than compensated." Hagerty writes that she "felt sorrier for their family and friends, who became the 'collateral damage' of the spiritual experience."[50]

Orthodox Christianity, Kolakowski points out, used the distinction between Creator and creation to emphasize that believers are bound to ordinary as well extraordinary duties. The God Within, on the other hand, can sometimes prove so overwhelming that devotees feel free to abandon their more quotidian responsibilities, entrusting merely finite goals and merely mortal companions—which often means spouses and children—to providence's care while they obey the promptings of their Supreme Self or Highest Thought. ("I have little use for the past and rarely think about it,"[51] writes Tolle, in a passage that chills rather more than inspires.)

One thinks here of Orwell's famous admonition that saints should be judged guilty until they are proven innocent. To be sure, often they are innocent: Christian orthodoxy doesn't exclude the possibility that God might call someone to abandon what can seem like their immediate moral responsibilities.Certainly nothing in the literature of the God Within is as radical as this Gospel admonition: "If anyone comes to me and does not hate his own father and mother and wife and children and brothers and sisters, yes, and even his own life, he cannot be my disciple."

But the strictures that orthodoxy places on its mystical seekers, the emphasis on hierarchies of goods and ordinary duties, also do honor to the words of Jesus—who insisted, after all, that he had come to fulfill the law rather than abolish it. And they're a useful reminder that the promptings of one's inner self aren't necessarily identical to the promptings of the Holy Spirit. Sometimes the God Within isn't God at all, but just the ego or the libido, using spirituality as a convenient gloss for its own desires and impulses. Sometimes your books and teachers are right, and what seems your Highest Thought is really emanating from the lower reaches of your soul. Sometimes God might offer you a less consoling and more demanding insight than Gilbert's delighted discovery that He "dwells within you as you yourself, exactly the way you are." To exclude or minimize these possibilities, as so many modern mystics do, is to risk baptizing egomania, divinizing selfishness, and leaving few legitimate ways to distinguish the God within a Mother Teresa from the God within a Jim Jones or a David Koresh.

Most Americans are not Koreshes, mercifully. But neither are they full-time mystics or professional philosophers—or even professional writers like Gilbert, equipped with book contracts that enable them to spend a solid four months in spiritual seclusion. For people leading more ordinary lives, reducing religion to the God Within and only the God Within doesn't create a vast population of budding Teresas of Ávila. It just provides an excuse for making religious faith more comfortable, more dilettantish, more self-absorbed—for doing what you feel like doing anyway, and calling it obedience to a Higher Power or Supreme Self.

The result isn't megalomania but a milder sort of solipsism, with numinous experience as a kind of spiritual comfort food rather than a spur to moral transformation—there when you need it, and not a bother when you don't. It's the church of the Oprah Winfrey Network, you might say: religion as a path to constant self-affirmation, heresy as self-help, the quest for God as the ultimate form of therapy.

The man who saw this coming was Philip Rieff, a midcentury psychologist and the philosopher, and the husband, briefly and unhappily, of the critic and essayist Susan Sontag. In 1966, while most observers of the religious scene were hailing Harvey Cox's union of Christian faith and secular ambition, Rieff produced *The Triumph of the Therapeutic: The Uses of Faith After Freud*, which was as densely written as *The Secular City* but more prophetic. The age of traditional Christian faith was over—in this much, Rieff agreed with his era's "death of God" theologians. But the new animating spirit of the age was likely to be personal desire rather than political ambition. Religious man was giving way to "psychological man," not ideological man. In place of a secularized Christianity building the kingdom of God on earth, Rieff foresaw an age of therapy, in which the pursuit of well-being would replace the quest for either justice or salvation.

"Religious man was born to be saved," he wrote, but "psychological man is born to be pleased."[52] This new man would be interested in neither political utopianisms nor moral idealisms. All existing orders would be equally acceptable to him, "so long as the powers that be preserve social order and manage an economy of abundance."[53] (The absence of political prescriptions in the literature of the God Within is almost as striking as the absence of moral exhortation.) So would all ethical systems: "If 'immoral' materials, rejected under earlier cultural criteria, are therapeutically effective, enhancing somebody's sense of well-being, then they are useful."[54] The only universal goal would be harmony and happiness—"more joy, right now!" runs *O, the Oprah Magazine* blurb for Tolle's *The Power of Now*—and the definitions of that happiness would prove as various as human personalities. The therapeutic revolution, Rieff wrote, "does not aim, like its predecessors, at victory for some rival commitment, but rather at a way of using all commitments, which amounts to loyalty to none."[55] In this new landscape, "'I believe!,' the cry of the ascetic," would lose precedence to "'one feels,' the caveat of the therapeutic."[56]

Crucially, though, the triumph of feeling over belief could still leave plenty of room for spirituality. Rieff, writing in the late afternoon of Freudianism, probably overestimated the extent to which psychoanalysis rather than mysticism would dominate the therapeutic era. But he predicted, with uncanny accuracy, the way the therapeutic mentality would dress itself in the garments of the religious traditions it had displaced. ("Psychological man, in his independence from all gods, can feel free to use all god-terms," Rieff suggested. "I imagine he will be a hedger against his own bets, a user of any faith that lends itself to therapeutic use."[57]) He foresaw, as well, the theological forms that this bets-hedging would take. The bulk of *The Triumph of the Therapeutic* is devoted to analyzing what amount to highbrow forerunners of the God Within—C. G. Jung's religion of the Unconscious, Wilhelm Reich's pantheistic religion of energy, and D. H. Lawrence's "Oceanic God."

Here is Rieff on what this would mean for the culture as a whole.

> In the emergent culture, a wider range of people will have "spiritual" concerns and engage in "spiritual" pursuits. There will be more singing and more listening. People will continue to genuflect and read the Bible, which has long achieved the status of great literature; but no prophet will denounce the rich attire or stop the dancing. There will be more theater, not less, and no Puritan will denounce the stage and draw its curtains. On the contrary, I expect that modern society will mount psychodramas far more frequently than its ancestors mounted miracle plays.[58]

In 2005, forty years after this uncanny anticipation of reality television, Christian Smith and Melinda Lundquist Denton conducted a long investigation into the religious lives of American teenagers, and discovered exactly the kind of therapeutic theology that Rieff had seen coming. Smith and Denton found no evidence of real secularization among their subjects: 97 percent of teenagers professed some sort of belief in the divine, 71 percent reported feeling either "very" or "somewhat" close to God, and the vast majority self-identified as Christian.[59] There was no sign of deep alienation from their parents' churches, no evidence that the teenagers in the survey were poised to convert outright to Buddhism or Islam, and no sign that real atheism was making deep inroads among the young.

But neither was there any evidence of a recognizably orthodox Christian faith. "American Christianity," Smith and Denton suggested, is "either degenerating into a pathetic version of itself," or else is "actively being colonized and displaced by a quite different religious faith."[60] They continued: "Most religious teenagers either do not really comprehend what their own religious traditions say they are supposed to believe, or they do understand it and simply do not care to believe it."[61]

What they believe instead is remarkably consistent across different denominations and traditions. According to Smith and Denton, the "de facto creed" of America's youth has five main premises. 1. "A God exists who created and ordered the world and watches over human life on earth." 2. "God wants people to be good, nice, and fair to each other, as taught in the Bible and by most world religions." 3. "The central goal of life is to be happy and to feel good about oneself." 4. "God does not need to be particularly involved in one's life except when God is needed to resolve a problem." 5. "Good people go to heaven when they die."[62]

Smith and Denton dub this theology Moralistic Therapeutic Deism. It's a resonant term but not an entirely accurate one. Therapeutic this religion certainly is, but "Deism" suggests a distance between God and man, and a sense of divine detachment from the affairs of the world, that the teenagers in the survey don't actually seem to accept. Indeed, the sociologists acknowledge as much, writing that "the Deism here is revised from its classical eighteenth-century version by the therapeutic qualifier, making the distant God selectively available for taking care of needs. . . . God is something like a combination Divine Butler and Cosmic Therapist: he is always on call, takes care of any problem that arises, professionally helps his people to feel better about themselves."[63]

The theology's supposed "moralism," meanwhile, is astonishingly weak. The God of MTD "is not demanding," the authors note. "He actually can't be, because his job is to solve our problems and make people feel good." Therapeutic religion doesn't call its adherents to prayer or repentance, to works of charity, or even the observance of a Sabbath. Instead, being a moral person "means being the kind of person that other people will like," which is to say pleasant, respectful, well-behaved, and nondisruptive.[64] Niceness is the highest ethical standard, popularity the most important goal, and high self-esteem the surest sign of sanctity.

"What appears to be the actual dominant religion among U.S. teenagers," Smith and Denton write, "is centrally about feeling good, happy, secure, at peace. It is about attaining subjective well-being, being able to resolve problems, and getting along amiably with other people." If there's "an essential aspect of living a moral life" in therapeutic faith, they conclude, it's the obligation to always persist in "feeling good about oneself." And if there's a central ethical commandment, it's summed up by the many teenagers who defined morality as follows: "Just don't be an asshole, that's all."[65]

*   *   *

A spirituality of niceness is not without its selling points. Therapeutic religion is immensely tolerant: since the only true God is the one you find within, there's no reason to impose your faith on someone else. The idea of persecution—historically a temptation for nearly every Christian sect—seems not only wrong but hopelessly anachronistic. In a diverse and pluralistic society, this kind of easygoing religion has obvious advantages. "Theologically speaking," Damon Linker has written of Moral Therapeutic Deism, "this watered-down, anemic, insipid form of Judeo-Christianity is pretty repulsive. But politically speaking, it's perfect: thoroughly anodyne, inoffensive, tolerant . . . [and] perfectly suited to serve as the civil religion of the highly differentiated twenty-first-century United States."[66]

Therapeutic religion's intertwining goals of happiness and self-esteem, too, are not so easily dismissed. Even Rieff, whose book has the tone of a jeremiad, could understand the case for such a faith. "I am aware that these speculations may be thought to contain some parodies of an apocalypse," he wrote. "But what apocalypse has ever been so kindly? What culture has ever attempted to see to it that no ego is hurt?"[67]

But a tolerant society is not necessarily a just one. Men may smile at their neighbors without loving them and decline to judge their fellow citizens' beliefs out of a broader indifference to their fate. An ego that's never wounded, never trammeled or traduced—and that's taught to regard its deepest impulses as the promptings of the divine spirit—can easily turn out to be an ego that never learns sympathy, compassion, or real wisdom. And when contentment becomes an end unto itself, the way that human contents express themselves can look an awful lot like vanity and decadence.

This growing vanity may even be quantifiable. Between 1982 and 2006, sixteen thousand American college students filled out the Narcissistic Personality Inventory, a psychological evaluation that asks for responses to statements like "If I ruled the world, it would be a better place," "I think I am a special person," and "I can live my life any way I want to." The trend was consistent: the average student in 2006 had a higher narcissism score than 65 percent of college students a generation earlier. The Millennials were more likely to agree with statements like "I find it easy to manipulate people" and "I insist upon getting the respect that is due to me." Other surveys have showed similar results. In the 1950s, only 12 percent of teenagers identified with the statement, "I am an important person." A half century later, it was 80 percent.[68]

As narcissism has waxed, empathy has waned. In 2010, researchers at the University of Michigan reported that contemporary college students scored about 40 percent lower than their predecessors in the 1970s on tests assessing their ability to put themselves in other people's shoes. They were more likely than their parents' generation to agree with statements like "other people's misfortunes do *not* usually disturb me a great deal," and less likely to agree with prompts like "I sometimes try to understand my friends better by imagining how things look from their perspective" and "I often have tender, concerned feelings for people less fortunate than me."[69]

This sounds a lot like what Christian Smith discovered, when he followed up on his study of teenagers with a similar project focusing on the spiritual lives of American twentysomethings:

The majority of those interviewed stated . . . that nobody has any natural or general responsibility or obligation to help other people. . . . Most of those interviewed said that it is nice if people help others, but that nobody has to. Taking care of other people in need is an individual's choice. If you want to do it, good. If not, that's up to you. . . . Even when pressed—What about victims of natural disaster or political oppression? What about helpless people who are not responsible for their poverty or disabilities? What about famines and floods and tsunamis?—No, they replied. If someone wants to help, then good for that person. But nobody has to.[70]

This growing narcissism has been a spur to excess on an epic scale. The narcissist may find it easy to say no to others, but he's much less likely to say no to himself—and nothing defines the last decade of American life more than our inability to master our own impulses and desires. A nation of narcissists turns out to be a nation of gamblers and speculators, gluttons and gym obsessives, pornographers and Ponzi schemers, in which household debt rises alongside public debt, and bankers and pensioners and automakers and unions all compete to empty the public trough.

Therapeutic theology is hardly uniquely responsible for these trends. Our appetites have increased in proportion to our unprecedented wealth, and our immediate-gratification culture has been made possible by material abundance and technological progress. Obesity is a disease of civilization. The credit boom is the fruit of clever innovations in the financial sector. Mass media and mass advertising have made overconsumers of us all. The advance of narcissism may have a great deal to do with the explosion of social media, and the constant self-cultivation and self-marketing that it requires. ("We found the biggest drop in empathy after the year 2000,"[71] one of the University of Michigan researchers noted—which is to say, just as MySpace and then Facebook came online.)

What the cult of the God Within *has* done, though, is make American religion an enabler of this excess rather than a potential curb against it. America would no doubt be an intensely consumerist society with or without therapeutic religion, and a solipsistic society with or without the God Within. But the triumph of the therapeutic has steadily undercut American religion's ability to serve as a corrective or a critique. For all their claims to ancient wisdom, there's nothing remotely countercultural about the Tolles and Winfreys and Chopras. They're telling an affluent, appetitive society exactly what it wants to hear: that all of its deepest desires are really God's desires, and that He wouldn't dream of judging.

This message encourages us to justify our sins by spiritualizing them. The covetousness of the American consumer becomes a path to self-actualization: Think of the way Oprah's network suggests that peace of mind goes better with a new Hyundai; think of the vast market for high-end products and luxury goods that promise "simplicity" and "authenticity." (Everything from their vacations to their kitchens, David Brooks wrote of the current American upper class in 2000's *Bobos in Paradise,* seems designed to be "the physical expression of some metaphysical sentiment."[72]) The gluttony of the Whole Foods–shopping gourmand is redefined as a higher form of asceticism: if you put enough thought (and money) into your locally grown artisanal grass-fed free-range organic farm-to-table diet, then a lavish meal can be portrayed as one part philosophical statement, one part eucharistic feast. The physical vanity of the diet-and-exercise obsessive is recast as the pursuit of a kind of ritual purity, hedged about with taboos and guilt trips and mysticized by yoga. (Not for nothing does

Amazon.com include diet and exercise books on its "Religion and Spirituality" bestseller list. . . .)

Nowhere is the spiritualization of what used to be considered sinfulness more apparent than in our sexual and romantic lives. The decline
of marriage, the weakening of family structures overall, the shift from a
child-centric to a romance-centric model for adult sexual relationships—all
of these trends would exist if Oprah Winfrey was still anchoring a local
news show and Deepak Chopra had never given up endocrinology for
mysticism. But therapeutic religion has often provided the narrative that
Americans use to justify their abandonment of what used to be considered
basic moral obligations. This was true during the divorce revolution of the
1970s, when pop-culture figures like Wayne Dyer—a proto-Chopra who
urged his readers to connect with "the Source," his favored term for the
God Within—emerged to minister to people looking for a spiritual justification for deserting their families. It's just as true today—and not only
because Dyer himself is still churning out pamphlets. From our Hallmark
cards to our divorce courts, the American way of love has become therapeutic to its very core. It emphasizes feelings over duties, it's impatient with
institutional structures of any sort, and it's devoted to the premise that the
God or Goddess Within should never, ever have to settle.

Think of the way Elizabeth Gilbert's spiritual odyssey plays out. *Eat,
Pray, Love* begins with her throwing over her husband of five years (a man
whose devotion and decency she praises to the skies) because she's bored
and frustrated and isn't ready to have kids, and ends with her finding love
with a handsome Brazilian in Bali. In the interim, God's intercession is
sought to smooth her divorce proceedings and then to ease her sense of
guilt over her own conduct. It's hard to imagine a better encapsulation of
religion's role in post–sexual revolution America—as an enabler of adult
desire, whether gluttonous or libidinous, and a source of endless justifications for whatever the heart already prefers to do.

"Historically," Rieff notes in *The Triumph of the Therapeutic,* "the rejection of sexual individualism . . . was the consensual matrix of Christian
culture."[73] With the crisis of orthodox belief, the Christian matrix has
been shattered, and a different set of moral standards has emerged. One is
the rule of consent, the idea that whatever adults do with their bodies is
their business, so long as neither party is harmed in the process. (Accord-

ing to Neale Donald Walsch, God's only specific sexual commandment is that "no action involving another may be taken without the other's agreement and permission"[74]—which makes the Deity sound rather like the bouncer at an S&M club.) Another is a rule of love: the idea that some forms of promiscuity may well be wrong, but that a strong emotional attachment, whether in or out of marriage, is enough to elevate sex from "casual" to licit. Undergirding both of these standards are two deeper assumptions. First, that the urge to have sex is both more irresistible and more fundamental to personal identity than other impulses and appetites. Second, that the act of sex itself is basically a small thing, a little spasm of delight which an all-powerful God can't possibly care that much about, at least so long as you're a kind and charitable person whose heart is fundamentally in the right place.

In James Frey's *The Final Testament of the Holy Bible* (2011), one of many recent literary attempts to improve on the gospels, the latter sentiment even gets attributed to Jesus Christ himself. "Love and laughter and fucking are what make life better," Frey's modern-day messiah tells a Catholic priest. "God doesn't care about the petty dramas that mean so much to us. God doesn't care what we say or who we fuck or what we do with our bodies or who we love or who we marry."[75]

This idea has become so commonplace that it's worth pausing to consider how extraordinary it is. I don't just mean extraordinary in the context of a religious culture that's still obsessed with Jesus of Nazareth, who was as hard on sins against chastity as he was on sins against the widow and the orphan. I mean extraordinary in the context of basic moral reasoning and simple common sense. Almost nothing that human beings do in life is freighted with as many potential consequences as sexual relations: emotional consequences, physical consequences, and above all, the world-altering consequence of creating an entirely new human life. The promises of the sexual revolution notwithstanding, neither contraception nor abortion has done away with these realities. Sex may be "safer" with pills and condoms, but it's never anything remotely close to safe.

Acknowledging this truth doesn't require accepting Christian conclusions on every controversial question. But for a culture as putatively religious as our own, it requires giving more consideration to the Christian premise that bright lines and absolute standards may have, if anything, a stronger role to play in sexual matters than in other areas of human life. True, this perspective can be a warrant for prudishness, hypocrisy, and sexism. But it can also be a way to afford human sexuality a kind of deep respect that acknowledges sex's promise but also its perils—for the couples involved and for the ever-widening circle of people that any sexual encounter can affect and (more importantly) create. Fidelity within lifelong relationships and continence outside them: these are hard standards, but when lived out successfully, they have been the basis for a remarkable amount of human flourishing—from the ordinary grace of a happy childhood to the extraordinary lives of the saints.

Since the 1960s, though, this is an argument that the Christian churches have found themselves increasingly helpless to promote. According to the sociologist Mark Regnerus, for a small minority of religious Americans—the devoutest of the devoutest—there's still a strong correlation between Christian faith and Christian sexual conduct, manifested in lower-than-average rates of out-of-wedlock childbearing, abortion, and divorce.[76] But outside this inner circle, the impact of religion seems if anything to run the other way. Overall, Evangelical teenagers are more likely to have sex at an early age; Evangelical mothers are more likely to bear children outside marriage; Evangelical marriages are more likely to end in divorce.[77] Catholics have more abortions than the national average.[78] African-Americans and Hispanics are among the most religious demographics in America, yet they have the highest rates of out-of-wedlock births.

The same is true when you zoom out and compare America to the rest of the developed world. Our vaunted religiosity is real enough, but our ostensibly Christian piety doesn't have the consequences a casual observer might expect. We have some of the most liberal divorce laws in the Western world, and the high divorce rates to go with it. We sentimentalize the family more than certain cultures, yet we also have one of the highest rates of unwed births. Our opinion polls suggest that we're more pro-life than Europeans, but we tolerate a much more permissive abortion regime than countries like Germany or France. We're more likely to fight over stem cell research than other developed countries, but our fertility clinics are among the least regulated in the world. We nod to God, and then we do as we please.

* * *

Again, the advantages of this therapeutic culture should not be easily dismissed. Tolerance, freedom, personal choice—what Rieff calls the "kindly" aspects of the new spiritual order—can loom very large indeed, especially when set against the web of shame that the older Christian culture sometimes bound around believers and nonbelievers alike.

But it's striking that the things that therapeutic, God Within religion doesn't seem to have delivered to Americans are the very things that it claims to be best suited to provide—contentment, happiness, well-being, and, above all, the ability to forge successful relationships with fellow human beings.

Instead, the solipsism and narcissism that shadow God Within theology seem to be gradually overwhelming our ability to live in community with one another. Just as Christopher Lasch predicted, in a therapeutic culture "the cult of intimacy conceals a growing despair of finding it," and "personal relations crumble under the emotional weight with which they are burdened."[79] Americans are less happy in their marriages than they were thirty years ago; women's self-reported happiness has dipped downward overall. Our social circles have constricted: declining rates of churchgoing have been accompanied by declining rates of just about every sort of social "joining," and Americans seem to have fewer and fewer friends whom they genuinely trust. Our familial networks have shrunk as well. More children are raised by a single parent; fewer people marry or have children to begin with; and more and more old people live and die alone. A Duke University study found that Americans reported having an average of three people with whom they discussed important matters in 1985, but only two in 2004; the percentage with exactly zero confidants doubled, and the percentage who talked only to family members rose from 57 percent to about 80 percent.[80] We're freer than we used to be, but also more isolated, lonelier, and more depressed.

In *The Triumph of the Therapeutic,* Rieff quotes a line from Goethe: "Speaking for myself, I too believe that humanity will win in the long run; I am only afraid that at the same time the world will have turned into one huge hospital where everyone is everybody else's humane nurse."[81] As ordinary human relationships have attenuated—families weakening, true friendship waning—this is roughly what's been happening. As Ronald Dworkin pointed out in a 2010 *Policy Review* essay, the United States has witnessed a hundredfold increase in the number of professional caregivers since 1950. Our society boasts 77,000 clinical psychologists, 192,000 clinical social workers, 105,000 mental health counselors, 50,000 marriage and family therapists, 17,000 nurse psychotherapists, 30,000 life coaches—and hundreds of thousands of nonclinical social workers and substance abuse counselors as well.[82] "Most of these professionals spend their days helping people cope with everyday life problems," Dworkin writes, "not true mental illness." This means that "under our very noses a revolution has occurred in the personal dimension of life, such that millions of Americans must now pay professionals to listen to their everyday life problems."[83]

Such a "culture of care," as Dworkin calls it, is a logical end point for a society in which the religious instinct is oriented more and more toward every individual's own Highest Thoughts and innermost spirits. Therapeutic theology raises expectations, and it raises self-regard. It isn't surprising that people taught to be constantly enamored of their own godlike qualities would have difficulty forging relationships with ordinary human beings. (Two Supreme Selves do not necessarily a happy marriage make.) Learning to love ourselves and love the universe isn't necessarily the best way to learn to love our neighbor as ourselves, it turns out, and an overemphasis on the essential unity of all things—the Creator and creation, God and man, Yahweh and Elizabeth Gilbert—may be a good way to dissolve more intermediate loyalties completely.

The result is a nation where gurus and therapists have filled the roles once occupied by spouses and friends, and where professional caregivers minister, like seraphim around the throne, to the needs of people taught from infancy to look inside themselves for God. Therapeutic religion promises contentment, but in many cases it seems to deliver a sort of isolation that's at once comfortable and terrible—leaving us alone with the universe, alone with the God Within.

EIGHT

THE CITY ON THE HILL

On August 28, 2010, the Washington Mall played host to an unusual gathering. Dubbed the Restoring Honor rally by its organizer and emcee, the talk show host Glenn Beck, the day's events resembled few of the protest marches that usually filled the public space in front of the Lincoln Memorial. Its cause was neither religious nor political but a distinctive fusion of the two. The tens of thousands of Americans spread out around the Reflecting Pool were mostly Republicans and Christians, but they weren't there for a specific church or a specific political program. Rather, they were there to celebrate a political theology—one as old as the republic itself and as fresh as the latest cable news broadcast.

The idea for the rally had come to Beck almost a year before, and he had originally intended it to be explicitly partisan—another show of the strength of the Tea Party movement that he had done so much to elevate, and a chance to broadcast the same themes that he was then propagating every night on the Fox News Channel. Those themes began with Beck's attack on the radicalism of Barack Obama's presidency, but then swiftly broadened into a sweeping critique of the contemporary American political order. Night after night, Beck argued that both parties had been corrupted by a totalitarian temptation . . . that big business and big government were in bed together . . . that radicals inside the government were pursuing a "the worse, the better" strategy to undermine the American economy . . . that anti-American global elites were intent on using the present crisis to consolidate their power . . . and that the whole vast conspiracy went back to the Progressive Era and the presidency of Woodrow Wilson, the great villain of American history. Finally, returning to where he began, Beck assured his viewers that all of these nightmarish forces could best opposed by rallying against the Obama agenda and all the Democratic Party's works.

But Beck had a change of heart about his Washington event. As he told it, he was at a Tea Party rally in Florida, watching as 25,000 people cheered for him, when suddenly he "broke out in a cold sweat" and realized that God had something else in mind. "I grabbed my assistant by the lapels," Beck said, "and I pulled him in close and I screamed in his ear, 'I don't know how, but we're wrong!'"[1]

With this realization echoing in his head, the *Fox News* host decided that instead of another Tea Party gathering, his D.C. rally would be an explicitly nonpartisan event. It would be a celebration of American values rather than a forum for political assaults, a moment of national unity rather than another attempt to stop Barack Obama's socialist agenda in its tracks. And so it came to pass: Save for an occasional Don't Tread on Me banner, the crowded Mall was nearly free of partisan signs and T-shirt slogans, and there was barely a whisper of the crusade against liberalism that consumed most of Beck's on-air hours.

Instead, there was patriotism: fund-raising for children of slain Special Forces vets; paeans to military heroism (delivered by Sarah Palin, among others); encomia to the Founding Fathers, whose faces appeared in images modeled on the famous Shepard Fairey pop-art poster of Obama. John Adams's face was emblazoned with *Faith,* George Washington's with an Obama-esque *Hope,* and Ben Franklin's with *Charity.* There was an awards ceremony, in which community-service prizes were handed out to a black minister, a Mormon businessman, and the Saint Louis Cardinals' Albert Pujols. And since this was all happening on the anniversary of the "I Have a Dream" speech—the source of much controversy, needless to say—there was a long tribute to Martin Luther King Jr.

Above all, though, there was piety. Speaker after speaker demanded that Americans rededicate themselves to God, while gospel choirs swayed and ministers intoned and Beck himself indulged in a wandering, quasi-biblical, "God and country" patter. As the *Atlantic*'s Chris Good wrote, watching the day unfold: "Everything Glenn Beck says during the rally has to do with the discovery of faith, American history, or some connection between the two. He lists more American historical figures than it's possible to count. He tells the crowd to discover faith. He tells them the future of America rests on their personal discoveries of faith, and on the nation's collective discovery of faith."[2]

Or, in Beck's own words: "It happens the same way, it has since the Burning Bush. Moses. Freedom. And then they forget. They wander until they remember that God is the answer. He always has been. And then they begin to trust."[3]

To many of the professional Beck-watchers in the press, this was all somewhat baffling. They were used to his high-rated political ranting and the anti-Obama fervor of his fans, and they had him pegged as a more amped-up and paranoid version of the other radio and cable-news shouters—the Keith Olbermanns and Sean Hannitys, the Limbaughs and O'Reillys. But this was something strange and different and entirely unclassifiable. It was a tent revival crossed with a pep rally intertwined with a history lecture married to a USO telethon . . . and that was just in the first hour.

But really it was all of a piece. The nonpartisan, revivalish festivities on the Mall were the theological expression of Beck's political rants. The analogies between the American founding and Moses's encounter with the burning bush, the heavy emphasis on a link between religious apostasy and American decline, the calls to restore the country's greatness and "honor" by returning to the piety of our ancestors—even the presence, in a rally pitched primarily to Evangelical Christians, of surreptitious flourishes from Beck's adopted Mormon faith—all of this was intimately connected to the more explicitly political worldview that the autodidact TV personality was promoting every night at 5 p.m. In those connections—between the worship of the founders and the hatred of Woodrow Wilson, between a theological reading of American history and a paranoid reading of present-day politics, and much more besides—we can see the outlines of the heresy that increasingly disfigures our politics, on the left and right alike: the heresy of American nationalism.

Universal faiths are a relative novelty in human history. The religious impulse intertwines with communal life somewhere deep within our psyches, and religion has long found its most natural expression through the cults of a particular place or clan or ethnic group—or, later, a particular city or nation-state. Even if they supposedly represented a more universal principle, the gods of the ancient world were usually local gods—bound to a particular region or tribe or city, invoked as protectors for parochial interests and hailed as defenders of specific peoples.

At the very least, this meant that there could be no real separation between religion and politics. At the most, in societies that deified their rulers, it meant that there was no separation between the political structure and the gods themselves. Either way, the local gods could sometimes accept rivals, but they could never accept being slighted or ignored. Syncretists might associate Rome's Jupiter with Egypt's Ammon or Greece's Zeus, and the sophisticated might even flirt with monotheism or agnosticism. But formally honoring the gods of the community was a requirement for both piety and patriotism. It's telling that both Socrates and the first Christians were denounced for "atheism" when they failed to acknowledge the gods of the *polis* or the empire.

But the same human nature that made localized religion immensely potent also left it vulnerable. If religion is a response, in part, to man's mortality, then a tribal god is by his very nature a potentially insufficient god, because the tribe as well as the individual is subject to decay and death. This was the argument of Franz Rosenzweig, a great Jewish intellectual of the early twentieth century:

> Just as every individual must reckon with his eventual death, the peoples of the world foresee their eventual extinction, be it however distant in time. Indeed, the love of the peoples for their own nationhood is sweet and pregnant with the presentiment of death. Love is only surpassing sweet when it is directed toward a mortal object, and the secret of this ultimate sweetness only is defined by the bitterness of death. Thus the peoples of the world foresee a time when their land with its rivers and mountains still lies under heaven as it does today, but other people dwell there; when their language is entombed in books, and their laws and customs have lost their living power.[4]

Their laws and customs—and their deities as well. The more local and personal the god, the greater the instinctive human attachment to the cult.

But the local god perishes when his cults and rituals perish, and no such deity can hope to redeem a people from the bitterness of death. This reality inspires peoples and races to what David Goldman, Rosenzweig's most provocative contemporary popularizer, calls a "fragile and ultimately futile effort to preserve their physical continuity through blood and soil. . . . Their hope for immortality takes the form of a perpetual fight for physical existence, which one day they must lose."[5] Real hope requires a different theology. Only a universal god, transcending time and space, language and geography, can plausibly save the countless tribes of humanity from their otherwise inevitable fate.

When this universal God actually entered history, though, it was as the champion of a very particular race and people. This is the strange revelation at the heart of the Old Testament story: a Being who seems at first like a particularly powerful tribal deity gradually reveals himself as the eternal YHWH, the great I AM, without ever abandoning his unique covenant with the Jewish people. Indeed, the Old Testament, or at least the prophetic tradition therein, argues that Yahweh's particularity is actually the *means* through which His universality will be ultimately manifested to the world. Of all the scandalous claims embedded in the Hebrew Bible, perhaps none is more scandalous than this: that Israel, alone among the peoples of the earth, will have immortality *as a people,* and that if the rest of the world claims a share of that same immortality, they will claim it through the Jews.

What Jewish prophecy envisioned, Christian history has operationalized. "Salvation is from the Jews," Paul told his readers, and then invited them to share Israel's destiny by joining themselves to the New Israel of the Christian Church. Or, as Goldman puts it: "In the West, nations came by the hope of immortality through Christianity, which offered the promise of Israel to the Gentiles, but only on the condition that they cease to be Gentiles, through adoption into an Israel of the Spirit."[6] Pagans could become Jews, in effect, so long as they ceased to be pagans. They could have a god who was simultaneously local and universal, but their own local gods would have to go.

Those gods went (albeit slowly), but the tribal impulse that motivated their worshipers endured. Often Christianity has been able to successfully accommodate some version of it, by adapting pagan cults to Christian purposes and allowing that God's interest in the fate of particular nations might not be confined to His relationship with the Twelve Tribes of Israel. Catholicism, in particular, through devotions to the saints and the Virgin Mary, has managed to balance the universalism of Christianity with a strong localism, which respects the possibility that the Creator's purposes might encompass a special providence for other races, regions, and cultures as well—from France to Mexico, Prague to Walsingham, Akita to Medjugorje.

But this balancing act can teeter into a kind of idolatry, as Protestants have always been eager to point out. And even when it doesn't, a Joan of Arc or a Virgin of Guadalupe hasn't always sufficed to satisfy the human desire to be especially loved, not just for oneself, but for one's clan or country or polity as well. Thus the persistence, throughout Christian history, of what you might call Jew-envy, which objects to the unique role that the Chosen People play in the history of salvation. Anti-Semitism has many taproots in the Christian world, but perhaps none is so potent as the resentment of Jewish chosenness and the desire to claim Israel's unique birthright for one's own.

The Gnostic/God Within answer to this resentment, as we've seen, is to make every individual into his own Chosen Person, with his own private Yahweh somewhere deep inside. (Rosenzweig saw Christianity's historical connection to Judaism as crucial to its ability to resist this impulse: "It is only the Old Testament that enables Christianity to defend itself against [Gnosticism], its inherent danger.") But another, equally popular, solution has been to simply substitute one's own nationality for the Twelve Tribes of Israel—or better still, to claim that one's own nation is actually *descended* from ancient Israel.

Christianity's greatest rival, Islam, was influenced by this impulse. In the more ethnocentric forms of the Muslim faith, the Arabs are implicitly cast as both the heirs of Abraham (through Ishmael rather than Isaac) and the real New Israel, superseding Christianity's pan-ethnic Church and the original Twelve Tribes alike. But the heresy of nationalism reached its fullest flower only with the rise of the modern nation-state. Religious nationalism influenced the ethno-Catholicism of Spain and France, the Protestant chauvinism of Puritan England, the Orthodox nationalism of czarist Russia, and many more besides. It shaped theologies as diverse as the

Sino-Christianity of Hong Xiuquan (who conquered half of China in the 1840s while claiming to be Jesus' Asian younger brother) and the "Aryan Christianity" of Nazi Germany.

Indeed, in a sense the entire age of romantic nationalism, and the subsequent carnage of the two world wars, can be seen as an extended revolt against Christian universalism. As Goldman puts it, "Europe arose from universal Christian empire and it fell when the nationalities mutinied against their foster mother the church and fought until their mutual ruin."[7]

In his remarkable parable *The Portage to San Cristobal of A.H.* (1981), George Steiner captures the impulses behind this revolt by putting words in the mouth of Adolf Hitler—a Hitler, in his story, who has been found alive in South America and put on trial in the jungle by his Israeli commando captors. Conducting his defense, Hitler argues that his vision was borrowed directly from the Jews, forged in envy and in imitation:

> It was there that I understood your secret power. The secret power of your teaching. Of yours. A chosen people. Chosen by God for His own. The only race on earth chosen, exalted, made singular among mankind. . . .
>
> The pride of it, the brute cunning. Whatever you are, wherever you are, be it ulcerous as Job, or Neumann scratching his stinking crotch . . . what does it matter if you're one of the chosen people? One of God's familiars, above all other men, set apart for His rages and His love. In a covenant, a singling out, a consecration never to be lost. . . .
>
> From you. Everything. To set a race apart. To keep it from defilement. To hold before it a promised land . . . Your beliefs. Your arrogance. In Nuremburg, the searchlights. That clever beaver Speer. Straight into the night. Do you remember them? The pillar of fire. That shall lead you to Canaan. . . .
>
> My racism was a parody of yours, a hungry imitation. What is a thousand-year *Reich* compared with the eternity of Zion?[8]

We can be grateful that the American story hasn't opened into such abysses. On these shores, classic ethno-nationalism has been swallowed up by a new and different understanding of the nation-state—one that resembles the self-understanding of Christianity itself. Like Gentiles entering the Church, every race and tribe is expected to leave its particular totems and traditions behind when it enters the democratic empire of the New World. As with pagans who turned Christian, the old deities of ethnicity must be set aside in favor of a more universal human brotherhood.

The impulse toward conflating religion and ethnicity has persisted, of course—in the ethnic subchurches established by Italian Catholics and German Lutherans, in the white-supremacist readings of the Bible popular in the antebellum South, and in the varieties of Afrocentric religion popular among black nationalists down to the present day. But it's persisted in an increasingly attenuated form. Our immigrant churches lose influence and potency with every successive generation, and the idea of a "white man's Christianity" is as dead as the eugenics movement. Outside the wilder reaches of the Internet, there is simply no meaningful American equivalent of European nationalism's nostalgia for the ethno-religion of the pagan past. (Neil Gaiman's novel *American Gods* cleverly envisions the pagan deities of Europe and Africa surviving as supernatural hobos in the New World, subsisting on scraps of worship from immigrants who have largely forgotten them.) This may explain, in turn, why the lure of anti-Semitism has always been weaker in the New World than in the Old: the Jewish claim to a kind of blood relationship with God inspires less envy among peoples who have put aside their own blood ties.

But if the lack of a blood-and-soil tradition has weakened the temptation toward imagining one's own tribe as God's real Chosen People, the obvious resemblance between America and the Christian Church—both pan-ethnic, universalizing bodies that promise to create a new man out of the old one, and redeem a fallen and corrupted world—has tempted many Americans to regard the United States *as a whole* as a New Israel, a holy nation, a people set apart. This inclination has been woven into every chapter of our national history, from the Puritan "errand in the wilderness" down to the presidential campaign of Barack Obama. The language of our politics casts the American story in explicitly religious terms: We're a "promised land" and our government a "new order for the ages," with a "manifest destiny" defined by "American exceptionalism." This can easily shade from the generic providentialism of presidential speeches ("May God bless you, and may God continue to bless the United States of America . . .") into something more powerful and comprehensive—a faith in "Americanism," in our mission and destiny and God's influence therein, that David Gelernter describes as "The Fourth Great Western Religion."[9]

This sense of the American narrative as a continuation of the biblical story transcends ethnic divisions. In 2010, a survey conducted by the Public Religion Research Institute found that 60 percent of Americans believed that "God has granted America a special role in human history." The view was strongest among white Evangelicals, upwards of 80 percent of whom agreed with the exceptionalist credo. But it was "strikingly robust" among minorities as well: 64 percent of Hispanics and 60 percent of African-Americans endorsed the idea of America's providential purpose.[10] Neither the residual power of tribalism nor even the legacy of chattel slavery, it turns out, is a match for the power of Americanism. Whether we claim descent from the first colonists, from subsequent immigrants, or from African slaves, we are all likely to be exceptionalists of one sort or another.

Depending on how far it's taken, a version of exceptionalism is entirely compatible with Christian orthodoxy. If God is the lord of history, then there's no reason to dismiss the possibility that a nation as significant (and particularly fortunate) as the United States shouldn't have an important role to play in His unfolding plan. If French Catholics are permitted to believe that Joan of Arc fulfilled God's will by saving her nation from invaders, then why shouldn't Americans believe the same thing about George Washington or Abraham Lincoln? If Russian Orthodox believers have license to regard their empire as a "Third Rome," why shouldn't Americans feel something similar about their republic?

But such a compatibility is possible only if the belief in exceptionalism is tempered by a realism about the mysteries of providence and the limits of human perfectability. Christian orthodoxy makes room for particular loves and loyalties, but not for myths of national innocence or fantasies about building the kingdom of heaven on earth. Love of country is one thing; chauvinism and utopianism are quite another.

Happily, such realism has often been present in our public life. Consider John Winthrop's famous vision of America as a "city on a hill," which is regularly invoked as the defining image of American exceptionalism—and just as often dismissed as an example of nationalist mythologizing. The Puritan lawyer's actual language admits of a more complicated reading:

"Consider that we shall be as a city upon a hill," he wrote to his daughters, "the eyes of all people are upon us, so that if we shall deal falsely with our God in this work we have undertaken and so cause him to withdraw his present help from us, we shall be made a story and byword through the world." As Mark A. Signorelli noted in a perceptive 2011 essay, the point of this passage isn't to boast of the new colony's special virtue, but to demand that it live up to its high ideals:

> Winthrop intended the preeminence of a city on a hill to signify not the inherent superiority of the Plymouth settlement, but its notoriety. His point was that the whole world would be aware of the outcome of the Pilgrims' expedition, so that a failure to establish a just community in the new world would inevitably become known throughout the old world, and become an occasion for the Puritans' enemies to deride their faith. . . . He did not wish to soothe the Pilgrims' complacency by extolling their virtues, but rather to awaken their moral vigilance by reminding them of the iniquity towards which the human soul is always inclined. . . . The image of a city upon a hill is, for Winthrop, the image of *preeminent responsibility*.[11]

You can hear the same combination of notes—exhortatory but cautionary, providentialist but anti-utopian—running through the public rhetoric of America's most impressive leaders. As Walter McDougall notes in *Promised Land, Crusader State* (1998), for the Founding Fathers and their wisest heirs, "the flip of the boast of Exceptionalism was a warning"—a caution against arrogance and folly, lest America follow the path of "Israel and Judah and Athens and Rome" and succumb "to decadence, hubris, even self-hatred, and enter its decline and fall."[12]

Thus George Washington, in his farewell address, balanced American optimism and Christian realism: On the one hand, he invoked "Providence" to summon Americans to an "experiment . . . recommended by every sentiment which ennobles human nature," but on the other hand he was careful to note that our experiment might be "rendered impossible" by the "vices" of that same fallen nature.[13] Likewise Calvin Coolidge, in his address on the 150th anniversary of 1776, warned Americans basking "in an age of science and of abounding accumulation of material things" that "the things of the spirit come first," and unless "we cling to that, all our material prosperity, overwhelming though it may appear, will turn to a barren sceptre in our grasp."[14] Likewise Dwight Eisenhower, in *his* farewell address a century and a half later, balanced an invocation of American exceptionalism . . .

> Throughout America's adventure in free government, such basic purposes have been to keep the peace; to foster progress in human achievement, and to enhance liberty, dignity and integrity among peoples and among nations. To strive for less would be unworthy of a free and religious people.[15]

. . . with a rejection of any sort of blind optimism or utopianism:

> Crises there will continue to be. In meeting them, whether foreign or domestic, great or small, there is a recurring temptation to feel that some spectacular and costly action could become the miraculous solution to all current difficulties . . .

This passage segues, of course, into Eisenhower's famous warning against the "military-industrial complex," and then into his less-celebrated, but equally prescient, critique of the pretensions of "a scientific-technological elite"—both of which would be ignored, with disastrous consequences, by the policy makers of the subsequent decade.

Nowhere is this balancing act more artfully accomplished than in Abraham Lincoln's famous Second Inaugural Address. On the one hand, Lincoln's rhetoric effectively sanctifies the American Civil War, transmuting the horror of a bloody conflict into a kind of Old Testament narrative, in which a just God acts to simultaneously chastise and redeem the New Israel of America:

> If we shall suppose that American slavery is one of those offenses which, in the providence of God, must needs come, but which, having continued through His appointed time, He now wills to remove, and that He gives to both North and South this terrible war as the woe due to those by whom the offense came, shall we discern therein any

departure from those divine attributes which the believers in a living God always ascribe to Him? Fondly do we hope, fervently do we pray, that this mighty scourge of war may speedily pass away. Yet, if God wills that it continue until all the wealth piled by the bondsman's two hundred and fifty years of unrequited toil shall be sunk, and until every drop of blood drawn with the lash shall be paid by another drawn with the sword, as was said three thousand years ago, so still it must be said "the judgments of the Lord are true and righteous altogether."[16]

Not for nothing have the more vigorous apostles of America's civil religion seen Lincoln as a martyred prophet of their creed—a man who "put Judeo-Christianity's holiest beliefs at America's disposal," as Gelernter puts it, and "mixed them into the very concrete of which Americanism is made."[17]

But note that Lincoln's Second Inaugural invokes providentialism to explain a *chastisement,* rather than to boast of America's particular virtue or celebrate its particular mission in the world. And note, as well, the way that the passage reproduced above is framed. First, with this introduction:

Neither party expected for the war the magnitude or the duration which it has already attained. Neither anticipated that the *cause* of the conflict might cease with or even before the conflict itself should cease. Each looked for an easier triumph, and a result less fundamental and astounding. Both read the same Bible and pray to the same God, and each invokes His aid against the other. It may seem strange that any men should dare to ask a just God's assistance in wringing their bread from the sweat of other men's faces, but let us judge not, that we be not judged. The prayers of both could not be answered. That of neither has been answered fully. The Almighty has His own purposes.

And then the famous conclusion:

With malice toward none, with charity for all, with firmness in the right as God gives us to see the right, let us strive on to finish the work we are in, to bind up the nation's wounds, to care for him who shall

have borne the battle and for his widow and his orphan, to do all which
may achieve and cherish a just and lasting peace among ourselves and
with all nations.

Again and again, Lincoln frames his providentialism in the language of
humility and mystery. ("Let us judge not, that we be not judged . . . With
malice toward none, with charity for all . . . The Almighty has his own
purposes . . . as God gives us to see the right.") Again and again, he eschews
the temptation to assert that the Union cause is pure and perfect, or that
the North is God's agent in a holy war.

If we follow his admonitions and example, we may believe, as he came
to believe, that God's intentions can sometimes be discerned in the pages of
the American story. But we must not boast of being God's instruments, or
pretend that we understand the full scope and direction of the story. Our
exceptionalism must be a provisional exceptionalism, in other words—
expectant but not presumptuous, perpetually tempered by humility and
open to correction and surprise.

Moreover, if we think of ourselves as in any way analogous to Israel,
it must be *only* by way of analogy. There is only one true Israel, and even
the greatest nation can hope only to be an "*almost*-chosen people."[18] That
phrase, too, is Lincoln's, from an 1861 address—and in that single word,
"almost," a healthy patriotism is defended, while the heresy of nationalism
stands rebuked.

But not every American leader has been a Washington, a Coolidge, an
Eisenhower, a Lincoln. In the right hands, the idea of American exceptionalism can reflect a healthy union of patriotism and piety. But in the wrong
hands, it can be a source of dangerous theological temptations.

One such temptation is messianism. Not content with the possibility
that God has particularly favored the United States, the messianic view
holds that American democracy can actually *fulfill* God's purposes on
earth—whether by building the New Jerusalem at home, or by spreading
the blessings of liberty to every race and people overseas. As the conservative sociologist Robert Nisbet observed, "in the New World as in the Old,
the compounding of the idea of progress and the idea of the nation-state

could result in an intensity of millennialism and messianism the like of which had never been seen on earth."[19] Piggybacking on the parallels between American universalism and Christian universalism, messianic Americanism turns liberal democracy into a religion unto itself, capable of carrying out the kind of redemptive work that orthodoxy reserves for Christ and his Church. It historicizes and secularizes the story of salvation, transforming the eschatological promises of the New Testament into political promises here on earth. Instead of seeking the kingdom of God, it seeks the end of history. Instead of trying to make all nations Christian, it hopes to make them all American—and looks for the day when, in Woodrow Wilson's phrase, the nations of the world recognize that our Stars and Stripes are "the flag, not only of America, but of humanity."

The other heresy of nationalism, messianism's mirror image, is doom-laden and apocalyptic. Not content to note the parallels between the story of Israel and the settlement of America, the apocalyptic view suggests that the American founding was literally a covenanted event, akin to the biblical establishment of Israel. We are not just "almost chosen," but *actually* chosen, and our constitution is not only consonant with Christian principles but literally divinely inspired. The Founding is our Eden and our Sinai; everything else is a tragic falling away, a descent into idolatry that God will justly punish. Indeed, modern America's various departures from the wisdom of the Founding places it in the same position—and under the same divine judgment—as ancient Israel during its flirtations with the gods of Assyria or Babylon. And given these realities, God-fearing Americans must either withdraw entirely from the corruptions of the United States's current Babylonian captivity, or else dedicate themselves, like King Josiah restoring God's Law to Judah, to the overthrow of the idols, and the restoration of the Founders' holy writ.

The first temptation is naturally progressive. The messianic mind is perpetually fastening on whatever seems like the coming thing in Western politics, from liberal imperialism in the 1890s to the cult of Obama in 2007–2008, and declaring it the new thing that the God of history is doing in the world. The accommodationist theology of Harvey Cox, which we considered in detail earlier, represented the New Frontier's version of this temptation, in which Christians were supposed to take instruction from the "mature secularity" of JFK and his whiz kids. But Cox's claim that "what God is doing in the world is politics" has been the recurring theme of messianic Americanism all the way back to the Founding generation (when Ezra Stiles, Yale's president, described the new republic as "God's New Israel," with George Washington as its Joshua) and the Puritan era before it. Over the last 150 years, the messianic temptation has variously yoked Christian zeal to Social Darwinism, to "white man's burden" colonialism, to progressivism and socialism, Marxism and New Deal liberalism, the Great Society and the sexual revolution. It has put its stamp on nearly every cause and crusade of the American left. And it has endured even as that same left has grown more hostile to organized Christianity. For all its notional secularity, much of today's liberalism is still informed by the essentially messianic assumption that "achieving our country," in the words of Richard Rorty, the post-Christian grandson of the great Social Gospel theologian Walter Rauschenbusch, can be a substitute for the consolations of traditional religious faith.

The second temptation is naturally reactionary. Everything that messianic Americanism embraces and celebrates, apocalyptic Americanism rejects or damns. It's often a heresy for the disappointed and dispossessed, and it finds its strongest adherents among populations for whom the story of American history is a story of gradual marginalization or defeat: nineteenth-century Nativists and neo-Confederates, Charles Coughlin's listeners in the 1930s and John Birchers in the 1950s, and religious fundamentalists in nearly every time and place. As messianism tempts liberal Christians, apocalypticism tempts their conservative cobelievers: The vision of American history as a long apostasy, a steadily downhill slide, blurs easily into the fundamentalist vision of the modern age as the gradual fulfillment of the book of Revelation. As messianism inspires an unwarranted optimism about human perfectability, apocalypticism inspires an unwarranted paranoia about foes abroad and enemies within, and invents vast anti-American conspiracies—Catholic in the nineteenth century, Jewish and then Communist in the twentieth, and nowadays a dark combination of the United Nations and the global Caliphate—to explain whatever ills beset the United States. As messianism awaits a great leader to deliver hope and change and finally lead America to the promised land, apocalypticism looks for a villain on whom to blame the betrayal of the Founding. Hence the the right-wing vendettas against Franklin Roosevelt;

hence Glenn Beck's fixation on the evils of Woodrow Wilson and Barack Obama alike.

These vendettas, though, are often interwoven with a strange kind of admiration. The midcentury Calvinist theologian R. J. Rushdoony, whose fringe vision of "Christian Reconstructionism" urged the American Republic to return to its supposed theocratic roots, was known to speak admiringly of John F. Kennedy's soaring, messianic, "pay any price" speeches. ("They've lost the theology," he said of the New Frontiersmen, "but they haven't lost the faith."[20]) So too with Beck, who has urged his conservative listeners to imitate the tactics of Marxist radicals like Saul Alinsky, and who implies that the right has a lot to learn about discipline and strategy from the vast left-wing conspiracies he claims to have exposed. It's a dynamic that hints at the kinship between the apocalyptic and messianic styles of nationalism: their mutual hatred doesn't prevent them from half-recognizing one another, through a glass darkly, as theological and political twins.

This relationship is nowhere more evident—and nowhere more illuminating—than in Beck's high-profile crusade against America's twenty-eighth president. On one level, fixating on a figure like Wilson (who comes in first on the list of the "Top Ten Bastards of All Time" in Beck's *Arguing with Idiots,* edging out Pol Pot and Pontius Pilate) seems like an odd way for a political talk show host to tackle the issues of the day. But understood as an exercise in ideological self-definition, it makes every kind of sense. Beck looks at Wilson and sees his own crack'd-mirror image: nine decades apart, the patrician president and the populist loudmouth perfectly embody the two poles of the heresy of nationalism.

More important, their respective follies offer telling examples of where its twin temptations can lead.

Few American presidents have been more pious than Woodrow Wilson. His administration's dedication to progressive reform at home, and eventually to humanitarian war-making abroad, represented the culmination of a particularly messianic period in American politics and religion. This was the golden age of the liberal Protestantism that we discussed in chapter 1, which steeped itself in Hegel and Darwin and emerged with a vision of an "applied Christianity" that would eschew metaphysics and seek to operationalize the Sermon on the Mount. ("Until the Holy City of the seer's vision has become the reality of earth," as a progressive clergyman wrote in 1911.[21]) The zealous Wilson was in the thick of this movement, transmuting the missionary impulse of his ancestral Presbyterianism into a missionary politics. The "mighty task before us," he told a convocation of Protestants a decade before he won the presidency, "is to make the United States a mighty Christian nation, and to Christianize the world."[22]

The latter quest came to define his presidency, and not for the good. Like George W. Bush almost a century later, Wilson came into office promising a kind of Christian humility in foreign policy. But as with Bush, when crisis struck and his attempts at a "new and more wholesome diplomacy" turned out to be insufficient to restore the peace, he donned the armor of a crusader instead. "What would Christ have done in our day, in our place, with our opportunities?" he had asked his fellow liberal Protestants in 1905.[23] In 1917, the answer turned out to be "make war on the Central Powers," a war that Wilson's messianic temper cast in the most absolutist and uncompromising terms—and that Wilson's fellow progressive Christians rushed to embrace. "I have no hesitation," declared one of the many strident ministers quoted in Richard Gamble's *The War for Righteousness* (2003), a grimly fascinating history of progressivism's martial Wilson-era turn, "in saying that the voice of a just God summons us to this War and that it is in the highest sense of the word a Holy War."[24] Jesus Christ himself, a Unitarian minister intoned as doughboys landed in Europe, "would take bayonet and grenade and bomb and rifle and do the work of deadliness against that which is the most deadly enemy of his Father's kingdom in a thousand years."[25]

In this atmosphere, it was not enough to fight for limited objectives. America's war aims, Wilson insisted, included "destruction of *every* arbitrary power anywhere . . . settlement of *every* question . . . upon the basis of the free acceptance of that settlement by the people immediately concerned . . . and an organization of peace which shall make it *certain* that the combined power of free nations will check *every* invasion of right and serve to make peace and justice the more secure."[26] Fine words, but in that march of "everys," one hears the jingle-jangle of fanaticism, rather than the more measured notes of a genuinely Christian statesmanship. In the results, meanwhile—Wilson's inability to prevent the victorious Allies from imposing a Carthaginian peace, the grisly riot of nationalisms that his demand for self-determination released, and the impotence of his dreamed-of League of Nations—one can see the costs of a messianism untempered by humility or self-doubt.

Where Wilson rushed in, too many subsequent presidents have followed. Peter Beinart calls this pattern the Icarus syndrome, a disease that has afflicted our policy makers in moments of apparent American preeminence, from the 1960s to the Bush era. James Kurth, somewhat more theologically, terms it the Protestant Deformation, linking it explicitly to the secularized, Hegelian Protestantism of the World War I era. Whatever term you give it, Wilsonianism has been a constant in twentieth-century American history, echoing in speeches (Kennedy's first inaugural, George W. Bush's second) that claim the mantle of providence without the humility of Lincoln, and then playing itself out in wars that vindicated the warnings of Washington and Eisenhower.

Nor has this spirit been confined to foreign policy. "War is the health of the state," Randolph Bourne argued, and our Wilsonian moments have tended to coincide with vast domestic expansions of government, sometimes with favorable consequences but just as often with unfortunate ones. Lyndon Johnson's strategy in Vietnam, Richard A. Hunt wrote in *Pacification: The American Struggle for Vietnam's Hearts and Minds* (1998), "had its origins in the same presidential impulses that gave birth to the Great Society."[27] Or as Johnson himself put it in 1966: "Our foreign policy must always be an extension of our domestic policy. Our safest guide to what we do abroad is what we do at home."[28]

The same essential unity suggests itself, albeit on a lesser scale, in the way that George W. Bush's arguments for No Child Left Behind and other "compassionate conservative" initiatives dovetailed with his arguments for trying to plant democracy in Muslim soil. In both cases, his critics were guilty of the "soft bigotry of low expectations" for doubting the transformative power of good intentions.

Thus utopianism abroad breeds utopianism at home, and vice versa. And because there's no need to balance the books in utopia, Wilsonianism tends to be a guns-and-butter political theology, a grasshopper ideology that spends today and lets tomorrow take care of itself. Which is why,

when tomorrow finally comes, our Wilsonian eras have tended to give
way to periods of stagnation, retrenchment, and decay.

Periods, that is, like the one we are living through now.

There is much in the enduring legacy of Woodrow Wilson's presidency,
in other words, to justify the kind of obloquy that Glenn Beck recently
decided to heap upon his head. But if Wilson embodied messianic nationalism unbound, his latter-day antagonist embodies apocalyptic nationalism
at its most perfervid. Indeed, the Beckian worldview, as elucidated across
his two years' plus as cable news's brightest-burning comet, is an almost
comical concatenation of every apocalyptic tic and tendency.

There is the Founder worship, often taken to a "What Would George
Washington Do" extreme. There are the constant predictions of the republic's imminent collapse and the near-inevitability of a totalitarian regime rising in its stead. There is the frantic hunt for enemies within (the
Marxists burrowing into the Obama White House, the threat posed by
domestic radicals and illegal immigrants) and enemies abroad (the riots
engulfing the Arab world in 2011 inspired Beck to extraordinary flights
of fancy about the links between American leftists and the looming pan-
Islamic Caliphate). There are the attacks on any religious system that
doesn't line up perfectly with Beck's limited-government interpretation
of the American founding. ("I beg you, look for the words 'social justice'
or 'economic justice' on your church Web site. If you find it, run as fast
as you can. Social justice and economic justice, they are code words.
Now, am I advising people to leave their church? Yes!"[29]) There is the
Manichaean language, aping the rhetoric of the totalitarian movements
Beck claims to be opposing. ("Progressivism is the cancer in America
and it is eating our Constitution[30] . . . our political leaders have become
nothing more than parasites who feed off our sweat and blood."[31]) And
there is the extension of this apocalyptic style to the political situation of
Israel, where Beck recently held a follow-up rally, on the theme "Restoring Courage"—the courage, that is, to resist what he sees as a looming
second Holocaust.

The particular channel through which these themes filtered down to
Beck is the work of Cleon Skousen, a prolific figure from the John Birch

era of American apocalyptism. Skousen leaped to prominence as a conspiracy theorist with 1958's *The Naked Communist,* which painted the global Marxist threat using wild colors and outrageous claims. He followed it up with *The Naked Capitalist,* which revealed that the Ivy League Establishment and international Communism were both part of the same vast conspiracy—a conspiracy that had been kicked off, naturally, in the presidency of Woodrow Wilson. Then in 1981's *The 5,000-Year Leap* (which Beck's enthusiastic recommendation turned into a surprise bestseller), Skousen spun a providential account of the American experiment as the culmination of God's long-term plan for humanity, and the country's recent history as a gradual falling away from the marriage of Christian piety and limited government that the founding generation envisioned.

Like Beck, Skousen was a member of the Church of Jesus Christ of Latter-day Saints, and his works offered a paranoid gloss on familiar Mormon themes. (In 1960, the president of the LDS, David McKay, urged every member of his church to read *The Naked Communist.*) With its vision of Jesus ministering in the New World after his resurrection and its insistence that true Christianity was restored to earth only shortly after the founding of the United States, Joseph Smith's faith sometimes hints at a literalized version of the heresy of American nationalism. Popular Mormon piety has taken these ideas a step further, spinning eschatological scenarios in which the United States Constitution will hang "upon a single thread" and an elder of the Mormon Church will be called upon to save it.

Ordinarily, the LDS influence running through Skousen's work (and Beck's popularization of the same) would be a turn-off to conservative Evangelicals, who tend to bristle at what they regard as Mormonism's cultish pseudo-Christianity. But the heresy of nationalism is an ecumenical faith. Both folk Mormonism and popular Evangelical piety incline toward highly theologized readings of American history, and Skousen's revisionist history of the United States maps onto the kind of "Christian America" historiography that's long been popular among fundamentalists. If you filter out the more conspiratorial elements of their political theology, Skousen and Beck can sound a lot like David Barton, the prolific amateur historian whose books and pamphlets have persuaded many Evangelicals that the American Founders had the divine mandate of King David and the politics of a contemporary Tea Partier.

As modern Evangelicalism matured across the 1980s and 1990s, this "God and the Constitution" political theology was gradually eclipsed by more sophisticated understandings of American history and of the Christian role in politics. But since the collapse of the Bush administration, the older attitudes have come rushing back to the fore. The political theology of a Michele Bachmann, for instance, sometimes resembled the heresy of nationalism at its most unvarnished, and many of her Republican rivals made more subtle forays in the same direction.

To the extent that the chasm between Evangelicals and Mormons can be bridged, the heresy of God and country is the obvious place to fling out a rope bridge. This is exactly what Beck did during his *Fox News* run. From his boosterism for *The 5,000-Year Leap* to the blend of civic religion and nondenominational Christianity on display at the Lincoln Memorial, the entire Beck project represented a subtle invitation to Evangelicals to get over their anxieties about Mormonism by finding common ground with the Latter-day Saints in a shared appreciation of the Father, the Son, and the Holy Constitution.

To many observers, this is scary stuff—much scarier by far than anything Woodrow Wilson did or didn't do as president. (She holds a "set of beliefs more extreme than those of any American politician of her stature," *The New Yorker* fretted about Bachmann during her primary-season rise to prominence.[32]) Here, too, the Wilson-Beck comparison illuminates the way the heresy of nationalism has been received and remembered in American life. Messianism is the respectable version of the heresy, the strain that high-minded politicians use to elevate their speeches and that swath of the intelligentsia embraces without apology. Apocalypticism is the madwoman in the attic, whose screeching, though it often finds an audience, is disdained as crazy by the great and good. "Wilsonianism" is a respectable school of foreign policy rather than an epithet, and our most messianic leaders—a John F. Kennedy, a Teddy Roosevelt—have never lacked for hagiographers. Whereas apocalypticism in all its myriad forms remains the preserve of cranks and fanatics, and there are precious few revisionist historians willing to make the case that Charles Coughlin and Cleon Skousen were misunderstood humanitarians, or geniuses before their time.

This is all understandable. Messianism invokes the better angels of our nature; apocalyptism plays to our fears and paranoias. Messianism tends to attract genuine idealists; apocalyptism is often the preserve of genuine bigots. And the messianic impulse, for all its faults, has great accomplishments to its credit. Many of the great moral crusades of American history would be unimaginable without a touch of heresy, a touch of religious utopianism, in the attitudes of their activists and champions. (If Wilson's ineffective Fourteen Points were messianic, so was Martin Luther King's "I Have a Dream" speech, with its vision of the mystic renovation of an entire racism-corrupted society.) The apocalyptic style, on the other hand, tends to be more purely negative. It may call for moral renewal, but its millenarian hostility toward present-day decadence tends to make it a poor vehicle for any kind of real reform. It's been responsible for far more witch hunts than genuine restorations of lost virtue. It scorches the earth but rarely turns it over.

But if messianism has done more good than apocalyptism, it has probably done more damage as well. Precisely because the messianic style has been more influential among the American elite, the consequences of messianic excess have generally been more comprehensively disastrous. Apocalyptism is rarely harmless, but its very marginalization limits its destructive power. Witch hunts are dangerous and deadly, to be sure. But "wars for righteousness" often have far more victims, and they do more lasting harm.

This is not how our history is usually remembered. But far more people suffered, at home and abroad, because messianic chief executives like Wilson and Teddy Roosevelt took the country repeatedly to war than suffered because of the excesses of Protestant fundamentalism in the same era. (*Inherit the Wind* bestrides high school reading lists, but the Roosevelt-championed Filipino War, America's first exercise in disastrous nation-building, has been more or less erased from the national memory.) More harm was probably done in the 1930s by the high-minded Protestant ministers who put an idealistic Christian stamp on the era's sweeping eugenic programs than by all of Charles Coughlin's radio broadcasts put together. In the Cold War era, the John Birch Society made life miserable for left-wing playwrights and State Department functionaries . . . but tens of thousands of Americans perished in the jungles of South Vietnam because of John F. Kennedy's "God's work must truly be our own" idealism. There was an apocalyptic thread running through Barry Goldwater's 1964 presidential campaign, but his "extremism in the defense of liberty is no vice" rhetoric isn't the reason that we're staring at trillions in unfunded liabilities as the baby boomers retire. Those debts can be laid at the door of Lyndon Johnson's messianic temper, and his quest to build a "Great Society" that would not only relieve want and poverty forever but also "establish a harmony between man and society which will allow each of us to enlarge the meaning of his life."[33]

So to the present day. In the presidency of George W. Bush, the apocalyptic side of American Evangelicalism was invoked to explain almost everything that liberal partisans hated about the occupant of the White House. Fundamentalist theories about the Rapture explained Republican indifference to global warming. ("Why care about the earth when the droughts, floods, famine, and pestilence brought by ecological collapse are signs of the apocalypse foretold in the Bible?" Bill Moyers wrote. "Why care about global climate change when you and yours will be rescued in the Rapture?"[34]) The malign influence of figures like Rushdoony—who was briefly elevated to an absurd level of prominence by liberal conspiracy theorists—explained the entire right-wing domestic agenda, from abortion and gay marriage to deregulation and tax cuts. Bush's Middle Eastern adventurism was regularly cast as an expression of his political coalition's apocalyptic worldview—the Christian Zionist belief in Israel's divine title to the Holy Land, the general fundamentalist hostility toward Islam, and even the end-times scenarios that featured Mesopotamian conflagrations and Megiddan battles royal. (It is "eerie," wrote Kevin Phillips in *American Theocracy*, "to see so many Bush administration foreign-policy qualities anticipated" in the Left Behind novels.[35])

Some apocalyptic ideas were certainly floating in the right-wing ether during the early 2000s. But there's no evidence that any of them actually influenced Bush's inner circle or shaped the choices and considerations that led America to war. The president's own piety was as substantial as Wilson's, but like Wilson's it owed far more to the messianic temperament than to its dark apocalyptic twin. If Bush sometimes talked about America's overseas commitments in the language of holy war, it was a Wilsonian war for freedom that he had in mind, not a world-ending Götterdämmerung or an anti-Islamic crusade. His goal wasn't to defeat Muslims but to free them from bondage, and he seemed bent on hastening Francis Fukuyama's end of history rather than hurrying Armageddon. His political-theological touchstone wasn't the dark view of an America fallen from grace and surrounded by enemies. Instead, he enjoyed the blithe confidence of an evangelist for democracy. "I do believe there is an Almighty," he told journalists during the grimmest days of the Iraq War, "and I believe a gift of that Almighty to all is freedom."[36] Proclaiming that gift, he said in his second inaugural, has been America's mission "across the generations." Spreading it is "the calling of our time."[37]

In the Bush era, in other words, the apocalyptic streak in American conservatism was culturally significant but politically marginal. Messianic nationalism was in the saddle, and it rode American foreign policy deep into the quicksand of the Middle East.

With the example of the Bush presidency, we come to what's distinctive about religion and politics in our own era. It isn't the presence of the heresy of nationalism in both its apocalyptic and messianic aspects; that's been a constant throughout American history. Rather, it's the coexistence of *both* aspects within *both* of the country's political coalitions. Instead of the normal pattern of American history, in which conservatives are tempted by the reactionary pessimism of the apocalyptic style, and liberals by the seductions of utopianism, now messianism and apocalyptism have increasingly become bipartisan afflictions. The right has become more Wilsonian, the left steadily more apocalyptic, and the two forms of the nationalist heresy have intertwined within the Republican and Democratic parties alike.

This shift happened first on the left, amid the disappointments of the 1970s. The liberal-Christian vision of history as the steady unfolding of God's purposes runs into trouble when history doesn't cooperate, and between the agonies of Vietnam, the miseries of stagflation, and the shock of a sudden conservative ascendancy, history dealt messianic liberalism a very bad hand in the two decades following JFK's assassination. As we saw in chapter 1, the last time this happened—following the agonies of two world wars—there was a turn back toward a more traditionally Christian understanding of politics in a fallen world, and even a temporary remarriage of modern liberalism and Christian orthodoxy. But institutional Christianity's post-1960s crisis foreclosed the possibility of this happening again. There would be no turn to Barthian or Niebuhrian neo-orthodoxy, no reembrace of Christian realism, for the disappointed liberals of the 1970s and 1980s.

Instead, the left embraced the kind of declinism and conspiracy theorizing that had long been the preserve of the far right. They wallowed in apocalyptic scenarios (the population bomb! the climate crisis! the looming nuclear winter!) that resembled the book of Revelation with the supernatural element edited out. They indulged in the darkest sort of paranoia about the institutions of American government, training the same sort of Manichaean lens on the military-industrial complex that right-wing millenarians had long brought to bear on the modern administrative state. And they embraced a vision of American history that resembled nothing so much as the "it's all been downhill since [insert your least favorite era]" narratives of the reactionary style. For many disillusioned progressives, the American story reached its fruition with blessed, martyred JFK, and everything after November 22, 1963, was a gradual slide into the abyss.

The older liberal mentality, with its nineteenth-century roots and utopian ambitions, has resurfaced whenever there seems to be a progressive restoration. The election of Bill Clinton inspired a spasm of New Frontier–style posturing, and Barack Obama's campaign for the presidency brought the messianic style back in a big way. Obama might just be "the rare kind of attuned being," a writer for the *San Francisco Chronicle* gushed in the summer of 2008, with "the ability to lead us not merely to new foreign policies or health care plans or whatnot, but . . . actually help usher in *a new way of being*."[38] He's "the One," Oprah Winfrey declared when she broke with her usual nonpartisan stance to endorse Obama (briefly uniting the therapeutic and messianic heresies in the process). "What Barack Obama has accomplished," Representative Jesse Jackson Jr. announced after the Illinois senator captured the Democratic nomination (not the presidency, mind you—just the nomination), is "so extraordinary that another chapter could be added to the Bible to chronicle its significance."[39]

But whenever liberals have found themselves shut out of power, this utopianism has been trumped by the paranoid style, which sees fascism lurking behind every right-wing policy proposal and hears intimations of the apocalypse in every news bulletin, and which has directed the kind of disproportionate, Big Villain venom toward Ronald Reagan and then George W. Bush that had once been aimed at FDR and Company.

As the left found room for its own version of the paranoid style, the right found room for an unexpected utopianism. Here Reagan was the transformational figure. A conservative in politics, he was essentially a romantic in his philosophical and religious premises—an heir of Emerson and Whitman, a religious believer with a deep faith in providence but no time for original sin (or any sort of institutional Christianity, judging by his barely intermittent church attendance), a right-wing utopian who was more likely to quote Thomas Paine's famous promise that "We have it in our power to begin the world over again" than any line of Edmund Burke. As John Patrick Diggins wrote, "Reagan offered three of the most radical thoughts ever held by an American president: We have no history at our back; the people know no evil because our God-given desires are good; and only the state knows how to sin."[40] The Gipper took elements from modernist theology and adapted them to right-of-center politics. Instead of History's God working out His purposes through the development of the modern bureaucratic state, it was democratic capitalism that reflected God's ultimate will for humanity. Reagan's was a utopianism of free men and free markets, rather than of a benevolent administrative body—but it was a utopianism nonetheless, unconstrained by traditional conservatism's sense of tragedy.

If this shift wasn't entirely obvious during his own presidency, subsequent trends in conservative politics have made it crystal clear. The two most successful post-Reagan Republican politicians have arguably been Newt Gingrich and the younger Bush—respectively a right-wing futurist whose favorite book is Alvin and Heidi Toffler's *Future Shock* and a right-wing Wilsonian who committed the United States to the cause of democratic revolution in the Middle East. Pre-Reagan, Gingrich and Bush would have been unlikely leaders for American conservatism; post-Reagan, their messianic streaks have been tolerated or celebrated within the conservative fold.

In an ideal world, these trends would somehow balance each other out, on the left and right alike. Conservative messianism would leaven the right's natural predisposition to declinism and nostalgia. Left-wing apocalypticism would provide a corrective to the liberal tendency to over-romanticize the future, while dismissing the past as nothing but a sinkhole of cruelty and bigotry. And both political coalitions would be the better for the synthesis.

In a sense, this is what happened in Reagan's presidency—not coincidentally, the most successful presidential administration since the Eisenhower era. Reagan's Emersonian optimism about human nature was crucial to the unexpected diplomatic leap that helped end the Cold War, and his boundless faith in the power of economic growth was a necessary corrective to the green-eyeshade views of many Republicans. But there were important constraints on his utopianism: Reagan's was a rhetorical Wilsonianism, but without the martial follow-through that led to Vietnam and Iraq. His foreign-policy idealism was balanced by the realpolitik of many of his advisers (and by Reagan's own admirable horror of war). His supply-side economic policies were dialed backward somewhat when the deficit exploded. His presidency was a successful marriage of Emerson and Burke, you might say, rather than an era of utopianism unbound.

Happily for the country, Reagan's two terms were followed by a decade of divided government, in which partisan competition and political self-interest provided a natural check on messianism and apocalypticism alike. In the Bush-Obama era, though, we haven't been so lucky. Instead of balancing each other out, the two heresies of nationalism have taken turns in the driver's seat of both political coalitions, giving us messianism from the party in power and apocalypticism from the party out of power, regardless of which party is which.

In the White House and on Capitol Hill, big government conservatism has given way to big government liberalism, deficit spending justified by supply-side economics has given way to deficit spending justified by Keynesian economics, neoconservative wars of choice have been succeeded by liberal internationalist adventures, and an imperial presidency of the right has given way to an imperial presidency of the left. The only constant has been hubris—the hubris of "ending tyranny in the world" and "when someone's hurting, the government's got to move" in the Bush era, succeeded by the hubris of "the fierce urgency of now" and "never let a crisis go to waste" under Barack Obama.

For partisans of the out-of-power party, meanwhile, Michael Moore has given way to Glenn Beck, 9/11 trutherism has been succeeded by birth certificate hysteria, cries of "fascism!" have been replaced by cries of "socialism!," and the government has been transformed from an agent of right-wing tyranny to an agent of Marxist oppression. These mood swings have been swift, comprehensive, and completely unembarrassed. In 2006, Gallup asked the public whether the government in Washington posed an "immediate threat" to Americans. Only 21 percent of Republicans agreed, versus 57 percent of Democrats. In 2010, with the hated Bush safely retired and Barack Obama in the White House, Gallup asked again. This time, 21 percent of Democrats said yes, compared with 66 percent of Republicans.[41] (When a Republican wins the Oval Office back, the numbers will no doubt reverse themselves once more.)

The cycle of hubris and backlash, utopian hopes and millennial angst, is much bigger than any individual politician, but it tends to revolve more around the presidency specifically than the government as a whole. (The Congress is a poor focus for religious devotion of any sort.) In 1908, six years before ascending to the White House, Woodrow Wilson argued that the Constitution's separation of powers was outdated and that only a vastly more powerful executive branch could meet the challenges of the modern world. A century later, much of the public seems to have come around to this perspective, embracing what the Cato Institute's Gene Healy calls "the cult of the presidency." To the disciples of this cult, the president *is* the government: "He is a soul nourisher," Healy writes, "a hope giver, a living American talisman against hurricanes, terrorism, economic downturns, and spiritual malaise."[42] Anything good or bad that happens on his watch happens because of him, and any disasters can be pinned entirely upon his mistakes—or, more likely, his malignancy.

Both Bush and Obama, in different ways, sometimes tried to push back against this cult and the messianic-apocalyptic cycle it encourages. Bush ran as a "uniter not a divider" and promised a "humble foreign policy." Obama cast himself as a postpartisan healer and talked about his affinity for the pessimism of Reinhold Niebuhr. But both men just as frequently embraced it as well, in ways that helped them politically in the short term (in the aftermath of 9/11 for Bush, during the 2008 campaign for Obama) but ultimately guaranteed backlash and disillusionment. And both men seemed at times to be imprisoned by it. Think of Bush sticking with Donald Rumsfeld for months after the defense secretary's failures became apparent, out of fear of compromising his image as "the decider." Think of Obama, taking America into a quasi-war in Libya against his better judgment and with a rush of Bush-like rhetoric. And then think of the way that the two presidents' actual policies—on taxes and spending, foreign wars and civil liberties—have ended up overlapping far more than the frenzied rhetoric surrounding their presidencies would lead one to suspect.

The faces and partisan affiliations change, in other words, but the song remains the same. The party in power hero-worships its leaders (recall the evangelical kitsch-art showing Bush praying in the snow with the ghosts of Washington and Lincoln, or Will.I.Am's worshipful YouTube hymns to the glories of "the One"), and the other party turns them into hate figures. The party in power claims to be restoring American greatness; the party out of power insists that the current administration is actually deeply un-American—heretics in the holy temple of the U.S.A., you might say—and promises to take our country back. The party in power piles on new military commitments and new domestic programs, which the party out of power bitterly opposes right up until the moment that it takes power itself. Meanwhile America's commitments keep on multiplying, the tide of red ink keeps rising, and the country keeps cycling through savior figures, hoping each time that this one will be the One that we've been waiting for.

This trend has helped ratify a shift we examined in earlier chapters: the steady conflation of religious belief and partisan politics, to the detriment of both. As the two political coalitions have become theological worlds unto themselves, messianic and apocalyptic in equal measure, it's become harder and harder for Christians to find a place to stand on public issues that isn't straightforwardly partisan. The more that politics becomes the landscape of good versus evil, real Americans versus fascists or socialists, liberty versus tyranny, the greater the pressure to simply conform your theology to ideology. Whether they're Protestant or Catholic, lukewarm or zealous, believers inevitably find themselves pressured to "join the side they're on," instead of trying to do justice to the inevitable complexities of political life in the City of Man.

In both the apocalyptic and messianic mind-sets, all good things go together, and the idea that *both* liberal and conservative ideas could capture some element of divine justice is anathema. To believe is to choose: If you're theologically conservative you *must* be conservative on taxes and spending and everything, because otherwise you're just playing into the

hands of "the secular-socialist machine" (to borrow Newt Gingrich's mem-
orable phrase). If you're politically liberal then you should be theologically
liberal as well: It isn't enough to back welfare programs or environmental
protections; you're a bigot and a tool of the wingnuts if you don't also
support gay marriage. If you don't want to vote for George W. Bush because of the Iraq War then you're playing into the hands of Christianity's
left-wing enemies; if you can't vote for Barack Obama because of abortion
then you're an accomplice to the shredding of the Constitution. You simply *cannot* be a social democrat and an orthodox Catholic, or a conservative Christian who's also genuinely antiwar. In the Manichaean landscape
created by the heresy of nationalism, these categories are either incoherent,
sinful, or both.

Partisan co-optation is always a danger for religious believers who enter
into politics. This peril can be avoided entirely only by cultivating a perfect
quietism, or an Anabaptist renunciation of all things tainted by Caesar.
Christian orthodoxy has not traditionally called its adherents to such re-
nunciations, not least because of the forces such withdrawal is likely to
empower. (Exactly such a purer-than-thou rejection of political activism
was often urged on believers by segregationist clerics in the civil rights–
era South.) The realities of politics don't necessarily make for the most
Christlike displays. But every great moral crusade in American history has
ultimately become intertwined with one or both of the political parties—
because political parties are how movements get things done.

Still, that "or both" is crucial. The most successful Christian-influenced
reform movements have transcended partisan divisions, finding supporters
in both political parties instead of being associated with just one. (Tellingly,
the one great cause that *didn't* transcend ideological divisions, the antislavery movement, required a bloody civil war to win its victory.) The Social
Gospel movement, which did a great deal of good despite its messianic excesses, found support within both the Democratic and Republican parties:
From William Jennings Bryan to Robert La Follette, the cause of reform
was taken up by populist Democrats and progressive Republicans alike.
So too with the civil rights movement, as we've seen: though primarily associated with political liberalism, the cause of racial equality gained ground
under Republican presidents and with the support of Republican legislators, pushed along throughout by the nonideological moral witness of both

black and white churches. Even the anti–Vietnam War movement, though decisively oriented toward the political left, achieved its potency precisely because it didn't waver from attacking an incumbent Democratic president as well as the Republican who succeeded him. (The antiwar activism of the Bush era, by contrast, essentially evaporated once Barack Obama succeeded to the presidency: More American soldiers died overseas in 2010 than in 2008, but only Code Pink and Cindy Sheehan still cared.)

Today, it's increasingly difficult to imagine any movement for moral reform, religious or secular, transcending partisanship in this way. This has been tragically apparent in the case of the pro-life movement. For a time, in the 1970s, both parties included serious critics of abortion. Ted Kennedy expressed pro-life sentiments, as did Jesse Jackson, and in the 1972 presidential campaign the most pro-life politician on either ticket was the Democratic nominee for vice president, Sargent Shriver. Over time, though, the power of partisanship overwhelmed the influence of Christian principles. To be a Democrat was to be pro-choice, and so liberal Catholics and Protestants alike found excuses for embracing the "personally opposed, but . . ." line on the subject. Antiabortion liberalism persisted notionally in senators like Nevada's Harry Reid and Pennsylvania's Bob Casey Jr., who called themselves pro-life but rarely cast an actual vote to limit abortion, and somewhat more credibly in a smattering of Midwestern politicians like Bart Stupak, who represented blue-collar districts where the worldview of New Deal Catholics survived in a kind of political amber. But the health care debate of 2009 essentially put an end to their increasingly antiquated balancing act. (The agony of Stupak, forced to choose between his liberalism and his Church, neatly encapsulated the demands that a polarized, hyperpartisan landscape places on every politically engaged Christian.)

There is no perfect analogue to the abortion issue—no issue where the stakes are quite so high for Christians in politics, and the costs of compromise so great. But there are striking parallels to the eclipse of the pro-life Democrat in the sudden Bush-era enthusiasm among conservative Christians for waterboarding and other "enhanced interrogation" techniques. The definition of torture admits of more honest disagreement than the definition of abortion, and the use of violence to extract information or confessions has a complicated history among Christian moralists. Still, the contemporary institutional Christian consensus leans heavily against such practices. The Catholic Church's ban on torture is absolute, and prominent Evangelical institutions, from *Christianity Today* to the National Association of Evangelicals, took strong Bush-era positions against harsh interrogation practices as well.

But this consensus has been rejected, downplayed, or ignored among many otherwise orthodox Christians, lest it interfere with their ability to feel an uncomplicated goodwill toward the Republican Party. Indeed, now that waterboarding has become a right-wing litmus test, polls show that frequent churchgoers are *more* likely to voice explicit support for torture than other Americans, and that both conservative Catholics and (especially) Evangelicals are the most pro-torture groups of all.[43] From George W. Bush to Rick Santorum (whose campaign-trail case for waterboarding included the ridiculous claim that "John McCain doesn't understand enhanced interrogation"), where the rights and dignity of suspected terrorists are concerned many politicians otherwise known for their strong commitment to religious values in public life have embraced the un-Christian idea that the ends justify the means.

The failure of Catholic bishops and high-profile Evangelicals to influence their co-religionists on this issue isn't ultimately surprising. On the right and left alike, the heresy of nationalism's contemporary power is intimately bound up in the declining influence of religious institutions in American life. Many bishops and clerics and intellectuals still *try* to embody the kind of prophetic, above-the-fray role that their predecessors once played more successfully. The Catholic bishops still tilt leftward on some issues and rightward on others, and both Mainline Protestants and Evangelicals regularly boast of their independence from any party or clique. But institutional authority in American religion has diminished to a point where their interventions are easily dismissed as just another form of partisanship. A Catholic bishop who denies a pro-abortion politician communion will inevitably be dismissed by Democrats as a reactionary right-winger. A prominent pastor who criticizes Republican stances on poverty or the environment will find himself attacked by conservatives for substituting liberal nostrums for the Gospel.

If American nationalism appeals to Christians because of the resemblance between the idea of America and the idea of the universal

Church, then it stands to reason that the weakening of the major Christian churches, Catholic and Protestant alike, would make the Church of
America (in both its progressive and conservative forms) more appealing
than ever before. Almost every major Christian body has less moral authority today than it did a few generations ago, and while the idea of America
has been battered over this period as well, patriotism in its various forms
burns far brighter than most religious Americans' affections for their particular churches and denominations. "God and country" has a stronger pull
than "God and the Catholic bishops" or "God and the United Methodist
Church," and the partisan mind-set increasingly provides a greater sense of
solidarity, shared purpose, and even eschatological fervor than the weakened confessions of Protestantism or the faded grandeur of Rome.

The choice that many liberal Protestants made in the 1970s, when they
decided essentially to fold their Protestantism into their liberalism and
skip out on Sunday services, has been replicated less starkly and explicitly
by many contemporary believers as well. Without dropping their religious
commitments entirely, a large percentage of Americans seem to have decided that the liberal-conservative struggles over ownership of the American idea—Obama's "hope and change" versus Sarah Palin's "fundamental
restoration of America"—is a better place to invest not only their political
energies and loyalties but their religious ones as well.

In the Bush era, liberals consistently portrayed the right-wing version
of this temptation as a theocratic menace to American democracy. But the
real danger has less to do with the specter of an oppressive ecclesiastical
dominance of politics—which was never a plausible fear in a religiously
diverse society—than with the political corruption of religious witness.
The present danger to our democracy isn't that Christianity has gained too
much power and influence over our politics. Rather, it's that the heresy of
nationalism's co-option of Christian faith has left the faith too *weak* to play
the kind of positive role it has often played in our public life.

In our nation's better moments, Christianity has been intimately involved in American politics while standing somewhat apart from partisanship, summoning the country to reform without falling victim to the
conceit that political reform is religion's only purpose. At their most robust
and independent, our churches and religious leaders have reminded us that
America is only *almost* chosen, and that paradise isn't possible on earth. In

our finer hours, orthodoxy's universalism has been potent enough to temper nationalism in both its apocalyptic and messianic manifestations.

But we do not inhabit such an hour today.

The first chapter in this book ended with the civil rights movement, and
so it's fitting that the last one should end there as well. Five decades later,
the achievements of that era remain a model for Christian engagement
with politics and a salutary example of how a democratic republic can
benefit from the prophetic side of religious faith. It was a case where pastors led and politicians of both parties followed, where the institutional
churches proved their worth as both sources of moral authority and hubs
of activism, and where religious witness helped forge a genuine national
consensus on an issue where even presidents feared to tread. Though the
movement had a messianic flavor and an eschatological edge, it never lost
sight of practical realities; though its hopes were idealistic, its demands
were always plausible; though its leaders were morally flawed in many
ways, their flaws never overwhelmed the message they carried. If there
was a great secret to the movement's success, as I suggested earlier, it was
distilled in King's "Letter from Birmingham Jail"—in which a black Protestant pastor drew on the heritage of Christendom, Catholic and Protestant alike, to persuade an audience of white Protestants of the justice of
his cause. In that document, as in the movement it served, the idea of a
"mere orthodoxy" or "mere Christianity" was temporarily vindicated, as
the resources of the entire Christian past were marshaled to effect a great
and necessary social change.

Today's America does not lack for causes where a similar spirit could
be brought to bear, or for religious actors and activists with the desire to
imitate the achievements of the past. But with the eclipse of orthodoxy and
the decline of institutional religion, it lacks a Christianity that's capable of
translating those desires into something other than just another spasm of
messianism or millenarianism, or another partisan crusade.

This has been a challenge for Christians in every time and place. There
is no single Christian politics, and no movement can claim to have arrived
at the perfect marriage of religious faith and political action. Christianity is
too otherworldly for that, and the world too fallen.

In the message of the Gospels, as Pope Benedict XVI has written, "political arrangements are no longer treated as a sacred law," fixed for all the ages. Instead, "the concrete political and social order is released from the directly sacred realm, from theocratic legislation, and is transferred to the freedom of man."[44]

But this freedom doesn't free believers from the obligation to strive in political affairs, as they strive in all things, to do what God would have them do. And while the heresy of nationalism is natural to man, it is fatal to this quest.

CONCLUSION

THE RECOVERY OF CHRISTIANITY

The story of Christianity has always featured unexpected resurrections. Eras of corruption give way to eras of reform; sinners and cynics cede the floor to a rush of idealists and saints; political and intellectual challenges emerge and then are gradually surmounted. There is no single form of Christian civilization, in the same sense that there is no stereotypical Christian life; across two millennia, the faith has found ways to make itself at home in the Roman court and the medieval monastery, the Renaissance city and the American suburb alike.

In *The Everlasting Man,* G. K. Chesterton describes what he calls the "five deaths of the faith"—the moments in Western history when Christianity seemed doomed to either perish entirely or else fade to the margins of a post-Christian civilization. It would have been natural for the faith to decline and fall with the Roman Empire, or to disappear gradually after the armies of Islam conquered its ancient heartland in the Near East and North Africa. It would have been predictable if Christianity had dissolved along with feudalism when the Middle Ages gave way to the Renaissance, or if it had vanished with the ancien regimes of Europe amid the turmoil of the age of revolutions. And it would have been completely understandable if the faith had gradually waned during the long nineteenth century, when it was dismissed by Marx, challenged by Darwin, denounced by Nietzsche, and explained away by Freud.

But in each of these cases, an age of crisis was swiftly followed by an era of renewal, in which forces threatening the faith either receded or were discredited and Christianity itself revived. Time and again, Chesterton noted, "the Faith has to all appearance gone to the dogs." But each time, "it was the dog that died."[1]

The same pattern extends to the history of Christianity in America. From Puritan moralists bemoaning the eclipse of colonial virtues to confident Deists anticipating the extinction of Trinitarian belief, prophecies of Christianity's imminent demise were already common at the beginning of our national story, and the faith's revivals have always taken the skeptics by surprise. I have already quoted Jefferson's prediction "that there is not a young man now living in the United States who will not die an Unitarian" (offered just a few short years before the Second Great Awakening), and the dean of the Harvard Divinity School's 1946 claim, at the dawn of Billy Graham's career, that the revivalist tradition in American religion was completely "discredited." Perhaps someday my own comments on the present age of heresy will look similarly presumptuous and premature.

Nothing would give me greater pleasure. This book has been written in a spirit of pessimism, but for both Americans and Christians, pessimism should always be provisional. Even in an era of disarray, Americans can draw confidence from our nation's remarkable past, with its stories of expectations confounded, obstacles overcome, declines reversed, and better futures attained. Christians have an even stronger source of confidence: the belief that history has an Author and that the destiny of both their country and their creed is in God's hands.

It would be heresy and hubris to assume that a renewal of either is inevitable. Christianity's overall resilience hasn't prevented particular Christendoms from decaying and dissolving, and Jesus never said that the gates of hell would not prevail against the United States of America. But to hope for a revival is every believer's obligation. And perhaps, just perhaps, a more robust and rigorous American Christianity is something that even non-believers should consider hoping for as well.

With that in mind, here are four potential touchstones for a recovery of Christianity. The first might be called the *postmodern opportunity:* the possibility that the very trends that have seemingly undone institutional Christianity could ultimately renew it. The rootlessness of life in a globalizing world, the widespread skepticism about all institutions and authorities, the religious relativism that makes every man a God unto himself—these forces have clearly weakened the traditional Christian churches. But they are also forces that Christianity has confronted successfully before. From a weary Pontius Pilate asking Jesus "what is truth?" to Saint Paul preaching beside the Athenian altar to an "unknown God," the Christian gospel originally emerged as a radical alternative in a civilization as rootless and cosmopolitan and relativistic as our own. There may come a moment when the loss of Christianity's cultural preeminence enables believers to recapture some of that original radicalism. Maybe it is already here, if only Christians could find a way to shed the baggage of a vanished Christendom and speak the language of this age.

In scholarly circles, this hope is often associated with the theology known as "radical orthodoxy," which seeks to use the architecture of post-modern theory—of Michel Foucault and Jacques Derrida and their various epigones—to make the case for Christianity afresh. Like Paul preaching to the sophisticates of Athens, these theologians present Jesus Christ's selfless love as the answer to postmodernism's obsession with power, and God as the bedrock that remains when every merely human foundation has been deconstructed. At the popular level, a similar impulse animates the so-called "emerging church" movement, which has won a growing constituency among younger Evangelical Christians. Born out of disillusionment with existing Christian structures, the "emergent" movement tries to answer the deracination of contemporary life with a faith that meets seekers where they are: in conversation rather than in Sunday preaching, in house churches and small groups rather than in archdioceses and megachurches, in prayer and storytelling rather than in explicit apologetics.

In different ways, both of these movements are attempting to rebuild Christianity from the ground up—bypassing failing institutions, avoiding culture-war flashpoints, and casting the faith as a lifeline for an exhausted civilization rather than just a return to the glories of the past. Both have a particular interest in reaching the urban, the academic, and even the *cool*—which points to the possibility of a kind of revolution from above, in which our cultural elite is reconverted and the country comes along. It's happened before: the midcentury revival was driven, in part, by a greater openness to Christianity among tastemakers and trendsetters and arbiters of intellectual fashion. From Oxford to Brooklyn, Ivy League faculty clubs to hipster watering holes, both radical orthodoxy and emergent Evangelicalism are trying kindle a similar highbrow revival.

The challenge for both groups, and others like them, is to avoid simply becoming a kind of warmed-over accommodationism. The Harvey Cox–James Pike generation was also excited by the idea of a postmodern Christianity, and there was a great vogue in the 1960s and 1970s for house churches and small prayer groups and rediscovering the radicalism of the early Church. But much of that excitement came to nothing, because the accommodationists were ultimately more interested in adapting to the culture than in changing it; they made relevance an end unto itself, while severing their connection to doctrine and authority and the wider Christian past. The same perils face today's missionaries to the hip and highbrow. R. R. Reno notes that the thinkers behind radical orthodoxy often "demonstrate an overall ambivalence about the role of Scripture, creed, and inherited ecclesial practice" that resembles earlier generations of accommodationist theologians.[2] Likewise, leading "emergent" pastors like Brian McLaren and Rob Bell tend to be more famous for downplaying the harder Christian teachings, from hell to homosexuality, than they are for showcasing Christianity itself.

These perils help explain the appeal of a second possible source of Christian renewal: not a renewed engagement with the postmodern world and a more successful quest for relevance, but an extended period of withdrawal, consolidation, and purification. The American Conservative's Rod Dreher has dubbed this the *Benedict option,* after the saint of late antiquity (and namesake of the current pope) whose monastic rule helped preserve both Christianity and Greco-Roman culture—and with them, the seeds of civilizational renewal—amid the Roman Empire's slow collapse. The Benedict option tends to assume that Christianity (whether Catholic or Protestant) must contract before it grows, with faithful believers forming communities that stand apart from postmodern culture and inspire by example rather than engagement.

There are various models for such a mustard seed strategy. The community of Latin Mass Catholics, which has recently been given encouragement and support from Rome, has long sought to sustain a purer church within the Church—one that's more liturgically rich and doctrinally rigorous than the American norm, and less compromised by Catholicism's current disarray. The "neo-Anabaptist" movement in Protestantism, associated with figures like the Duke Divinity School theologian Stanley Hauerwas, envisions Christianity as a kind of parallel culture—pacifist, apolitical, and ascetic—within the decadent American imperium. (The actual Anabaptists, Amish and Mennonite, take this separatism a few hundred steps further.) The spread of the Christian home-schooling movement represents an ecumenical attempt to create religious subcultures uncorrupted by the secular culture and the bureaucratic state. And, doctrinal issues aside, the example of Mormonism's vigor and cohesion is often cited as a testament to what a certain degree of self-segregation can accomplish, and as a model that more orthodox Christian churches would do well to emulate.

At their best, such separatist movements can offer believers a kind of liberation from many of the temptations discussed in this book—worldliness and partisanship, the cult of Mammon and the worship of the nation-state. Such communities have a vibrancy and solidarity that other strains of American Christianity often lack, and frequently a greater intellectual sure-footedness as well. (Of Christopher Hitchens's many Christian debating partners, none was more eloquent and effective than Douglas Wilson, a Reformed pastor associated with New Saint Andrew's, a Moscow, Idaho, college dedicated to providing a classical Christian education to a largely homeschooled student body.) In an age of stagnant or declining birthrates, too, these communities' willingness to heed the admonition to be fruitful and multiply has led to speculation about what the demographer Philip Longman calls "the survival of the godliest."[3] Drop in on the right enclave of Latin Mass Catholics or neo-Calvinist homeschoolers, and it's easy to come away convinced that traditional believers will eventually inherit the earth.

But separatist Christians also risk falling into the same traps that snared the fundamentalists of the 1920s and 1930s—paranoia, crankishness, and all the other pathologies of the religious ghetto. (When he wasn't tangling with Hitchens, Douglas Wilson was known to describe himself as a "paleo-Confederate" and flirt with theocratic sentiments.[4]) What's more, they risk effectively giving up on those cobelievers who aren't capable of opting out of their existing communities and churches and schools. In its quest for a greater purity and a more perfect solidarity, the Benedict option often seems to have little to say about the millions of baptized Christians whom separatism would effectively leave behind. Even if their faith is lukewarm and compromised, the undercatechized Catholic and the Oprahfied Protestant are still only a good confession or an altar call away from a more authentic Christian life. Even if America is retracing the Roman Empire's decline, it's worth remembering that the Christians of late antiquity didn't just withdraw from a collapsing civilization. They took responsibility for it as well—and for the nations and peoples that crowded into the Mediterranean world in the wake of Rome's collapse.

In a rather different way, the migrations of our own era may offer an unexpected opportunity for Western Christianity. This is the vision of renewal that one might call the *Next Christendom,* after Philip Jenkins's 2002 book of the same name, which documents the extraordinary growth of Christianity in Africa, Asia, and Latin America. By the end of the twenty-first century, Jenkins argues, the real heartlands of Christian belief will no longer be in Europe and North America; they'll be in Nigeria and Brazil, in Mexico and Uganda, and perhaps even in China as well. In the 1960s and '70s, globalization helped undercut orthodox Christian faith, by making religious truth seem relative and theology culturally contingent. In this century, the new global Christianity could help restore orthodoxy's vitality, and the next Christendom could help revive the old one.

To some extent this is happening already. What growth there is in American Catholicism is largely driven by Hispanic immigration, and cities like Los Angeles and Miami and San Antonio are replacing Boston and Chicago and Philadelphia as the most important centers of the twenty-first-century American Church. Thanks to decades of missionary activity and aid work, nearly every major Evangelical body has deep ties to churches in Africa and Asia, and influential pastors like Rick Warren and T. D. Jakes increasingly minister to communities that transcend borders and straddle oceans. Catholic priests from Africa and South Asia have been imported to fill vacancies created by the priest shortage in the United States. Conservative Episcopalians in Virginia have placed themselves under the authority of Anglican bishops in Africa. From the outer boroughs of New York to the D.C. suburbs, the Christian presence in America's cultural and political capitals is increasingly dominated by thriving immigrant churches—Vietnamese Catholics, Egyptian Copts, Korean Evangelicals, Latino Pentecostalists.

This looks like a new thing in world history—the developed West as a mission field; the Third World as the source of missionaries and parishioners, clergy and zeal. But in some ways it's a familiar story, since immigrant churches and cultural exchanges have long played a role in American Christianity's revivals—the midcentury renaissance very much included. Reinhold Niebuhr grew up speaking German at home; Eisenhower-era Catholicism was in many ways still as Irish as it was American; and Billy Graham became Billy Graham in part because he saw an opportunity to take Evangelical Christianity to a global as well as a national stage. Given that international influences helped renew American Christianity in the twentieth century, no one should be surprised if something similar were to happen in the even more globalized third millennium.

But influence runs both ways, and not every form of cross-pollination is healthy. From prosperity preaching to religious nationalism, the emerging Christianity of the developing world already shares many faults with American religion, and its institutions are heavily dependent on American dollars as well. We may still be generations away from a world where the churches of Africa and Asia could plausibly re-evangelize the West, and it's easy to imagine a very different scenario unfolding—in which the age of heresy goes global, and the American way of religion changes Mexican and Nigerian and Korean immigrants more than they change us.

In the end, then, renewal can't come just from outside this country; it has to come from within as well. The revival of midcentury was prompted, in part, by economic and political shocks—by a depression and a world war, and the spirit of humility and realism and reassessment that they helped inspire. God willing, no horrors of that magnitude await us, but our current economic turmoil does raise the possibility that a similar reassessment might be in the offing—that an *age of diminished expectations* might also be an age that's willing to reckon with the ways that bad theology and bad religion have helped bring us to our present pass.

Like W. H. Auden wandering amid the shuttered churches of 1930s Spain, perhaps Americans will survey the wreckage all around them and turn once again to a more rigorous and humble form of Christian faith. Perhaps the experience of a financial meltdown will help vindicate orthodox Christianity's critique of avarice and greed. Perhaps the lived reality of family breakdown and social isolation will make Christianity's emphasis on chastity, monogamy, and fidelity more compelling. Perhaps the spectacle of polarization and gridlock will inspire greater realism about the ability of politics to serve God's purposes, and put an end to the persistent conflation of partisan and religious loyalties.

Against this hope, though, we need to set the example of the last few years. From the "hope and change" messianism of the Obama campaign to Joel Osteen's sold-out tours to Glenn Beck's meteoric rise, our post-boom, post-Iraq, post-bailout present seems only to have further empowered many of the forces discussed in this book. A grim economic picture may be making prosperity preaching's promises seem that much more urgent and compelling. A period of political crisis may be making both messianic hopes and apocalyptic fears more intuitively appealing. An age of institutional failure may just end up inspiring Americans to be even more suspicious of any sort of religious authority, and more inclined to put their faith only in the God they find within.

Sometimes cultural crises lead to reassessments and renewals. But sometimes they just make people double down on their original mistakes.

"For us, there is only the trying," T. S. Eliot wrote. "The rest is not our business." The deeper trends that might inspire a Christian renaissance are beyond any individual believer's control. But the kind of faith that should animate such a renaissance can be lived out Christian by Christian, congregation by congregation, day by day, without regard to whether it succeeds in changing the American way of religion as a whole.

First, such a faith should be *political without being partisan*. This means avoiding the nationalist temptations described in the last chapter without falling prey to quietism or indifference. The fact that there is no single model for a Christian politics, no uniquely godly leaders or nations or parties, doesn't absolve Christian citizens of the obligation to bring their faith to bear on debates about justice and the common good. Instead, it sharpens all Christians' obligation to be *a* model unto themselves—to make it clear, in words and deeds, how their faith informs their voting and their activism, and to constantly test their ideological convictions against their theological worldview. When believers practice politics, there should be a clear Christian difference—an allegiance to principle over party that sets the Christian voter and the Christian politician apart from the typical Republican or Democrat.

This difference should begin with the rule that Jesus gave his followers: "First take the log out of your own eye; and then you will see clearly to take the speck out of your brother's eye." Christians can disagree about public policy in good faith, and a libertarian and a social democrat can both claim to be living out the gospel. But the Christian libertarian has a particular obligation to recognize those places where libertarianism's emphasis on freedom can shade into an un-Christian worship of the individual. Likewise the Christian liberal: even as he supports government interventions to assist the poor and dispossessed, he should be constantly on guard against the tendency to deify Leviathan and wary of the ways that government power can easily be turned to inhuman and immoral ends.

In the contemporary United States, a host of factors—from the salience of issues like abortion to the anti-Christian biases of our largely left-wing intelligentsia—ensure that many orthodox Christians feel more comfortable affiliating with the Republican Party than with the Democrats. But this comfort should not blind Christians to the GOP's flaws. Instead, they should be the Republican Party's most vocal internal critics, constantly looking for places where the right-wing party line deserves correction, and constantly aware that Rush Limbaugh's take on tax policy and Donald Rumsfeld's views on waterboarding are not inscribed in the New Testament. Similarly, those Christians for whom the Democratic Party still seems to provide a more natural home should make it their business to speak out loudly against the ways that liberalism can provide a warrant for libertinism. And Christian activists who work outside the party system— from pro-life groups to antipoverty crusaders—should wear their outsider status as a badge of honor, rather than thinking of themselves as team players for one faction or another.

Our politics do not exactly overflow with examples of this kind of engagement. But there are bright spots here and there. One need not agree with the exact balance they've struck to admire the consistency with which the Catholic bishops have defied easy partisan categorization over the years, taking conservative positions on issues like abortion and gay marriage even as they tilt leftward on issues like immigration and health care. In the Evangelical world, it's been encouraging to watch the new head of Focus on the Family, Jim Daly, try to reconnect with his organization's original mission as a pro-family advocacy group, emphasizing cultural forays like Tim Tebow's pro-life Super Bowl ad over the attempts at Republican Party kingmaking that consumed James Dobson's later years at the helm of the organization.

In the political arena itself, meanwhile, we are not *that* far removed from an era when America's leading Evangelical politician was the antiwar environmentalist Republican Mark Hatfield, and one of its leading Catholic officeholders was the pro-life Democrat Sargent Shriver. We are not *so* distant from the days when the civil rights movement united Christians from many different traditions in a cause that ultimately transcended party affiliations entirely. We don't need to imagine what a Christian politics less corrupted by ideology and partisanship would look like. We only need to remember what was possible not all that long ago.

Second, a renewed Christianity should be *ecumenical but also confessional*. From the postdenominational appeals of Billy Graham and his megachurch-building heirs, to the "deeds not creeds" activism of Mainline Protestant accommodationists, to the culture war co-belligerency of Evangelicals and Catholics Together, the quest for greater Christian unity has been one of the defining projects of the modern era. Newer movements like radical orthodoxy and the emergent church partake of the same vision. So does this book: both my emphasis on the distinction between orthodoxy and heresy and my argument that Protestants and Catholics have an interest in distinguishing their shared patrimony from the pseudo-Christianities of Oprah and Osteen and Glenn Beck assume that what unites Christians is more important than the issues that divide them.

This vision must not be abandoned. But neither can ecumenism become the source and summit of the Christian life. "Parachurch" efforts and "emergent" communities cannot replace institutional churches. The common ground of a "mere Christianity" cannot be allowed to become a lowest common denominator. The political causes that often unite believers from different churches cannot be allowed to become more important than the gospel itself.

This has happened too often in contemporary Christianity. In their quest to woo the biggest possible audience, megachurch pastors have watered down Evangelical theology and ignored much of their own Reformation heritage. In the pursuit of relevance and dialogue, a large swath of post–Vatican II Catholicism has made itself liturgically and theologically indistinguishable from Mainline Protestantism. In the pursuit of social change, both the accommodationist project of the 1960s and '70s and the resistance movement that followed have too often confused political and religious goals, and made elections and legislation an end unto themselves.

Here C. S. Lewis is worth heeding. The man who coined the term "mere Christianity" also warned against its misapplication and abuse:

> I hope no reader will suppose that "mere" Christianity is here put forward as an alternative to the creeds of the existing communions—as if a man could adopt it in preference to Congregationalism or Greek Orthodoxy or anything else. It is more like a hall out of which doors open into several rooms. If I can bring anyone into that hall I shall have done what I attempted. But it is in the rooms, not the hall, that there are fires and chairs and meals. The hall is a place to wait in, a place from which to try the various doors, not a place to live in.[5]

Similarly, believers who inhabit the various rooms can enter the hall for the sake of dialogue and mutual support. But they cannot afford to remain there, chatting and cooperating and maybe even throwing up some tents, while their own rooms fall into neglect. A conversation has to reach conclusions in order to actually stand for something; a community has to define itself theologically in order to be able to sustain itself across the generations. In an age of institutional weakness and doctrinal drift, American Christianity has much more to gain from a robust Catholicism and a robust Calvinism than it does from even the most fruitful Catholic-Calvinist theological dialogue.

Again, this doesn't mean that this dialogue should disappear, or that Christians should lose sight of what they have in common. One of the most effective exponents of "mere Christianity" in today's culture is Timothy Keller, the pastor of New York City's Redeemer Presbyterian Church and the author of *The Reason for God* (2008), one of the more lucid responses to the New Atheism. Keller's books usher the reader into Lewis's hallway of faith and emphasize the common theological premises shared by Catholics, Protestants, and Orthodox churches alike. But while Keller is ecumenical in public dialogue, he is proudly confessional in worship and communion. The New Yorker who joins his church will be welcomed, not into the generic Jesus worship of the typical megachurch, but into a more specific and rigorous confessional tradition: the Reformed Presbyterianism of Knox and Calvin, bound to a particular interpretation of Scripture and rooted in the Westminster Confession of Faith.

This combination has made Keller's ministry one of the true success stories of contemporary Christianity. Without making doctrinal compromises and transparent bids for relevance, Redeemer Presbyterian has managed to attract a youthful, affluent, and cosmopolitan congregation, drawing in "a cross-section of yuppie Manhattanites—doctors, bankers, lawyers, artists, actors, and designers"[6] (as a *New York* magazine profile put it) with an essentially orthodox message. At the same time, its pastor's books and writings reach an audience wider than both his Manhattan home base and his particular confessional tradition. When it comes to dealing with the skepticism and prejudices of the American elite, a Christianity with more Timothy Kellers among its ministers, priests, and laypeople would be a Christianity with less to fear and more to offer.

Third, a renewed Christianity should be *moralistic but also holistic*. No aspect of Christian faith is less appealing to contemporary sensibilities than the faith's long list of "thou shalt nots," and no prohibition attracts more exasperation and contempt than the Christian view of chastity and sex. But recurring efforts to downplay the faith's moralistic side—to make its commandments general rather than particular, to recontextualize Bible passages that offend contemporary sensibilities, to make the faith seem more hospitable to America's many millions of divorced people, cohabitating couples, and (especially) gays and lesbians—have usually ended up redefining Christianity entirely. The traditional Christian view of sexuality is more essential to the faith as a whole than many modern believers want to acknowledge. Like most Christian dogmas, from the identity of Christ to the doctrine of the Trinity, it doesn't just rest on a literal reading of a few passages in Scripture, which can be easily revised or reinterpreted. Rather, it's the fruit of centuries' worth of meditation and argument on the whole of the biblical narrative, from the creation of Adam and Eve to Jesus' prohibition on divorce. It seems easy enough to snip a single thread out of this pattern, but often the whole thing swiftly unravels once you do.

Yet many conservative Christians often make a similar mistake; they emphasize the most hot-button (and easily politicized) moral issues while losing sight of the tapestry as a whole. There are seven deadly sins, not just one, and Christianity's understanding of marriage and chastity is intimately bound to its views on gluttony and avarice and pride. (Recall that in the *Inferno,* Dante consigns gluttons, misers, and spendthrifts to lower circles of hell than adulterers and fornicators.) Christians often complain, with some justice, that journalists want to quote religious leaders only when they're talking about sex. But sexual issues are one of the few places where many ministers and bishops are comfortable issuing specific condemnations, as opposed to general love-thy-neighbor appeals. It's rare to hear a rip-roaring Sunday sermon about the temptations of the five-course meal and the all-you-can-eat buffet, or to hear a high-profile pastor who addresses the sin of greed in the frank manner of, say, Saint Basil the Great in the fourth century A.D.:

> The bread that you possess belongs to the hungry. The clothes that you store in boxes, belong to the naked. The shoes rotting by you, belong to the bare-foot. The money that you hide belongs to anyone in need. You wrong as many people as you could help.[7]

Note that Basil isn't arguing for a slightly higher marginal tax rate to fund modest improvements in public services. He's passing judgment on individual sins and calling for individual repentance. There are conservative Christians today who seem terrified of even remotely criticizing Wall Street tycoons and high-finance buccaneers, lest such criticism be interpreted as an endorsement of the Democratic Party's political agenda. But a Christianity that cannot use the language of Basil—and of Jesus—to attack the cult of Mammon will inevitably be less persuasive when the time comes to attack the cult of Dionysus.

In much the same way, the Christian case for fidelity and chastity will inevitably seem partial and hypocritical if it trains most of its attention on the minority of cases—on homosexual wedlock and the slippery slope to polygamy beyond. It is the *heterosexual* divorce rate, the *heterosexual* retreat from marriage, and the *heterosexual* out-of-wedlock birthrate that should command the most attention from Christian moralists. The Christian perspective on gay sex only makes sense in light of the Christian perspective on straight sex, and in a culture that has made heterosexual desire the measure of all things, asking gays alone to conform their lives to a hard teaching will inevitably seem like a form of bigotry.

Obviously the Christian position on homosexuality will be widely described as bigotry in any event. I have no easy answers to the question of how churches should minister to gays and lesbians in a post-closet age, and great sympathy for same-sex-attracted Christians who regard the traditional teaching as impossible. But it's worth emphasizing that one reason the Christian insistence on chastity for homosexuals seems particularly cruel and unreasonable is that the Christian churches no longer successfully hold up heterosexual chastity as a clearly defined, successfully lived-out ideal. The prevalence of homosexuality in the Catholic priesthood, for instance, has become a source of corruption and scandal not because gay men can't be holy priests (they can), but because without a large enough straight presence in seminaries and rectories the ideal of a "celibate" priesthood can come to feel like a richly brocaded closet for gay Catholics rather than a genuine way of life. Likewise the "defense of marriage" by a parade of womanizers: all men are sinners, but a conservative Christianity that lets figures like Newt Gingrich and David Vitter serve as its public champions shouldn't be surprised when its claim to be protecting the sacredness of the family falls on deaf ears.

Too often, contemporary Christian treatments of sexuality make the idea of chastity seem like a kind of divine punishment, whether for a failed marriage or an unchosen sexual orientation. This concept would have been entirely foreign to earlier eras of Christian history, which valorized celibacy as the highest and holiest of callings and elevated various forms of committed friendship and nonfamilial community as viable alternatives to Christian marriage—equal in dignity and perhaps superior in holiness. From the early Church to the Victorian era, rituals and gestures grew up to exalt and commemorate chaste same-sex affection, and forms of communal life were made available to unmarried Christians who didn't feel called to take monastic vows. When the historian John Boswell argued that medieval Christianity conducted same-sex weddings, he was clearly mistaken about the nature of the ceremonies, but he wasn't wrong about the existence of a Christian culture that, as Andrew Sullivan puts it, "taught the primacy of *caritas* to eros, and held out the virtue of friendship as equal to the benefits of conjugal love."[8]

Elements of this culture survive, primarily in Catholicism. (In both its Mainline and Evangelical forms, Protestantism has had more difficulty advancing positive models for celibate life.) But to a great extent, the understandable Christian zeal to defend the institution of marriage has created a vacuum where the case for chaste modes of living should exist. It isn't a coincidence that some of the most eloquent celebrations of the ancient emphasis on friendship and community have come from gay and lesbian Christians—from writers like Sullivan, who dissents from the traditional teaching on gay marriage, but also from writers who accept it, such as the Catholic Eve Tushnet and the Evangelical Wesley Hill. Recovering this older strain of Christian thought would be only a partial answer to the issue of homosexuality, but it seems like a more plausible response than either the complete abandonment of the Christian view of marriage or the blinkered quest for psychiatric "cures" (itself a Christian surrender to the cult of therapy).

A renewed emphasis on nonmarital forms of community could have broader applications as well. A recent *Atlantic* essay on contemporary single womanhood, Kate Bolick's "All the Single Ladies," concluded with the author visiting the Begijnhof, an all-female Dutch collective that began as a religious organization in the mid-twelfth century, in search of what Bolick describes as "bigger, and more intentional" forms of same-sex community.[9] Hers is a not uncommon impulse: with the eclipse of the nuclear family, we increasingly inhabit a culture of singletons and divorcés, unwed parents and unmarried retirees, in which millions upon millions of people pass through life without the stability of a two-parent family and then find themselves growing old alone. There is a void here, in other words, that a more holistic Christianity should find ways to fill—rediscovering the resources of the Christian past to address the needs of the American present.

Finally, a renewed Christianity should be *oriented toward sanctity and beauty*. In every crisis in the Christian past, it has been saints and artists—from Saint Francis down to John Wesley, Dante to Dostoevsky—who resurrected the faith from one of its many deaths. The example of a single extraordinary woman, Mother Teresa, did more for Christian witness in the twentieth century than every theology department and political action committee put together. The critic Alan Jacobs points out that what remains of highbrow Christian culture in the United States is sustained, to a remarkable extent, by literary works rather than by institutions—by *Wise Blood* and Walker Percy, Auden's verse and *The Chronicles of Narnia,* Thomas Merton's memoirs and "The Four Quartets."

As Joseph Ratzinger put it, shortly before becoming Benedict XVI: "The only really effective apologia for Christianity comes down to two arguments, namely, the saints the Church has produced and the art which has grown in her womb."[10] Today we have too few of both. There are high-profile Christian artists—the novelist Marilynne Robinson, the poet (and editor of *Poetry* magazine) Christian Wiman, even the demon-haunted Mel Gibson—but nothing that even resembles a significant Christian presence in literature and architecture, television and film. The ghost of a Christian worldview haunts many of our finest creative minds, from David Chase to Terence Malick, but the kind of belief that infused the midcentury Christian renaissance is much harder to find. Worse, many Christians are either indifferent to beauty or suspicious of its snares, content to worship in tacky churches and amuse themselves with cultural products that are well-meaning but distinctly second-rate. Few Americans think of religion as a great wellspring of aesthetic achievement anymore, and the Christian message is vastly weaker for it.

As for saints, there are no doubt many holy men and women in America whose sanctity is known to God alone. But Christian witness needs to be public and evangelistic as well as intimate and personal, and our highest-profile evangelists—Catholic as well as Protestant—have been far more likely to fall prey to the culture of celebrity than to follow in the footsteps of a Jonathan Edwards or a Dorothy Day. The future of American religion depends on believers who can demonstrate, in word and deed alike, that the possibilities of the Christian life are not exhausted by TV preachers and self-help gurus, utopians, and demagogues. It depends on public examples of holiness, and public demonstrations of what the imitation of Christ can mean for a fallen world. We are waiting, not for another political savior or television personality, but for a Dominic or a Francis, an Ignatius or a Wesley, a Wilberforce or a Newman, a Bonhoeffer or a Solzhenitsyn. Only sanctity can justify Christianity's existence; only sanctity can make the case for faith; only sanctity, or the hope thereof, can ultimately redeem the world.

This book has often made a more instrumental case for Christian ortho-doxy—defending its exacting moralism as a curb against worldly excess and corruption, praising its paradoxes and mysteries for respecting the com-plexities of human affairs in ways that more streamlined theologies do not, celebrating the role of its institutions in assimilating immigrants, sustaining families, and forging strong communities. My hope throughout has been to persuade even the most skeptical reader that traditional Christian faith might have more to offer this country than either its flawed defenders or its fashionable enemies would lead one to believe.

But whether I have succeeded or failed in that argument, neither reli-gions nor cultures can live on instrumentality alone. It is not enough for Americans to respect orthodox Christianity a bit more than they do at present. To make any difference in our common life, Christianity must be *lived*—not as a means to social cohesion or national renewal, but as an end unto itself. Anyone who seeks a more perfect union should begin by seek-ing the perfection of their own soul. Anyone who would save their country should first look to save themselves. *Seek first the kingdom of God and his righteousness, and all these things will be added to you.*

That quest begins with a single step—over the threshold of your local church, back through the confessional door, or simply into an empty room for a moment's silent prayer. Even if you do not consider yourself a Christian, chances are that your values and beliefs owe more to Christianity than you think. Even if you think that you have left your ancestors' faith behind en-tirely, chances are that you are still partially within the circle—more a heretic than a true apostate, more Christian-ish than post-Christian. If so, then there is something to be said for returning to the source, for looking again at your half-forgotten patrimony, for considering anew the possibility that Christian-ity might be an inheritance rather than a burden.

You may be disappointed in what you find. But then again you may be joyfully surprised. And just as importantly, your very presence might make a difference to what others find, when they come to look themselves.

NOTES

Prologue: A Nation of Heretics

1. Joseph Bottum, "The Death of Protestant America," *First Things*, August/September 2007.
2. Alister McGrath, *Heresy: A History of Defending the Truth* (New York: Harper-Collins, 2009), 11–12.
3. Thomas C. Oden, *The Rebirth of Orthodoxy: Signs of New Life in Christianity* (New York: HarperCollins, 2003).
4. G. K. Chesterton, *Orthodoxy* (San Francisco: Ignatius Press, 1995), 107.
5. Jonathan Wright, *Heretics: The Creation of Christianity From the Gnostics to the Modern Church* (New York: Houghton Mifflin Harcourt, 2011), 8.
6. Robert Inchausti, *Subversive Orthodoxy: Outlaws, Rebels and Other Christians in Disguise* (Grand Rapids, MI: Brazos Press, 2005).

One: The Lost World

1. W. H. Auden, in *Modern Canterbury Pilgrims*, ed. James A. Pike (New York: Morehouse-Gorham., 1956), 41.
2. Ibid.
3. Arthur Kirsch, *Auden and Christianity* (New Haven: Yale University Press, 2005), 22.
4. Auden, *Modern Canterbury Pilgrims*, 40.
5. Auden, "As I Walked Out One Evening," in *Collected Poems*, ed. Edward Mendelson (New York: Vintage, 1991), 133.
6. Auden, "A Thanksgiving," in *Collected Poems*, 891–92.
7. Martin E. Marty, *Modern American Religion, Volume 3: Under God, Indivisible: 1941–60* (Chicago: The University of Chicago Press, 1996), 279.
8. Sydney E. Ahlstrom, *A Religious History of the American People* (New Haven and London: Yale University Press, 1972), 952.
9. Will Herberg, *Protestant-Catholic-Jew: An Essay in American Religious Sociology* (Chicago: The University of Chicago Press, 1983), 51.
10. Ahlstrom, *A Religious History*, 953.
11. Patrick Allitt, *Religion in America Since 1945: A History* (New York: Columbia University Press, 2003), 34.

12. Herberg, *Protestant-Catholic-Jew*, 4.
13. *Publishers Weekly*, January 23, 1954, quoted in Herberg, *Protestant-Catholic-Jew*, 68–69.
14. Herberg, *Protestant-Catholic-Jew*, 2.
15. Charles R. Morris, *American Catholic: The Saints and Sinners Who Built America's Most Powerful Church* (New York: Random House, 1997), 197.
16. Thomas C. Reeves, *America's Bishop: The Life and Times of Fulton Sheen* (San Francisco: Encounter Books, 2001), 240.
17. Ahlstrom, *A Religious History*, 952.
18. Herberg, "The Religious Stirring on the Campus," *Commentary*, March 1952.
19. Herberg, *Protestant-Catholic-Jew*, 55.
20. Herberg, *Protestant-Catholic-Jew*, 53.
21. Reinhold Niebuhr, "Is There a Revival of Religion?," *The New York Times Magazine*, November 19, 1950.
22. Herberg, *Protestant-Catholic-Jew*, 55.
23. Richard Wightman Fox, *Reinhold Niebuhr: A Biography* (New York: Pantheon Books, 1985), 28.
24. Ibid., 111–12.
25. Walter Rauschenbusch, *Christianity and the Social Crisis* (New York: HarperCollins, 2007), 338.
26. Ahlstrom, *A Religious History*, 934.
27. Barth, *The Epistle to the Romans,* trans. Edwyn C. Hoskyns (London: Oxford University Press, 1968), 51.
28. Karl Adam, quoted in Ahlstrom, *A Religious History*, 934.
29. Reinhold Niebuhr, "Ten Years That Shook My World," *The Christian Century*, April 26, 1939.
30. H. Richard Niebuhr, *The Kingdom of God in America* (Middletown: Wesleyan University Press, 1988), 193.
31. Charles C. Brown, *Niebuhr and His Age: Reinhold Niebuhr's Prophetic Role and Legacy* (Harrisburg, PA: Trinity Press International, 2002), 66–67.
32. Reinhold Niebuhr, *The Nature and Destiny of Man* (Louisville: Westminster John Knox Press, 1996), 207.
33. Ahlstrom, *A Religious History*, 933.
34. Jason Stevens, *God-Fearing and Free: A Spiritual History of America's Cold War* (Cambridge: Harvard University Press, 2010), 2.
35. Ibid., 8.
36. Ibid., 90–91.
37. Marty, *Under God, Indivisible*, 144–47.
38. Peter Kihss, "President Participates in Church Rites Here," *The New York Times*, October 13, 1958.

39. Ibid.

40. David Aikman, *Billy Graham: His Life and Influence* (Nashville: Thomas Nelson, 2007), 131.

41. John Calvin, *Commentary on Genesis, Volume I*, Christian Classics Ethereal Library. http://www.ccel.org/ccel/calvin/calcom01.html.

42. Marty, *Under God, Indivisible*, 103–4.

43. Ibid., 149.

44. Peter Boyer, "The Big Tent: Billy Graham, Franklin Graham, and the Transformation of American Evangelicalism," *The New Yorker*, August 22, 2005.

45. Aikman, *Billy Graham*, 126.

46. Carl F. W. Henry, *The Uneasy Conscience of Modern Fundamentalism* (Grand Rapids: Wm. B. Eerdsman, 2003), xviii.

47. Ibid., 67–68.

48. George Marsden, *Reforming Fundamentalism: Fuller Seminary and the New Evangelicalism* (Grand Rapids: Wm. B. Eerdsman, 1987), 158.

49. Marty, *Under God, Indivisible*, 153.

50. Pope Pius X, *Lamentabili Sane Exitu*, 1907. http://www.papalencyclicals.net/Pius10/p10lamen.htm.

51. James Hitchcock, "Post-Mortem on a Rebirth: The Catholic Intellectual Renaissance," in *Years of Crisis: Collected Essays, 1970–1983* (San Francisco: Ignatius Press, 1985), 104.

52. Jay P. Dolan, *The American Catholic Experience* (New York: Image Books, 1985), 319.

53. Morris, *American Catholic*, 281.

54. Kenneth Woodward, "Memories of a Catholic Boyhood," *First Things*, April 2011.

55. Garry Wills, *Bare Ruined Choirs* (New York: Doubleday, 1971), 17.

56. John T. McGreevy, *Catholicism and American Freedom* (New York: W.W. Norton, 2003), 151.

57. "Radio Religion," *Time*, January 21, 1946, http://www.time.com/time/magazine/article/0,9171,934406,00.html.

58. Morris, *American Catholic*, 225–26.

59. McGreevy, *Catholicism and American Freedom*, 166.

60. Ibid., 167.

61. Fulton Sheen, *Whence Come Wars* (Sheed and Ward, 1940), 60.

62. Wilfrid Parsons, S.J., "Philosophical Factors in the Integration of American Culture," 1942. Quoted in McGreevy, *Catholicism and American Freedom*, 193.

63. Jacques Maritain, *Reflections on America* (New York: Scribner's, 1958), 83.

64. Pope Pius XII, *Humani Generis*, 1950. http://www.vatican.va/holy_father/pius_xii/encyclicals/documents/hf_p-xii_enc_12081950_humani-generis_en.html.

65. W.E.B. Du Bois, *The Philadelphia Negro: A Social Study* (Philadelphia: University of Pennsylvania, 1899).

66. E. Franklin Frazier, *The Negro Church in America* (New York: Pantheon Books, 1973), 54.

67. Ibid., 51.

68. Patrick Allitt, *Religion in America Since 1945*, 48–50.

69. David L. Chappell, *A Stone of Hope: Prophetic Religion and the Death of Jim Crow* (Chapel Hill: The University of North Carolina Press, 2004), 88.

70. Allitt, *Religion in America Since 1945*, 51.

71. Marty, *Under God, Indivisible*, 392.

72. Chappell, *Stone of Hope*, 99.

73. Marty, *Under God, Indivisible*, 385.

74. Ibid., 386.

75. Chappell, *Stone of Hope*, 97.

76. Ibid.

77. Ben Schwarz, "What to Read This Month," *The Atlantic*, November 2003.

78. Steven Patrick Miller, *Billy Graham and the Rise of the Republican South* (Philadelphia: University of Pennsylvania Press, 2009), 95.

79. Chappell, *Stone of Hope*, 107.

80. Morris J. MacGregor, *Steadfast in the Faith: The Life of Patrick Cardinal Boyle* (Washington, DC: Catholic University of America Press, 2006), 195–96.

81. McGreevy, *Catholicism and American Freedom*, 211.

82. Martin Gardner, *The Flight of Peter Fromm* (Amherst, NY: Prometheus Books, 1994), 189.

83. Joseph Bottum, "A Room With a View," *First Things*, August/September 2009.

Two: The Locust Years

1. Dolan, *The American Catholic Experience*, 391.

2. Martin Luther King, Jr., "I Have a Dream," August 28, 1963.

3. Wills, *Bare Ruined Choirs*, 146–48.

4. Dean M. Kelley, *Why Conservative Churches Are Growing* (New York: Harper and Row, 1972), 1.

5. Thomas Jefferson, "A Letter to Dr. Benjamin Waterhouse," June 26, 1822.

6. Dean R. Hoge, Benton Johnson, and Donald A. Luidens, *Vanishing Boundaries: The Religion of Mainline Protestant Baby Boomers* (Louisville, KY: Westminster/John Knox Press, 1994), 2.

7. Kelley, *Conservative Churches*, 2–8.

8. Hoge et al., *Vanishing Boundaries*, 5.

9. Thomas C. Reeves, *The Empty Church: The Suicide of Liberal Christianity* (New York: Free Press, 1996), 11–12.

10. Diana L. Eck, *A New Religious America: How a "Christian Country" Has Become the World's Most Religiously Diverse Nation* (New York: HarperCollins, 2001), 2.

11. Morris, *American Catholic*, 308.

12. Leo Rosten, ed., *Religions of America: Ferment and Faith in an Age of Crisis* (New York: Simon and Schuster, 1975), 431–32.

13. Roger Finke and Rodney Stark, *The Churching of America 1776–2005: Winners and Losers in Our Religious Economy* (New Brunswick, NJ: Rutgers University Press, 2005), 255–61.

14. Ibid., 255–61.

15. Kelley, *Conservative Churches*, 20-31.

16. Ibid., 21–25.

17. Claude S. Fischer and Michael Hout, *Century of Difference: How America Changed in the Last One Hundred Years* (New York: Russell Sage Foundation, 2008), 208.

18. Hillary D. Rodham, "1969 Student Commencement Speech," Wellesley College, May 31, 1969.

19. Robert Ellwood, *The Sixties Spiritual Awakening: American Religion Moving From Modern to Postmodern* (New Brunswick, NJ: Rutgers University Press, 1994), 7.

20. Hoge et al., *Vanishing Boundaries*, 198.

21. Wills, *Bare Ruined Choirs*, 33.

22. Peter Beinart, *The Icarus Syndrome: A History of American Hubris* (New York: HarperCollins, 2010), 170.

23. R. J. Biggar et al., "Trends in the Number of Sexual Partners among American Women," *Journal of Acquired Immune Deficiency Syndrome* (1989) 2(5): 497–502.

24. Fischer and Hout, *Century of Difference*, 90.

25. Arland Thornton and Linda Young-DeMarco, "Four Decades of Trends in Attitudes Toward Family," *Journal of Marriage and Family*, November 2001.

26. David J. Harding and Christopher Jencks, "Changing Attitudes toward Premarital Sex: Cohort, Period, and Aging Effects," *Public Opinion Quarterly*, summer 2003.

27. Barbara Dafoe Whitehead, *The Divorce Culture: Rethinking Our Commitments to Marriage and Family* (New York: Vintage Books, 1998), 82.

28. Charles Murray, *Coming Apart: The State of White America, 1960–2010* (New York: Crown Forum, 2010), 153.

29. Hoge et al., *Vanishing Boundaries*, 199.

30. Ibid., 184.

31. Finke and Stark, *Churching of America*, 263.

32. Fischer and Hout, *Century of Difference*, 200.

33. Matthew J. Price, "Male Clergy in Economic Crisis," *The Christian Century*, August 15–22, 2001.

34. Paul Wilkes, "The Hands That Would Shape Our Souls," *The Atlantic*, December 1990.
35. Hoge et al., *Vanishing Boundaries*, 46–47.

Three: Accommodation

1. "Is God Dead?" *Time* magazine, April 8, 1966.
2. Robert Ellwood, *The Sixties Spiritual Awakening*, 139.
3. Harvey Cox, *The Secular City* (Toronto: Macmillan, 1965), 221.
4. Ibid., 186–87.
5. Ibid., 27–32.
6. Ibid., 35.
7. Ibid., 55.
8. Ibid., 72–73.
9. Ibid., 201–6.
10. David M. Roberston, *A Passionate Pilgrim: A Biography of Bishop James A. Pike* (New York: Random House, 2004), 104.
11. "Teachings and Practice on Marriage, Divorce and Remarriage," American Lutheran Church, 1982.
12. *The Didache*, Roberts-Donaldson translation, EarlyChristianWritings.com.
13. Chris Herlinger, "'God Box' in New York More Diverse as It Turns 50," *The Christian Century*, November 24, 2010.
14. Mark Oppenheimer, *Knocking on Heaven's Door: American Religion in the Age of Counterculture* (New Haven: Yale University Press, 2003), 143.
15. Allitt, *Religion in America Since 1945*, 124.
16. Carl Braaten, "An Open Letter to Bishop Mark Hanson," July 11, 2005. http://wordalone.org/docs/wa-braaten.shtml.
17. Cox, *The Secular City*, 232.
18. Richard John Neuhaus, *The Catholic Moment: The Paradox of the Church in the Postmodern World* (San Francisco: Harper and Row, 1987), 51.
19. John Wilkins, "Ratzinger at Vatican II: A Pope Who Can and Cannot Change," *Commonweal*, June 4, 2010.
20. Malachi Martin, *The Jesuits: The Society of Jesus and the Betrayal of the Roman Catholic Church* (New York: Simon and Schuster, 1987), 405.
21. George A. Kelly, *The Battle for the American Church* (New York: Doubleday, 1980), 291.
22. Ibid., 296.
23. Theodore Hesburgh et al., "The Idea of the Catholic University," July 23, 1967.
24. "Gay Priests Commit No More Abuse . . . ," Religion and Ethics Newsweekly, PBS, April 5, 2002. http://www.pbs.org/wnet/religionandethics/week531/feature.html.
25. James Hitchcock, *The Recovery of the Sacred* (New York: Seabury Press, 1974), 9.

26. Ibid.

27. Wills, *Bare Ruined Choirs*, 158.

28. Philip F. Lawler, *The Faithful Departed: The Collapse of Boston's Catholic Culture* (New York: Encounter Books, 2008), 74.

29. Thomas Sheehan, "The Revolution in the Church," *The New York Review of Books*, June 14, 1984.

30. Kelly, *The Battle for the American Church*, 245.

31. Leon Podles, *Sacrilege: Sexual Abuse in the Catholic Church* (Baltimore: Crossland Press, 2008), 454-56.

32. James Hitchcock, *The Decline and Fall of Radical Catholicism* (New York: Herder and Herder, 1971), 58-59.

33. Kelly, *Battle for the American Church*, 238.

34. Sheehan, "Revolution in the Church."

35. Wills, *Bare Ruined Choirs*, 161.

36. Ibid., 186.

37. Finke and Stark, *Churching of America*, 269-271.

38. Hitchcock, *Recovery*, 23.

39. Harvey Cox, *Feast of Fools: A Theological Essay on Festivity and Fantasy* (Cambridge, MA: Harvard University Press, 1969).

40. Sheehan, "Revolution in the Church."

41. Kelley, *Conservative Churches*, 84-85.

42. Wills, *Bare Ruined Choirs*, 212-213.

43. Hitchcock, *Decline and Fall*, 31-32.

44. Robertson, *Passionate Pilgrim*, 214.

45. Ibid., 218.

Four: Resistance

1. "Evangelicals and Catholics Together: The Christian Mission in the Third Millennium," *First Things*, May 1994.

2. Jacques Maritain, *The Peasant of the Garonne: An Old Layman Questions Himself About the Present Time* (New York: Holt, Rinehart and Winston, 1968), 152.

3. Neuhaus, *The Catholic Moment*, 135.

4. Michael Novak, "The Peasant of the Garonne, by Jacques Maritain," *Commentary*, September 1968.

5. McGreevy, *Catholicism and American Freedom*, 261.

6. Pope Paul VI, *Humanae Vitae*, July 25, 1968, http://www.vatican.va/holy_father/paul_vi/encyclicals/documents/hf_p-vi_enc_25071968_humanae-vitae_en.html.

7. George Weigel, *The Courage to Be Catholic: Crisis, Reform and the Future of the Church* (New York: Basic Books, 2002), 221.

8. Ibid.
9. Holy Mass for the American Priests, Homily of His Holiness John Paul II, October 4, 1979, http://www.vatican.va/holy_father/john_paul_ii/homilies/1979/documents/hf_jp-ii_hom_19791004_usa-philadelphia_en.html.
10. Robert George, "He Threw It All Away," *First Things*, March 20, 2009.
11. Marsden, *Reforming Fundamentalism*, 111.
12. "People and Ideas: Francis Schaeffer," *God in America*, PBS, http://www.pbs.org/godinamerica/people/francis-schaeffer.html.
13. Alister McGrath, *J. I. Packer: A Biography* (Grand Rapids, MI: Baker Books, 1997), 200.
14. Mark Noll, *The Scandal of the Evangelical Mind* (Grand Rapids, MI: W. B. Eerdsman Publishing, 1994), 109.
15. Laurie Goodstein and David Kirkpatrick, "On a Christian Mission to the Top," *The New York Times*, May 22, 2005.
16. Mark Noll and Carolyn Nystrom, *Is the Reformation Over? An Evangelical Assessment of Contemporary Roman Catholicism* (Grand Rapids, MI: Baker Publishing, 2005), 73.
17. Robert Putnam and David Campbell, *American Grace: How Religion Divides and Unites Us* (New York: Simon and Schuster, 2010), 108.
18. Ibid., 138.
19. Peter Steinfels, "Further Adrift," *Commonweal*, October 22, 2010.
20. For instance, "Catholics Similar to Mainstream on Abortion, Stem Cells," Gallup, March 20, 2009. http://www.gallup.com/poll/117154/catholics-similar-mainstream-abortion-stem-cells.aspx.
21. For instance, "American Catholics Revere Pope, Disagree With Some Major Teachings," Gallup, April 4, 2005, http://www.gallup.com/poll/15478/american-catholics-revere-pope-disagree-some-major-teachings.aspx.
22. Christian Smith and Melinda Lundquist Denton, *Soul Searching: The Religious and Spiritual Lives of American Teenagers* (New York: Oxford University Press, 2005), ch. 2 and 6.
23. Karen Terry et al., *The Nature and Scope of the Problem of Sexual Abuse of Minors by Priests and Deacons*, prepared by the John Jay College of Criminal Justice for the U.S. Conference of Catholic Bishops (Washington, DC: USCCB, 2004).
24. For instance, Pat Wingert, "Priests Commit No More Abuse Than Other Men," *Newsweek*, April 7, 2010.
25. Podles, *Sacrilege*, 441–87.
26. Christian Smith, *American Evangelicalism: Embattled and Thriving* (Chicago: University of Chicago Press, 1998), 20.
27. Ibid., 22.
28. Daniel M. Hungerman, "Substitution and Stigma: Evidence on Religious

Competition from the Catholic Sex-Abuse Scandal," University of Notre Dame and NBER, November 2011.

29. Putnam and Campbell, *American Grace*, 108.
30. Ibid., 126.
31. Smith, *American Evangelicalism*, 181.
32. Ibid., 178.
33. David F. Wells, *The Courage to Be Protestant: Truth-Lovers, Marketers and Emergents in the Postmodern World* (Grand Rapids, MI: W. B. Eerdsman, 2008), 10.
34. James Davison Hunter, *To Change the World: The Irony, Tragedy and Possibility of Christianity in the Late-Modern World* (New York: Oxford University Press, 2010), 16.
35. Michael Hout and Claude S. Fischer, "Why More Americans Have No Religious Preference: Politics and Generations," *American Sociological Review*, April 2002.
36. Putnam and Campbell, *American Grace*, 126.
37. Cathy Lynn Grossman, "More Americans Tailoring Religion to Fit Their Needs," *USA Today*, September 13, 2011.
38. Hunter, *To Change the World*, 89.
39. Ibid., 92.
40. Ibid., 89.
41. Andrew Sullivan, "There's a New Power in America—Atheism," *The Times of London*, March 14, 2009.
42. Daniel Dennett, "The Evaporation of the Powerful Mystique of Religion," from *What Are You Optimistic About?*, John Brockman, ed., TheEdge.org, 2007.

Five: Lost in the Gospels

1. Joan Accocella, "Should We Hate Judas Iscariot?" *The New Yorker*, August 3, 2009.
2. Elaine Pagels, "The Gospel Truth," *The New York Times*, April 8, 2006.
3. Thomas Bartlett, "The Betrayal of Judas," *The Chronicle of Higher Education*, May 30, 2008.
4. John Noble Wilford and Laurie Goodstein, "In Ancient Document, Judas, Minus the Betrayal," *The New York Times*, April 7, 2006.
5. April DeConick, "Gospel Truth," *The New York Times*, December 1, 2007.
6. Thomas Jefferson, "Letter to John Adams," October 13, 1813.
7. Paul Boyer, *When Time Shall Be No More: Prophecy Belief in Modern American Culture* (Cambridge, MA: Belknap Press of Harvard University Press, 1992), 98.
8. Henry Emerson Fosdick, "Shall the Fundamentalists Win?," *Christian Work*, June 10, 1922.

9. Bart Ehrman, *Lost Christianities: The Battle for Scripture and the Faiths We Never Knew* (Oxford: Oxford University Press, 2005), 4.

10. Richard B. Hays, "The Corrected Jesus," *First Things*, May 1994.

11. Pagels, *Beyond Belief: The Secret Gospel of Thomas* (New York: Random House, 2003), 48.

12. Marcus Borg, *Jesus: Uncovering the Life, Teachings and Relevance of a Religious Revolutionary* (New York: HarperCollins, 2006), 307.

13. John Dominic Crossan, *Who Killed Jesus? Exposing the Roots of Anti-Semitism in the Gospel Story* (New York: HarperCollins, 1995), 217.

14. Luke Timothy Johnson, *The Real Jesus: The Misguided Quest for the Historical Jesus and the Truth of the Traditional Gospels* (New York: HarperCollins, 1996), 8.

15. Pagels, *The Gnostic Gospels* (New York: Random House, 1989), xx.

16. Elisabeth Schüssler Fiorenza, *In Memory of Her: A Feminist Theological Reconstruction of Christian Origins* (New York: Crossroad, 1983), 107.

17. Ibid., 52.

18. Borg, *Meeting Jesus Again for the First Time* (New York: HarperCollins, 1994), 32.

19. Crossan, *The Historical Jesus: The Life of a Mediterranean Jewish Peasant* (New York: HarperCollins ,1991), 422.

20. Johnson, *The Real Jesus*, 12–13.

21. Robert Funk, "The Coming Radical Reformation: Twenty-One Theses," *The Fourth R*, July/August 1998, http://www.westarinstitute.org/Periodicals/4R_Articles/funk_theses.html.

22. Pagels, *Beyond Belief*, 31.

23. Crossan, *God and Empire: Jesus Against Rome, Then and Now* (New York: HarperCollins, 2008), 5.

24. Borg, *Jesus*, 305.

25. Funk, "Twenty-One Theses."

26. Pagels, *Beyond Belief*, 48.

27. Ehrman, *Jesus, Interrupted: Revealing the Hidden Contradictions in the Bible (And Why We Don't Know About Them)* (New York: HarperCollins, 2009), 222.

28. Pagels, *Beyond Belief*, 328.

29. Johnson, *The Real Jesus*, 54.

30. Adam Gopnik, "What Did Jesus Do?" *The New Yorker*, May 24, 2010.

31. Timothy Beal, "The Bible Is Dead; Long Live the Bible," *The Chronicle of Higher Education*, April 17, 2011.

32. Andreas J. Kostenburger and Michael J. Kruger, *The Heresy of Orthodoxy: How Contemporary Culture's Fascination With Diversity Has Reshaped Our Understanding of Early Christianity* (Wheaton, IL: Crossway, 2010), 81.

33. C. E. Hill, *Who Chose the Gospels?: Probing the Great Gospel Conspiracy* (New York: Oxford University Press, 2010), 235.

34. Ehrman, *Lost Christianities*, 9.
35. Ehrman, *Jesus, Interrupted*, 219.
36. Ehrman, *Lost Christianities*, 5.
37. *Gospel of Thomas*, Stephen Patterson and Marvin Meyer, transl., the Gnostic Society Library, http://www.gnosis.org/naghamm/gosthom.html.
38. Hill, *Who Chose the Gospels?*, 229.
39. Gopnik, "Jesus Laughed," *The New Yorker*, April 17, 2006.
40. Crossan, *Jesus: A Revolutionary Biography* (New York: HarperCollins, 1994), 190.
41. Ibid., 188.
42. Pagels, *Gnostic Gospels*, 9.
43. Ibid., 47.
44. Carl Olson, "Dan Brown Rushes in Where Angels (and Demons) Fear to Tread," *This Rock*, April 2009.
45. Dan Brown, *The Da Vinci Code* (New York: Random House, 2003), 327.
46. "Freemasons Await Dan Brown Novel," *Associated Press*, September 15, 2009.
47. Gopnik, "Jesus Laughed."
48. Hitchcock, "Does Christianity Have a Future?," in *Years of Crisis*, 129.
49. Pagels, *Gnostic Gospels*, xx.
50. Mark Lilla, "Getting Religion," *New York Times Magazine*, September 18, 2005.
51. *The Glenn Beck Program*, May 27, 2010, transcribed by Mark Shea, "But I Learn So Much from Glenn Beck!," *National Catholic Register*, June 7, 2010.

Six: Pray and Grow Rich

1. Joel Osteen, *Your Best Life Now: 7 Steps to Living at Your Full Potential* (New York: Time Warner, 2004), 5.
2. Alexis de Tocqueville, *Democracy in America, Vol. 2*, Henry Reeve, trans. (New York: J. and H. G. Langsley, 1840), 261.
3. Russell Conwell, *Acres of Diamonds* (New York: Harper and Brothers, 1915), 18.
4. Rhonda Byrne, *The Secret* (New York: Atria Books, 2006), 32.
5. Hank Hanegraaf, *Christianity in Crisis* (Eugene, OR: Harvest House, 1997), 332.
6. David Jones and Russell Woodbridge, *Health, Wealth and Happiness: Has the Prosperity Gospel Overshadowed the Gospel of Christ?* (Grand Rapids, MI: Kregel Publications, 2011), 53.
7. D. R. McConnell, *A Different Gospel* (Peabody, MA: Hendrickson Press, 1988), 57.
8. William Lobdell, "Pastor's Empire Built on Acts of Faith, and Cash," *Los Angeles Times*, September 19, 2004.

9. Burkhard Bilger, "God Doesn't Need Ole Anthony," *The New Yorker*, December 6, 2004.
10. Hanna Rosin, "Did Christianity Cause the Crash?" *The Atlantic*, December 2009.
11. Carolyn Tuft and Bill Smith, "From Fenton to Fortune in the Name of God," *St. Louis Post-Dispatch*, November 15, 2003.
12. William Martin, "Prime Minister," *Texas Monthly*, August 2005.
13. Osteen, *Your Best Life*, 165.
14. Ibid., 125.
15. Ibid., 168.
16. "Changing Faiths: Latinos and the Transformation of American Religion," Pew Hispanic Center, 2008, 32.
17. Jonathan L. Walton, *Watch This! The Ethics and Aesthetics of Black Televangelism* (New York: NYU Press, 2009), 47.
18. Ibid., xiii.
19. Ibid., xiv.
20. Ted Olsen, "What Really Unites Pentecostalists?" *Christianity Today*, December 5, 2006.
21. "Spirit and Power: A 10-Country Survey of Pentecostalists," Pew Research Center, October 5, 2006, 30.
22. Bruce Wilkinson, *The Prayer of Jabez: Breaking Through to the Blessed Life* (Sister, OR: Multnomah Publishers, 2000), 17.
23. Ibid., 33.
24. Ibid., 31–32.
25. T. D. Jakes, *The Great Investment: Balancing Faith, Family and Finance to Build a Rich Spiritual Life* (New York: Berkley Publishing, 2000), 31.
26. Larry Eskridge, "Money Matters: The Phenomenon of Financial Counselor Larry Burkett and Christian Financial Concepts," in *More Money, More Ministry: Money and Evangelicals in Recent North American History*, Eskridge and Mark Noll, eds. (Grand Rapids, MI: W. B. Eerdsman, 2000), 318.
27. Eskridge, "Money Matters," 312.
28. Ibid., 329–30.
29. Jakes, *The Great Investment*, 15.
30. Michael Hamilton, "More Money, More Ministry: The Financing of American Evangelicalism Since 1945," in *More Money, More Ministry*, 104.
31. Hamilton, "More Money," 104.
32. Ibid., 107.
33. David Van Biema and Jeff Chu, "Does God Want You to Be Rich?" *Time* magazine, September 10, 2006.
34. Leo XII, *Rerum Novarum,* May 15, 1891.
35. Pope Benedict XVI, "Europe and Its Discontents," *First Things*, January 2006.

36. Michael Novak, *The Spirit of Democratic Capitalism* (New York: Simon and Schuster, 1982), 79–82.
37. Ibid., 342.
38. Ibid., 349.
39. Bill McKibben, "The Christian Paradox: How a Faithful Nation Gets Jesus Wrong," *Harper's*, August 2005.
40. McKibben, "Christian Paradox."
41. "U.S. Charitable Giving Estimated to Be $307.65 Billion in 2008," Giving USA Foundation, June 10, 2009; for international comparisons, see "Americans Give Record $295B to Charity," *Associated Press*, November 25, 2007.
42. Arthur Brooks, *Who Really Cares: The Surprising Truth About Compassionate Conservatism* (New York: Basic Books, 2007), 34–39.
43. Arthur Brooks, "Religious Faith and Charitable Giving," *Policy Review*, October 1, 2003.
44. Rob Reich and Christopher Rimer, "Has the Great Recession Made Americans Stingier?" *Pathways*, fall 2011: 5.
45. Hamilton, "More Money, More Ministry," in *More Money, More Ministry*, 130.
46. Michael Phillips, "In Swaziland, U.S. Preacher Sees His Dream Vanish," *The Wall Street Journal*, December 19, 2007.
47. Ibid.
48. Novak, *Business as a Calling: Work and the Examined Life* (New York: Simon and Schuster, 1996), 22.
49. Osteen, *Your Best Life Now*, 3.
50. Rosin, "Did Christianity Cause the Crash?"
51. Ibid.
52. Ibid.
53. Ibid.
54. Ibid.
55. Osteen, *It's Your Time: Activate Your Faith, Achieve Your Dreams, and Increase in God's Favor* (New York: Simon and Schuster, 2009), xi.
56. Ibid., 73.
57. Ibid., 35.
58. Ibid., 131.
59. Ibid., 125.

Seven: The God Within

1. Elizabeth Gilbert, *Eat Pray Love* (New York: Penguin Books, 2006), 10-16.
2. Ibid., 18–21.
3. Ibid., 26–28.
4. Ibid., 33.
5. Ibid., 158.

6. Ibid., 176.

7. Ibid., 199–200.

8. Ibid., 205.

9. Ibid., 208.

10. Ibid., 192.

11. Ibid., 122.

12. Ibid., 122.

13. Ibid., 120.

14. Eckhart Tolle, *The Power of Now: A Guide to Spiritual Enlightenment* (Navoto, CA: New World Library, 2004), 13.

15. Ibid., 13.

16. Neale Donald Walsch, *Conversations with God: An Uncommon Dialogue, Vol. I* (New York: Putnam, 1996), 8.

17. Paulo Coelho, *The Alchemist* (New York: HarperCollins, 1993), 152.

18. Pagels, *Beyond Belief*, 133.

19. Deepak Chopra, *The Third Jesus: The Christ We Cannot Ignore* (New York: Three Rivers Press, 2008), 20.

20. Gilbert, *Eat Pray Love*, 328.

21. James Redfield, *The Celestine Prophecy* (New York: Grand Central Publishing, 2006), 242.

22. "An Interview with Paulo Coelho," in Coehlo, *The Alchemist*, 182.

23. Ahlstrom, *A Religious History*, 1019.

24. Kathryn Lofton, *Oprah: The Gospel of an Icon* (Berkeley: University of California Press, 2011), 4.

25. Nathan Schneider, "What Is Oprah?: An Interview with Kathryn Lofton," The Immanent Frame, January 26, 2011, http://blogs.ssrc.org/tif/2011/01/26/what-is-oprah-an-interview-with-kathryn-lofton/.

26. Ibid.

27. Gilbert, *Eat Pray Love*, 14.

28. Redfield, *The Celestine Prophecy*, 241.

29. Ralph Waldo Emerson, "Harvard Divinity School Address," July 15, 1838.

30. Leszek Kolakowski, *Religion: If There Is No God: On God, the Devil, Sin and Other Worries of the So-called Philosophy of Religion* (London: Fontana Press, 1993), 116.

31. Kolakowski, *Religion*, 104.

32. Harold Bloom, *The American Religion: The Emergence of the Post-Christian Nation* (New York: Simon and Schuster, 1992), 15.

33. Kolakowski, *Religion*, 104.

34. Walsch, *Conversations With God: An Uncommon Dialogue: Living in the World With Honesty, Courage and Love* (Charlottesville, VA: Hampton Roads Publishing, 1997), 99.

35. Gilbert, *Eat Pray Love*, 203.

36. Alexis de Tocqueville, *Democracy in America, Vol. 2*, Henry Reeve, trans. (New York: J. and H. G. Langsley, 1840), 30.
37. Richard Dawkins, *The God Delusion* (New York: Houghton Mifflin, 2008), 40.
38. Sam Harris, *The End of Faith* (New York: W. W. Norton, 2004), 221.
39. Karen Armstrong, *The Case for God* (New York: Random House, 2009), xii.
40. Ibid., xviii.
41. Ibid., 113.
42. Ibid., 142.
43. Ibid., 118.
44. Ibid.
45. Kolakowski, *Religion*, 108–9.
46. "An Interview with Paul Coelho," in Coelho, *The Alchemist*, 181.
47. Gilbert, *Eat Pray Love*, 144.
48. Luke Timothy Johnson, "Dry Bones: Why Religion Can't Live Without Mysticism," *Commonweal*, February 26, 2010.
49. Walsch, *Living in the World*, 97.
50. Barbara Bradley Hagerty, *Fingerprints of God: The Search for the Science of Spirituality* (New York: Riverhead Books, 2009), 43.
51. Tolle, *The Power of Now*, 3.
52. Philip Rieff, *The Triumph of the Therapeutic: The Uses of Faith After Freud* (Wilmington, DE: ISI Books, 2006), 19.
53. Ibid., 20.
54. Ibid., 21.
55. Ibid., 16.
56. Ibid., 19.
57. Ibid., 20.
58. Ibid., 19–20.
59. Christian Smith and Melinda Lundquist Denton, *Soul Searching: The Religious and Spiritual Lives of American Teenagers* (New York: Oxford University Press, 2005), 40–41.
60. Ibid., 171.
61. Ibid., 134.
62. Ibid., 162-63.
63. Ibid., 165.
64. Ibid., 163–65.
65. Ibid., 163–64.
66. Damon Linker, "The Future of Christian America," The New Republic Online, April 7, 2007.
67. Rieff, *Triumph*, 21.
68. Jean Twenge, *Generation Me: Why Today's Young Americans Are More Confident, Assertive, Entitled—and More Miserable Than Ever Before* (New York: Free Press, 2006), 69–70.

69. "Empathy: College Students Don't Have as Much as They Used To," University of Michigan News Service, May 27, 2010.

70. Christian Smith and Patricia Snell, *Souls in Transition: The Religious and Spiritual Lives of Emerging Adults* (New York: Oxford University Press, 2009), 68.

71. "Empathy," University of Michigan News Service.

72. David Brooks, *Bobos in Paradise: The New Upper Class and How They Got There* (New York: Simon and Schuster, 2000), 99.

73. Rieff, *Triumph*, 13.

74. Walsch, *Conversations*, 129.

75. James Frey, *The Final Testament of the Holy Bible* (New York: Gagosian Gallery, 2011).

76. Margaret Talbot, "Red Sex, Blue Sex," *The New Yorker*, November 3, 2008.

77. Talbot, "Red Sex, Blue Sex"; also, Ronald J. Sider, *The Scandal of the Evangelical Conscience* (Grand Rapids, MI: Baker Books, 2005); Mark A. Smith, "Religion, Divorce, and the Missing Culture War in America," *Political Science Quarterly*, spring 2010.

78. Rachel K. Jones et al., "Patterns in the Socioeconomic Characteristics of Women Obtaining Abortions in 2000–2001," *Perspectives on Sexual and Reproductive Health*, September/October 2002.

79. Christopher Lasch, *The Culture of Narcissism* (New York: W. W. Norton, 1991), 188.

80. "Americans Have Fewer Friends Outside the Family, Duke Study Shows," *Duke Today*, June 23, 2006.

81. Rieff, *Triumph*, 262.

82. Ronald Dworkin, "The Rise of the Caring Industry," *Policy Review*, June 1, 2010.

83. Ibid.

Eight: The City on the Hill

1. Chris Good, "Glenn Beck Comes to Town," theAtlantic.com, August 28, 2010.

2. Ibid.

3. Ibid.

4. Franz Rosenzweig, *The Star of Redemption*, translated and quoted in David Goldman, "Christian, Muslim, Jew," *First Things*, August 2007.

5. Goldman, "Christian, Muslim, Jew."

6. David Goldman, writing as Spengler, "Overcoming Ethnicity," *Asia Times* Online, January 6, 2009, http://www.atimes.com/atimes/Front_Page/KA06Aa01.html.

7. Ibid.

8. George Steiner, *The Portage to San Cristobal of A.H.* (Chicago: University of Chicago Press, 1981), 163–164.

9. David Gelernter, *Americanism: The Fourth Great Western Religion* (New York: Doubleday, 2007).

10. E. J. Dionne and William Galston, "The Old and New Politics of Faith: Religion in the 2010 Election," Brookings Institution, November 17, 2010.

11. Mark A. Signorelli, "A City Upon a Hill," Front Porch Republic, March 27, 2011. http://www.frontporchrepublic.com/2011/03/a-city-upon-a-hill/.

12. Walter McDougall, *Promised Land, Crusader State: The American Encounter with the World Since 1776* (New York: Houghton Mifflin, 1997), 37.

13. George Washington, "Farewell Address," September 19, 1796.

14. Calvin Coolidge, "Speech on the Occasion of the One Hundred and Fiftieth Anniversary of the Declaration of Independence," July 5, 1926.

15. Dwight D. Eisenhower, "Farewell Address," January 17. 1961.

16. Abraham Lincoln, "Second Inaugural Address," March 4, 1865.

17. Gelernter, *Americanism*, 139.

18. Abraham Lincoln, "Address to the New Jersey State Senate," February 21, 1861.

19. Richard M. Gamble, *The War for Righteousness: Progressive Christianity, the Great War, and the Rise of the Messianic Nation* (Wilmington, DE: ISI Books, 2003), 66.

20. Jeff Sharlet, "Through a Glass, Darkly: How the Christian Right is Reimagining U.S. History," *Harper's*, December 2006.

21. Gamble, *The War for Righteousness*, 66.

22. Ibid., 56.

23. Ibid., 56.

24. Ibid., 148.

25. Ahlstrom, *A Religious History*, 885.

26. McDougall, *Promised Land*, 138.

27. Ibid., 190.

28. Ibid.

29. "Glenn Beck: 'Leave Your Church,'" *Christianity Today*, March 12, 2010.

30. Full transcript of Glenn Beck's Keynote Speech at CPAC," Gather.com, February 22, 2010, http://www.gather.com/viewArticle.action?articleId=281474978060978.

31. Glenn Beck, *Glenn Beck's Common Sense: The Case Against an Out-of-Control Government* (New York: Simon and Schuster, 2009), 21.

32. Ryan Lizza, "The Transformation of Michele Bachmann," *The New Yorker*, August 15, 2011.

33. Lyndon Johnson, "State of the Union Address," January 4, 1965.

34. Bill Moyers, "Welcome to Doomsday," *Beliefnet*, March 2005, http://www.beliefnet.com/News/2005/03/Welcome-To-Doomsday.aspx?p=1.

35. Kevin Phillips, *American Theocracy: The Peril and Politics of Radical Religion, Oil, and Borrowed Money in the 21st Century* (New York: Viking, 2006), 253.

36. Rich Lowry, "A Theology of Freedom," *National Review* Online, July 17, 2007.

37. George W. Bush, "Second Inaugural Address," January 20, 2005.

38. Mark Morford, "Is Obama an Enlightened Being?," *San Francisco Chronicle*, June 6, 2008.

39. Josephine Hearn, "Black Lawmakers Emotional about Obama's Success," *Politico*, June 4, 2008.

40. John Patrick Diggins, *Ronald Reagan: Fate, Freedom and the Making of History* (New York: W. W. Norton, 2007), 16.

41. "Republicans, Democrats Shift on Whether Government Is a Threat," Gallup, October 18, 2010, http://www.gallup.com/poll/143717/republicans-democrats-shift-whether-gov-threat.aspx.

42. Gene Healy, "The Cult of the Presidency," *Reason*, June 2008.

43. "The Religious Dimensions of the Torture Debate," Pew Research Center, April 29, 2009. http://pewforum.org/Politics-and-Elections/The-Religious-Dimensions-of-the-Torture-Debate.aspx.

44. Pope Benedict XVI, *Jesus of Nazareth: From the Baptism in the Jordan to the Transfiguration* (San Francisco: Ignatius Press, 2008), 118.

Conclusion: The Recovery of Christianity

1. G. K. Chesterton, *The Everlasting Man* (San Francisco: Ignatius Press, 1993), 255.

2. R. R. Reno, "The Radical Orthodoxy Project," *First Things*, February 2000.

3. Philip Longman, "Survival of the Godliest," Big Questions Online, November 11, 2010.

4. Molly Worthen, "The Controversialist," *Christianity Today*, April 17, 2009.

5. C. S. Lewis, *Mere Christianity* (New York: HarperCollins, 1980), xv.

6. Joseph Hooper, "Tim Keller Wants to Save Your Yuppie Soul," *New York*, November 29, 2009.

7. Saint Basil the Great, *Homily on Avarice*.

8. Andrew Sullivan, *Love Undetectable: Notes on Friendship, Sex and Survival* (New York: Vintage Books, 1999), 199.

9. Kate Bolick, "All the Single Ladies," *The Atlantic*, November 2011.

10. Vittorio Messori, *The Ratzinger Report* (San Francisco: Ignatius Press, 1985), 129.

ACKNOWLEDGMENTS

This book has been years in the making, and it owes something to a great many people's influence and help. I might not be a Christian without the ministry of Grace James in Connecticut, and I might not be a Catholic were it not for Father Carleton Jones, Father Paul Keller, and Christopher Thacker. I would certainly be neither without my family: my sister, my companion on many adventures; my father, who knows that I really should have been a fantasy novelist; and especially my mother, who took us on the journey that made mine possible, and whose story is the foundation of this book.

Rafe Sagalyn, my agent, patiently shepherded this project through multiple iterations. Adam Bellow and Andrew Miller offered a great deal of constructive advice during the early going. Emily Loose, my editor, projected exactly the right mix of patience and pressure through a drawn-out writing process, and then delivered a searching edit that improved the book immensely. I am indebted to Michael Cromartie, Michael Brendan Dougherty, and Rod Dreher for their comments and advice.

Particular thanks are due to the many editors who have let me explore this book's themes in print and in pixels: Andy Rosenthal, David Shipley, Linda Cohn, and Peter Capatano at *The New York Times*; James Bennet at *The Atlantic*; Rich Lowry and Mike Potemra at *National Review*; Jody Bottum at *First Things*; Jenny Schuessler and Sam Tanenhaus at *The New York Times Book Review*; John Kienker at the *Claremont Review of Books*; and Jonathan Last at the *Weekly Standard Online*.

My friends have endured my near-complete disappearance from their lives with immense forbearance over the last two years. My mother-in-law and sister-in-law, Maureen and Judith, have endured my perpetually harried state with immense kindness and good grace.

Finally, all of this belongs to my beloved wife, Abby, who participated in the madness, and my daughter, Gwendolyn, who I trust was blissfully unaware that it was unfolding around her.

INDEX

economic growth, 78–79

ecumenism:

accommodationist Christianity and, 94, 95, 104, 109

Benedict option and, 281

Evangelical Christianity and, 140

of Graham, 35, 53, 128, 139–140, 286

John Paul II and, 129

Kelley and, 109

Murray and, 43

political theology and, 261

in post–World War II era, 21, 30, 113

prosperity theology and, 185

renewal of American Christianity and, 286–288

resistant Christianity and, 115, 118, 141, 143

Roman Catholic Church and, 55, 56, 113, 128, 129

of Sheen, 40

Vietnam War and, 66

Eddy, Mary Baker, 6, 8, 64, 152, 155, 185

Edwards, Jonathan, 292

Ehrman, Bart, 150, 152, 158, 160, 161, 162, 163, 167, 168, 170, 175, 178, 179

Eikerenkotter, Frederick J., II, 192

Einstein, Albert, 89, 223

Eisenhower, Dwight D., 31–32, 36, 38, 42, 52, 58, 68, 252, 254, 259

Eliot, T. S., 24, 50, 85, 138, 284

Ellington, Duke, 45

Ellwood, Robert, 63

emerging church movement, 279, 280, 286

Emerson, Ralph Waldo, 6, 8, 152, 219, 220, 228–229, 267, 268

The End of Faith (Harris), 223

entertainment industry:

American Catholic Church and, 39

marginalization of religious faith, 2

religious films in post–World War II era, 22–23

environmentalism, 106, 107

Episcopal Church:

accommodationist Christianity and, 89–90, 91, 92–93, 106, 118

membership in, 31, 58, 59, 61

Epistle to the Romans (Barth), 28, 51

Equal Rights Amendment, 106, 122

ethics:

Christianity and, 27, 28, 29, 71, 118

See also morality

sexual ethics, 70–73, 81, 87, 90, 91, 100–101, 102, 104–105, 119, 120, 122, 136, 239, 289–291

war on, 51

eugenics, 263

Europe:

cultural influence of, 74

modernist theology and, 28

state-supported Christianity of, 14

euthanasia, 128, 129

Evangelical Christianity:

American Catholic Church and, 113–116, 118, 121, 123, 128, 129–131, 135–136, 137, 141–142, 143

convergences with other churches, 14

denouncing of harsh interrogation, 273

emerging church movement, 279, 280, 286

Graham and, 32–33, 35–37

growth of, 60–61, 63, 137

influence of, 137–138

institutional weaknesses of, 139–140

intellectuals of, 124, 125–126, 129, 138–139

Israel and, 76

marginalization of, 39, 52

nationalism and, 250

neo-evangelicals, 35–37, 52, 62, 68, 124, 139–140

philanthropy and, 203–204

political theology and, 261–262

prosperity theology and, 52, 139, 195–198

reemergence in post–World War II era, 21

Republican Party and, 69, 122, 123, 124, 141, 142, 203, 204

resistant Christianity and, 121–122

segregation and, 49

stigma of fundamentalism and, 33, 34–35, 36, 52, 62, 123, 125, 128, 139, 161

universities and, 125–127

Methodists, 6, 58, 64, 90, 118
Metzger, Bruce, 169
Meyer, Joyce, 188, 196, 217
military operations, effect on American
    attitudes, 1
millenarianism:
    apocalyptism and, 263
    fundamentalism and, 34, 36, 139
    spirituality and, 63
Millennial Generation, 138, 234–235
Miller, Henry, 99
Miller, Walter, 6, 24, 133
Millerites, 63, 64
missionaries:
    developed West as mission field, 283
    Evangelical Christianity and, 126, 129,
        204, 282
    prosperity theology and, 195, 196
    Protestantism and, 31, 59
Missouri Synod Lutherans, 60
modernist theology:
    accommodationist Christianity and,
        85–86, 115
    Darwinism and, 27, 28
    fundamentalism and, 60
    Jesus Christ and, 156
    Niebuhr and, 29
    progress and, 28, 33, 34, 85
    rationalism of, 8
    Reagan and, 267
    Roman Catholic Church and, 37–38, 42
modernity:
    Christian center and, 14
    Christian orthodoxy and, 56
    post–World War II era and, 23
    prosperity theology and, 184
Monnet, Jean, 202
Montgomery bus boycott of 1955, 45–46
Moore, Michael, 268
Moore, Paul, 92–93
Moralistic Therapeutic Deism, 233
morality:
    accommodationist Christianity and, 92,
        103
    civil rights movement and, 57, 66
    conservative churches and, 62
    contraception and, 70–72

God Within theology and, 228, 237, 238
Jesus Christ and, 154
political theology and, 272–274, 275
priests' sexual abuse and, 132
private sphere and, 72
Protestant intellectuals and, 26
relativism and, 87
religion as bulwark against totalitarian-
    ism, 21
renewal of American Christianity and,
    288–291
resistant Christianity and, 114–115, 123
See also ethics
Ten Commandments and, 10
Vietnam war and, 66
Moral Majority, 122, 140
Moran, Gabriel, 96
Mormons, 6, 61, 64, 261, 262, 281
Morris, Charles, 22, 38, 41
Morse, Wayne, 98
Mother Teresa, 291–292
Mount Saint Mary's Seminary, 97
Mouw, Richard, 114
Moyers, Bill, 264
Murray, John Courtney:
    death of, 85
    democracy and, 42–43, 51–52, 200
    ecumenism and, 43
    as intellectual, 24, 55, 177
    Neuhaus and, 129
    Second Vatican Council and, 44, 94
    as theological adviser to Vatican, 56
Muslims and Islam:
    as antagonist to Christianity, 247
    Christian paradoxes and, 11
    political theology and, 264–265
    population of, 59
mysteries:
    Christian orthodoxy and, 10–12
    modernist theology and, 28
    Niebuhr and, 29
mystics and mysticism:
    accommodationist Christianity and,
        106–108, 109, 111
    Christian paradoxes and, 11
    God Within theology and, 219, 220,
        223, 226–227, 228, 229–230

ABOUT THE AUTHOR

Ross Douthat is a columnist for the *New York Times* op-ed page. He is the author of *Privilege: Harvard and the Education of the Ruling Class* and the coauthor, with Reihan Salam, of *Grand New Party: How Republicans Can Win the Working Class and Save the American Dream*. Before joining the *New York Times* he was a senior editor for *The Atlantic*. He is the film critic for *National Review*, and he has appeared regularly on television, including *Charlie Rose*, *PBS Newshour*, *Real Time*, and *The Colbert Report*. He lives with his wife and daughter in Washington, D.C.

53695